Hydrology and the Management of Watersheds

A forested wetland in northern Minnesota. Such wetlands are expressions of shallow groundwater and are sensitive to human activities.

Mountain stream. Forested watersheds form the head-water areas for most major rivers. This is the Madison River in Montana, a tributary of the Missouri River.

HYDROLOGY AND THE MANAGEMENT OF WATERSHEDS

Kenneth N. Brooks
Peter F. Ffolliott
Hans M. Gregersen
John L. Thames

IOWA STATE UNIVERSITY PRESS/AMES

TO

Pam, Linda, and in memory of Anne and Ethel

Kenneth N. Brooks is professor of forest hydrology and director of graduate studies, College of Natural Resources, University of Minnesota, St. Paul.

Peter F. Ffolliott is professor of watershed management, School of Renewable Natural Resources, College of Agriculture, University of Arizona, Tucson.

Hans M. Gregersen is professor of forest economics, Department of Forest Resources, College of Natural Resources, University of Minnesota, St. Paul.

John L. Thames is professor emeritus of watershed management, School of Renewable Natural Resources, College of Agriculture, University of Arizona, Tucson.

© 1991 Iowa State University Press, Ames, Iowa 50010
All rights reserved

Authorization to photocopy items for internal or personal use, or the internal or personal use of specific clients, is granted by Iowa State University Press, provided that the base fee of $.10 per copy is paid directly to the Copyright Clearance Center, 27 Congress Street, Salem, MA 01970. For those organizations that have been granted a photocopy license by CCC, a separate system of payments has been arranged. The fee code for users of the Transactional Reporting Service is 0-8138-0137-0/91 $.10.

♾ Printed on acid-free paper in the United States of America

First edition, 1991
Second printing, 1992

Library of Congress Cataloging-in-Publication Data

Hydrology and the management of watersheds / Kenneth N. Brooks . . . [et al.]. — 1st ed.
    p. cm.
  Includes bibliographical references.
  ISBN 0-8138-0137-0
  I. Watershed management. 2. Watersheds. I. Brooks, Kenneth N.
TC409.H93 1991
  627 — dc20   90-34860

CONTENTS

Streamflow in a forested watershed, a source of water for many uses including scenic beauty.

PREFACE

■ This book provides fundamental information and practical methodology necessary to solve hydrologic problems on watersheds, and to understand and develop watershed management programs. Parts 1 and 2 are basic to courses on forest hydrology, range hydrology, or watershed management, as taught in many forestry and natural resource management programs. Part 3 deals with watershed management planning, implementation, and evaluation and emphasizes the multidisciplinary aspects, including social and economic factors. Part 4 consists of special topics that provide emphasis tailored to specific problems and to different regions of the United States and elsewhere in the world.

This book also is intended as a reference for administrators, planners, managers, and technicians who deal with the management and utilization of natural resources, but who may not be educated formally in hydrology and watershed management. It should be useful for national and international agencies in the development of short courses and continuing education programs. Most parts of this book have been used in formal college courses taught in the United States and training courses offered for international audiences.

Metric units are used in this book, except where original figures, tables, or unit-dependent mathematical relationships are presented that were developed from English units.

We have provided a table of English to metric unit conversion factors in the Appendix to assist the reader.

The authors thank Clara M. Schreiber for her invaluable typing and editorial assistance. We are also grateful to Judith D. Hasbrouck and to Paul K. Barten for preparing many of the illustrations, and to the literary executor of the late Sir Ronald A. Fisher, F.R.S., to Dr. Frank Yates, F.R.S., and the Longman Group Ltd., London, for permission to reprint Table 18.1 from their book *Statistical Tables for Biological, Agricultural, and Medical Research* (6th Edition 1974).

DEFINITION OF TERMS

Hydrology is the science of water that is concerned with the origin, circulation, distribution, and properties of waters of the earth.

Forest Hydrology/Range Hydrology/Wildland Hydrology refer to a branch of hydrology that deals with the effects of vegetation and land management, in respective settings, on water quantity and quality, erosion, and sedimentation.

Watershed, or catchment, is a topographically delineated area that is drained by a stream system, that is, the total land area above some point on a stream or river that drains past that point. The watershed is a hydrologic unit often used as a physical-biological unit and a socio-economic-political unit for the planning and management of natural resources.

River basin is similarly defined but is of a larger scale. For example, the Mississippi River Basin, the Amazon River Basin, and the Congo River Basin include all lands that drain through those rivers and their tributaries into the ocean.

Watershed management is the process of guiding and organizing land and other resource use on a watershed to provide desired goods and services without affecting adversely soil and water resources. Embedded in the concept of watershed management is the recognition of the interrelationships among land use, soil, and water, and the linkages between uplands and downstream areas.

Watershed management practices are those changes in land use, vegetative cover, and other nonstructural and structural actions that are taken on a watershed to achieve watershed management objectives.

Landslide in Nepal, the result of road construction in a mountainous watershed. Human activities should be carefully planned for steep, mountainous watersheds.

Hydrology and the Management of Watersheds

*A lake scene in northern Minnesota with red pine in the
foreground. The close association between forests and
water is evident in many regions of the world.*

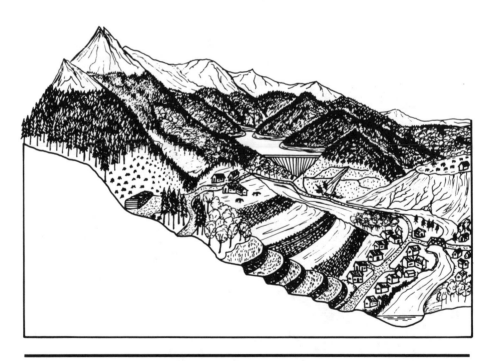

1.1. Many different types of land use can occur on a watershed; each affects a particular site but also has potential impact on downstream areas as well (redrawn from *Protect and Produce,* Food and Agriculture Organization of the United Nations, Rome, Italy).

CHAPTER 1

Introduction

Our perspective of watershed management differs from some of the more traditional ones that concentrate only on hydrology. While hydrology is an essential component of watershed management and is the subject of much of this book, we also recognize the importance of land productivity as an integral part of watershed management. That is, watershed management not only deals with the protection of water resources but also the capability and suitability of land and vegetation resources to be managed for the production of goods and services. Few watersheds in the world are managed solely for the production of water—some municipal watersheds are the exception. Yet, watersheds serve as a logical and practical unit for analysis, planning, and management of multiple resources.

A basic understanding of hydrology is fundamental to the planning and management of renewable natural resources for sustainable use on a watershed. Hydrology enters explicitly and directly into the design of water resource projects, including reservoirs, flood control structures, navigation, irrigation, and water quality control. Knowledge of hydrology helps us in our attempt to balance demands for water with supplies, to avoid floods, and to protect the quality of streams and lakes. Thus, basic hydrology and the hydrologic effects of land use are the subjects of Part 1.

One of our concerns and an incentive for writing this book is that hydrology is not always explicit in the management of forests, rangelands, and croplands, even though it should be! Ignoring the effects of land management activities on soil and water resources is shortsighted, and can lead to unwanted effects on a particular site and on downstream areas (Fig. 1.1). Many of these effects are discussed in parts 2 and 3. For example, soil erosion can lead to losses of plant productivity and/or soil stability. Changes in vegetation and soils can alter streamflow, sediment flow, and water quality that affect the health and welfare of people living downstream.

With the perspective of a watershed and a clear awareness of the linkages between uplands and downstream areas, we should be able to plan and develop long-term, sustainable solutions to many natural resource problems—and, at the same time, avoid many kinds of environmental degradation. The linkage between upland use and downstream effects provides the central tenet of watershed management. Part 3 focuses on how we can better identify, analyze, and quantify the benefits associated with watershed management.

Part 4 considers special topics that are of interest in particular areas or that are needed to quantify hydrologic responses; it serves as a supplement to parts 1 and 2.

▪ WATERSHED MANAGEMENT STRATEGIES AND RESPONSES TO PROBLEMS

Watershed management involves an array of nonstructural (vegetation management) practices, as well as an array of structural (engineering) activities when conditions warrant them. Soil conservation practices and land use planning activities can be tools employed in watershed management, as can agroforestry, establishing protected reserves, building dams, and regulations guiding roadbuilding, timber harvesting, and other types of activities. The unifying focus in all cases is on how these various activities affect the relationship between water and other natural resources on a watershed. The common denominator or the integrating factor is water. This focus on water and its interrelationship with other natural resources and their use is what distinguishes watershed management from other natural resource management strategies.

On the one hand, watershed management is an integrative way of thinking about all the various human activities on a given area of land (the watershed) that have effects on, or are affected by, water. On the other hand, watershed management practices also include a set of "tools" or techniques—the physical, regulatory, or economic means for responding to problems or potential problems involving the relationship between water and land uses. What sometimes confuses people is the fact that these tools or techniques are not employed by a watershed manager as such, but rather by farmers, foresters, soil conservation officers, engineers, and so forth.

This fact is both the dilemma and the strength of watershed management. In practice, activities using natural resources are decided upon and undertaken by individuals, local governments, and various groups that control land in a political framework that has little relationship to, and in fact most often ignores, the boundaries of a watershed. For example, in Figure 1.1 the forested uplands may be under the control of a federal forestry agency, but the middle elevations and lowlands may be a composite of private, city, and community ownerships. Activities are undertaken independently, often with little regard to how they affect other areas. Yet, despite this real world of disaggregated, independent political, and economic actions, it remains a fact that water and its constituents flow downhill and ignore political boundaries. What one person or group does upstream can affect the welfare of those downstream. Somehow, the physical facts of watersheds and the political realities have to be brought together. That is the focus of *integrated watershed management*. Within this broad focus, there is concern both with how to prevent deterioration of an existing sustainable, productive relationship between the use of water and other natural resources and how to restore or create such a relationship where it has been destroyed in the past.

Watershed management actions and activities, thus, are employed in *preventative strategies*—ones aimed at preserving existing sustainable land use practices, or more commonly, they are employed in *restorative strategies*—ones designed to overcome identified problems or restore conditions to a desirable level, where desirable is defined both in environmental and in political terms. Both strategies respond to the same types of problems, only in one case the objective is to prevent a problem from occurring, while in the other case, the objective is to restore conditions once the problem has occurred. In reality, of course, we are dealing with a continuum, going from regulatory support and reinforcement of existing sustainable land use practices (preventative strategy) to emergency relief, building of temporary gully control structures, removing cattle, or restricting land use on fragile, eroded lands (restorative strategy).

In most watershed management situations, we are somewhere in between the two extremes—some measures will be preventative, some will be direct responses to existing problems. The point to stress is that routine preventative strategies and actions are fully as important as the more dramatic and visible restorative actions: losses avoided (through preventative strategies) can be just as important to people as gains from solving a problem. In economic terms, the cost of preventing losses of productivity in the first place can be much lower than the cost of achieving the same benefit through more dramatic actions to restore productivity on problem lands that already have been degraded.

With this as background, a summary is presented of the most common situations encountered and alternative solutions (preventative or restorative) to overcoming them as they relate to watershed management objectives (Table 1.1).

Table 1.1. The role of watershed management in developing solutions to natural resource problems

Problem	Possible Alternative Solutions	Associated Watershed Management Objectives
Deficient water supplies	Reservoir storage and water transport	Minimize sediment delivery to reservoir site; maintain watershed vegetative cover
	Water harvesting	Develop localized collection and storage facilities
	Vegetation manipulation; evapotranspiration reduction	Convert from deep-rooted to shallow-rooted species or from conifers to deciduous trees
	Cloud seeding	Maintain vegetative cover to minimize erosion
	Desalinization of ocean water	Not applicable
	Pumping of deep groundwater and irrigation	Management of recharge areas
Flooding	Reservoir storage	Minimize sediment delivery to reservoir site; maintain watershed vegetative cover
	Construct levees, channelization, etc.	Minimize sediment delivery to downstream channels
	Flood plain management	Zoning of lands to minimize human activities in flood-prone areas; minimize sedimentation of channels
	Revegetate disturbed and denuded areas	Plant and manage appropriate vegatative cover
Energy shortages	Utilize wood for fuel	Plant perpetual fast-growing tree species; maintain productivity of sites; minimize erosion

Table 1.1. Continued

Problem	Possible Alternative Solutions	Associated Watershed Management Objectives
Energy shortages	Develop hydroelectric power project	Minimize sediment delivery to reservoirs and river channels; sustain water yield
Food shortages	Develop agroforestry	Maintain site productivity; minimize erosion; promote species compatible with soils and climate of area
	Increase cultivation	Restructure hill slopes and other areas susceptible to erosion; utilize contour plowing, terraces, etc.
	Increase livestock production	Develop herding-grazing systems for sustained yield and productivity
	Import food from outside watershed	Develop forest resources for pulp, wood and wildlife products, etc. to provide economic base
Erosion/sedimentation from denuded landscapes	Erosion control structures	Maintain life of structures by revegetation and management
	Contour terracing	Revegetate, mulch, stabilize slopes and institute land use guidelines
	Revegetate	Establish, protect, and manage vegetative cover until site recovers
Poor quality drinking water	Develop alternative supplies from wells and springs	Protect groundwater from contamination
	Treat water supplies	Filter through wetlands or upland forests
Polluted streams/reduced fishery production	Control pollutants entering streams	Develop buffer strips along stream channels; maintain vegetative cover on watersheds; develop guidelines for riparian zones
	Treat wastewater	Use forests and wetlands as secondary treatment systems for wastewater

■ WATERSHED MANAGEMENT: A GLOBAL PERSPECTIVE

Resource use and management practices around the world are a function of not only the physical and biological characteristics of watersheds, but also institutional factors and social characteristics such as the cultural background of rural populations and the nature of governments. How these factors are interrelated can best be illustrated by looking at specific examples.

Steep and Mountainous Lands

Steep and mountainous lands accentuate most watershed problems. One-quarter of the earth's land surface is mountainous and is inhabited by 10% of the world's population. Most of this area has a mesic climate, forest or shrub cover with little arable soil, and a low population density. At the same time, many mountain watersheds are the headwater areas of major rivers that directly impact large populations living downstream.

In the coastal range of Oregon, for example, timber production is an important contributor to the economy, yet, some timber-harvesting activities threaten another important part of Oregon's economy—the salmon fishery. Clearcutting on steep hillsides with accompanying road construction has led to numerous landslides, many of which deposit soil and debris directly into streams. Although landslides are natural occurrences in this terrain, road construction and forest harvesting clearly can accelerate their frequency and extent. Landslides then become a watershed management problem; what measures are needed to reduce landslides to protect the salmon fishery and other resource uses, and yet sustain timber production?

In approaching the answer to this question, we have to consider the physical and biological input-output relationships, or production functions, that are involved and then attempt to find ways of altering them by changing land use practices or introducing new elements into existing ways of doing things. Appropriate measures have to be tempered by the social and economic implications of the alternatives available. Some measures are more acceptable than others by affected groups. Also, the costs of different alternatives will vary, so the cost-effectiveness or economic efficiency of the alternatives must be considered to meet budget constraints and other economic criteria.

As a result of landslide problems in Oregon, road construction practices that minimized road-caused landslides were implemented, increasing construction costs 50–100%. It was determined, however, that reducing road-caused landslides was not enough; clearcutting trees in landslide-prone areas continued to promote landslides. As a result, about 25% of the commercial forestland in one district was protected from commercial operations. In this district, watershed management resulted in increased costs of road construction and a reduction of commercial timber area in exchange for protection of a valuable fisheries resource. Sometimes, the seemingly high costs of achieving watershed management objectives in the short term are difficult to balance with the long-term, sustainable benefits that accrue. This is a dilemma of watershed management; clarifying the balance is a challenge for those working in watershed management.

The densely populated mountains of Nepal exhibit serious natural and human-caused erosion that contributes 250 million m^3 of silt to the Gangetic Plain each year. According to observers, the beds of the rivers in the Terai Plain of southern Nepal are rising 15–30 cm annually, resulting in flooding and changing river courses. The Kosi River, for example, has shifted its course 115 km westward within the past 150 yr, leaving 15,000 km^2 of once fertile land buried under a mass of sand and rubble.

The increasing populations of Nepal and other countries in this part of the world are moving further into the mountains and higher up the slopes to seek a means of livelihood. Even with the aid of terracing, which the farmers of Nepal have been practicing for centuries, these slopes are too steep and the soils too thin for sustainable, intensive cultivation. Nevertheless, a single hectare of cultivated land must now support ten people in many areas. The demands of an increasing population result in the cultivation of less suitable soils and steeper lands, causing a reduction of productivity per unit area. In the densely populated eastern hills of Nepal, as much as 40% of what once was farmland has been abandoned and allowed to revert to bush because it is no longer fertile enough to support crops. These lands are the sites and sources of severe erosion, massive landslides, and gully erosion. However, cultivation is only partially responsible for the rapid deterioration of the watersheds. Nepal's remaining forestlands stand in jeopardy because of overgrazing and fodder harvesting due to increasing numbers of livestock. Forest and range fires also add to the problem.

Degraded mountainous watersheds usually can be restored, but the costs are great and the time for recovery is usually long. Overgrazing by livestock and burning on many high-elevation watersheds in the western United States during the early 1900s led to intensive restoration projects. Between 1923 and 1930, high-intensity summer rainstorms triggered flooding and mud-rock flows from denuded watersheds in northern Utah. Lives were lost, valuable lowlands were flooded, and homes were destroyed. Watershed rehabilitation projects that combined contour trenching and revegetation measures began in the early 1930s. These projects were so successful in stabilizing steep slopes and reducing mud-rock flows that by 1969 about 30,000 acres of fragile lands in five western states had undergone similar restoration.

Korea is an example of a country that has made major progress in the management of its mountainous watersheds. The urgency in Korea was related to both protection of an expanding network of major hydropower installations and its need to protect the well-defined, but relatively small, area of productive, irrigated agricultural lowlands, which depend on water from the northern mountains. The Korean approach has been one of integrating watershed management with forestry and of community development efforts through its "new community movement." This program has been successful so far, largely because watershed management practices were developed and applied at the grass-roots level.

Watershed degradation already has taken place over much of the East African highlands. At one time, 75% of Ethiopia was covered with forests, which moderated the process of soil loss. However, recent surveys indicate that substantial forest cover has diminished to only 4% of that nation's total land area. Erosion from the mountainous 6000-ft-high Amhara Plateau produced silt, which was carried by the Nile and which fertilized the agricultural flood plain of Egypt for centuries. Now, the high dam at Aswan helps to control the Nile's floods and traps the silt. The dam has created a lake of over 5000 km² and receives an estimated 90 million tons of sediment each year, giving the lake a life expectancy of 500 yr in a land with a cultural history of more than 5000 yr. The rate of sedimentation may increase in the future.

Few forests remain on great portions of the Andes mountain range of South America. In the high plateaus of Peru, which include more than one-third of the country, the population has doubled and redoubled in this century. The mountain farmers have been forced into large-scale deforestation, overgrazing, and overcropping. Drastic reductions of crop yields have occurred during shifting agriculture, and in some areas the hill people have even been driven to digging up the roots of trees and shrubs to burn for fuel and fertilizer, greatly increasing the susceptibility of the soil to severe erosion. As in the Andes, intensive use of steep and mountainous watersheds is accelerating in eastern India, Pakistan, Thailand, the Philippines, Indonesia, Malaysia, Nigeria, Tanzania, and many other countries.

Drylands

Water relationships of arid and semiarid regions are perhaps more critical to a greater number of people on earth than those of more humid regions. Water is usually in short supply and in great demand by dense populations of people and their livestock.

Dry regions cover more than one-third of the earth's land surface, and slightly over half of that area is inhabited by 630 million people. The remainder is climatically so arid and unproductive that it cannot support human life. But, the degradation of land and water resources by human activities is turning potentially productive drylands into unproductive deserts in Asia, Africa, and America. This process is called *desertification*. It has been estimated that a total area larger than Brazil, with rainfall above the level classified as semiarid, has been degraded to desertlike conditions. This does not take into account the far greater degradation that is taking place within the potentially productive semiarid zones.

About 60 million people in the developing countries live on the semiarid interface between deserts and more humid areas. Desert encroachment in West Africa has received the greatest international attention. It has been estimated that 650,000 km² of land suitable for agriculture or grazing have undergone desertification in West Africa over the past 50 yr.

The arid lands of India, which include the sandy waters of the Thor Desert of western Rajasthan, experience population densities over 60 people/km². The practical consequence of the pressure this population exerts has been the extension of farming to submarginal lands, which may be fit only for range, helping to make this perhaps the most dusty area in the world. Meanwhile, as the land available for forage shrinks, the number of grazing animals swells. The area in Western Rajasthan available exclusively for grazing dropped from 13 to 11 million ha between 1951 and 1961, while the population is still growing. During the 1960s, the farmed area expanded from 26 to 38% of the total area, shrinking the grazing area even more.

As long as current land use patterns continue, the livelihood of tens of millions living in the arid lands of India will, at best, remain at its current dismal level. At worst, and most probably, a prolonged drought in the future will mercilessly rebalance the number of people with the available resources. As it is, relief programs for the arid zones are seriously draining the governments' funds and food stores. Present land use patterns in desert environments must be reshaped in order that delicate water relations are not pushed beyond their limits.

Humid Tropical Lands

There is a common misconception that no matter how much steep and mountainous lands might lose their production potential by erosion, or how much marginal land is degraded into desert, the world always can fall back on its abundant tropical forestlands. One-quarter of the Asian, African, and Latin American tropics are occupied by forest. While the Amazon Basin, for example, covers nearly 7.8 million km², or 40% of the South American continent, it is inhabited by less than 3% of the population.

Because these lands support a rich and diverse plant cover, it is sometimes assumed that they also must be highly productive and suited for intensive agriculture. But, the available nutrients in tropical rain forests are tied up mainly in the vegetative canopy and are returned to the soil after the slash is burned. Thus, sustained slash-and-burn agriculture has been practiced in tropical regions for thousands of years. However, this form of agriculture becomes a serious threat when population pressure on the land becomes too great to allow a sufficiently long recovery period, or fallow, between slash-and-burn cycles. There is evidence that such pressures contributed to the collapse of several civilizations, notably the Mayan civilization of Central America and the ancient Khmer Empire of Cambodia, whose agricultural practices led to cementation and loss of fertility of the lateritic soils they farmed.

Increasing demands for food and fiber are now placing pressure upon tropical watershed lands on a global scale. For instance, in eastern Nigeria, the most densely populated part of Africa south of the Sahara, shifting agriculture has been forced into shorter and shorter rotation cycles to the point that it has become continuous farming. The result is a loss of nutrients and a breakdown of soil structure.

One of the best examples of the problems of tropical watershed lands are those in the Amazon Basin. By any account, the soils of most of the Amazon Basin are poor and could perhaps best be exploited through forestry or other perennial crop practices. Only about 4% of the Brazilian portion of the Amazon has soils with medium to high fertility. Most of the better soils are in narrow plains along the banks of rivers, and their development for large-scale agriculture would require large expenditures for drainage and flood control. Nevertheless, programs to help new farmers from other regions to settle in the basin have been tried. Since 1971, 50,000 families have settled along a proposed highway between Peru and the Atlantic. With few financial and administrative resources, and less knowledge of tropical farming techniques, only the most successful barely attain production at subsistence levels. It is probable that many more colonists will find it impossible to make a living and will abandon their plots after the soil has been severely degraded by over-intense, inappropriate cultivation.

■ PREVENTATIVE STRATEGIES: THE KEY TO WATERSHED MANAGEMENT

The preceding global perspective leaves an impression that watershed management is mostly the restoration of degraded lands. Problems of soil erosion, gully formation, localized flooding, or water shortages resulting from abusive land use call for action—usually in the form of engineering structures and widespread revegetation schemes. Much like in the popular press, the natural disasters and problems of human suffering associated with resource depletion and degradation get more attention than the quiet successes. Likewise, the mobilization of people and equipment to renovate devastated areas gets attention. It is an effective way, sometimes, to attract attention to serious problems; however, we do not want to leave the impression that watershed management comes into play only when problems arise.

A more positive picture of watershed management is that of establishing and sustaining preventative practices. This means instituting guidelines of land use and implementing land use practices on a day-to-day basis that result in long-term, sustainable resource development and productivity without causing soil and water problems. In fact, land management agencies in the United States and many other countries have established land management policies that embody sound watershed management principles. These preventative measures, when listed and described, may not make for exciting reading, but in total they represent the ultimate goal of watershed management programs. To achieve this goal requires that resource managers recognize the implications of their actions and that they work effectively within the social and political setting in which they find themselves.

The role of natural resource managers in any area should be to achieve the needed goods and services desired by society, but without adversely impacting long-term productivity and downstream communities, and without causing unwanted environmental change. People who occupy watersheds must be an integral part of any watershed management solution. For example, creating new sources of water does not necessarily solve water shortages in arid areas; an increased use of new supplies or an influx of people from water-poor areas can quickly deplete new sources of water. Nor will reservoirs that are designed to store flood flows and attenuate flood peaks provide the solution to flooding. Floodplain occupancy is a continuing problem and one that cannot be solved only with hydrologic engineering practices.

The dilemma in watershed management is that land use changes needed to promote the survival of society over the long term can be at cross purposes with what is essential to the survival of the individual over the short term. Requirements for food and natural resources today should not be met at the expense of future generations. Any discussion of sustainable natural resource development should consider watershed boundaries, the linkages between uplands and downstream areas, and the effects of land use practices on long-term productivity. Land use that is at cross purposes with the environment cannot be sustained. Sustainable productivity and environmental protection can be achieved with the integrated, holistic approach that explicitly considers hydrology and the management of watersheds.

A V-notch weir, measuring streamflow from an upland watershed in northern Arizona.

PART 1

Hydrologic Processes and Land Use

■ The *hydrologic cycle* represents the processes and pathways involved in the circulation of water from land and water bodies to the atmosphere and back again. The cycle is complex and dynamic but can be simplified if we categorize components into input, output, and storage (Fig. 2.1). Based on the principle of conservation of mass, inputs such as rainfall, snowmelt, and condensation must balance with changes in storage and outputs, which include streamflow, groundwater seepage, and evapotranspiration (inflow less outflow is equal to the change in storage). This hydrologic balance, or *water budget,* is an application of the conservation of mass law expressed by the equation of continuity:

$$I - O = \Delta S$$

where I = inflow; O = outflow; and ΔS = change in storage.

The water budget is both a fundamental concept of hydrology and a useful method for the study of the hydrologic cycle; this basic equation and its modifications allow the hydrologist to trace the pathways and changes in water storage in a watershed.

The quantities of water in the atmosphere, soils, groundwater, surface water, and other components are constantly changing because of the dynamic nature of the hydrologic cycle. At any one point in time, however, quantities of water in each component can be approximated. If we consider the total water resource on the earth, only about 2.6% is fresh water (Baumgartner and Reichel 1975). About 77% of this fresh water is tied up in the polar ice caps and glaciers, and 11% is stored in deep groundwater aquifers, leaving about 12% for active circulation. Of this 12%, only 0.57% exists in the atmosphere and in the biosphere. The biosphere is from the top of trees to the lowest roots. The atmosphere redistributes evaporated water by precipitation and condensation. Components of the biosphere partition this water into runoff, soil and groundwater storage, groundwater seepage, or evapotranspiration back to the atmosphere.

The hydrologic processes of the biosphere and the effects of vegetation and soils on these processes are of particular interest in forest hydrology and watershed management. Precipitation and the flow of water into, through, and out of a watershed all can be affected by land use and management activities. Likewise, the magnitude of various storage components including soil water, snowpacks, lakes, reservoirs, and rivers can be altered by human activities. With the water budget approach, we can examine existing watershed systems, quantify the effects of management impacts on the hydrologic cycle, and in some cases predict or estimate the hydrologic consequences of proposed activities.

Part 1 of this textbook (chapters 2 through 6) focuses on basic hydrology. Hydrologic processes are described and the effects of land use and management activities on the respective processes are given special attention. The information contained herein is fundamental to understanding hydrology. Further, it provides the background necessary for a more complete understanding of land use impacts on soil and water resources.

CHAPTER 2

Precipitation and Interception

■ INTRODUCTION

Precipitation and interception affect the amount, timing, and spatial distribution of water added to a watershed from the atmosphere (Fig. 2.1). Hydrologists view precipitation as the major input to a watershed and a key to its water yield characteristics. Ecologists recognize the role of precipitation in determining the types of soils and vegetation that occur on a watershed. As a process, however, most people have only a cursory understanding of why precipitation occurs and why it occurs where it does.

Precipitation is the result of meteorological factors and, therefore, is largely outside of human control. However, land use and associated vegetation alterations can affect the deposition of precipitation by changing interception, at least to some extent. This chapter examines the process of precipitation, its deposition and occurrence in time and space. Basic methods of analyzing precipitation and of estimating interception are presented.

■ MOISTURE IN THE ATMOSPHERE

Air masses take on the temperature and moisture characteristics of underlying surfaces, particularly when they are stationary or move slowly over large water or land surfaces. Air masses moving from an ocean to land bring to that land surface a source of moisture. Air masses from polar regions will be dry and cold. The movement of air masses modifies the temperature and moisture conditions of the atmosphere over a watershed and determines the climatic, and more specifically, the precipitation characteristics that occur. To understand the precipitation process, the relationship between atmospheric moisture and temperature must be understood.

Moisture is added to the atmosphere by the process of *evaporation,* the change in state from liquid water to water vapor, resulting in a net loss of liquid water from the underlying surface (a detailed discussion follows in Chapter 3). At the water-air interface the pressure resulting from evaporation is called the vapor pressure of water. Once in air, the water vapor exerts its own partial pressure, called simply *vapor pressure.*

The relationships among moisture content in the atmosphere, temperature, and

15

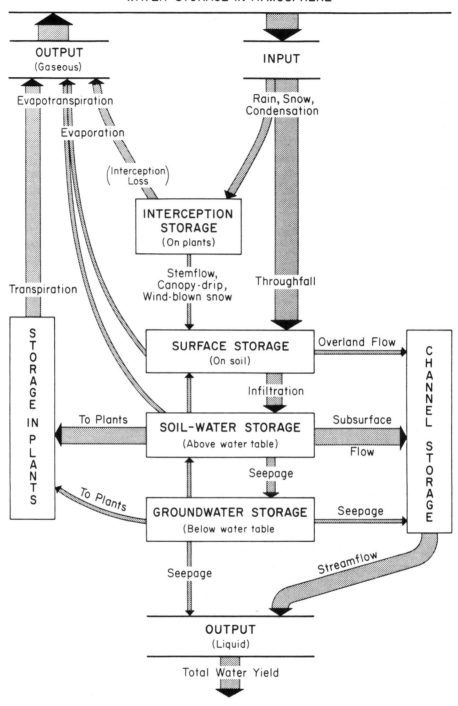

2.1. The hydrologic cycle consists of a system of water-storage compartments and the solid, liquid, or gaseous flows of water within and between the storage points (from Anderson et al. 1976).

vapor pressure determine the occurrence and amounts of evaporation and precipitation (Fig. 2.2). The *saturation vapor pressure* (e_s) is determined by air temperature alone and is the partial pressure of water vapor in a saturated atmosphere as described by Lee (1978):

$$\ln e_s = 21.382 - \frac{5347.5}{T} \tag{2.1}$$

where T = absolute temperature in °K.

A parcel of unsaturated air (point A in Figure 2.2) can become saturated by either cooling (A–C) or by adding moisture to the air mass (A–B). Unsaturated air can be characterized by its *relative humidity,* the ratio of vapor pressure of the air to saturation vapor pressure at a given temperature and expressed as a percentage. For example, at 25°C in Figure 2.2, the relative humidity of the air parcel A is 100 (17 mb/31mb) = 55%. The difference between the saturation vapor pressure (e_s) and the actual vapor pressure of an unsaturated air parcel (e_a) is the *vapor pressure deficit* (for A it is 31 mb − 17 mb = 14 mb). The temperature at which a parcel of unsaturated air reaches its saturation vapor pressure is the *dew point temperature* (15.56°C in Figure 2.2 for the air parcel A).

Atmospheric pressure decreases with height, causing a rising parcel of air to expand. Therefore, the temperature of the air will decrease, while that of a descending parcel of air will become compressed and warmed. The process is called *adiabatic* if no heat is gained or lost by mixing with surrounding air. The rate at which unsaturated air cools by adiabatic lifting is approximately 1°C / 100 m, called the *dry adiabatic*

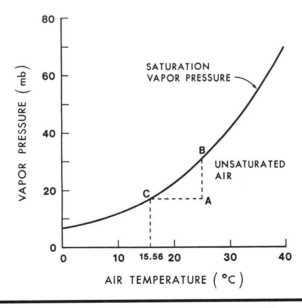

2.2. Saturation vapor pressure-air temperature relationship; a parcel of unsaturated air (A) must be cooled (A to C) or moisture must be added (A to B) before saturation occurs.

lapse rate. Movements of large air masses can change the lapse rate, and conditions can even reverse the lapse rate when large cold air masses underlay less dense warm air, a condition called an *inversion* (temperature increases with height).

■ PRECIPITATION

Precipitation occurs when three conditions in the atmosphere are met:

1. The atmosphere becomes saturated.
2. Small particles or nuclei are present in the atmosphere (e.g., dust and ocean salt) upon which condensation or sublimation can take place.
3. Water or ice particles must coalesce and grow large enough to reach the earth against updrafts.

Saturation results when either the air mass is cooled until the saturation vapor pressure is reached or when moisture is added to the air mass (Fig. 2.2). Rarely does the direct introduction of moist air cause precipitation. More commonly, precipitation occurs when an air mass is lifted, becomes cooled, and reaches its saturation vapor pressure. Air masses are lifted as a result of (1) frontal systems, (2) orographic effects, and (3) convection. Different storm and precipitation characteristics result from each of these lifting processes (Fig. 2.3).

Frontal precipitation occurs when two air masses of different temperature and moisture content are brought together by general circulation and air becomes lifted at the frontal surface. A cold front results from a cold air mass replacing and lifting a warm air mass that already has a tendency to rise. Cold fronts are characterized by high-intensity rainfall of relatively short duration and usually cover a zone narrower than that of warm fronts. Conversely, a warm front results when warm air rides up and over a cold air mass; it is generally characterized by widespread, gentle rainfall.

Orographic precipitation occurs when general circulation forces an air mass up and over mountain ranges. As the air mass becomes lifted, a greater volume of the air mass reaches saturation vapor pressure resulting in more precipitation with increasing elevation. A striking example of orographic precipitation is on the windward side of Mt. Rainier, Washington, where annual precipitation varies from about 1346 mm at 305 m to 2921 mm at 1690 m. Once the air mass passes over mountains, a lowering and warming of the air occurs, creating a dry rain shadow effect on the leeward side.

Convective precipitation, as characterized by summer thunderstorms, is the result of excessive heating of the earth's surface and the adjacent layer of moist air. When the air adjacent to the surface becomes warmer than the air mass above it, lifting occurs. As the air mass rises, condensation takes place, the latent heat of vaporization is released, more energy is added to the air mass, and consequently more lifting occurs. Rapidly uplifted air can reach high altitudes where water droplets become frozen and hail forms or becomes intermixed with rainfall. Such rain or hail storms are some of the most severe precipitation events anywhere and are characterized by high-intensity, short-duration rainfall over rather limited areas. When numerous thunderstorms occur over a large enough area, flash flooding can result.

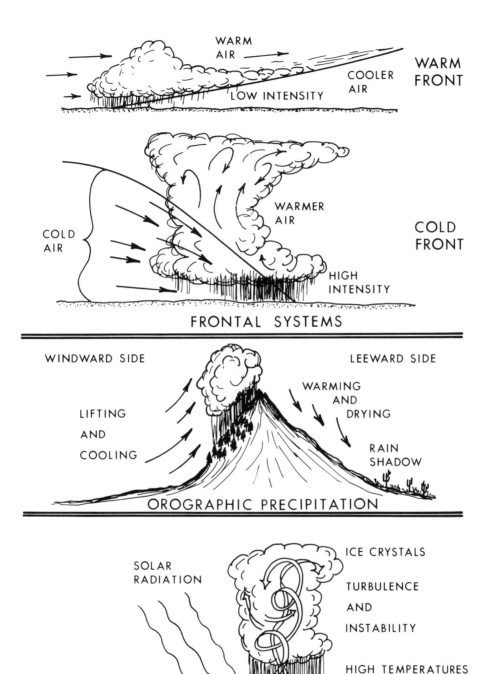

2.3. Examples of different mechanisms causing air masses to lift and cool, resulting in precipitation.

TYPES OF PRECIPITATION

Drizzle—waterdrops less than 0.5 mm in diameter; intensity less than 1 mm/hr.

Rain—waterdrops greater than 0.5 mm in diameter; upper limit is 6 mm in diameter.

Sleet—small frozen raindrops.

Snow—ice crystals formed in the atmosphere by the procss of sublimation.

Hail—ice particles greater than 0.5 mm diameter found by alternative freezing and thawing in turbulent air currents; usually associated with intense convective cells.

Fog, dew, and frost—not actually precipitation; the result of interception or condensation (or sublimation); can be important sources of moisture to watersheds in coastal areas and other areas subjected to persistent fog and/or clouds.

Measurement of Precipitation

Precipitation characteristics of interest include the total amount (or depth) over some period of time (daily, monthly, seasonally, or annually), the intensity of precipitation (depth per unit time), and the distribution of precipitation over time and space. Although precipitation often is measured on a routine basis at major towns and airports, precipitation is not routinely measured in many rural parts of a watershed. In addition, many records of precipitation are short term or discontinuous, which hamper our ability to better understand the likelihood of having droughts or floods.

Determining the depth of precipitation over watersheds requires precipitation to be measured at selected points within the watershed (or in adjacent areas), and these measurements must be extended to estimate the depth of precipitation that fell over the ungauged parts of the watershed. The purpose of such measurements is to estimate the total amount of precipitation that is representative of the area.

In higher latitudes and at high elevations of mountainous regions, both rainfall and snow may need to be measured. The following discussion will concentrate on rainfall. Snow measurements are discussed in Chapter 14.

METHODS OF MEASUREMENT

Three types of precipitation gauges that are now in general use are (1) the standard gauge, (2) the storage gauge, and (3) the recording gauge. The most common method of measuring rainfall is with a series of gauges, typically cylindrical containers 20.3 cm (8 in.) in diameter (Fig. 2.4A). Standard or nonrecording gauges often are used because of economy. Such gauges must be read periodically, normally every 24 hr at the same time each day. The standard gauge magnifies rainfall depth 10-fold by funneling rainfall into an internal cylinder of 10-fold smaller cross-sectional area. Storage gauges have the same size opening, but have a greater storage capacity, usually 1525–2540 mm in depth. They may be measured periodically, for example, once a week, once a month, or seasonally. Usually, a small amount of oil is added to gauges that are measured less frequently than 24 hr to suppress evaporation.

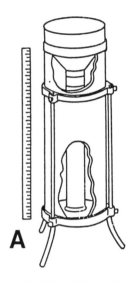 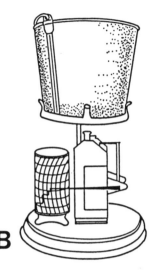

2.4. Rain gauges. A: Cut-away of the cylindrical standard Weather Service rain gauge; B: A weighing-type recording gauge with its cover removed to show the spring housing, recording pen, and storage bucket (from Hewlett 1982b; © Univ. of Georgia Press, by permission).

Recording instruments that allow for continuous measurement of rainfall are more limited because of their higher cost. Examples of recording rain gauges are the weighing-type (Fig. 2.4B) and the tipping-bucket gauge. The weighing-type gauge records the weight of water with time by means of a calibrated pen on a clock-driven drum; the chart on the drum indicates the accumulated rainfall with time. Rainfall intensity is obtained by determining incremental increases in amount per unit of time (typically 1 hr). A tipping-bucket gauge records intensity, making a recording each time a small cup (usually 1 mm) fills with water and then empties as it tips back and forth. Because about 0.2 sec are required for each bucket to tip, high-intensity rainfall may not be accurately measured.

The accuracy of rainfall measurements is affected both by gauge site characteristics and the relationship of the location of gauges to the watershed. As a rule, a rain gauge should be located in a relatively flat area with the funnel opening in a horizontal plane. In the United States, the standard is to situate the gauge so that the funnel orifice is 1 m above the ground surface. The gauge should be far enough away from surrounding objects so that the rainfall catch is not affected. A clearing defined by a 30–45° angle from the top of the gauge to the closest object is usually sufficient (Fig. 2.5). If gauges are located too close to trees or structures, the wind patterns around the gauge can result in gauge catches far different from the rainfall that actually occurred. Ideally, one should select small openings in a forest or in other areas that are sheltered from the full force of the wind but that meet the above criteria. Sometimes, gauges are located in a large enough opening when they are initially installed but become affected by forest growth in adjacent areas over time. This is particularly important in areas where vegetation grows quickly. Also, high wind speeds diminish the efficiency of

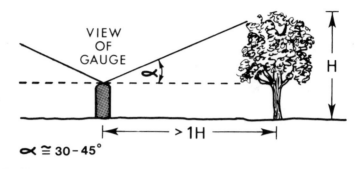

2.5. Proper siting of a rain gauge with respect to the nearest surrounding object.

gauge catch (Table 2.1). Wind shields, such as Nipher or Alter shields, should be used to reduce eddy effects in areas of high wind speeds. Errors caused by catch deficiencies are called instrumentation errors.

Gauges should be located throughout watersheds so that spatial and elevational differences in precipitation can be measured. Such factors as topographic barriers, elevational differences, and storm track patterns, or "tracking," should be considered in developing a rain-gauge network. Practical considerations such as economics and accessibility usually limit the number, type, and location of gauges.

Precipitation over an area can be estimated indirectly by radar sensing. Radar senses the backscatter of radio waves caused by water droplets and ice crystals in the atmosphere. The area and relative intensity of precipitation can be estimated up to a distance of 208 km. Radar echoes can be correlated with measured precipitation, but such a calibration is hampered by ground barriers, drop size, distribution of rainfall, and other storm factors. Radar has been most useful for tracking storm systems and identifying areas of intense or violent storm activity.

Table 2.1. Effect of wind velocity on the catch of precipitation by standard precipitation gauges

Wind Velocity (mi/hr)	Catch Deficiency (% of true amount)	
	Rainfall	Snowfall
0	0	0
5	6	20
15	26	47
25	41	60
50	50	73

Source: From Gray (1973), by permission.

NUMBER OF GAUGES REQUIRED

The number of rain gauges required to measure precipitation should generally increase with the size of the watershed and with the variability of precipitation. Sampling requirements can be determined with standard statistical methods (see Chapter 18). Use of random sampling as a means of excluding bias in the selection of gauge sites and for estimating the number of gauges needed is suggested. However, in areas of dense brush or forest, this type of rainfall sampling may not be practical owing to the difficulty of obtaining adequate sampling sites. Accessibility also limits the "ideal" siting of gauges in remote watersheds. As a result, insufficient sampling more often is the norm than the exception.

Rainfall variability on a watershed for monthly, seasonal, or annual periods can be estimated by using a regular network that is read after each storm event. By reading storage gauges monthly or seasonally, the effects of storm types on variability may be lost, but systematic differences in precipitation between parts of the watersheds for these longer periods can be estimated.

METHODS OF CALCULATING MEAN WATERSHED PRECIPITATION

The mean depth of precipitation over a watershed is required in many hydrologic investigations. Several methods are used in deriving this value. The three most common are the arithmetic mean, the Thiessen polygon, and the isohyetal methods (Fig. 2.6).

Arithmetic Mean Method. A straight arithmetic average is the simplest of all methods for estimating the mean rainfall on a watershed (Fig. 2.6). This method yields good estimates in level terrain if the gauges are numerous and uniformly distributed. Even in mountainous country, averaging the catch of a dense rain-gauge network will yield good estimates if the orographic influence on precipitation is considered in the selection of gauge sites. However, if gauges are relatively few, irregularly spaced, or precipitation over the area varies considerably, more sophisticated methods may be warranted.

Thiessen Polygon Method. When gauges are nonuniformly distributed over a watershed, this method may improve estimates of precipitation amounts over the entire area. Polygons are formed from the perpendicular bisectors of lines joining nearby gauges (Fig. 2.6). The watershed area within each polygon is determined and is used to apportion the rainfall amount of the gauge in the center of the polygon. It is assumed that the depth of water recorded by the rain gauge located within the polygon represents the depth of rain over the entire area of the polygon. The results usually are more accurate than the arithmetic average when the number of gauges on a watershed are limited and when gauges are located outside of the watershed boundary.

The Thiessen method allows for nonuniform distribution of gauges but assumes linear variation of precipitation between gauges and makes no attempt to allow for orographic influences. Once the area-weighing coefficients are determined for each station, they become fixed, and the method is as simple to apply as the arithmetic method.

Source Data: Daily rainfall measured at each gauge in centimeters

A	B	C	D
4	8	10	6

$$\text{Arithmetic mean} = \frac{4 + 8 + 10 + 6}{4}$$

$$= 7 \text{ cm}$$

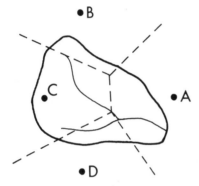

Thiessen Polygon:

Station	Depth (cm)		Area in Polygon[a]		Volume (cm)
A	4	×	0.28	=	1.12
B	8	×	0.09	=	0.72
C	10	×	0.49	=	4.90
D	6	×	0.14	=	0.84
				sum =	7.58

[a]As a fraction of total area.

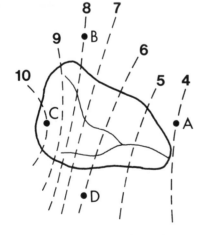

Isohyetal:

Mean Depth (cm)		Area between Isohyets[a]		Volume (cm)
4.5	×	0.12	=	0.54
5.5	×	0.25	=	1.38
6.5	×	0.14	=	0.91
7.5	×	0.13	=	0.98
8.5	×	0.18	=	1.53
9.5	×	0.14	=	1.33
10.5	×	0.04	=	0.42
			sum =	7.09

[a]As a fraction of total area.

2.6. Methods of estimating the average rainfall for a watershed: Arithmetic mean; Thiessen polygon; Isohyetal.

Isohyetal Method. With the isohyetal method, gauge location and amounts are plotted on a suitable map and contours of equal precipitation (isohyets) are drawn (Fig. 2.6). Rainfall measured within and outside of the watershed can be used to estimate the pattern of rainfall, and isohyets are drawn according to gauge catches. The average depth then is determined by computing and dividing by the total area. Many investigators indicate this as theoretically the most accurate method of determining mean watershed precipitation. But, it is also by far the most laborious.

The isohyetal method is particularly useful when investigating the influence of storm patterns on streamflow and for areas where orographic precipitation occurs. In some instances, relationships between precipitation and elevation can be used advantageously with only a few gauges (typically located in the lower elevations). Where orographic precipitation occurs, contour intervals sometimes may be used to help estimate (locate) the lines of equal precipitation. Precipitation amounts then are determined for each elevation zone or band and the respective areas weighed to obtain estimates for the entire watershed.

The accuracy of the isohyetal method depends upon the skill of the analyst. An improper analysis can lead to serious error. If linear interpolation between stations is used, the results will be essentially the same as those obtained with the Thiessen method.

ERRORS ASSOCIATED WITH PRECIPITATION MEASUREMENT

Hydrologic studies of watersheds often are constrained by an inadequate number of precipitation gauges, by the absence of long-term precipitation records, or both. Two types of error must be considered when determining precipitation measurement: *instrument error* is related to the accuracy with which gauges catch the true precipitation amount at a point; *sampling error* is associated with how well the gauges in a watershed represent the precipitation over the entire watershed area. Taking care in siting a gauge correctly and proper maintenance can minimize instrumentation error. Sampling error is minimized by properly designing a network with an adequate number of gauges.

Analysis of Precipitation

Once we have precipitation records, there are a number of analyses that can be performed to enhance our knowledge of hydrology and climate. This section briefly describes some of the more common types of analysis.

ESTIMATING MISSING DATA

All too often, one or more gauges in a precipitation network become nonfunctioning for some period of time. One way to estimate the missing record for such a station is to use existing relationships with adjacent gauges. For example, if the precipitation for a storm is missing for station C and precipitation at C (seasonal or annual) is correlated with that of stations A and B, the storm precipitation for station C can be estimated by the normal ratio method:

$$P_C = \frac{1}{2}\left(\frac{N_C}{N_A}P_A + \frac{N_C}{N_B}P_B\right) \tag{2.2}$$

where P_C = estimated storm precipitation for station C (mm); N_A, N_B, N_C = normal annual (or seasonal) precipitation for stations A, B, and C, respectively (mm); and P_A and P_B = storm precipitation for stations A and B (mm). The generalized equation for missing data is:

$$P_x = \frac{1}{n}\left(\frac{N_x}{N_1}P_1 + \ldots + \frac{N_x}{N_n}P_n\right) \tag{2.3}$$

Equation 2.3 is recommended only if there is a high correlation with other stations.

DOUBLE MASS ANALYSIS

Double mass analysis is a convenient method of checking the consistency of a precipitation station against that of one or more nearby stations. The application of this method is best explained by an example. Consider that station E has been collecting rainfall data for 45 yr. Originally, the station was located in a large opening in a conifer forest, but over the years the surrounding forest has grown up to the point where you suspect that the catch of this gauge is now affected. Based on your knowledge of the precipitation patterns in the region, you recognize that stations H and I are influenced by the same storm patterns, although their elevational differences and other factors cause annual rainfall to differ. There was a consistent correlation between the average of stations H and I with that of E in the early years of station E. By plotting the accumulated annual rainfall of E against the accumulated average annual rainfall of H and I, the relationship clearly changed after 1970 (Fig. 2.7). The relationship then can be used to correct existing rainfall catch at E so that it better represents the "true" catch at the location without the interference of nearby trees.

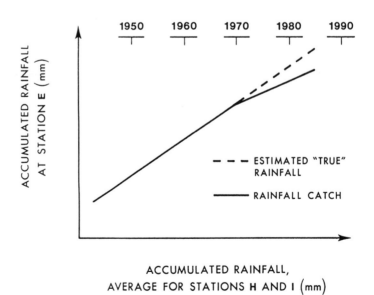

2.7. Double mass plot of annual precipitation at station E vs. average annual precipitation of stations H and I.

FREQUENCY ANALYSIS

Water resource systems such as small reservoirs, waterways, irrigation networks, and drainage systems for roads should be planned and designed for future events, the magnitude of which cannot be accurately predicted. Weather systems vary from one year to the next, and no one can accurately predict what the next year, season, or even month will bring. Therefore, we rely on statistical analyses of rainfall amounts over certain time periods. From these analyses the frequency distributions of past events are determined; the probability or likelihood of having certain events occur over a specified period of time then can be estimated. This approach, called *frequency analysis,* will be discussed for precipitation events.

The objective of frequency analysis is to develop a *frequency curve,* which is a relationship between the magnitude of events and the associated probability or recurrence interval (Fig. 2.8). The details of developing a frequency distribution function are outlined in Chapter 18 (see also Haan 1977). The recurrence interval (T_r) can be approximated by:

$$T_r = \frac{n + 1}{m} \tag{2.4}$$

where n = number of years of record and m = rank of the event.

The recurrence interval or return period (T_r) that corresponds to a given probability (p) is determined as the reciprocal of the probability:

$$T_r = \frac{1}{p} \tag{2.5}$$

The return period associated with the 0.05 event in Example 2.1 is 20 yr. The chance or risk of having certain events occur in any given year can be estimated from such a

---

EXAMPLE 2.1

Using rainfall frequency information to determine the correct size of a culvert for a road system

A road is to be constructed in a forested area and should be designed with sufficient culverts (numbers and sizes) to minimize washouts. It has been decided that the acceptable risk for this road is 5%, that is, we only want to take a 5% chance in any given year that it will be washed out. The 24-hr maximum rainfall frequency curve in Figure 2.8 was developed from data from a nearby station. From this curve, the 24-hr rainfall corresponding to the 0.05 probability is about 88 mm. The 88-mm rainfall over a 24-hr period then would be used to estimate the corresponding runoff (using a method such as the rational method discussed in Chapter 17). This approach should only be used for small, relatively homogeneous watersheds. As watershed size and complexity increases, it becomes less likely that the 0.05 rainfall event would produce a runoff event with the same probability.

PROBABILITY ≥ ORDINATE VALUE

2.8. Frequency curve of daily rainfall for a single station.

curve. For example, in Figure 2.8, the probability of having a 24-hr rainfall of 100 mm or more in any given year is about 0.02. Precipitation frequency curves can be developed for purposes of evaluating maximum annual events (Ex. 2.1) or can be developed for evaluating dry periods or droughts (for example, a frequency curve can be developed for the minimum 12-mo precipitation amounts).

Once a frequency curve is developed, the probability of exceeding certain rainfall amounts over some specified period of time can be determined. The probability that an event with probability p will be equalled or exceeded x times in N years is determined by:

$$\text{Prob }(x) = \frac{N!}{x!(N-x)!}\,(p)^x(1-p)^{N-x} \tag{2.6}$$

This relationship can be simplified by considering the probability of *at least one* event with probability p being equalled or exceeded in N years as follows:

$$\text{Prob(no occurrences in } N \text{ yr)} = (1-p)^N \tag{2.7}$$

therefore,

$$\text{Prob(at least one occurrence in } N \text{ yr)} = 1 - (1-p)^N \tag{2.8}$$

For example, the probability of having a 24-hr rainfall event of 100 mm or greater (Fig. 2.8) over a 20-yr period is determined by:

$$\text{Prob}(x \geq 100) = 0.025$$

or

$$\text{Prob}(x \geq 100 \text{ mm over 20 yr}) = 1 - (1-0.025)^{20} = 0.40, \text{ or } 40\%$$

DEPTH-AREA-DURATION ANALYSIS

The above frequency analysis is based upon rainfall characteristics at a point or a specific location. The design of storage reservoirs and other water resource–related activities requires that the watershed area be taken into account. Because rainfall does not occur uniformly, it is expected that as larger watersheds are considered, the depth of rainfall associated with any given probability will decrease (Fig. 2.9). Furthermore, on a given area, the greater the depth of rainfall for a given duration, the lower the probability of equalling or exceeding that amount.

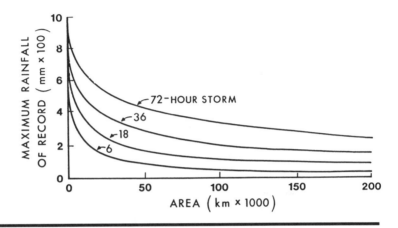

2.9. Relationship between maximum rainfall amounts for specified durations and area (from Hewlett 1982, © Univ. of Georgia Press, by permission).

■ INTERCEPTION AND NET PRECIPITATION

Once rainfall or snowfall occurs, the type, extent, and condition of vegetation influences the pattern of deposition and amount of precipitation reaching the soil surface. Dense coniferous forests in northern latitudes and the multistoried canopies of the tropics catch and store large quantities of precipitation, which directly returns to the atmosphere by evaporation and thus becomes a loss of water from the watershed. In tropical forests, over 30% of the annual precipitation may be lost via canopy interception. Interception losses are less in more arid or semiarid environments with more sparse vegetation. Although we generally consider forests to have the highest interception losses, shrublands and prairie vegetation can intercept 10–20% of gross precipitation during periods when maximum growth has been attained. Forest floor litter also can store large quantities of precipitation, which partly evaporates directly to the atmosphere.

Not all the precipitation caught by a forest canopy is lost to the atmosphere. Much can drip off the foliage or run down the stems (stemflow), ultimately reaching the soil surface. Similarly, drainage from forest floor litter will reach the soil surface.

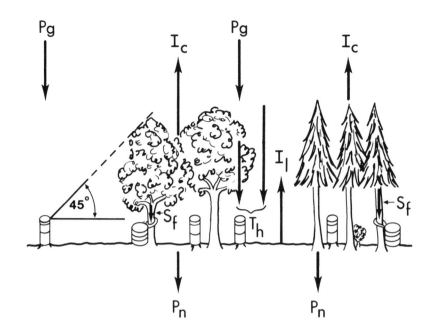

Interception total = I = I_c + I_l
The amount reaching the forest floor = T_h + S_f
Interception by canopy (overstory + understory) I_c = P_g − T_h − S_f
Net precipitation P_n = T_h + S_f − I_l

2.10. Components of interception (from Hewlett 1982, © Univ. Georgia Press, by permission). I_c = canopy interception; I_l = litter interception; P_g = gross percipitation; P_n = net precipitation; S_f = stemflow; T_h = throughfall.

Components of Interception

The components of the interception process, methods of measurement, and resulting deposition of precipitation are illustrated in Figure 2.10. Interception by the forest canopy is defined as:

$$I_c = P_g - T_h - S_f \tag{2.9}$$

where I_c = canopy interception loss (mm); P_g = gross precipitation (mm); T_h = throughfall, precipitation that passes through the vegetative canopy or as drip from vegetation (mm); and S_f = stemflow, water that flows down the stems to the ground surface. Collars are fixed to the stems of trees and divert stemflow to containers for measurement (mm).

The partitioning of a given quantity of rainfall into the above pathways depends upon vegetative cover characteristics such as leaf and branch surface area, branch attitude, shape of the canopy, and roughness of the bark. The interception components of a growing forest, from seedling stage to mature forest, would change as follows: (1) T_h would diminish over time as the canopy cover increases; (2) S_f would increase over time, but would always be a small quantity; and (3) the storage capacity of vegetation and litter, as related primarily to leaf surface area, would increase substantially.

THROUGHFALL

Canopy coverage, total leaf area, the number of layers of vegetation, and rainfall intensity determine how much of the gross rainfall reaches the forest floor. The size and shape of canopy openings affect the amount, intensity, and spatial distribution of throughfall. The shape of the overstory, particularly the branch and leaf angles, can concentrate throughfall in drip points, which can result in greater amounts and intensities of rainfall at these points, with a corresponding greater kinetic energy than in the open. Other locations under a dense forest canopy can receive little throughfall. Throughfall relationships have been determined for forest types in many parts of the world. Relationships between throughfall and precipitation (Ex. 2.2) have been devel-

---

EXAMPLE 2.2

Throughfall relationships for different vegetative canopies

1. Eastern U.S. Hardwood Forests (Helvey and Patric 1965):
Growing Season

$$T_h = 0.901P - 0.031n$$

Dormant Season

$$T_h = 0.914P - 0.015n$$

where T_h = throughfall (in.); P = total precipitation (in.); and n = number of storms.

2. Southern U.S. Pine Forests (Roth and Chang 1981):
Longleaf Pine

$$T_h = 1.002P - 0.0008P^2 - 1.397$$

Loblolly Pine

$$T_h = 0.930P - 0.0011P^2 - 0.610$$

where T_h = throughfall (mm); and P = total rainfall (mm).

3. New Zealand Vegetation Communities (Blake 1975):
Kauri Forest

$$T_h = 0.60P - 3.71$$

Manuka Schrub

$$T_h = 0.44P - 0.10$$

Mountain Beech Forest

$$T_h = 0.69P - 1.90$$

where T_h = throughfall (mm); and P = total rainfall (mm).

oped for mature forest stands in particular areas. Because throughfall depends on tree canopy surface area and cover, descriptors of forest stands that relate to these characteristics should be included in prediction equations to allow for wider application.

STEMFLOW

Stemflow, usually less than 2% of gross annual precipitation, is affected by branch attitude, shape of tree crowns, and roughness of bark. Generally, tree species with rough bark retain more water and exhibit less stemflow than those with smooth bark.

Although stemflow is not a large quantity in terms of an annual water budget, the process can be an important mechanism of replenishing soil moisture. Stemflow concentrates water in a small area near the base of the tree stem; this water can flow quickly and penetrate deeply into the soil through root channels.

Interception Process

Observations of interception losses for individual storms indicate that the precipitation and associated storm characteristics as well as vegetation characteristics influence the interception process. The type of precipitation, whether rain or snow, the intensity and duration of rainfall, wind velocity, and evaporative demand affect interception losses. The interception of snow, although clearly visible for a conifer forest immediately after snowfall, usually is not a significant loss. Much of the snow caught by foliage usually reaches the soil surface by the mechanical action of wind or by melt and drip (Ex. 2.3).

The process of interception during a rainstorm usually results in greater losses than with snowfall. The total interception loss is the sum of (1) water stored on vegetative surfaces (including forest litter) at the end of a storm and (2) the evaporation from these surfaces during the storm. If a storm were to last over a long period of time

EXAMPLE 2.3

Deposition of intercepted snowfall in a southwestern ponderosa pine forest (Tennyson et al. 1974)

Time-lapse imagery and meteorological records of precipitation, temperature and relative humidity, wind velocity, and solar radiation were employed to study the deposition of intercepted snowfall in a southwestern ponderosa pine forest throughout a winter season. From an analysis of 10 snowfall events, each of which was in excess of 250 mm in depth, it was determined that over 95% of the intercepted snow eventually reached the ground. The important processes of removal of intercepted snow were wind erosion and snowmelt with subsequent dripping and freezing in the snowpack on the ground. While snowfall interception was not a significant loss to the water budget for the site, the deposition of intercepted snow on the ground resulted in a redistribution of the snowpack.

under windy conditions, the interception loss would be expected to exceed that from a storm of equal duration with calm conditions. Conversely, a high-intensity, short-duration thunderstorm with high wind speeds can have the least amount of interception loss. This can be explained by the action of wind, which can mechanically remove water from the canopy and, therefore, not allow the storage capacity of the canopy to be reached. The effects of wind on evaporative loss would be minimal for a storm of short duration.

Potential interception loss (I) for a storm can be expressed as (Horton 1919):

$$I = S + RtE \tag{2.10}$$

where S = water storage capacity of vegetative surfaces, expressed as depth over the projection area of canopy (mm); R = ratio of evaporating surface to the projected area (decimal fraction); E = evaporation rate (mm) during the storm; and t = time duration of storm (hr).

Equation 2.10 assumes that rainfall is sufficient to satisfy the total storage capacity (S). Equation 2.11 has been used to account for rainfall amount (Meriam 1960, as presented by Gray 1973):

$$I = S(1 - e^{-P/S}) + RtE \tag{2.11}$$

where P = rainfall (mm); and e = the base of natural logarithms.

The storage capacity of mature conifers is generally greater than that of mature hardwoods. Comparisons among conifer stands have yielded a wide range of values in contrast to less variability among mature hardwood stands in North America. Interception losses of deciduous hardwoods vary with season as a result of leaf fall. In many instances the total interception loss from a natural forest is attributed to both understory and overstory species, and often a mixture of conifers and hardwoods.

Hydrologic Importance of Interception

The hydrologic importance of interception is dependent upon several climatic, physical, and vegetative characteristics. In most water budget studies, interception is an important storage term that should be subtracted from gross precipitation. The result is *net precipitation,* or that amount of precipitation available to either replenish soil water deficits or become surface, subsurface, or groundwater flow. Net precipitation can be determined from:

$$P_n = P_g - I \tag{2.12}$$

where P_n = net precipitation (mm); P_g = gross precipitation measured by rain gauges in openings (mm); and I = interception loss (mm).

The above terms can be measured rather easily with simple plot studies (Fig. 2.10); however, determining net precipitation over a watershed can be more difficult. The spatial variability of canopy cover type and extent, canopy stratification or layering, and the storage capacity of plant litter all affect the total interception loss for a watershed. Under certain climatic conditions, the interception storage differences between species results in water yield differences. In regions where annual precipitation exceeds potential evapotranspiration (see Chapter 3) and soil water rarely limits transpiration, differences in interception between conifers and hardwoods also can result in differences in water yield. Converting from hardwoods to conifers in the humid southeastern United States, for example, has increased interception losses and reduced annual streamflow volume. Such differences likely would not be observed in semiarid regions because of the higher ratio of annual potential evapotranspiration to annual precipitation. The reasoning is that the difference in net precipitation reaching the soil surface, due to differences in interception, will on the average not result in streamflow but rather will satisfy soil water deficits. These differences in net precipitation simply will be transpired at some other time and will not necessarily represent differences in water yield.

Forest canopies affect the deposition pattern of precipitation. In the case of snow, such effects have management implications for water yield improvement. Snow has a high surface to mass ratio and, consequently, is strongly affected by wind patterns. Small openings within a conifer stand, for example, experience eddies, which deposit more snow than the adjacent forest. Also, wind mechanically deposits much of the snow intercepted by surrounding trees into these openings. By clearcutting strips in conifer stands and orienting them perpendicular to wind, the deposition of snow can be increased within the strips and thus increase the water yield in some cases (see Chapter 14).

Up to this point in our discussion, interception has been considered a loss from a watershed. However, in some coastal areas and high elevations in the humid tropics, which experience a large number of days with low clouds or fog, interception can add moisture to the soil. Fog that is intercepted by foliage coalesces and drips off, adding moisture that would otherwise remain in the air. In such cases, the greater the foliage surface area, the greater the interception *input* to the water budget.

Interception has been studied widely and the literature cites interception values for many different vegetative types and tree species. Unfortunately, few have related interception storage values or total interception loss to forest stand (or other vegetative) characteristics so that the values can be estimated from field data. Examples of stand characteristics and associated interception storage values for red pine stands in Minnesota are presented in Table 2.2. These storage relationships then were used with precipitation records to calculate with Equation 2.11 the growing season interception losses for the respective stands (Table 2.3). Interception storage represents both canopy and associated understory vegetation. Based on these tables, the interception loss for dense conifer plantations can be over 30% of the precipitation occurring during the growing season.

The hydrologic role of litter interception can be considered twofold: (1) the storage of part or all of the throughfall, and (2) the protection that litter provides for the mineral soil surface against the energy of rainfall. The storage capacity of forest litter depends on the type, thickness, and level of decomposition of the litter. Generally, the storage capacity of conifer litter exceeds that of hardwood litter. Litter storage capacities of conifer plantations in Minnesota were similar to canopy storage capacities (Table 2.2). However, the moisture content of litter generally remains high because the forest floor is usually protected from wind and direct solar radiation. As a result, litter may not be able to absorb much additional water, a point emphasized by contrasting litter storage capacities in Table 2.2 with seasonal litter interception losses in Table 2.3. Forest stands that are more open, such as ponderosa pine in the southwestern

Table 2.2. Interception storage for red pine stands at Cloquet Forestry Center

Stand	Stand Characteristics			Canopy Storage		Litter Storage Capacity (in.)
	Age (Yr)	Basal area (ft²/acre)	Stems (no./acre)	P_g<1 in. (in.)	P_g>1 in. (in.)	
A	21	85	1030	.06	.14	.07
B	20	165	1512	.14	.28	.12
C	29	234	1150	.10	.22	.16
D	71	174	427	.09	.15	.16

Source: From unpublished data, S. J. Fox. 1985. Interception–net rainfall relationships of red pine stands in northern Minnesota. Plan B Paper, College of Forestry, University of Minnesota, 56 pp.

Table 2.3. Simulated interception components for the growing season (June, July, and August) for four red pine stands

Year	Gross Rainfall (P_g)(in.)	Stand	Simulated Net Rainfall (in.)	Canopy Interception (in.)	Litter Interception (in.)	Stemflow (in.)
1953	21.55	A	18.19	3.50	0.42	0.57
		B	16.49	5.07	0.62	0.64
		C	17.46	4.02	0.62	0.45
		D	17.43	3.46	0.74	0.08
1970	6.13	A	4.68	1.16	0.41	0.12
		B	3.48	2.10	0.67	0.13
		C	3.87	1.66	0.69	0.09
		D	4.06	1.30	0.78	0.02
1976	11.74	A	9.79	1.77	0.46	0.28
		B	8.48	2.90	0.67	0.31
		C	9.02	2.23	0.71	0.22
		D	9.12	1.82	0.85	0.04

Source: From unpublished data, S. J. Fox. 1985. Interception–net rainfall relationships of red pine stands in northern Minnesota. Plan B Paper, College of Forestry, University of Minnesota, 56 pp.

United States, can experience significant litter interception; ponderosa pine litter storage capacities of over 200% by weight have been reported.

The protection against rainfall that litter provides for the soil surface influences the surface soil conditions directly and, therefore, infiltration, surface runoff, and surface soil erosion (discussed in greater detail in chapters 4 and 7).

■ SUMMARY

You should now have a general understanding of the important factors that influence the occurrence of precipitation over an area and how vegetation affects the amount and spatial deposition of that precipitation. Specifically, you should be able to:

1. Describe the conditions necessary for precipitation to occur.

2. Explain the different precipitation and storm characteristics associated with frontal storm systems, orographic influences, and convective storms.

3. Understand how precipitation is measured at a point and how such measurements can be used to estimate the average depth of precipitation over a watershed area.

4. Estimate values of precipitation that are missing for a particular storm.

5. Explain the purpose of performing double mass analysis and frequency analysis.

6. Understand the ways in which vegetation influences the deposition of precipitation.

7. Explain and be able to calculate stemflow, throughfall, and interception storage when given appropriate data.

8. Calculate net precipitation, given values of gross precipitation and interception values.

9. Explain and discuss the hydrologic importance of interception under different vegetative cover and climatic regimes.

CHAPTER 3

Evapotranspiration and Soil Water Storage

INTRODUCTION

Evaporation from soils, plant surfaces, and water bodies, together with water losses through plant leaves, are considered collectively as *evapotranspiration* (*ET*). Evapotranspiration affects water yield, largely determines what proportion of precipitation input to a watershed becomes streamflow, and is influenced by forest, range, and agricultural practices that alter vegetation. The water budget equation can be used to estimate *ET* as follows:

$$ET = P - Q - \Delta S - \Delta l \tag{3.1}$$

where ET = evapotranspiration (mm); P = precipitation over time period (mm); Q = streamflow (mm); ΔS = change in the amount of storage in the watershed = $S_2 - S_1$ (mm), where S_2 = storage at the end of a period of time, and S_1 = storage at the beginning of a period of time; and Δl = change in deep seepage, $l_o - l_i$ (mm), where l_o = seepage out of the watershed, and l_i = seepage into the watershed.

The *ET* component of the above water budget can be over 90% of the annual precipitation in some watersheds. Changes in vegetation that reduce annual *ET* will increase streamflow and/or groundwater recharge; increases in annual *ET* have the opposite effect.

Rates of *ET* influence water yield by affecting the antecedent water status of a watershed: high rates deplete water in the soil and in surface-water impoundments; more storage space is then available for precipitation. Low rates leave comparatively less storage space in the soil and surface water impoundments. The amount of storage space in the watershed subsequently determines the amount and, to some extent, the timing of streamflow resulting from precipitation.

THE PROCESS

Evaporation is the net loss of water from a surface resulting from a change in the state of water from liquid to vapor and the net transfer of this vapor to the atmosphere. Before evaporation or transpiration can occur, there must be (1) a flow of energy to

37

the evaporating or transpiring surface, (2) a flow of liquid water to these surfaces, and (3) a flow of vapor away from these surfaces. If one or more of these flows are changed, there is a corresponding change in the total *ET* loss from a surface.

Energy Flow

Solar energy drives the hydrologic cycle. Conditions that control the net flow of energy determine the amount of energy available for the latent heat of vaporization. The flow of energy to evaporating and transpiring surfaces is usually described with an energy budget, components of which can be partitioned and related to parts of the water budget. The linkage between water and energy budgets is direct; the net energy available at the earth's surface is apportioned largely in response to the presence or absence of water. Reasons for studying the energy budget and the relation to the water budget are to develop a better understanding of the hydrologic cycle and to be able to quantify or estimate evaporation from bodies of water, potential evapotranspiration for terrestrial systems, and snowmelt.

The earth's surface neither gains nor loses significant quantities of energy over long periods of time, but there may be a net gain or loss for any given time interval. The following discussion emphasizes the general concepts of the energy budget.

RADIATION

All substances with a temperature above absolute zero (O°K) emit electromagnetic radiation, as determined by:

$$W = \varepsilon \, \sigma \, T^4 \tag{3.2}$$

where W = emission rate of radiation in cal/cm²/min (langleys min⁻¹); ε = emissivity, the ratio of radiation emitted from a substance divided by the radiation emitted from a perfect black body (solid terrestrial objects have emissivities of 0.95–0.98 and are often assumed to equal 1.0); σ = Stefan-Boltzman constant (8.132×10^{-11} cal/cm²/°K⁴/min); and T = *absolute* temperature in °K (°C + 273).

The amount of radiation at a particular wavelength is temperature dependent, just as is the emission rate of radiation. A perfect black body absorbs and emits radiation in all wavelengths. By convention, radiation is separated into (1) shortwave or solar radiation (sometimes called insolation), which includes wavelengths up to 4.0 μ, and (2) longwave or terrestrial radiation, which is radiation above 4.0 μ. As temperature increases, the greatest magnitude of emitted radiation occurs at shorter wavelengths, that is, the hotter the substance, the shorter the wavelength; therefore, the sun emits radiation at shorter wavelengths than do terrestrial objects. A doubling of the absolute temperature increases the emission rate of radiation 16-fold. The sun has a temperature of about 6000°K and emits about 10⁵ cal/cm²/min, while a soil surface with a temperature of 300°K (27°C) emits about 0.66 cal/cm²/min. The radiant environment of soil, plants, water, and snow surfaces is determined by both shortwave and longwave processes of radiation.

Shortwave radiation comprises direct solar radiation (W_s) and diffuse radiation (w_s), which includes scattered and reflected solar radiation. Scattering is caused mainly by air molecules; reflection is from clouds, dust, and other atmospheric particles.

ENERGY RELATIONSHIPS OF WATER

Latent heat of fusion: 80 cal/g required to change water from solid ice (at 0°C) to liquid without changing the temperature.

Specific heat of ice: 0.5 cal/g/°C.

Latent heat of vaporization (L): energy required to change from liquid to vapor state without changing temperature; varies with temperature as follows:

Temperature (°C)	L (cal/g)
0	597.3
5	594.5
10	591.7
15	588.9
20	586.0
30	580.4

Specific heat of liquid water: 1 cal/g/°C.

Diffuse skylight averages about 15% of the total downward stream of solar radiation.

The total amount of shortwave radiation that is absorbed by terrestrial surfaces depends on the *albedo* or shortwave reflectivity of terrestrial objects. The albedo (α) is the proportion of the total shortwave radiation ($W_s + w_s$) that is reflected by an object. Light-colored surfaces have a higher albedo than dark-colored surfaces (Table 3.1). The net shortwave radiation at a surface is then determined as ($W_s + w_s$) − $\alpha(W_s + w_s)$, or $(1 - \alpha)(W_s + w_s)$.

Longwave radiation is emitted by the atmosphere and all terrestrial objects. The

Table 3.1. Albedos of natural terrestrial surfaces

Terrestrial Surface	Albedo (α) (%)
Fresh, new snow	80–95
Old snow	40
Dry, light sand	35–60
Dry grass	20–32
Cereal crops	25
Eucalyptus	20
Mixed hardwood forests (in leaf)	18
Rain forests	15
Pine forests	10–14
Bare wet soil	11

Source: From Lee (1980), Reifsnyder and Lull (1965), U.S. Army Corps of Engineers (1956).

primary longwave emitting constituents in the atmosphere are CO_2, O_3, and liquid and vapor forms of H_2O. Only a small portion of the total downward longwave radiation (I_a) is reflected by soil or plant surfaces; therefore, terrestrial objects usually are considered to be black bodies in terms of longwave radiation. The net longwave radiation at a surface is the difference between incoming (I_a) and emitted (I_g) longwave radiation, $I_a - I_g$.

   Net radiation, or the net all-wave radiation (R_n), is the resulting radiant energy available at a surface:

$$R_n = (W_s + w_s)(1 - \alpha) + I_a - I_g \tag{3.3}$$

By measuring incoming and outgoing shortwave and longwave radiation over a surface, net radiation is the residual term.

ENERGY BUDGET

   Net radiation can be either positive or negative for any particular time interval. A positive R_n represents excess radiant energy for some time interval, which according to the conservation of energy principle must be converted into other nonradiant forms of energy. When positive, R_n can be allocated at a surface as follows (for a snow-free condition):

$$R_n = (L)(E) + H + G + P_s \tag{3.4}$$

where L = latent heat of vaporization (cal/g); E = evaporation (g or cm^3/cm^2); H = energy flux that heats the air, or sensible heat (cal/cm^2); G = heat of conduction to ground or rate of energy storage in terrestrial system (cal/cm^2); and P_s = energy of photosynthesis (cal/cm^2). The latent heat of vaporization (L) and evaporation (E) usually are expressed as a product (LE), which represents the energy available for evaporating water.

   Net radiation is important from a hydrologic standpoint because it is the primary source of energy for evaporation, transpiration, and snowmelt. The allocation of net radiation in snow-free systems is dependent upon the presence of liquid water. If water is abundant and readily available at the evaporating surface, as much as 80–90% of the net radiation can be consumed in the evaporative process (LE). Little energy is left to heat the air (H) or ground (G), which remain relatively cold. If water is limiting, a greater amount of net radiation energy is available to heat the air, the ground surface, and other terrestrial objects. Losses (or gains) of energy to the interior earth do not change rapidly with time and usually are small in relation to the net radiation. Similarly, energy consumed in photosynthesis, although of immeasurable importance to life on earth, is a small portion of the net radiation and is usually not considered. When snow is present, the majority of net radiation may be apportioned to snowmelt (see Chapter 14).

   Energy budget applications to watersheds are concerned mainly with net radiation (R_n), latent heat (LE), and sensible heat (H). When the energy available for evaporating water from a watershed, latent heat, is considered, the contribution of sensible heat from adjacent areas cannot be neglected. The best example of lateral sensible heat contributions is that of an oasis, where a well-watered plant community can receive large amounts of sensible heat from the surrounding dry, hot desert.

EXAMPLE 3.1 _____

> **The following energy budget components were measured for oasis conditions at Aspendale, Australia (adapted from Penman et al. 1967)**
>
> LE = energy used in evaporation
> R_n = net radiation = 433 cal/cm²/day
> G = heat of conduction to ground = 21 cal/cm²/day
> H = sensible heat = −183 cal/cm²/day
>
> The energy consumed in evapotranspiration was:
>
> $$LE = R_n - G - H = 433 - 21 - (-183) = 595 \text{ cal/cm}^2/\text{day}$$
>
> Assuming the latent heat of vaporization to be 585 cal/cm³, the actual evapotranspiration would be:
>
> $$ET = \frac{595 \text{ cal/cm}^2/\text{day}}{585 \text{ cal/cm}^3} = 1.02 \text{ cm/day}$$
>
> where ET = evapotranspiration.

Energy budgets for an oasis and two different surface conditions at the same site are compared in Table 3.2. Note that for the bare soil condition, much of the net radiation is used to heat the air (H = 220 cal/cm²/day). In contrast, for the oasis condition, 180 cal/cm²/day sensible heat are added into the oasis. This energy is *in addition to* net radiation. Example 3.1 illustrates the energy budget calculations for an oasis condition. Similarly, a tall "island" of forest vegetation presents more surface area than low-growing vegetation (for example, crops). The greater, laterally exposed surface area intercepts more solar radiation and more sensible heat from moving air masses if the vegetation is cooler than the air. The total latent heat flux then is determined by:

$$LE = R_n + H \tag{3.5}$$

Table 3.2. Energy budget measurements at Akron, Colorado, for three different conditions

Site Description	R_n	G	H	LE
		(cal/cm²/day)		
Dry bare soil	284	18	220	46
Wet bare soil	226	58	−52	220
Oasis condition	388	18	−180	550

Source: Adapted from Hanks et al. (1968), as reported by Hanks and Ashcroft (1980).
Note: R_n = net radiation; G = heat of conduction to ground; H = sensible heat; LE = energy used in evaporation.

Such lateral movement of warm air to cooler plant-soil-water surfaces is called *advection.* *Convection,* in contrast, describes the vertical component of sensible heat transfer. The combination of advection and convection over and within irregular tree canopies can contribute significant quantities of sensible heat for evapotranspiration.

Water Flow

For purposes of discussion, the flow of water through the soil-plant-atmosphere system is analogous to the flow of electrical current in an electrical circuit (Fig. 3.1A). The soil can be represented as a variable resistor that changes with soil water content and soil-root interfaces. As the soil dries, more resistance is offered to flow. However, as roots grow into moist soil, the resistance to flow becomes offset.

Evaporation and transpiration from the soil-plant system require that liquid water must flow either to the *soil-atmosphere* interface or to plant roots, from where it then moves to the *leaf-atmosphere* interface (Fig. 3.1B). Therefore, we also must understand how liquid water flows in soils and plants.

WATER FLOW IN SOIL

Processes of evaporation and transpiration in most watersheds are controlled by the water flow through unsaturated soils. The driving force in the system is the difference in water potential (ψ) between two points; the concept being that water flows from a region of higher free energy (higher ψ) to a region of lower free energy (lower ψ). *Water potential* is the amount of work that a unit volume of water is capable of doing in reference to an equal unit of pure, free water at the same location in space. It also can be considered as the minimum work needed to move a unit of water from the soil that is in excess of the work needed to move an equal unit of pure, free water from the same location in space.

The water potential concept is derived from the second law of thermodynamics and relates to the free energy of water. A system that physically or chemically restricts the free energy of water results in negative values of water potential ($-\psi$). Gradients of negative water potentials are most common in soil-plant-atmosphere systems.

Soil water potential (ψ_s) is determined by several potentials:

$$\psi_s = \psi_g + \psi_p + \psi_o + \psi_t + \psi_m \tag{3.6}$$

where ψ_g = gravitational potential; ψ_p = pressure potential; ψ_o = osmotic or solute potential; ψ_t = thermal potential; and ψ_m = matric potential.

The gravitational potential exerts a downward pressure as a function of the weight of water as determined by the height of the water column, gravity, and density. It is the difference in elevation of a point in the system with respect to a stable reference datum, often mean sea level.

For a point in saturated soil or groundwater situations, the pressure potential is positive. The sum of gravitational and pressure potential is the total hydraulic potential. In the example in the top frame of Figure 3.2, the pressure potential (ψ_p at C) corresponds to the depth below the free water surface, a depth of 15 cm. The pressure potential is zero at the water table level (ψ_p at W.T. in Figure 3.2) and becomes negative above the water table. *Matric potential* (ψ_m) describes the physical attraction of

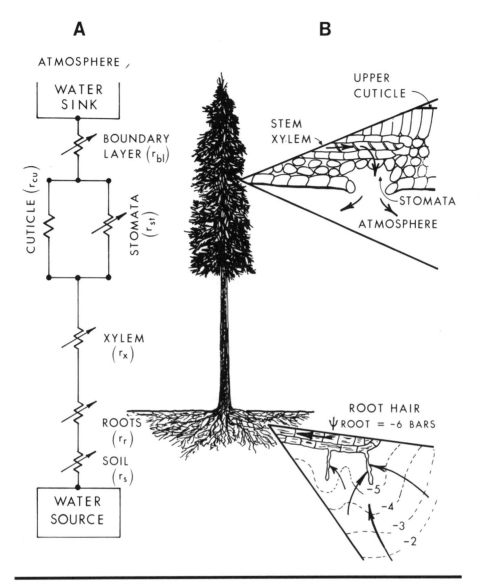

A

ATMOSPHERE

WATER SINK

BOUNDARY LAYER (r_{bl})

CUTICLE (r_{cu})

STOMATA (r_{st})

XYLEM (r_x)

ROOTS (r_r)

SOIL (r_s)

WATER SOURCE

B

UPPER CUTICLE

STEM XYLEM

STOMATA

ATMOSPHERE

ROOT HAIR
ψ ROOT = -6 BARS

-5
-4
-3
-2

3.1. A representation of soil-plant-atmosphere resistances to water flow (A) and corresponding flow through roots and leaves (B) (adapted from Rose 1966, © Pergamon Books Ltd., by permission). Flow of water can be described by $v = \Delta\psi/r$, analagous to Ohm's Law.

UNITS COMMONLY USED TO EXPRESS WATER POTENTIAL

1 kilopascal (kPa) = 10 millibars (mb)
= 10.2 cm H_2O
= .01 atmosphere
= .75 cm Hg

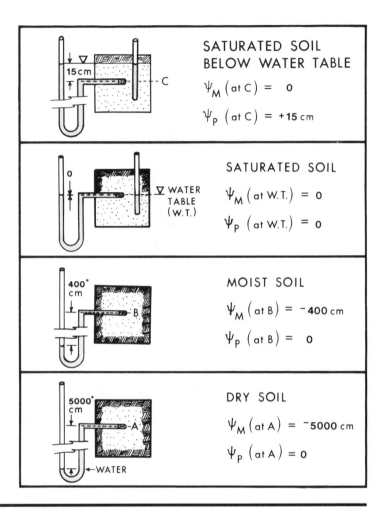

3.2. Matric potential (ψ_m) and pressure potential (ψ_p) of a dry soil (A), moist soil (B), at the water table (W.T.), and in a saturated soil (C) measured with a water manometer or tensiometer (adapted from Hanks and Ashcroft 1980). *Vertical distance not to scale; porous ceramic cup at *A, B, W.T., C.*

water to soil particles by both capillary and adsorptive forces. As the soil dries, matric forces in the soil increase and tend to oppose water flow. Thus, more energy must be exerted to move a quantity of water in a drier soil than in a more moist soil. If the moist and dry soils in Figure 3.2 were connected, water would flow from B to A.

Osmotic potential (ψ_o) is caused by solutes in the soil water solution. Solutes lower soil water potential (ψ_s) because they attract water molecules in the form of hydrated shells. This component normally has little effect on liquid water flow in soils except at the soil-root interface. Here, a semipermeable membrane (permeable only for water molecules) must be crossed for water to enter the root vascular system.

Thermal potential (ψ_t) is usually neglected. It would appear, however, that soil temperature gradients (over time and space) would affect ψ_s under certain conditions.

Higher thermal energy would increase ψ_s and, thereby, change the flow of water in soil.

Water flow in unsaturated soils is primarily a function of matric potential gradients ($d\psi_m/dx$), which are directly related to gradients in soil water content. As water is taken up by the roots, the soil water content immediately adjacent to the roots is depleted. The lower moisture content results in a greater attraction between water and the soil particles next to the root. A gradient in soil water content and, hence, water potential is then established. In all cases, water flow is from a region of higher ψ_s to a region of lower ψ_s (Fig. 3.1).

The driving forces operating in unsaturated flow have been described, but the velocity of soil water flow (v) is determined by:

$$v = \frac{\Delta\psi}{r_s} = -k_v \frac{d\psi}{dx} \tag{3.7}$$

where v = velocity (cm/sec); $\Delta\psi$ = water potential difference (kPa); r_s = resistance of any component (kPa·sec/cm); k_v = hydraulic conductivity (cm/kPa·sec); x = distance over which gradient is present (cm); and $d\psi/dx$ = total water potential gradient.

The velocity of water flow is proportional to $d\psi/dx$ and k_v. The pore size, pore geometry of the soil, and the soil water content affect the value of k_v for unsaturated conditions. Soil texture and structure affect soil water flow in unsaturated conditions and, as discussed in Chapter 5, in saturated conditions as well. Total flow through a cross-sectional area becomes:

$$Q = Av \tag{3.8}$$

where Q = flow (cm³/sec); A = cross-sectional area (cm²); and v = velocity (cm/sec).

WATER FLOW IN PLANTS

Water flow through soils is relatively passive until intercepted by the roots of plants. Once soil water is absorbed by the root, different forces become operative as the major constituents of water potential. The primary components of plant water potential are:

$$\psi_{pl} = \psi_o + \psi_p + \psi_t + \psi_g + \psi_m \tag{3.9}$$

where ψ_{pl} = plant water potential; and ψ_o, ψ_p, ψ_t, ψ_g, and ψ_m are defined as in Equation 3.6.

Isothermal conditions usually are assumed within the plant system, thereby eliminating ψ_t. Matric potential, an important part of soil water potential, is a minor constituent of ψ_{pl} and is usually ignored. Gravitational potential generally is not considered for herbaceous plants but can be important in tall trees. For example, about 0.3 bar/m of tree height must be overcome for water to move to the top of a tree. Water potential gradients between cells of plants, therefore, are due to the interaction of the osmotic potential (ψ_o) with the pressure potential (ψ_p).

In metabolizing plant cells, fluctuations of solute concentrations affect the energy status of cellular water. When solutes are added to cellular water, the ψ_{pl} of the cell is lowered. This steepens the water potential gradient between surrounding cells causing water to move through differentially permeable membranes into the cell. Water can enter from intercellular regions as well. The increased water content in the cell causes an increased turgidity (like blowing up a balloon), which in turn, opposes water entry. The final water potential of the cell is determined by these opposing forces, which can be expressed in terms of pressure as follows:

$$\psi_{pl} = P_t - P_o \tag{3.10}$$

where P_t = turgor pressure; and P_o = osmotic pressure.

Whereas the addition of solutes lowers ψ_{pl}, increased turgor pressure increases ψ_{pl}.

The analogy to Ohm's Law can again be used in describing water flow through the plant:

$$q = -k_w A(\Delta\psi_{pl}) = -A\frac{\Delta\psi_{pl}}{r_{pl}} \tag{3.11}$$

where q = water flow (cm³/sec); k_w = water permeability (cm/sec·kPa); A = membranous area (cm²); $\Delta\psi_{pl}$ = water potential difference (kPa); and r_{pl} = resistance of plant components (kPa·sec/cm).

The leaf of a plant, which is the primary food manufacturing center, maintains the water potential gradient since solute concentrations are increased by photosynthesis. This osmotic potential gradient alone is probably sufficient to cause some water flow up the stem. Transpiration reduces the pressure potential in the leaf and thereby steepens the total potential gradient from root to leaf. Liquid water moves through the cells in the leaf and eventually reaches substomatal cavities of the leaf from where it is evaporated. Water vapor then diffuses out and through the leaf boundary layer to be dissipated by turbulent mass transport into the atmosphere.

Vapor Flow

Evapotranspiration requires both energy and conditions that permit water vapor to flow away from evaporating or transpiring surfaces. Water molecules migrate from the liquid surface as a result of their kinetic energy. This transfer involves a change of state from liquid to vapor, during which the energy inputs to the vaporization (or transpiration) process occur. Vapor flow is initially a *diffusion* process in which water molecules diffuse from a region of higher concentration (evaporating surface or source) toward a region of lower concentration (sink) in the atmosphere. Water molecules at the soil-atmosphere or leaf-atmosphere interface must first diffuse through the *boundary layer*. This is also the layer through which sensible heat is transferred by molecular conduction only. The thin layer of air adjacent to evaporating and transpiring surfaces, which is at maximum thickness under still-air conditions, can be as thin as only 1 mm or less. Wind and air turbulence reduce the boundary layer thickness, but there is no turbulent flow in the boundary layer itself.

After water molecules exit the boundary layer, they move into a turbulent zone of the atmosphere where further movement is primarily by *mass transport* (turbulent eddy movement). In mass transport, whole parcels of air or eddies with water vapor and sensible heat flow in response to atmospheric pressure gradients, which cause the air parcels to flow both vertically and horizontally.

Evaporation describes the *net* flow of water away from a surface. Therefore, water molecules also return to the evaporating surface by mass transport and diffusion processes. If the amount of vapor arriving equals the amount leaving, a steady state exists and no evaporation occurs. If more molecules arrive than leave, a net gain results, called *condensation*.

The vapor pressure of water molecules at the evaporating surface must exceed the vapor pressure in the atmosphere for evaporation to occur. Under natural circumstances the vapor pressure of liquid water is mainly a function of its temperature, although solute content, atmospheric pressure, and water-surface curvature in capillaries also can be important. The vapor pressure of water molecules in the atmosphere is primarily a function of air temperature and the humidity of the air (Fig. 2.2). The vapor pressure gradient between evaporating surfaces and the atmosphere is the driving force that causes a net movement of water molecules. For this reason, the vapor pressure deficit between an evaporating surface and the atmosphere (the difference between point A and B in Figure 2.2) is often a component of empirical equations like the following (Dunne and Leopold 1978):

$$E_o = N(e_s - e_a)f(u) \tag{3.12}$$

where E_o = evaporation from a water body (mm); N = mass transfer coefficient, determined empirically; e_s = vapor pressure of water surface (mb); e_a = vapor pressure of the air (mb); and $f(u)$ = function of wind speed (km/day).

Formulas like Equation 3.12 are useful for estimating vapor flow away from *free-water* surfaces, such as a lake, but cannot be directly applied to *nonsaturated* conditions that prevail in watersheds. The vapor pressure deficit (*vpd*) or gradient ($e_s - e_a$) above a free-water surface can be determined from measurements of surface water temperature, air temperature, and the relative humidity of the air.

Conceptual relationships of the evaporative process that are applicable to complex surfaces, including plants and soil, have been developed. Such "models" assume that the vapor flow away from evaporating (E) or transpiring (T) surfaces is proportional directly to the vapor pressure deficit and inversely proportional to the resistance (R_v) of air to the molecular diffusion and mass transport of water vapor. That is:

$$E \text{ or } T = \frac{vpd}{R_v} \tag{3.13}$$

The R_v term includes a resistance for the turbulent layer of the atmosphere (r_e) and the boundary layer (r_{bl}), and internal resistances characterizing air-filled soil pores (r_s) or plant pores (r_{st}), called *stomates*. For convenience, the two atmospheric resistances sometimes are combined as r_a and the two internal resistances as r_n. The internal resistance is necessary because the liquid-air interface often is beneath the external surface of soil or plants. Water vapor diffusing outward encounters resistance from the air in soil and plant pores before reaching the boundary layer. For a wet external surface, the diffusive path length consists only of the boundary and turbulent layers of the atmosphere. The extra path length for *dry* soil or plants increases the total resistance to flow.

■ EVAPORATION FROM SOIL

Previous sections of this chapter described the flow of energy and liquid water to evaporating or transpiring surfaces and the flow of water vapor away from these surfaces into the atmosphere. In this section, these three flows are discussed for the simplest watershed situation—evaporation from a bare soil surface.

Given a bare, flat, wet soil surface, the water supply initially is unlimited and the amount of evaporation depends on the energy supply and the vapor pressure gradient. Under open atmospheric conditions, sufficient vapor pressure gradients usually exist and are maintained, causing only the *energy supply* to limit evaporation from the wet, exposed soil. If a piece of transparent plastic sheeting were laid over this soil, evaporation would cease because vapor flow would be blocked, even though energy and water flows would still converge at the active surface. In natural environments, however, energy inputs to the active surface increase the vapor pressure of water, steepening the vapor pressure gradient. In this case, evaporation proceeds at rates similar to those of free-water surfaces, assuming equal energy input. As evaporation occurs, lost water is replaced by water moving up from below the active surface in connecting water films around soil particles and through capillary pores. As the soil surface dries, a gradient in total water potential ($d\psi/dx$) is established; water is forced to move from the zone of higher potential (lower layer, wet zone) to the region of lower potential (upper layer, drier evaporating surface). As the soil dries, hydraulic conductivity also decreases. After a period of drying, water flow through the soil limits the rate of evaporation at the soil surface.

Water flow in moist soil is primarily liquid, but as soils dry, vapor diffusion through pores becomes more dominant. At about -1500 kPa water potential, the flow must be mainly as vapor or some combination of vapor and liquid. Liquid flow is reduced greatly at -1500 kPa because the continuity of capillary water and water films becomes disrupted. This is the point at which most plants become wilted and is referred to as the *permanent wilting point*. Water cannot move as rapidly through soils in vapor form as in liquid form; consequently, as the soil dries, a deficient water supply limits evaporation at the active surface, regardless of energy input. This condition is reached sooner in sandy soils than in clay soils, which have smaller pores that permit water films to remain intact for a longer period. Fine-textured soils retain pore water continuity at lower water contents than coarse-textured soils.

In summary, evaporation from wet soil initially will occur at a rate limited by *energy flow* to the active surface. With time, evaporation rates decrease because the *water flow* to the active surface is too slow to keep pace with the energy input. How much water will be evaporated from a soil under these conditions depends, in large part, on soil texture.

■ TRANSPIRATION

Transpiration is a biological modification of the evaporation process, because it is a function of the plant system and the environment. This modification is more efficient because of the large evaporating surface presented by plant foliage that is exposed directly to turbulent airflows above the soil boundary layer. Plants affect the amount of water transpired by stomatal regulation (the variable stomatal resistor in Figure 3.1), structural and physiological adaptations, and rooting characteristics. In essence, plants provide a variable conduit for water to flow from the soil water reservoir to the active evaporating surface at the leaf-atmosphere interface. This conduit bypasses the higher resistance offered by dry surface soils. To understand the importance of transpiration and associated land management implications, the basic process is examined below.

Once liquid water reaches cell surfaces within the leaf, 585–590 cal gm^{-1} (for temperatures of most terrestrial systems) are required for vaporization. After vaporization, the water vapor flows through intercellular spaces to the substomatal cavity, between guard cells of stomata, and into the atmosphere in response to the *vapor pressure gradient* at the leaf surface. Water vapor also can take a parallel path through leaf cuticles, but this pathway usually offers more resistance (r_{cu}) to flow than through stomata, except when stomata are closed tightly. Consequently, r_{cu} is considered large, making the variable resistor of stomata (r_{st}) the primary regulator of transpiration. The magnitude of r_{st} is proportional to the degree of opening of the stomatal pore, or stomatal aperture, while the magnitude of r_{cu} is a function of cuticular integrity and thickness.

The total resistance offered to vapor flow by the leaf (r_l) is:

$$\frac{1}{r_l} = \frac{1}{r_{st}} + \frac{1}{r_{cu}} \tag{3.14}$$

or

$$r_l = \frac{r_{st}\, r_{cu}}{r_{st} + r_{cu}} \tag{3.15}$$

The affect that the stomatal opening has on transpiration depends on the thickness of the boundary layer (r_{bl}) surrounding leaf surfaces; this is evident in Figure 3.1, because r_{bl} is in series with r_{st}. The total diffusive resistance (r) is described by:

$$r = r_{bl} + r_l \tag{3.16}$$

Because boundary layer resistance is related inversely to wind speed, r_{bl} will be large under still-air conditions, causing r_t to have less effect on transpiration. Under windy conditions, changes in stomatal aperture strongly affect rates of transpiration (Fig. 3.3).

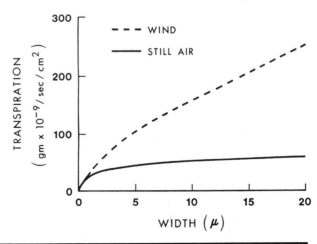

3.3. Relation between stomatal width and transpiration in still air and in wind (from Slatyer 1967, after Bange, 1953, by permission).

The vapor pressure gradient, which causes vapor to flow from the substomatal cavity, usually is created and maintained by energy inputs to the leaf. This energy causes the vapor pressure of leaf water to be greater than the partial pressure of water vapor in the surrounding atmosphere. Consequently, more water molecules exit the liquid-air interface than enter, and the gradient in liquid water potential, $(d\psi/dx)$, is steepened from the leaf down to the root surface. Water flows into the plant until some permanently limiting level of soil water content is reached. This critical level varies for each plant species, although $\psi_s = -15$ bars $(-1500$ kPa$)$ often is considered the limit for most plants (Fig. 3.4).

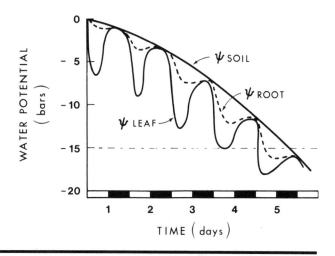

3.4. Changes in water potential (ψ) of the soil, plant root, and leaf as transpiration occurs, beginning with a soil near field capacity and proceeding until the permanent wilting point (-15 bars) is reached (from Slatyer 1967, by permission).

Measurement of Transpiration

Most methods of measuring transpiration have been developed for crop plants, thus few are applicable for field measurements of larger trees and shrubs that are of interest in forest hydrology. For the most part, transpiration cannot be measured directly in the field without some type of major disturbance to the plant. This section provides a brief overview of some of the most common methods used in the field.

POTTED PLANTS AND LYSIMETERS

Soil-plant systems that are contained in small covered pots or larger tanks, called *lysimeters,* can be used to measure transpiration. Water budget analyses, in which every component is measured directly except transpiration, are performed on these systems.

The potted-plant method is suited for small, individual plants. The bottom of the pot is perforated to allow water to drain freely. Typically, the soil is wetted thoroughly, the soil surface is covered (usually with plastic sheeting) to prevent soil evaporation, and the soil is allowed to drain. After all free water drains from the soil, the potted plant is weighed—the soil is assumed to be near field capacity at this point. At some determined time period, the potted plant is reweighed, and the difference in weights is equated to transpiration loss over the time period. Although not suited for large plants, small trees and shrubs can be measured and transpiration rates compared for different environmental conditions or treatments.

Lysimeters are tanks that are designed to hold a larger mass of soil and usually more than one plant and can be either a weighing type (similar to the potted-plant method) or a drainage type. With the drainage type, any surface runoff or drainage from the bottom is collected and measured. As with the potted-plant method, the only unmeasured part of the water budget is transpiration, or total *ET*. To obtain estimates of transpiration, the soil surface must be covered.

Because of the greater volume of soil, lysimeters allow plant roots to develop more naturally and boundary conditions are not as severe as with potted plants. Although usually designed for smaller plants, Fritschen et al. (1977) developed a lysimeter to measure transpiration of a 28-m-high Douglas-fir tree. The lysimeter weighed 28,900 kg and could detect changes in weight of 6.3 g. The difficulty of construction and costs associated with such lysimeters make them impractical for most situations.

TENT METHOD

The tent method encloses a plant with plastic sheeting and monitors the rate and moisture content of air entering and leaving the tent (Fig. 3.5). When the amount of moisture in the air leaving the tent exceeds that entering the tent, the difference is due

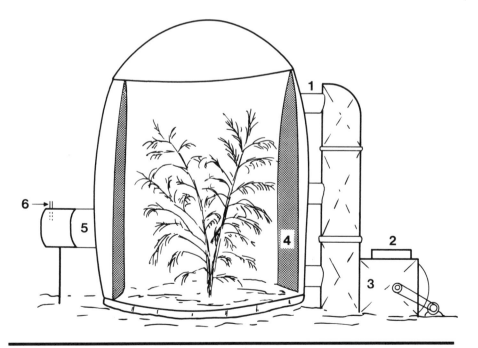

3.5. Triple-inlet evapotranspiration tent (from Mace and Thompson 1969). 1 = inlet; 2 = squirrel cage blower; 3 = inlet humidity thermometer; 4 = perforated polyvinyl curtain; 5 = outlet; 6 = outlet humidity thermometer.

to transpiration if the soil surface is covered, or *ET* if soil evaporation is permitted. The method excludes rainfall interception from the *ET* process.

The transpiration of rather large shrubs and small trees can be measured by this method without transplanting or disturbing the soil. One disadvantage is the build-up of heat in the tent caused by the trapping of radiation, that is, the "greenhouse effect." This can be overcome partly by maintaining adequate air circulation in the tent. The same principle is used for small enclosures for individual leaves. Nevertheless, the environment surrounding the plant is artificial, and the measured transpiration rates may not coincide with rates outside a tent. The method can be used to indicate relative transpiration differences between plant species in adjacent plots or the same species under different treatments.

SAP MOVEMENT METHOD

Measurement of the rates of flow within a plant's water-conducting tissue is the basis for the sap movement method. Some type of tracer is injected into the sap stream at a point in the main stem of a tree; subsequent measurements of the tracer are made both upstream and downstream from the source (Fig. 3.6). Most commonly, a heat pulse is used as a tracer to indicate sapflow rates.

This method assumes that the net upward velocity of sap is an index of transpiration rate and is useful for indicating periods when transpiration is occurring. However, the difficulty of determining the cross-sectional area through which sap is flowing prevents an accurate estimate of actual fluxes of transpiration over time.

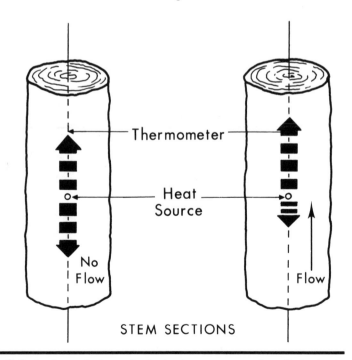

3.6. Sapflow-velocity method using heat as a tracer; heat dissipation in stem on the left has no transpiration, but the stem on the right indicates transpiration (from Swanson and Lee 1966).

OTHER METHODS

There are several indirect methods of estimating transpiration activity that do not indicate rates or volumes over time. One such method, called "quick-weighing," has been used to overcome the difficulty of weighing large plants in the field. A leaf or small branch is cut off, weighed immediately, then reweighed after some short time period. The change in weight is related to transpiration. The severity of plant disturbance makes this a questionable method. However, one can get comparative data in the field that can be used to indicate relative transpiration activity.

Another indirect method uses small chambers, or porometers, to indicate stomatal openings. Usually, the degree of penetration of some solvent or dye is measured and related to stomatal aperture. This method indicates relative transpiration activity but does not measure volume over time.

Methods of determining evapotranspiration (discussed later in this chapter) sometimes can be modified to estimate transpiration rates of plants. Soil water depletion measurements in the field, for example, can be indicators of transpiration rates when soil-surface evaporation is prevented.

Interception and Transpiration Relationships

When a vegetative surface intercepts rainfall, part of the energy normally allocated for transpiration is used in evaporation at the leaf surface. Some compensation occurs in that transpiration rates are often reduced when the foliage is wet. The net effect, however, is usually a greater total loss of water by vaporization than would have occurred via transpiration alone. Evaporation rates of wet canopies have been reported to be two to three times greater than transpiration rates for forest stands, largely because evaporation of a wet surface is not affected by stomatal resistance. Also, forest canopies are rough surfaces that are projected into the more turbulent upper air, where a greater exchange of advective energy results in high evaporation rates. Wet forest canopies generally exhibit higher evaporation rates than those of wet low-growing crops or grasses, and the evaporation rates can exceed potential evapotranspiration rates as estimated by traditional methods discussed later in this chapter. Furthermore, evaporation rates at night can far exceed transpiration rates because the stomata of most plants close at night.

Effects of Vegetative Cover

The type, density, and coverage of plants on a watershed influence transpiration losses over time. Differences in transpiration rates among individual plants and plant communities can be attributed largely to differences in rooting characteristics, stomatal response, and albedo of plant surfaces. Annual transpiration losses are affected by the length of a plant's growing season. Grasses, herbaceous vegetation, and crops generally have shorter growing seasons, hence shorter active transpiration seasons than forest vegetation. Likewise, deciduous hardwood forests may transpire over a shorter period than do conifers.

Effects of changing vegetative cover on transpiration and total *ET* can be illustrated by comparing a bare soil, a herbaceous grass cover, and a mature forest (Fig. 3.7). If soil water is abundant in all three sites, evaporation and transpiration will occur at rates primarily dependent on available net energy, vapor pressure gradients, and

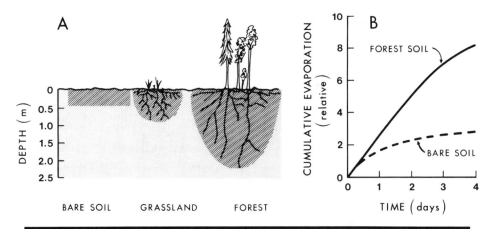

3.7. Effects of changing vegetative cover on transpiration and total evapotranspiration. A: Soil water depletion (cross-hatched areas) of bare soil, herbaceous grass cover, and a mature forest (vertical scale exaggerated); B: The associated accumulative evaporation/evapotranspiration for the bare soil and forest condition (from Lee 1980, © 1980 Columbia Univ. Press, by permission).

wind conditions. Differences in overall vapor loss would be largely the result of differences in advective energy. In such instances, transpiration by plants with a large leaf area and a canopy extending higher aboveground may surpass that of smaller plants. With an extensive, dense forest canopy, advection may only affect transpiration at the edges of stands or stand openings. Plant canopies also may increase the rate of vapor flow by creating more turbulent air flow around transpiring surfaces. This effect would be particularly pronounced with some conifers, whose needlelike leaves create numerous small eddies. Therefore, larger-canopied plants potentially can transpire larger amounts of water than would otherwise evaporate from a bare soil or transpire from communities dominated by plants of smaller stature, such as grasses and forbs.

Once the soil begins to dry, the film of water around soil particles becomes thinner, the pathways of flow become more tortuous, and the hydraulic conductivity decreases. Eventually, the slower rate of water movement through the drier soil limits the rate of evaporation at the soil surface.

Soil water depletion may occur only to a depth of 0.4 m after a given period of time. Except for very coarse soils, evaporation seldom depletes soil water below a depth of 0.6 m. The flow of water to the evaporating (transpiring) surface of herbaceous vegetation can continue for a longer time because plant roots grow and extend into greater depths (1 m in grassland, Figure 3.7A) and extract water that would otherwise not evaporate from a bare soil in the given time period. Deep-rooted forest vegetation can extract water to depths greater than 2 m and, thereby, have greater access to the soil water reservoir. Over time the differences in evaporation from a bare soil versus *ET* from a forest can be substantial (Fig. 3.7B). Such differences in soil water depletion result in differences in water yield. For a given rainfall or snowmelt event, more water is required to recharge soils under forest vegetation than soils with herbaceous cover. The least amount of water would be needed to recharge bare soil areas. Consequently, the proportion of rainfall or snowmelt that will be yielded as streamflow will be greatest for the bare soil and least for the forested area.

By reasoning alone, it may be possible to estimate relative differences in *ET* among different soil-plant systems. One obstacle to many hydrologic investigations, however, is that of quantifying *ET*. Approaches that can be used to approximate *ET* losses are discussed below.

■ POTENTIAL EVAPOTRANSPIRATION

The concept of *potential evapotranspiration* (*PET*) has its origin in evapotranspiration studies of irrigated crops. Potential evapotranspiration was defined as "the amount of water transpired in unit time by a short green crop, completely shading the ground, of uniform height, and never short of water" (Penman 1948). This definition was supposedly an expression of the maximum *ET* that could occur and was limited only by available energy. This led to thinking that all well-watered soil-plant systems and open bodies of water will lose equal amounts of water, amounts that are controlled by available energy. Of course, available energy (discussed earlier) can differ appreciably among vegetative types, different soils, and bodies of water. Empirical models of energy availability have been developed as "workable" definitions or indices of *PET*.

Several methods of estimating *PET* are available in the literature but only a few will be reviewed here. In all cases, equations and relationships used to calculate *PET* should be considered only as indices of *PET*. Before applying any *PET* equation, one should review its origin and understand its limitations and range of applications.

Pan Evaporation

The simplest method of determining a *PET* index is to obtain evaporation from a pan and apply a coefficient as follows:

$$PET = C_e E_p \tag{3.17}$$

where C_e = pan coefficient; and E_p = pan evaporation (mm/day).

The standard pan in the United States, a National Weather Service Class A pan, is a metal cylinder 122 cm in diameter and 25 cm deep. Water depth is maintained at 18–20 cm and is measured daily with a hook gauge in a stilling well.

The pan evaporation method has been used extensively to estimate lake evaporation, for which C_e usually ranges from 0.5 to 0.8. Average annual pan coefficients of 0.70–0.75 often are used in areas where they have not been derived experimentally. Seasonal relationships of C_e have been derived to simulate changes in transpiration for certain plant species.

Simple Empirical Models

The *PET* indices that require only air temperature data are attractive to hydrologists because they only require one simple variable to be measured. Thornthwaite's equation (Thornthwaite and Mather 1955) estimates *PET* for 12-hr days and a 30-day month with the equation:

$$PET = 1.6 \left(\frac{10\, T_a}{I}\right)^a \tag{3.18}$$

where PET = annual potential evapotranspiration (cm); T_a = mean monthly air temperature (°C); I = annual heat index =

$$\sum_{i=1}^{12} \left(\frac{T_{ai}}{5}\right)^{1.5};$$

and $a = 0.49 + .0179I - 0.0000771\, I^2 + 0.000000675\, I^3$.

Values of PET determined above must be adjusted for the number of days per month and day length (latitudinal adjustment).

Hamon's equation (1961) determines PET by:

$$PET = 5.0\, \rho_s \tag{3.19}$$

where PET = daytime potential evapotranspiration (mm); and ρ_s = saturation vapor density at mean air temperature (g/m^3).

Penman (1948) combined a simplified energy budget with aerodynamic considerations to estimate evaporation. The Penman equation, perhaps the most widely known method of estimating daily PET, is defined as:

$$PET = \frac{\Delta R_n + \gamma E_a}{(\Delta + \gamma)\, L} \tag{3.20}$$

where PET = evaporation or potential evapotranspiration (g/cm^2/day); Δ = slope of saturation vapor curve (0.66 mb/°C); γ = psychometric constant (mb/°C); R_n = net radiation (cal/cm^2/day); $E_a = (e_s - e_a)f(u)$, $(e_s - e_a)$ = vapor pressure deficit at 2 m height (mb); $f(u)$ = wind function (km/day), approximating atmospheric diffusivity near evaporating surface (g/cm^2/day); and L = latent heat of vaporization (585 cal g^{-1} at 21.8°C).

Penman's equation originally was developed to predict evaporation from an open water surface rather than PET from a vegetated surface. Modifications to Equation 3.20 have been numerous and include the addition of plant coefficients that express physiological and aerodynamic resistance of vegetation. Although such equations represent more physically based approaches than earlier empirical models, they have limited application in hydrology because of their extensive data requirements.

■ ESTIMATING ACTUAL EVAPOTRANSPIRATION

Actual evapotranspiration from watersheds cannot be measured directly by any practical field method. The best estimates of vegetative effects on actual evapotranspiration come from water budget analyses and paired watershed experiments (Ex. 3.2). An example of the latter was an experiment conducted at Hubbard Brook, New Hampshire, in which two similar watersheds with mixed hardwood forests were calibrated and one was subsequently cleared of all living vegetation (Hornbeck et al. 1970). By suppressing vegetative regrowth with herbicides on the cleared watershed,

EXAMPLE 3.2

The paired watershed method

This method often is used for evaluating effects of timber harvesting on streamflow. Two watersheds first must be selected on the basis of similar soils, vegetative cover, geology, topography, and size; they should be in close proximity of one another. Streamflow is measured at the outlet of both watersheds (as discussed in Chapter 4) over a sufficient time so that streamflow from one (Fig., watershed B) can be predicted from streamflow measurements at the other (Fig., watershed A). Depending on the similarity of the two watersheds, a calibration period, usually from 5 to 10 yrs, is needed to achieve an acceptable regression relationship for annual streamflow (see Chapter 18 for discussion on ession analysis). After calibration, the vegetation on watershed B can be cleared; however, streamflow measurements continue for both watersheds. Observed streamflows Q_B after treatment then are compared to streamflow values from watershed B that were predicted from the regression relationship based on streamflow measurements Q_A. The treatment period following vegetation clearing shows an increase in streamflow at watershed B. The change in streamflow is usually attributed primarily to changes in evapotranspiration.

PAIRED WATERSHED EXPERIMENT

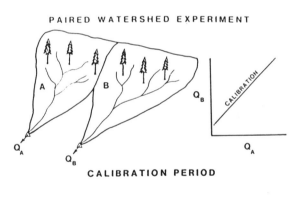

CALIBRATION PERIOD

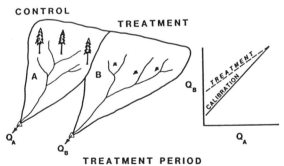

TREATMENT PERIOD

The paired watershed method as a means of estimating the effects of timber harvesting on streamflow.

water yield was increased an average of 290 mm/yr over a 3-yr period; these changes were equated with transpiration reductions. Total *ET* could not be measured because evaporation from soil and litter was not suppressed.

The absence of practical methods of measuring *ET* requires that hydrologists apply their knowledge of *ET* processes of plant and soil systems with which they are working. A commonly used approach is to employ some index of *PET* and relate *PET* to available water in the watershed. Such an approach requires knowledge of soil water characteristics and plant response to soil water changes.

A review of evaporation and transpiration experiments of forest vegetation exposed the weaknesses of *PET* methods (Calder 1982). Early work implied that all wet vegetative surfaces experienced similar *ET* (differences being attributed to albedo). This assumption was attractive to practitioners because maximum possible rates of *ET* could be estimated from physical and meteorological measurements. Experimental evidence indicates, however, that:

1. *ET* losses vary significantly among vegetative types, e.g., forest vs. grasses, even if both systems have abundant available water.
2. Forest interception losses can cause *PET* (as predicted by Penman's equation) to be exceeded.
3. Some forest stands, well supplied with water, will periodically transpire significantly less water than would be predicted from net radiation methods.

The departures from earlier *PET* concepts addressed in (1) and (2) above may be explained using the Penman-Monteith equation (Monteith 1965):

$$PET = \frac{\Delta R_n + \rho C_p (e_s - e_a)/r_a}{\Delta + \gamma(1 + r_{st}/r_a)} \qquad (3.21)$$

where ρ = air density; C_p = specific heat of air; r_a = aerodynamic resistance; and r_{st} = plant stomatal resistance.

When a film of water covers leaves (interception), r_{st} becomes negligible. In addition, r_a for forest vegetation is smaller than that of grasses or low-growing herbaceous vegetation. Both of these factors result in high interception losses for forests, particularly conifers. As much as 80% of the total energy input to wet forest canopies can be derived from advection; even in humid climates such as that in England, latent heat flux can exceed net radiation by 12%.

Equation 3.21 also helps to explain differences in transpiration losses among species that cannot be explained on the basis of energy exchange alone. Plants control transpiration through stomatal response. Stomata respond to changes in light intensity, soil moisture, temperature, and vapor pressure deficit. Most species close their stomata at night. Some close their stomata in response to wind. Many plant species close stomata when soils become dry.

Evapotranspiration/Potential Evapotranspiration Approach

Definitive relationships between transpiration or *ET* and soil moisture deficits (soil water content below field capacity) have been developed for few wildland species. Relationships of the form below have been used to relate actual *ET* to *PET*:

$$ET = (PET) f\left(\frac{AW}{AWC}\right)$$ **(3.22)**

where f = functional relationship; AW = available soil water (mm) = (soil moisture content − permanent wilting point) × rooting depth of mature vegetation; and AWC = available water capacity of the soil (mm) = (field capacity − permanent wilting point) × rooting depth of mature vegetation.

Field capacity (*FC*) refers to the maximum amount of water that a given soil can retain against the force of gravity. If a soil were saturated and allowed to drain freely, the amount of water remaining in the soil after all drainage ceased would be its field capacity. As a soil dries, the permanent wilting point eventually can be reached. Relationships of *FC* and the permanent wilting point for different soil textures are illustrated in Figure 3.8.

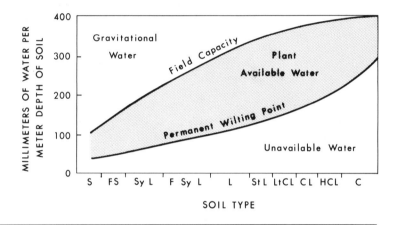

3.8. Typical water-holding characteristics of different textural soils (redrawn from U.S. Forest Service 1961). C = clay; F = fine; H = heavy; L = loam; Lt = light; S = Sand; St = silt; Sy = sandy.

Actual *ET* normally would be expected to be at or near *PET* when soil moisture conditions are near field capacity. However, quantifying the relationship $f(AW/AWC)$ requires experimental evidence of plant or plant community response to soil moisture deficits. Tan and Black (1976) found that transpiration rates of Douglas-fir were halved when $\psi_s = -1000$ kPa. They also indicated that high vapor pressure deficits accentuated the effects of soil moisture deficits. Leaf and Brink (1975) developed relationships for forest types and stand conditions in the Rocky Mountain region of the United States. The effects of clearcutting and regrowth on $f(AW/AWC)$ are illustrated in Figure 3.9. In all such approaches, it should be remembered that *PET* values are only an index.

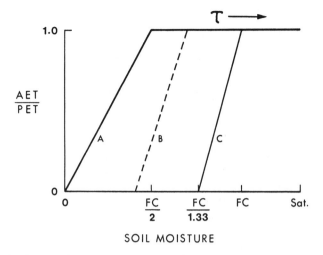

3.9. Actual evapotranspiration (*AET*) to potential evapotranspiration (*PET*) ratio as a function of soil water conditions for an old growth forest (*A*), an intermediate forest cover condition (*B*), and open or clearcut conditions (*C*) (adapted from Leaf and Brink 1975). *FC* = field capacity.

The point at which soil water deficit begins to limit *ET* varies both with stand condition (from clearcut to old growth) and forest tree species (Fig. 3.10), and can be estimated from:

$$\tau = (FC)e^{-k(t-t_c)} \qquad\qquad (3.23)$$

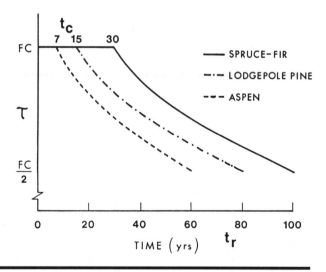

3.10. Time and forest tree species affect soil water deficit (adapted from Leaf and Brink 1975). τ = limiting soil water deficit with time for forest tree species; t_c = time (years) when soil water begins to limit *ET*; t_r = time (years) when the hydrologic effect of clearcutting becomes negligible.

for conditions $\tau = FC$, $t < t_c$, and $\tau = FC/2$, $t > t_r$, where τ = soil water deficit value at which *ET* becomes limited; k = index of rate of decline of τ; t_c = time (years) when soil water begins to limit *ET*; and t_r = time (years) when the hydrologic effect of clearcutting becomes negligible.

The approach used in the above example requires information that may not be available for many types of vegetation. Simpler approaches can be used to approximate existing evapotranspiration on a watershed basis.

Water Budget Approach

The application of a water budget as a hydrologic tool is relatively simple; if all but one component of a system can be either measured or estimated, then the unknown component can be solved directly.

A simplified water budget can be used to estimate annual *ET* of a watershed if changes in storage over a 1-yr period are normally small. Computations for the water budget could be made, beginning and ending with wet months (A–A') or dry months (B–B') as illustrated in Figure 3.11. In either case, the difference in soil water storage between the beginning and ending of the period should be small. The above assumes that all outflow of liquid water from the watershed has been measured, there was no loss of water by deep seepage to underground strata, and all groundwater flow from the watershed was measured at the gauging site. If geologic strata such as limestone underlie a watershed, the surface watershed boundaries may not coincide with boundaries governing groundwater flow. In such cases, there are two unknowns in the water budget, *ET* and groundwater seepage (l), which result in:

$$ET + l = P - Q \tag{3.24}$$

If groundwater seepage is suspected, it sometimes can be estimated by specialists in hydrogeology who have knowledge of geologic strata and their water conducting properties.

When annual changes in storage are significant, they must be determined. Estimates of change in storage become more difficult as the computational interval dimin-

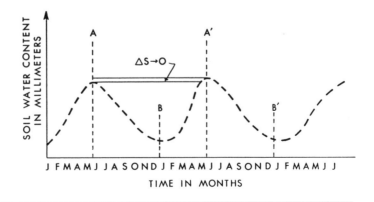

3.11. Hypothetical fluctuation of soil moisture on an annual basis.

ishes and as the size of the area increases. The change of storage for a small vegetated plot can involve only periodic measurements of soil water content. Soil water content can be estimated gravimetrically (weighing a known volume of soil, drying the soil in an oven, and reweighing), with neutron attenuation probes or by other methods. As the size of the watershed area increases, storage changes of surface reservoirs, lakes, and groundwater also must be considered. Reservoir-elevation-outflow data are needed to evaluate changes in lake or reservoir storage. These data are not difficult to analyze, when compared with storage changes in surface soils and geologic strata.

The water budget approach can be used for purposes other than estimating actual *ET*. In Example 3.3, actual *ET* is assumed to equal *PET* if soil moisture content is sufficient. Once available soil moisture is less than *PET*, the actual *ET* equals the available soil moisture content. This approach likely over-estimates *ET*, but it is useful for providing conservative estimates of water yield (runoff) from a watershed. If *ET/PET* relationships (such as illustrated in Figure 3.9) are known, they should be used in the analysis.

EXAMPLE 3.3

Water budget exercises for a forest-covered watershed, near Chiang Mai, Thailand

	Consecutive Months				
	OCT	NOV	DEC	JAN	FEB
	(mm)				
Average rainfall[a]	130	46	10	5	10
Initial soil moisture[b]	192	192	131	39	0
Total available moisture	322	238	141	44	10
Potential *ET*[c]	114	107	102	99	85
Actual *ET*[d]	114	107	102	44	10
Remaining available moisture	208	131	39	0	0
Final soil moisture[e]	192	131	39	0	0
Runoff[f]	16	0	0	0	0

[a]Average over the watershed for each month of record.

[b]At start of each month; same as "final soil moisture" of previous month.

[c]Average annual evapotranspiration (*ET*) values for the month, as estimated by Thornthwaite's method.

[d]Total available moisture, or potential *ET*, whichever is smaller.

[e]At end of month; same as "initial soil moisture" for next month. This value cannot be larger than the soil water holding capacity determined for the watershed, for this watershed 192 mm; effective rooting depth = 1.2 m × 160 mm/m of available water (field capacity–permanent wilting point).

[f]Runoff occurs when the remaining available moisture exceeds the water holding capacity for the watershed (192 mm).

■ SUMMARY

The importance of evapotranspiration and its strong influence on the water budget of any watershed should be recognized after reading this chapter. Evapotranspiration represents one of the most significant hydrologic processes that can be altered by human activities on a watershed—activities that alter the type and extent of vegetative cover on a watershed. Resource managers who manipulate soil-plant systems on a watershed should have a good fundamental understanding of the process of evapotranspiration and the factors that influence its magnitude. After reading this chapter, you should be able to:

1. Explain and differentiate among the processes of evaporation from a water body, evaporation from a soil, and transpiration from a plant.

2. Understand and be able to solve for evapotranspiration using a water budget and energy budget method.

3. Explain potential evapotranspiration and actual evapotranspiration relationships in the field. Under what conditions are they similar? Under what conditions are they different?

4. Understand and explain how changes in vegetative cover affect *ET*.

5. Describe methods used in estimating potential and actual *ET*.

CHAPTER 4

Infiltration, Runoff, and Streamflow

◼ INTRODUCTION

Once net precipitation reaches the ground, it either moves into the soil, forms puddles on the soil surface, or flows over the soil surface. Precipitation that enters the soil moves either downward to a groundwater aquifer or downward and laterally to a stream channel. The water that flows over the soil reaches the stream channel in a shorter period of time than that flowing through the soil. The allocation of net precipitation at the soil surface into either surface or subsurface flow determines, to a large extent, the timing and amount of streamflow that occurs.

The discussion in this chapter shifts emphasis from soil moisture movement governed by matric potential to soil moisture movement governed by gravity.

◼ INFILTRATION

The process by which water enters the soil surface is called *infiltration,* which results from the combined forces of capillarity and gravity. If water is applied to a dry, medium-textured soil under a well-managed pasture condition, a rapid initial infiltration rate will be observed (Fig. 4.1). This high initial rate is due to the physical attraction of soil particles to water or the matric potential gradient. As water fills the micropores, the rate of infiltration typically drops and eventually becomes constant. At this time, infiltration is only as rapid as the rate at which water moves through the soil macropores or drains under the influence of gravity; this downward movement of water through the soil is *percolation.*

The rate at which net precipitation enters the soil surface depends upon several soil surface conditions and the physical characteristics of the soil itself. Plant material or litter on the soil surface influences infiltration and can be viewed as two hydrologically distinct layers: an upper horizon composed of leaves, stems, and other undecomposed plant material; and a lower horizon of decomposed plant material that behaves much like mineral soil. The upper layer protects the soil surface from the energy of raindrop impact, which can displace smaller soil particles into pores and effectively seal the soil surface. Plant debris also slows or detains surface runoff, allowing water to enter the soil. The lower layer can have a substantial storage capacity, over 200%

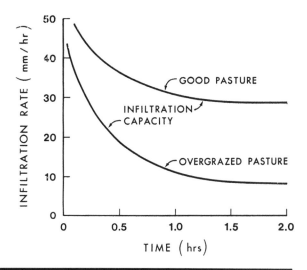

4.1. Infiltration-capacity curves for soils subjected to different levels of grazing.

by weight in some instances. Plant litter, therefore, is important as both a storage component and as a protective cover that maintains an "open" soil surface condition favorable for high rates of infiltration. Conditions that reduce vegetative cover and compact the soil surface, such as the overgrazed pasture condition in Figure 4.1, cause infiltration to diminish.

Infiltration capacity diminishes over time in response to several factors that affect the downward movement of the wetting front. The size of individual pores and the total amount of pore space in a soil generally decrease with increasing soil depth. Air entrapment within the pores and the swelling of soil colloids also can reduce infiltration rates.

Infiltration Capacity

The maximum rate at which water can enter the soil surface is called *infiltration capacity*. The actual infiltration rate equals the infiltration capacity only when the rainfall (or snowmelt) rate equals or exceeds the infiltration capacity. When rainfall rates exceed infiltration capacity, surface runoff, or ponding of water on the soil surface occurs (Fig. 4.2). Under conditions where surface ponding reaches a sufficient depth, the positive pressure of water (head) can cause infiltration to exceed the infiltration capacity. Conversely, when rainfall intensity is less than the infiltration capacity, the rate of infiltration equals rainfall intensity. In such instances, water enters the soil and is either held within the soil (when soil moisture content is less than or equal to field capacity) or percolates downward under the influence of gravity (when soil moisture content is greater than field capacity).

The infiltration capacity of a soil depends on several factors, including texture, structure, surface conditions, the nature of soil colloids, organic matter content, soil depth or presence of impermeable layers, and the presence of macropores or "small

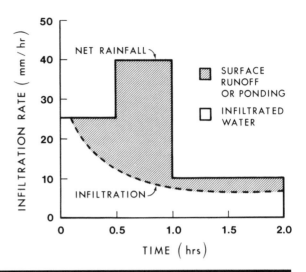

4.2. Relationship between rainfall rate and infiltration rate resulting in surface runoff, or ponding.

channel" systems within the soil. Soil water content, soil frost, and the temperature of soil and water all influence infiltration characteristics of a soil at any point in time. Many of the above factors are also influenced by land use and vegetation management practices.

The size and interconnections of pores within a soil affect infiltration and the subsequent movement of a wetting front through the soil. As pore size increases, all other factors being equal, the maximum amount of water moving through a pore or channel within the soil is proportional to the fourth power of the radius of the pore:

$$Q = \frac{\pi R^4 \, \Delta p}{8\eta L} \tag{4.1}$$

where Q = volume of water moving through a pore of length L; R = radius of pore; Δp = pressure drop over length L; and η = viscosity.

This equation, called Poiseuille's Law, is a fundamental relationship for the laminar flow of water in saturated soils or groundwater systems and explains why water moves at a faster rate through coarse-textured soils than fine-textured soils. Even though matric forces within fine-textured soils exceed those of coarse-textured soils at a given water content, pore size and the interconnected nature of pores ultimately govern infiltration capacity. Similarly, soil structure and the presence of soil fauna and old root channels create a macropore system that increases water conveyance through a soil.

Soil surface conditions can influence infiltration capacities. The roughness of the surface and the nature of pore openings at the surface largely govern the flow of water into (and air out of) the soil (Fig. 4.3). Air entrapment reduces infiltration capacity and storage. Soils with rough surfaces have a greater amount of depression storage; water in depressions is under a positive pressure (due to the depth of water) that is greater than atmospheric pressure. Large pores that are open to the atmosphere like-

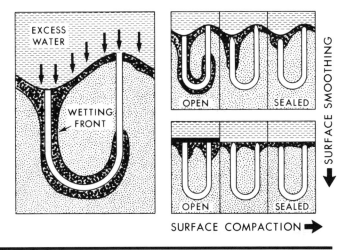

4.3. Effects of surface roughness and surface sealing on infiltration of a soil with a macropore and micropore system (from Dixon and Peterson 1975, © Am. Soc. Civil Eng., by permission).

wise promote rapid infiltration; water freely moves into the soil and displaced air freely escapes. Surface compaction or sealing diminishes the effectiveness of large pores, which then become barriers to water entry because of the back pressure of air trapped in the sealed pores. Different activities on the soil surface can affect surface and macropore relationships to either enhance or diminish infiltration capacity.

Measurement of Infiltration

The infiltration capacity of a soil can be estimated in the field with *infiltrometers,* the two most common of which are the flooding type and the rainfall-runoff plot type. With either approach, the entry of water into the soil surface is measured on a small plot of soil.

The flooding-type infiltrometer uses a cylinder that is driven into the soil. Water is added and maintained at a specified depth (usually 10 cm) in the cylinder and the amount of water needed to maintain the constant depth is recorded at specific times. Most often, a double-ring infiltrometer is used in which one cylinder is placed inside another. Typically, the inner ring is about 30 cm in diameter and the outer ring is 46–50 cm in diameter. Water is added to both cylinders or rings, but measurements are made only in the inner ring. The outer ring provides a buffer that reduces boundary effects caused by the cylinder and by lateral flow at the bottom of the ring. This method is easy and relatively inexpensive to apply, but the positive head of water usually is thought to cause higher infiltration rates than might occur from rainfall. Double-ring infiltrometers are useful for obtaining comparisons of infiltration rates for different soils, sites, vegetation types, and treatments.

The rainfall-runoff plot-type infiltrometer either applies water to the soil surface in a manner that simulates rainfall (sprinklers) or it provides a system for which natural rainfall events can be evaluated. The runoff plot has a boundary strip that forces any surface runoff to flow through a measuring device. Rainfall simulators can be adjusted to represent different drop sizes and rainfall intensities. Rainfall intensities can be increased until surface ponding or surface runoff occurs, at which time the infiltration capacity has been reached. The rainfall simulator approach is more costly and difficult to apply in remote areas, particularly where there is thick brush or dense trees that interfere with sprinkler rainfall simulation. Fewer replications are possible over a given time period unless more than one rainfall simulator is available. Infiltration capacities determined by this approach should be more representative of actual infiltration capacities than those determined by flooding-type infiltrometers. However, studies have shown that there is a consistent relationship between infiltration capacities determined by the two methods. Once the relationship is defined, the double-ring approach can be used and the values adjusted with a coefficient to represent more accurate estimates of infiltration.

Infiltration Equations

Infiltration rates have been determined for many types of soils and plant-cover conditions. Typically, the initial phase of infiltration (dry soils) is high and reduces to a relatively constant value as the soil becomes thoroughly wetted (Fig. 4.1). In the case of agricultural soils and under pasture or rangeland conditions, the curves can usually be approximated with several equations of the type described in Example 4.1.

EXAMPLE 4.1 _____

Infiltration Equations

Horton (1940): $I_t = f_c t + d e^{-kt}$

where I_t = cumulative infiltration in time t, (cm^3/cm^2); f_c = constant rate of infiltration after prolonged wetting of the soil (cm/hr); e = base of natural logarithms; and d, k = constants.

Philip (1957): $I_t = S_p t^{1/2} + at$

where I_t = cumulative infiltration (cm^3/cm^2) at time t; S_p = "sorptivity" parameter that relates to capillarity or soil matrix forces; and a = soil parameter relating to transmission of water through the soil or gravity forces.

Holtan (1971): $f_m = ci S_a^n + tf_c$

where f_m = infiltration capacity (cm/hr); c = 0.69 for cm (1.0 for in.); i = infiltration capacity per unit of available storage (cm/hr); S_a = available storage, which is the difference between the potential soil moisture storage and the cumulative infiltration (cm); n = coefficient that relates to soil texture; and f_c = constant rate of infiltration after prolonged wetting of soil (cm/hr) (same as in the Horton equation).

Infiltration measurements on wildland soils, particularly forested soils, indicate that infiltration rates change erratically and often do not conform to the smooth curves characterized by the equations in Example 4.1. Forested soils usually are porous and open at the soil surface with an extensive macropore system caused by old root cavities, burrowing animals, and earthworms. Initial and final infiltration rates of such soils can be several orders of magnitude higher than agricultural soils of similar texture. Deep, forested soils in humid climates often have infiltration capacities far in excess of any expected rainfall intensity. Under such conditions, surface runoff rarely occurs.

A simplified approach for quantifying infiltration has been frequently used in which infiltration (I_t) is estimated by:

$$I_t = A_i + f_c t \tag{4.2}$$

where A_i = initial loss or storage by the soil (mm); f_c = transmission rate or net infiltration rate (mm/hr); and t = time after A_i is satisfied.

This simplified approach can be used to estimate precipitation excess for stormflow and flood analyses. Precipitation excess (P_e) in millimeters then can be determined by:

$$P_e = P_n - A_i - f_c t \tag{4.3}$$

where P_n = net precipitation available at the soil surface (mm).

Values of f_c or net infiltration rates have been estimated for a variety of soil-vegetation-land use types (Table 4.1). Shallow bedrock or impervious layers within a soil can reduce net infiltration rates because of the limited available storage in the soil. Such influences have been reported even for soils under undisturbed forests. For example, in a tropical forest in Australia an impervious layer at 0.2 m depth caused the upper soil layer to become quickly saturated during rainstorms (Bonell et al. 1982). This resulted in surface runoff even though the pores of the undisturbed soils were apparently quite open at the surface.

Net infiltration rate refers to the relatively constant rate of infiltration that occurs after infiltration has taken place for some time (often 2 hrs), and usually is governed by the saturated hydraulic conductivity of a soil unless shallow bedrock or impervious

Table 4.1. Net infiltration rates for unfrozen soils

Soil Category	Bare Soil	Row Crops	Poor Pasture	Small Grains	Good Pasture	Forested
			(mm/hr)			
I	8	13	15	18	25	76
II	2	5	8	10	13	15
III	1	2	2	4	5	6
IV	1	1	1	1	1	1

Source: From Gray (1973), by permission.

Note: I = coarse-medium-textured soils over sand or gravel outwash; II = medium-textured soils over medium-textured till; III = medium- and fine-textured soils over fine-textured till; IV = soil over shallow bedrock.

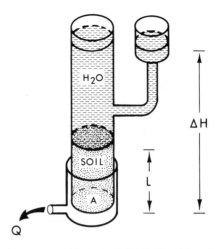

4.4. Darcy's laboratory method of determining the hydraulic conductivity (k_v) of a soil for a given head of water (ΔH) and length of soil column (L) and measuring the quantity of flow per unit time (Q).

layers are present. Hydraulic conductivity is a physical characteristic of a soil that is constant under saturated conditions. It is best illustrated with Darcy's Law (Fig. 4.4):

$$Q = k_v A \frac{\Delta H}{L} \tag{4.4}$$

where Q = rate of flow (cm³/sec); k_v = hydraulic conductivity (cm/sec); A = cross sectional area (cm²); ΔH = change in head (cm); and L = length of soil column (cm).

If the soil-pore system remains unchanged following saturation, Darcy's Law approximates the rate of flow. Again, wildland soils with a heterogeneous pore system may not respond as do more homogeneous media, such as agricultural soils or groundwater aquifers for which the equation is most useful.

Land Use Impacts on Infiltration

Activities that compact or alter the soil surface, soil porosity, or the vegetative cover can reduce the infiltration capacity of a soil. Driving vehicles or skidding logs over a soil surface, intensive grazing, and intensive recreational use can compact the surface and reduce infiltration. Exposing a soil to direct raindrop impact also will diminish the openness of the surface soil and reduce infiltration capacities.

Logging of a 110-yr-old Douglas-fir stand in Oregon with a low ground pressure, torsion suspension skidder resulted in 25–45% increases in soil bulk density to a depth of 15 cm (Sidle and Drlica 1981). The area affected by skidding amounted to 13.6% of the total area logged plus 1.5% of the area that was used as a landing. The greatest compaction resulted from frequent travel over wet soils.

The compaction of surface soils by yarding and skidding of logs reduces infiltration capacities and can result in surface runoff and erosion. If soils are allowed to recover, the effects of such operations usually are negligible after 3–6 yr except where soils were heavily disturbed (Johnson and Beschta 1980).

Grazing can reduce infiltration capacities by removing plant material, exposing mineral soil to raindrop impact, and compacting the surface. Surfaces compacted by intensive grazing can reduce infiltration capacities over a wider area than can activities such as skidding logs. Infiltration capacities for different grazing and vegetative conditions in Morocco are compared in Table 4.2. Comparisons of infiltration capacities among different grazing conditions are often confounded by differences in soils and vegetative cover. As a rule, rangelands that are in good to excellent condition with light grazing exhibit infiltration capacities at least twice those in poor condition with heavy grazing.

Land use also can affect infiltration capacities indirectly by altering soil moisture content and other soil characteristics.

Table 4.2. Comparisons of soils and infiltration relationships (double-ring infiltrometers) for three land-use conditions in northern Morocco

	Heavily Grazed, Doum Palm Vegetation	Moderately Grazed, Brushland	Ungrazed, Afforested (Aleppo pine)
Soil texture	Coarse	Medium	Fine
Soil organic matter content (%)	1.47	1.77	2.7
Soil bulk density (g/cm³)	1.44	1.42	1.22
Vegetative cover (%)	12.5	41.3	99
Slope (%)	0–10	5–25	5–40
Initial infiltration rate (mm/hr)	179	194	439
Infiltration rate after 2 hr (mm/hr)	43	65	226

Source: Adapted from Berglund et al. (1981).

WATER REPELLENT SOILS

Water repellent soils have been reported throughout the world in both wild and cultivated lands. Although the occurrence of hydrophobic soils appears to be widespread, the causes are not always known. Most hydrophobic soils repel water as a result of organic, long-chain hydrocarbon substances coating mineral soil particles. As a result, water will not spread readily nor penetrate into the soil.

The occurrence of hydrophobic soils under chaparral vegetation in southern California has received the most study (DeBano 1981). Organic matter accumulates in the litter layer that is leached to the soil under chaparral. Water repellency occurs as the organic substances accumulate and mix in the upper soil profile. Fires, which occur frequently in chaparral, intensify the hydrophobic condition and apparently volatilize organic substances, driving the water repellent layer deeper into the soil. The resulting layer restricts water movement into and through the soils, and inhibits infiltration (Fig. 4.5). The resulting change in the infiltration rate is illustrated in Figure 4.6. The effects of the nonwettable layer are essentially the same as any dense or hard pan layer that restricts water movement through the soil.

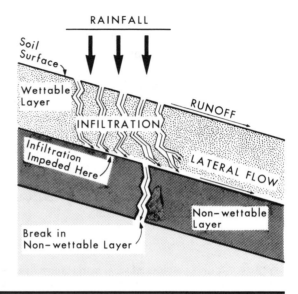

4.5. Effect of water repellent layer on infiltration and surface runoff (from DeBano 1981).

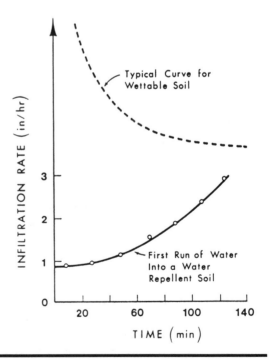

4.6. Infiltration rates of a water repellent soil (as shown in Fig. 4.5) in contrast with a typical wettable soil (from DeBano 1981).

Undisturbed peat soils are porous and exhibit high infiltration capacities, but a hydrophobic condition has been observed by the authors for these soils that have been mined. The mining of peat for horticulture or fuel exposes large areas of peat soil. Once the upper layer of sphagnum is removed and the darker, more decomposed peat becomes exposed to direct solar radiation and wind, the soil surface can dry to a point where it becomes hydrophobic. Once this occurs, surface runoff can increase. The cause of this hydrophobic condition is unknown, but it may be similar to that induced by fire.

SOIL FROST

Soil frost is common during winter and spring in cold, continental climates. It also can occur periodically in milder climates and can lead to serious flooding, particularly when high-intensity rainfall occurs on frozen soils. The influence of soil frost on infiltration capacity is determined largely by the moisture content of the soil when it freezes. A saturated soil upon freezing can act as a pavement with little infiltration, a condition referred to as concrete frost (Fig. 4.7). If the soil is not saturated when freezing occurs, a granular, more porous frost develops and the infiltration capacity is affected less. Under conditions of granular frost, some melting of soil frost occurs as infiltration continues; the soil pores then become, in effect, larger and able to transmit water at a faster rate. This explains the increase in infiltration over time.

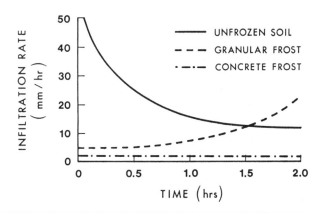

4.7. Effects of soil frost on infiltration rates (adapted from Gray 1973).

The occurrence of soil frost is affected by vegetative cover, soil texture, depth of litter, and depth of snow. Snow and litter act as insulators; the deeper the snow prior to freezing, the less likelihood of soil frost. By altering vegetative cover, particularly forest cover, frost can be affected indirectly by the influence of the forest canopy on snow accumulation and distribution. In general, removal of forest cover results in more frequent and deeper occurrences of soil frost. Compaction of soil surface horizons also can increase the depth of frost penetration. The effects of different forest cover conditions on soil frost in northern Minnesota are illustrated in Figure 4.8. The balsam fir

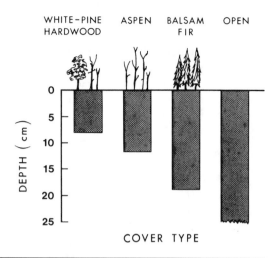

4.8. Depth of concrete frost during midwinter (January to mid-March) on loamy soils in northern Minnesota under different cover types; the vertical scale is exaggerated (from Weitzman and Bay 1963).

stand intercepts more snow than hardwood stands, resulting in less snow depth and deeper frost than the hardwood stands. Unforested areas experience the deepest frost penetration.

■ RUNOFF AND STREAMFLOW

Various processes and pathways determine how excess water becomes streamflow. Excess water represents the portion of total precipitation that runs off the land surface plus that which drains from the soil and thus is neither consumed by *ET* nor leaked into deep groundwater. Some water flows directly into a channel and quickly produces streamflow. Other pathways have a detention storage time, which can take weeks or months before excess precipitation enters a stream channel. Therefore, the magnitude of water flowing through the various pathways determines the ultimate shape and size of a *streamflow hydrograph*. A streamflow hydrograph is the graphical relationship of streamflow discharge (m³/sec) plotted against time (Fig. 4.9).

A *perennial stream* (one that flows continuously throughout the year) is most likely being fed by groundwater, pathway *D* in Figure 4.9. This component sustains streamflow between periods of precipitation or snowmelt. Because of the long and tortuous pathways involved, groundwater flow, or *baseflow*, does not respond quickly to moisture input.

Once rainfall or snowmelt occurs, several additional pathways of flow contribute to streamflow. The most direct pathway is precipitation that falls directly on the stream channel and associated saturated areas, called *channel interception* (*A* in Figure 4.9), causing the initial rise in the streamflow hydrograph; it ceases immediately after precipitation stops. *Surface runoff*, or *overland flow*, is water that flows over the soil surface and occurs from areas that are impervious, locally saturated, or areas where

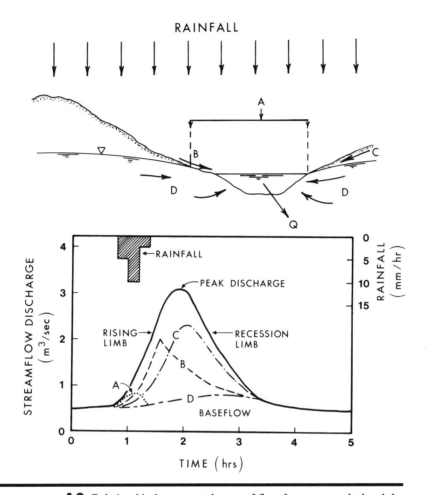

4.9. Relationship between pathways of flow from a watershed and the resultant streamflow hydrograph. A = channel interception; B = surface runoff, or overland flow; C = subsurface flow, or interflow; D = groundwater, or baseflow; Q = streamflow discharge.

the rainfall rate exceeds the infiltration capacity of the soil (B in Figure 4.9). Some surface runoff is detained by the roughness of the surface and can be slowed down. Overall, surface runoff represents a "quickflow" response that reaches the outlet of a watershed second only to channel interception. Surface runoff is a relatively large component of the hydrograph for impervious urban areas, but typically it is insignificant for forested areas with well-drained deep soils.

Overland flow in one part of a watershed can infiltrate at some downslope location before reaching a stream channel. This flow component reaches channels later than surface runoff but quicker than groundwater.

Subsurface flow, or *interflow,* is that part of precipitation that infiltrates, yet arrives at the stream channel over a short enough time period to be considered part of the storm hydrograph (C in Figure 4.9). This is considered to be the major flow pathway in most well-drained forested watersheds.

The sum of channel interception, surface, and subsurface flow is called *direct runoff, stormflow,* or *quickflow.* This is the part of the hydrograph of interest when floods and flood-producing characteristics of watersheds are analyzed. (The term stormflow will be used when describing this part of the hydrograph in the remaining chapters.)

Although the four major pathways of flow can be conceptually visualized, it is impossible to physically measure each pathway and separate one from the others. The actual pathway from rainfall to streamflow usually involves a combination of surface and subsurface flow. Water can infiltrate in one area and exfiltrate (return to the surface) downslope and run over the land surface for some distance. Conversely, some surface runoff may collect in depressions to be evaporated or infiltrated at some later time. The total streamflow hydrograph depicts the integrated response of a watershed to a given quantity of moisture input with a given set of watershed conditions.

Most hydrograph studies do not attempt to separate the various pathways of flow as illustrated in Figure 4.9. Rather, the streamflow response is evaluated by separating the stormflow component from the slow-responding baseflow. Because the hydrograph represents the integrated response to a precipitation event, the separation of a hydrograph in terms of time response rather than flow pathway is more realistic and useful for flood analysis (see Chapter 17).

Variable Source Area Concept

Wildland watersheds typically are heterogeneous mixtures of soils, vegetative cover, and land use. As such, there can be a wide range of rainfall (or snowmelt) runoff responses. At one extreme, forested watersheds with deep, permeable soils can have high infiltration capacities and exhibit predominantly subsurface flow. On the other extreme, rangelands with shallow soils can have low infiltration capacities and exhibit a quick or flashy streamflow response that is dominated by surface runoff. Perhaps, the most common situation is a watershed in which some areas produce surface runoff for any rainfall event (rock outcrops, roads, etc.) and where other areas seldom, if ever, produce surface runoff.

The variable source area concept (VSAC) explains the mechanisms of stormflow generation from watersheds that exhibit little surface runoff (Hewlett and Troendle 1975). Early concepts of stormflow runoff suggested that the only mechanism capable of producing quick-responding peak discharge was surface runoff. The VSAC suggests two mechanisms that are primarily responsible for the quickflow response: an expanding source (saturated) area that contributes flow directly to a channel, and a rapid subsurface flow response from upland to lowland areas that is principally the result of soil water displacement (Fig. 4.10).

A stream channel and the wet areas immediately adjacent to the channel respond most quickly to a rainfall event. As it rains, the wetter areas and shallow soil areas become saturated; this saturated zone expands upstream and upslope. Therefore, the area contributing directly to the channel becomes larger with the duration of the storm. This source area slowly shrinks again after the rain stops.

Water that is stored in the soil upslope from the channel system contributes to flow downstream by displacement and by direct flow out of saturated zones near the channel. Midslope and low areas can respond quickly due to the displacement of upslope water into the saturated zone. Ridgetop areas may contribute little to storm-

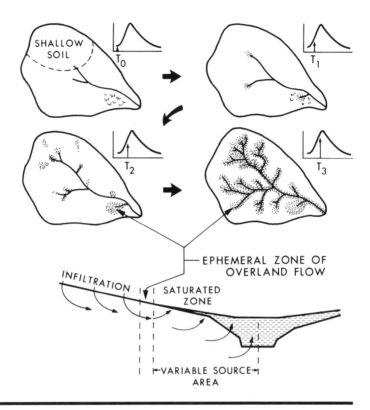

4.10. Schematic of the "variable source" area of stormflow and the relationship between overland flow and the zone of no infiltration. The small arrows on the hydrographs indicate streamflow response changes as the variable source area expands (modified from Hewlett and Troendle 1975, and Hewlett 1982b, © Univ. Georgia Press, by permission).

flow; much of the infiltrated water can be stored or the pathway can be long enough to delay the flow until long after the storm event has ended.

Stormflow Response

The stormflow response of a watershed often is characterized on the basis of separating stormflow from baseflow. The *unit hydrograph* (UHG), a widely used method of characterizing the stormflow response of a watershed, is defined as the stormflow, or direct runoff, response of a given watershed to 1 unit (1 mm) of precipitation excess that occurs uniformly over the area and over a given time increment. The method is described in Chapter 17.

Simpler approaches can be used, such as the hydrologic response (Woodruff and Hewlett 1970):

$$R_s = \left(\frac{\text{Annual stormflow}}{\text{Annual precipitation}} \right) 100 \qquad (4.5)$$

where R_s = hydrologic response (%).

The hydrologic response gives some indication of the stormflow response or "flashiness" of a particular watershed to rainstorms. For individual storms the hydrologic response can vary considerably ($< 1\%$ to $> 75\%$) depending on antecedent moisture conditions.

Factors Affecting Stormflow Response

The magnitude of stormflow volume and peakflow is determined by many factors; some are fixed and some vary in time for a given watershed. From earlier discussions, some of these factors should be apparent. Here, they are discussed in qualitative terms. Methods of estimating stormflow characteristics for a given watershed are discussed in Chapter 17.

Watershed characteristics that are fixed and have a pronounced influence on stormflow response include size and shape of the watershed, channel and watershed slopes, drainage density, and presence of wetlands or lakes. The larger the watershed, the greater the volume and peak of streamflow for rainfall or snowmelt events. Watershed shape affects how quickly surface and subsurface flow reaches the outlet of a watershed. For example, a round-shaped watershed concentrates runoff more quickly at the outlet than an elongated watershed and, all other factors being equal, will tend to have higher peakflows. Likewise, the steeper the hillslopes and channel gradients, the quicker the response and higher the peakflows. *Drainage density,* defined as the sum of all stream channel lengths divided by the watershed area, also affects the rapidity by which water can flow to the outlet. The higher the drainage density, the quicker the flow response and higher the peak. As the percentage of area in wetlands, lakes, or reservoirs increases, a greater attenuation or flattening of the stormflow hydrograph occurs. Again, the effect is due to the impact on travel time through the watershed to the outlet; wetlands and lakes detain (slow down) and retain (store) water flowing into them.

Factors affecting stormflow response that vary with time can be separated into precipitation or watershed factors. The magnitude of rainfall or snowmelt affects the magnitude of streamflow response. For rainstorms, the intensity and duration are important. As a rule, the higher the intensity and longer the duration, the higher the magnitude of peakflow. The areal distribution of rainfall or snowmelt and the movement or tracking of a storm affect the peak and volume of stormflow. For example, a storm that moves from the upper reaches of a watershed to the outlet will tend to concentrate flow at the outlet; one that tracts upland, will tend to spread out the flow response over time. Such a response is due to the timing of drainage from upland and from downstream parts of a watershed. The length of time between rainfall or snowmelt events affects the *antecedent conditions* of a watershed, which refers to the relative moisture storage status of a watershed at some point in time. If a watershed has experienced rainfall or snowmelt of any magnitude recently, it is primed to respond quicker and with a greater volume of streamflow (as there is less available storage) than one that has not had precipitation for weeks.

Watershed conditions that can vary and influence stormflow response include vegetation type and extent, soil surface conditions, and a variety of human-caused changes, such as roads, reservoirs, drainage systems, waterways, and stream channel alterations. These watershed factors are the ones that can be manipulated to achieve desired hydrologic objectives or become altered as parts of other management activities or projects.

All the above factors exert some influence on streamflow response. It is difficult to separate and quantify the contributions of individual components or factors. Hydrologic methods (discussed in Chapter 17), including computer simulation models, have been developed to study and quantify the various watershed and meteorological factors affecting stormflow.

STREAMFLOW MEASUREMENTS

Streamflow or discharge data are perhaps the most important information needed by the engineer and the water resource manager. Peakflow data are needed in planning for flood control or engineering structures (for example, bridges and culverts). Streamflow data during low-flow periods are required to estimate the dependability of water supplies. Total runoff and its variation must be known for design purposes (for example, reservoir storage as discussed in Chapter 15).

The *stage,* or height, of water in a stream is measured readily at some point on a stream reach with a staff gauge or water level recorder. The problem is to convert a record of the stage of a stream to discharge or quantity of flow per unit of time; this is done either by *stream gauging* or with precalibrated structures such as *flumes* or *weirs* constructed in the stream.

Measuring Discharge

One of the simplest ways of measuring discharge is to observe the time it takes a floating object tossed into the stream to travel a given distance. A measurement of the cross section of the stream should be made simultaneously and the two then are multiplied together:

$$Q = VA \tag{4.6}$$

where Q = discharge (m³/sec); V = velocity (m/sec); and A = cross section (m²).

This simple method is not always accurate, particularly for a large stream, because velocity varies from point to point with depth and width over the cross section of the stream.

The velocity at the surface is greater than the mean velocity of the stream. Generally, actual velocity is assumed to be about 80–85% of surface velocity.

If the cross section of a stream is divided into finite vertical sections, the velocity profile can be estimated by individually measuring the mean velocity of each section (Fig. 4.11). The area of each section can be determined, and the average discharge of the entire stream then is computed as the sum of the product of area and velocity of each section as follows:

$$Q = \sum_{1}^{n} A_i V_i \tag{4.7}$$

where n = the number of sections.

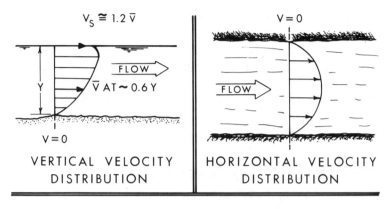

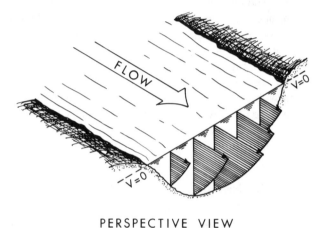

4.11. Measurements of channel cross section and velocity needed to determine streamflow discharge.

The greater the number of sections, the closer the approximation. However, for practical purposes, between 10 and 20 sections commonly are used. The actual number of sections depends upon the channel configuration and the rate of change in the stage with discharge. Depth and velocity should not vary greatly between points of measurement. Also, all measurements should be completed before the stage changes too much.

The velocity and depth of vertical sections can be measured by wading into the stream or from cable car, boat, or bridge. Velocity is usually measured with a current meter, using the following rules:

1. For depths greater than 0.5 m, two measurements are made for each section at 20% and 80% of the total depth and then averaged.
2. For depths less than 0.5 m, one measurement is made at 60% of the depth.
3. For shallow streams less than about 0.5 m, a pygmy meter or similar instrument is used instead of standard current meters (such as the Price meter).

The most critical aspect of stream gauging is the selection of a control section,

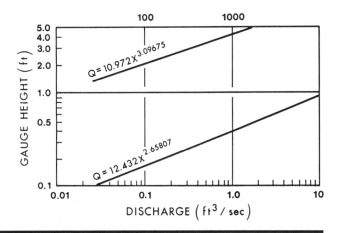

4.12. Example of a rating curve of streamflow discharge vs. water surface evaluation (from Brown 1969).

that is, a section of the stream for which a rating curve (Fig. 4.12) is to be developed. Such a section of stream should be stable and have a sufficient depth for velocity measurements at the lowest of streamflows. The control section should be in a straight reach without turbulent flow.

Precalibrated Structures for Streamflow Measurement

On small watersheds, usually less than 800 ha in size and particularly experimental watersheds, precalibrated structures often are used because of their convenience and accuracy. The most common types of precalibrated structures are *weirs* and *flumes*. Because of greater accuracy, weirs generally are preferred for gauging small watersheds, particularly those in which flows can become quite low. Where heavy sediment-laden flows are common, flumes are preferred.

Weirs or flumes can be constructed of concrete, treated wood, concrete blocks, metal, fiberglass, and other materials. The notch of a weir is often a steel blade set into concrete, and flumes frequently are lined with steel for permanence.

WEIRS

As used here, a weir includes all components of a stream-gauging station that incorporates a notch control (Fig. 4.13). The notch can be V-shaped, rectangular, or trapezoidal. An impoundment of water, the stilling basin, is formed upstream from the wall or dam containing the notch, and a stilling well with water-level recorder is connected to the weir basin. A gaugehouse or some other type of shelter is provided to protect the recorder. The cutoff wall or dam, used to divert water through the notch, is tied into bedrock or other impermeable material where possible so that no water can flow under or around it. Where leakage is apt to occur, the stilling basin sometimes is constructed as a watertight box.

The edge or surface over which the water flow is called the *crest*. Weirs can be either sharp crested or broad crested. A sharp-crested weir has a blade with a sharp

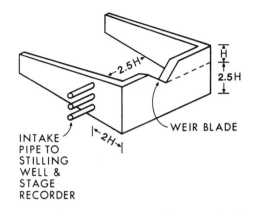

4.13. Schematic of a weir, with a V-shaped notch.

upstream edge so that the passing water touches only a thin edge and clears the rest of the crest. A broad-crested weir has a flat or broad surface over which the discharge flows. Broad-crested weirs generally are used where sensitivity to low flows is not critical and where sharp crests would be dulled or damaged by sediment or debris.

The rectangular weir has vertical sides and horizontal crest. Its major advantage is its capacity to handle high flows. However, the rectangular weir does not provide for precise measurement of low flows.

The trapezoidal weir is similar to the rectangular weir, but it has a smaller capacity for the same crest length; the discharge is approximately the sum of discharges from the rectangular and triangular sections.

Sharp-crested V-notch or triangular weirs often are used where accurate measurements of low flows are important. The V-notch weir can have a high rectangular section to accommodate infrequent high flows.

FLUMES

A flume is an artificial open channel built to contain flow within a designed cross section and length (Fig. 4.14). There is no impoundment, but the height of water in

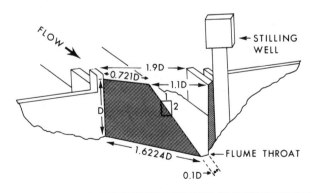

4.14. Schematic of a an H-flume.

the flume is measured with a stilling well. The types of flumes that have been used on small watersheds are described here.

HS-, H-, and HL-type flumes developed and rated by the U.S. Soil Conservation Service have converging vertical sidewalls cut back on a slope at the outlet to give them a trapezoidal projection. These have been used largely to measure intermittent runoff.

The Venturi flume is rectangular, trapezoidal, triangular, or any other regular shape with a gradually contracting section leading to a constricted throat and an expanding section immediately downstream. The floor of the Venturi flume is the same grade as the stream channel. Stilling wells for measuring the head are at the entrance and at the throat; the difference in head at the two wells is related to discharge. This type of flume is used widely in measuring irrigation water.

The Parshall flume (a modification of the Venturi flume) measures water in open conduits and is used frequently for measuring irrigation water. It consists of a contracting inlet, a parallel-sided throat with a depressed floor, and an expanding outlet, all of which have vertical sidewalls. It can measure flows under submerged conditions. Two water-level recorders are used when measuring submerged flow, one in the sidewall of the contracting inlet and the other slightly upstream from the lowest point of the flow in the throat. When measuring free flow, only the upper measuring point is used.

The San Dimas flume measures debris-laden flows in mountain streams. It is rectangular, has a sloping floor (3% gradient), and functions as a broad-crested weir except that the contraction is from the sides rather than the bottom; therefore, there is no barrier to cause sediment deposition. Depth measurements are made in the parallel-walled section at about the midpoint. Rapid flow keeps the flume scoured clean.

CONSIDERATIONS FOR USING PRECALIBRATED STRUCTURES

The type of flume or weir to be used depends upon several factors: magnitude of maximum and minimum flows; accuracy needed in determining total discharge for high flows and low flows; amount and type of sediment or debris that is expected; channel gradient; channel cross section; underlying material; accessibility of site; and the length of the project and associated funding (costs) for gauging. In general, weirs are more accurate than flumes at low flows, but flumes are preferred when streams transport high volumes of sediment or debris.

Maximum and minimum flows must be estimated before construction. Such estimates can be made from observation of high and low flows, high watermarks, and from information given by local residents. Flow estimates also might be based on the area of the watershed and records from other gauging stations in the region. Maximum expected flood peaks can also be estimated from rainfall, soil, and cover data, using a method developed by the U.S. Soil Conservation Service (see Chapter 17). The maximum and minimum flows to be measured at any degree of precision depend upon the objectives of the project and the extremes that might occur.

Flumes and weirs have been used together in tandem. Under high flows, the discharge flows through the flume and over the weir that is immediately downstream. Under low flows, there is not sufficient jump to clear the downstream weir. In such cases, the water trickles into the impoundment above the weir and accurate measurements of low flow can be obtained. Such configurations are costly and can be justified usually only for experimental purposes.

Empirical Estimations of Streamflow

In practice, streamflow data are often needed where there is no gauge. In many rural areas and particularly in developing countries, stream gauges are few and data may be completely lacking for large areas. An estimation of streamflow, no matter how rough, often is essential for appraising the condition of catchments or for design purposes. Most frequently, a main interest is in flood flows. Sometimes, reasonable estimates can be made by extrapolating information from a similar basin, but this must be done cautiously and by an experienced analyst. It must be emphasized that estimates, no matter how sophisticated, are never as good as direct measurements.

Several empirical methods are available to estimate streamflow where no gauge exists. Two commonly used methods for estimating stream discharge at known stages (depths) of flow are the Manning and the Chezy equations.

The *Manning Equation* is:

$$V = \frac{1.49}{n} R_h^{2/3} s^{1/2} \tag{4.8}$$

where V = the average velocity in the stream cross section (ft/sec); R_h = the hydraulic radius (ft), and $R_h = A/WP$ (Fig. 4.15), A = cross-sectional area of flow (ft²); WP = wetted perimeter (ft); s = energy slope as approximated by the water surface slope (ft/ft); and n = a roughness coefficient.

The *Chezy Equation* is:

$$V = C \sqrt{R_h s} \tag{4.9}$$

where C = Chezy roughness coefficient.

Equations 4.8 and 4.9 are similar. The relationship between the roughness coefficients is:

$$C = \frac{1.49}{n} R_h^{1/6} \tag{4.10}$$

The equations are used in similar fashion: the hydraulic radius and water surface slope are obtained from cross-sectional and bed slope data in the field (Fig. 4.15). The roughness coefficient is estimated (Table 4.3) and the average discharge Q is calculated by multiplying the velocity by the cross-sectional area (A in Figure 4.15).

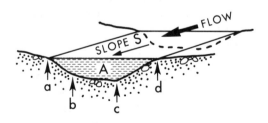

4.15. Stream channel section showing slope or gradient of streambed, wetter perimeter WP (line *a-b-c-d*) and cross-sectional area A.

Table 4.3. Examples of Manning's roughness coefficient "n"

Type of Channel	Minimum	Average	Maximum
Dredged			
Earth, straight, clean	0.016	0.018	0.020
Earth, winding, sluggish grass, some weeds	0.025	0.030	0.033
Natural Streams			
Mountain streams, no vegetation in channel, gravel bottom, cobbles	0.030	0.040	0.050
Sluggish reaches with weedy, deep pools	0.050	0.070	0.080
Flood plains			
Pasture, no brush, short grass	0.025	0.030	0.035
Scattered brush, heavy weeds	0.035	0.050	0.070
Dense willows, straight channel	0.110	0.150	0.200

Source: Adapted from Gray (1973).

In practice, the above equations are most often used to estimate some previous peakflow. High watermarks can be located after the stormflow event and used to estimate the depth of flow. Sometimes, this can be obtained by measuring the height of debris caught along the stream channel (Fig. 4.16) or by watermarks on structures. This should be obtained for a reach of channel where the cross section of the flow of interest can be measured with reasonable accuracy. The slope of the water surface can be approximated by the slope of the stream channel along the reach. The wetted perimeter can be measured by laying a tape on the channel bottom and sides between the high watermarks. The cross-sectional area should be measured by summing several segments.

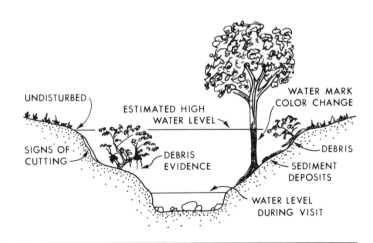

4.16. Looking for evidence of high water level in the field.

■ **SUMMARY**

The streamflow response from a watershed due to rainfall or snowmelt events represents the integrated effect of many factors. Some of these factors are affected directly by human activities on the watershed, while others are not. To this point in this book, many of the precipitation and watershed characteristics that affect the amount and pattern of streamflow have been discussed. By now, you should be able to:

1. Explain how the following affect infiltration rates:
   • soil moisture content
   • hydraulic conductivity of the soil
   • soil surface conditions
   • presence of impeding layers in the soil profile

2. Explain how land use activities affect infiltration capacities of a soil through each of the above.

3. Discuss how changes in infiltration capacities can result in different flow pathways through the watershed.

4. Illustrate and discuss the different pathways and mechanisms of flow that result in a stormflow hydrograph and baseflow for a forested watershed with deep soils vs. an urban or agricultural watershed; explain how the major pathways of flow differ in each case, and how these differences change the total streamflow hydrograph.

5. Determine streamflow discharge, given velocity and cross-sectional area data.

6. Describe different ways in which streamflow can be measured; discuss the advantages and disadvantages of each.

7. Define the terms in the Manning and Chezy equations, and give an example of how they can be used to estimate peak discharge of a streamflow event that was not measured directly.

CHAPTER 5

Groundwater

INTRODUCTION

Water that occurs in saturated zones beneath the soil surface is groundwater. In contrast with the more visible surface water in streams, rivers, ponds, lakes, and reservoirs, groundwater comprises over 97% of all fresh liquid water on the earth. About 30% of all streamflow in the United States is contributed by groundwater. Furthermore, nearly 50% of drinking water in the United States comes from wells. Although groundwater is an important source of fresh, liquid water, it does not always occur where it is most needed and sometimes is difficult to extract. Without proper management, large quantities of this valuable resource can become unusable because of contamination or by deep pumping to the point that further extraction is not feasible economically.

The purpose of this chapter is to focus on the relationships between watershed and groundwater management. A comprehensive discussion of groundwater is beyond the scope of this book, but we intend to familiarize the reader with some basic terminology and concepts. The emphasis is on land use impacts on groundwater, particularly those associated with upland watersheds and riparian-wetland systems.

BASIC CONCEPTS

Groundwater is perceived by some to occur as vast underground lakes and rivers, but for the most part, groundwater occurs in voids between soil or rock particles in the zone of saturation. To understand how a zone of saturation is formed, the forces that govern the downward movement of water in the soil first must be understood.

The process of infiltration and the subsequent movement of water through the soil are both the result of matric, or capillary, forces and gravity. Capillary forces represent the physical attraction of soil or rock particles to water; water flows from wetted particles (high-energy potential) to drier particles (low-energy potential). As the openings between particles become filled with water, gravity becomes more dominant. Once the field capacity of a well-drained soil is exceeded, a rapid flow of water begins in a downward direction. This downward movement of water continues through pores in the soil, parent material, and underlying rock. In general, pores become fewer and

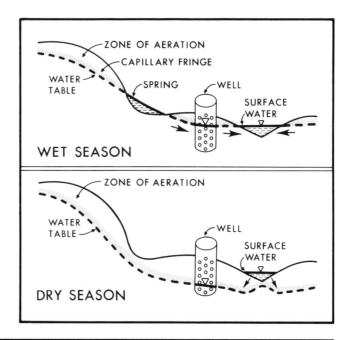

5.1. Groundwater characteristics and water table changes from a wet to dry season.

smaller with increasing depth, generating more resistance to flow. Furthermore, as water moves into deeper zones, it is no longer subjected to evaporation or transpiration. These conditions result in the formation of a zone of saturation.

The *zone of aeration* is that part of the profile that occurs between the soil surface and the top of the zone of saturation (Fig. 5.1). The zone of aeration consists of the soil water zone, which extends through the rooting zone; the *vadose zone,* which extends from the soil water zone to the *capillary fringe;* and the capillary fringe. The top of the zone of saturation, where the water potential is zero, is called the *water table.* It is measured by the elevation of water surfaces in wells that penetrate into the zone of saturation. Immediately above the water table is the capillary fringe, a zone in which water from the zone of saturation is "pulled up" by capillary forces into the zone of aeration. This capillary fringe has a negative water potential, and its irregular position varies with changes in water table elevation. The height of the capillary fringe above the water table is determined by the type of matrix; it is insignificant in coarse-grained sediments but can be several centimeters high in silts and clays.

The above terminology should not suggest that the zone of aeration cannot become saturated. In fact, this zone frequently can become saturated in some areas when rainfall or snowmelt become excessive. The distinguishing feature of the aeration zone is that saturated conditions are only temporary. It also must be emphasized that the water table is not a static surface; the elevation of a water table moves up and down in response to changing precipitation and evapotranspiration patterns, as illustrated in Figure 5.1. During the wet season, springs occur where the water table comes in contact with the soil surface and the groundwater system can be discharging water into streams (Fig. 5.1). Streams that are fed by groundwater are called *effluent streams;* if they are effluent year round, they also are *perennial streams*. During dry periods, the water table can drop and create situations where springs no longer flow and where streams are no longer fed by groundwater. Streams that lose runoff to the groundwater are *influent streams* (Fig. 5.1).

■ STORAGE AND MOVEMENT OF GROUNDWATER

Groundwater occurs in many different types of soil and rock strata. The amount of groundwater that is stored and released from water-bearing strata depends on the porosity, size of pore spaces, and the continuity of pores. Water-bearing porous soil or rock strata that yield significant amounts of water to wells are called *aquifers*. Any water-bearing soil or rock that does not transmit significant amounts of water is referred to as an *aquiclude*.

An aquifer can be an underground lens of sand or gravel, a layer of sandstone, a zone of highly fractured rock (even granite), or a layer of cavernous limestone. An aquifer can be from a few meters to hundreds of meters thick and can underlie a few hectares or thousands of square kilometers. The Ogallala aquifer underlies several states in the midwestern United States.

Porosity, the total void space between the grains or the cracks and solution cavities that can fill with water, is defined in terms of percent pore space as:

$$\text{Porosity} = \frac{100V_v}{V_t} \qquad (5.1)$$

where V_v = the volume of void space in a unit volume of rock or soil; and V_t = the total volume of earth material, including void space.

Porosity ranges from 10 to 20% for glacial till, from 25 to 50% for well-sorted sands or gravels, and from 33 to 60% for clay. The effective porosity is the ratio of the void space through which water can flow to the total volume.

If all the grains in a consolidated or unconsolidated material are about the same size and are well sorted, the spaces between them account for a large part of the total volume. If grains are sorted poorly, the larger pores can fill with smaller particles rather than water. Well-sorted materials tend to hold more water than materials that are sorted poorly.

Pores must be connected to each other if water is to move through a soil or rock. If pores are interconnected and of sufficient size to allow water to move freely, the soil or rock is *permeable*. Aquifers that contain small pores, or pores that are connected poorly can yield only small amounts of water, even if their total porosity is high.

Water flowing through a soil or rock material follows the pathway of least resistance. It will move through permeable materials and around impermeable ones. As the complexity of the geology of an area increases (that is, the amount of folding, uplifting, and fracturing of strata increases), the pathways of water flow likewise become complex. In some instances, groundwater can flow slowly for hundreds of kilometers before emerging as a natural spring, seeping into a stream, being tapped by a well, or emerging into the ocean. Just as discharge areas can be varied, recharge for an aquifer also can occur in many areas that are dispersed spatially over a large area. Recharge areas can be far distant from discharge areas of an aquifer, which sometimes makes it difficult to identify all important recharge areas. Because water moves through aquifers under the influence of gravity, one thing is certain: recharge zones are higher in elevation than areas of discharge.

Recharge usually takes place in areas where permeable soil and rock materials are relatively close to the land surface and where there is an excess of water from precipitation. The rate of recharge and the area over which recharge takes place are important considerations when groundwater pumping is being contemplated. If more groundwater is removed by pumping than is being recharged, the aquifer is being *mined*.

Unconfined and Confined Aquifers

Aquifers that contain water that is in direct contact with the atmosphere through porous material are called *unconfined aquifers*. The groundwater system illustrated in Figure 5.1 is unconfined; the soil system immediately above the water table readily allows the exchange of gases and water. In contrast, a *confined aquifer* is separated from the atmosphere by an impermeable layer, or aquiclude (Fig. 5.2). A confining stratum often forms a perched water table. An unconfined aquifer can become a confined aquifer at some distance from the recharge area.

Confined aquifers, also called *artesian aquifers*, contain water under pressure, in some cases sufficient to produce freely flowing wells. Water pressure (*P*), or pressure potential, is a function of the height of the water column at a point (h_p), the density of

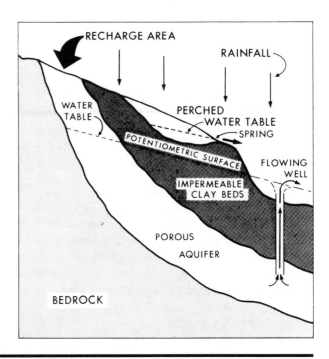

5.2. Artesian aquifer and recharge area with a perched water table above an impermeable layer (adapted from Baldwin and McGuinnes 1963).

water (ρ), and the force of gravity (g). For a system without energy loss due to flow friction, the pressure can be approximated by:

$$P = \rho g \, h_p \tag{5.2}$$

Pressure is proportional directly to the height of the water column above some point in the system. The total hydraulic head (h_t) includes the water pressure from that point down to an arbitrary but stable reference datum (z):

$$h_t = z + h_p \tag{5.3}$$

These components are illustrated in Figure 5.3. The difference in total hydraulic head from one point to another creates the hydraulic gradient dh_t/dx, where x is the distance between points.

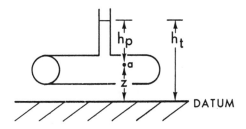

5.3. Pressure head (h_p), elevation head (z), and total hydraulic head (h_t) of water. Elevation head (z) is the distance from an arbitrary but stable reference datum to a point (a) where pressure head (h_p) is measured.

The piezometric, or *potentiometric,* surface of an artesian aquifer describes the imaginary level of hydraulic head to which water will rise in wells drilled into the confined aquifer (Fig. 5.2). The potentiometric surface is declining because of friction losses between points, but when the land surface falls below the potentiometric surface, water will flow from the well without pumping (artesian, or flowing well). Therefore, artesian pressure is the result of the actual water table in the downstream discharge area being at a much lower level than in the upstream recharge area and because it is suppressed in the aquifer by confining layers.

Aquifer Characteristics

When considering the development of groundwater for pumping, certain characteristics of the aquifer(s) from which the groundwater is to be extracted need to be understood. An important characteristic is the *transmissivity* of an aquifer, which is the amount of water that can flow horizontally through the entire saturated thickness of the aquifer under a hydraulic gradient of 1 m/m, and is defined as:

$$T_r = bk_v \tag{5.4}$$

where T_r = transmissivity (m² per unit time); b = saturated thickness (m); and k_v = hydraulic conductivity of the aquifer (m per unit time).

Any time the hydraulic head in a saturated aquifer changes, water will either be stored or discharged. *Storativity* is the volume of water that is either stored or discharged from a saturated aquifer per unit surface area per unit change in head. The storativity characteristic of an aquifer is related to the specific yield of the soil or rock material that constitutes the aquifer. *Specific yield* (S_y) is the ratio of the volume of water that can drain freely from saturated earth material due to the force of gravity to the total volume of the earth material.

The amount of water that is discharged from an aquifer can be approximated with Darcy's Law (see Chapter 4):

$$Q = k_v A \frac{dh_t}{dx} \tag{5.5}$$

The discharge from an aquifer (Ex. 5.1), thus, is dependent on the cross-sectional area through which flow occurs (A), the hydraulic conductivity of the material constituting the aquifer (k_v), and the hydraulic gradient (dh/dx). The value of k_v is dependent on the properties of the porous medium and of the fluid passing through it; the more viscous the fluid, the lower the k_v. Examples of hydraulic conductivities of earth material for pure water at a temperature of 15.6°C are listed in Table 5.1.

EXAMPLE 5.1

The problem presented is to determine the discharge of flow (Q) through a well-sorted gravel aquifer, given that $k_v = 0.01$ cm/sec, the change in head is 1 m over a distance of 1000 m, and the cross-sectional area of the aquifer is 500 m²

$$Q = k_v A \frac{dh_t}{dx}$$

$$= (0.01 \text{ cm/sec}) (500 \text{ m}^2) (\frac{10{,}000 \text{ cm}^2}{1 \text{ m}^2}) \, 0.001 \text{ m/m}$$

$$= 50 \text{ cm}^3/\text{sec}$$

$$= 4.32 \text{ m}^3/\text{day}$$

Table 5.1. Examples of hydraulic conductivities for unconsolidated sediments (pure water, 15.6°C)

Material	Hydraulic Conductivity (cm/sec)
Well-sorted gravel	10^{-2}–1
Well-sorted sands, glacial outwash	10^{-3}–10^{-2}
Silty sands, fine sands	10^{-5}–10^{-3}
Silt, sandy silts	10^{-6}–10^{-4}
Clay	10^{-9}–10^{-6}

Source: Adapted from Fetter (1980).

GROUNDWATER DEVELOPMENT

Assessing the potential for groundwater development requires knowledge of the local geology and aquifers. Surface features ordinarily do not allow one to determine the location, depth, and extent of water-bearing material or strata. Geologic maps can be used to help identify potentially productive water-bearing strata by examining the direction and degree of dipping strata, locating faults and fracture zones, and determining the stratigraphy of rocks with different water-bearing and hydraulic characteristics. Information from geologic maps can be used to determine whether special considerations, such as horizontal wells, may be appropriate. For example, areas that have old lava flows often exhibit considerable vertical development of secondary openings, such as lava tubes and fissures caused by escaping gases. Horizontal wells increase the chances of intercepting these larger water-bearing pores that generally are not widespread and are difficult to locate by vertical drilling.

As a rule, opportunities for groundwater development increase as one moves from upland watersheds to lower basins and flood plains. Extensive and high-yielding aquifers occur in most major river valleys and alluvial plains. On a smaller scale, the same features can be important sources of groundwater in upland areas. Small valleys in uplands and associated stream channel systems can have locally high water-yielding deposits of alluvium. Although usually not extensive, such deposits can provide water supplies during critically dry periods for local consumption or as a backup for other water supply systems.

Given sufficient aquifers and proper well location, groundwater can supply most of the water needs of many communities. Upland wells often are dug for local drinking water for humans and livestock. Some upland wells can also supply water for larger communities and limited irrigation. The amount of water that can be supplied from upland wells depends on the types of rocks underlying the area, the degree of weathering, the presence of faults or fracture zones, and the extent of unconsolidated sands and gravels that occur as alluvium or below stream channels. Well yields from consolidated and unconsolidated materials can vary considerably (Table 5.2).

Table 5.2. Water-bearing and yield characteristics of some common aquifers

	Specific Yield	Well Yields	
Type of Material	(%)	GPM	l/sec
Metamorphic/plutonic igneous	0–25	10–25	0.6–1.6
Volcanic	variable	< 1500	< 95
Granite	< 1	neg.	neg.
Sedimentary rocks			
Shales/claystones	0–5	< 5	< 0.3
Sandstones	8	5–250	0.3–16
Limestone, solid	2	neg–5	neg–0.3
Limestone with solution cavities	variable	> 2000	> 126
Unconsolidated deposits			
Clay	0–5	neg	neg
Sand/gravel	10–35	10–> 3000	0.6–> 189

Source: Adapted from Davis and DeWiest (1966) and Fetter (1980).
Note: GPM = gallons per minute; neg = negligible.

Wells

There are many types of wells, ranging from those that are dug by hand to those that are drilled with a cable-tool drilling rig (Table 5.3). Dug wells generally are not deep, but even a well dug by hand must be lined to keep the sides from falling in.

A drilled well is different from a dug well only in that the hole is made with drilling rigs; cable-bucket and rotary drill rigs commonly are used. A cable-bucket rig churns a heavy bit up and down, pounding it through the soil or rock. A rotary rig drills its way through. In either case, the hole is *cased* with a pipe to prevent cave-in. When a hole has been drilled some distance below the water table, the drilling is stopped and a water pipe is lowered inside the casing. The *well-point* is the lower end of the pipe to which a screen is attached; this screen consists of a length of pipe with many fine perforations that allow water to enter the pipe but exclude soil material. Water is forced out of the well by a motor-driven submersible pump or a pump driven by a windmill (unless, of course, it is an artesian well).

To test a well, one measures the water level, then pumps the well at a steady rate. The water level will drop quickly at first, and then more slowly as the rate at which water is flowing into the well approaches the pumping rate. The difference between the original water level and the water level after a period of pumping is called the *drawdown*. The discharge rate is determined by a flowmeter attached to the discharge pipe. The ratio between the discharge rate and the drawdown characterizes the well's *specific capacity* (m^3/sec). Hydrologists can use the result of controlled pumping tests to predict effects of future pumping on water levels.

Pumping water from a well lowers the water table around the well and creates a *cone of depression* (Fig. 5.4). Around small-yield wells in productive aquifers, the cone of depression is small and shallow. Wells pumped for irrigation or industrial use can withdraw so much water that the water table is lowered and the cone of depression can extend for many kilometers.

Locating wells too close together causes more lowering of a water table than spacing them far apart. This process is called *interference*. Interference can draw water levels so low that pumping costs will be greatly increased.

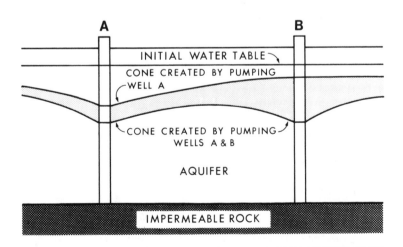

5.4. Cones of depression (from Baldwin and McGuiness 1963).

Management of Groundwater Resources

The continued use of large quantities of groundwater can create water problems. Under natural conditions, the hydrologic cycle tends to be in balance, but human's use of the water can upset this balance. Use of groundwater resources without knowledge of the effects of use or in disregard of them is unwise. In contrast, *good management* of groundwater is use with knowledge of the probable effects and with plans to minimize adverse effects.

Good management of groundwater depends upon knowledge of basic water facts. Detailed studies of groundwater in local areas are needed and basic research on replenishment and movement of groundwater is required. Also, information on groundwater quality is necessary, and methods of storing surplus water in underground reservoirs must continue to improve.

Groundwater can be managed using the concept of *safe yield,* which refers to the annual draft of groundwater at levels that do not produce undesirable effects. For example, groundwater should not be withdrawn at rates that result in excessive lowering of the water table and, hence, high pumping costs, or that result in saltwater intrusion. A water budget analysis can be performed on aquifers to study the quantitative aspects of safe yield; various inputs can be compared with outputs as follows:

$$I - O = \Delta S \qquad\qquad (5.6)$$

where I = inputs to groundwater, including groundwater recharge by percolation of rainwater and snowmelt, artificial recharge through wells, and seepage from lakes and streams; O = outputs from groundwater including pumping, seepage to lakes and streams, springs, and evapotranspiration; and ΔS = change in storage, determined as the product of change in water table elevation and specific yield for an unconfined aquifer, or the product of the change in potentiometric head and storativity for a confined aquifer.

Ideally, groundwater should be managed over long periods of time so that there is zero change in storage. Pumping sometimes can be offset by artificial recharge so that $\Delta S = O$. Depletion of groundwater storage not only affects groundwater use, but also can affect surface water supplies by reducing groundwater contributions to lakes and streams.

Groundwater that seeps into streams provides the baseflow for those streams. Therefore, if water levels decline because of heavy pumping, the baseflow of the streams also will be reduced. Surface water and groundwater are linked inextricably and should be evaluated together. River basin development can affect groundwater reservoirs and vice versa. However, plans for river basin development commonly neglect groundwater. The rate of natural replenishment need not limit the use of groundwater if floodwaters can be used to increase recharge. River basin development should include a coordinated program of flood control and artificial recharge.

SPECIAL CONSIDERATIONS—UPLAND AREAS

Several problems can result from extensive pumping of groundwater in both upland areas and in the valleys below. Land subsidence can occur when groundwater is mined over long periods of time. Such phenomena usually are associated with the reduction of artesian pressure in lower lying valley deposits and would not be of major

Table 5.3. Water well construction methods and applications

Method	Materials for which Best Suited	Water Table Depth for which Best Suited (m)	Usual Maximum Depth (m)	Usual Diameter Range (cm)	Usual Casing Material	Customary Use	Yield (m³/day)[a]	Remarks
Augering Hand	Clay, silt, sand, gravel less than 2 cm	2–9	10	5–20	Sheet metal	Domestic, drainage	15–250	Most effective for penetrating and removing clay. Limited by gravel over 2 cm. Casing required if material is loose
Power	Clay, silt, sand, gravel less than 5 cm	2–15	25	15–90	Concrete, steel, or wrought-iron pipe	Domestic, irrigation, drainage	15–500	Limited by gravel over 5 cm, otherwise same as for hand auger
Driven Wells Hand, air hammer	Silt, sand, gravel less than 5 cm	2–5	15	3–10	Standard-weight pipe	Domestic, drainage	15–200	Limited to shallow water table, no large gravel
Jetted Wells Light, portable rig	Silt, sand, gravel less than 2 cm	2–5	15	4–8	Standard-weight pipe	Domestic, drainage	15–150	Limited to shallow water table, no large gravel
Drilled Wells Cable tool	Unconsolidated and consolidated	Any depth	450[b]	8–60	Steel or wrought-iron pipe	All uses	15–15,000	Effective for water exploration. Requires casing in

Method	Geologic formation			Casing	Use	Yield[a]	Remarks
	medium hard and hard rock						loose materials. Mud-scow and hollow rod bits developed for drilling unconsolidated fine to medium sediments
Rotary	Silt, sand, gravel less than 2 cm; soft to hard consolidated rock	Any depth	450[b]	8–45	Steel or wrought-iron pipe	All uses	15–15,000	Fastest method for all except hardest rock. Casing usually not required during drilling. Effective for gravel envelope wells
Reverse-circulation rotary	Silt, sand, gravel, cobble	2–30	60	40–120	Steel or wrought-iron pipe	Irrigation, industrial, municipal	2500–20,000	Effective for large-diameter holes in unconsolidated and partially consolidated deposits. Requires large volume of water for drilling. Effective for gravel envelope wells
Rotary-percussion	Silt, sand, gravel less than 5 cm; soft to hard consolidated rock	Any depth	600[b]	30–50	Steel or wrought-iron pipe	Irrigation, industrial, municipal	2500–15,000	Now used in oil exploration. Very fast drilling. Combines rotary and percussion methods (e.g., drilling) cuttings removed by air. Would be economical for deep water wells

Source: From U.S. Soil Conservation Service (1969).

[a]Yield influenced primarily by geology and availability of groundwater.

[b]Greater depths reached with heavier equipment.

concern in upland areas. Perhaps of greatest concern is when upland watershed inhabitants become overly dependent upon groundwater resources that are not sufficient to support long-term, sustained demands. Increasing human and livestock populations in remote watershed lands can deplete local groundwater supplies quickly. Prolonged dry spells or droughts then can cause loss of life and serious economic losses. A point can be reached easily where digging another well or deepening existing wells are no longer viable solutions to water needs.

In some water-scarce areas, the development of wells for livestock watering can have detrimental effects on the watershed vegetation. For example, areas where water availability has limited livestock numbers can become subjected to overgrazing after the development of wells. In such instances, the design and development of wells should be accomplished in a manner that is compatible with a sound livestock management program.

To sustain water yields from wells, the rate of extraction or pumping cannot exceed the rate of recharge over long periods of time. The rate of recharge is governed by the availability of water and the infiltration and hydraulic characteristics of the soil and rock strata in the recharge area. The time required for water to move from recharge zones to well sites can be days, months, or years. For coarse sands and fine gravels, water can travel at rates of 20–60 m/day. Rates of travel in finer clays and dense rock aquifers can be less than 0.001 m/day. By altering the hydraulic properties of the soil system in recharge zones, rates of infiltration and recharge can be affected, but these impacts may not be observed at downstream well sites for long periods of time.

Naturally occurring springs can provide local sources of water for upland inhabitants and their livestock and are useful indicators of the location and extent of aquifers. The discharge of a spring is determined by the permeability of the aquifer and its recharge. The areal extent of the recharge area and its hydraulic characteristics govern the amount of recharge that takes place. As discussed earlier, springs occur where the water table intercepts the ground surface and when discharge is sufficient to flow in a small rivulet most of the time. If such flow is not evident, the resulting wet areas are called *seeps*. Springs normally can be found at the toe of hillslopes, along depressions such as stream channels, and where the ground surface intercepts an aquifer covered by an aquiclude.

Wells and springs can enhance water resource development in upland watersheds if they provide dependable, high-quality water. Dependability is a function of recharge, the extent of the aquifer, and its yield characteristics. Many perched, or temporary, zones of saturation occur in upland watersheds and can be identified by seeps or springs that flow only during the wet season. Even when flow occurs year round, extreme variability of flow can indicate an unreliable or temporary groundwater system.

The quality of groundwater sometimes can indicate whether the aquifer is perched or is part of a regional groundwater system. For example, the specific conductance (see Chapter 10) of groundwater in northern Minnesota is a good indicator of the type of groundwater present. Specific conductance readings of over 120 μmohs/cm indicate significant contributions of water from regional groundwater sources (Hawkinson and Verry 1975). Readings less than 50 μmohs/cm indicate a short residence time underground with low concentrations of minerals and salts in the water. In this illustrative case, specific conductance can be used to predict the dependability of the groundwater source. Areas that have calcareous soils would not show the same distinction; any underground water would tend to have high specific conductance readings.

GROUNDWATER RECHARGE ZONES

Upland forested watersheds commonly are viewed as being important recharge zones for aquifers, because forests occur in areas with high annual precipitation and are associated with soils that have high infiltration capacities. Given this to be true, then what are the effects of land management activities, including forest cutting and regeneration, or groundwater recharge? In considering this question, we first will examine the processes affected and then the implications of such changes for groundwater supplies. To provide a focal point for this discussion, we will examine forest management implications.

The removal of forest cover normally would increase the amount of water in soil storage and the amount available for groundwater recharge. If forest harvesting is accompanied by extensive road and skid trail development, total infiltration capacity can become reduced. If such disturbance is widespread and in proximity to stream channels, surface runoff can be increased at the expense of subsurface and groundwater flow. The conversion of cut-over areas to crops or pasturelands could result in a more widespread and "permanent" impact on infiltration capacity and recharge. The net effect of such activities depends on whether reductions in evapotranspiration or reductions in infiltration have the greatest impact on recharge.

Although not well documented through controlled catchment experiments, it is possible that widespread soil disturbance in a recharge zone could cause groundwater-fed, perennial streams to become dry during seasonal low-flow periods. Such occurrences would be rare, however, and would be significant only where small catchments feed a localized groundwater aquifer. Otherwise, the opportunities for water to recharge a groundwater aquifer are too great, especially when large distances and vast regional aquifers are involved. As stated in Chapter 6, most controlled watershed experiments have shown increases in recession flow and baseflow following forest harvesting and logging activities.

A realistic appraisal of land use impacts on the recharge of large, regional groundwater aquifers indicates that little impact would be expected under most conditions. For example, if forest management in the United States is considered, the effects on recharge of major aquifers would be slight because (1) at any point in time only a small portion of any recharge area is under clearcut or logging conditions; (2) recharge usually occurs over vast areas and aquifers store large amounts of water and do not respond quickly or noticeably to small changes in recharge; and (3) changes in evapotranspiration, infiltration, and permeability normally would not be severe, especially when compared to changes in precipitation and energy associated with natural fluctuations in climate.

■ VEGETATION-GROUNDWATER TOPICS

Most of the work in groundwater management is concerned with the geological aspects of location, extent, and hydraulic characteristics of aquifers that relate to dependability and performance. However, there are specific situations where changes in vegetative cover can affect groundwater directly. These changes will be discussed under two topics: phreatophyte-riparian communities and other wetland communities.

Riparian and Phreatophyte Communities

Several plant species have adapted to conditions of shallow water tables or wet areas adjacent to streams and lakes. Since soil water is available throughout the growing season in such cases, transpiration can occur at rates near potential evapotranspiration. Large quantities of groundwater can be lost annually as a result.

Riparian communities consist of plants that grow adjacent to streams or lakes and often have root systems in close proximity to the water table. Such communities exist in both wet and dry climates. Although riparian vegetation consumes large amounts of water, including groundwater, such communities often are valuable for streambank protection, wildlife habitat, and the protection of adjacent aquatic ecosystems. Under most conditions, the riparian communities are best left alone or even protected from logging, grazing, and other types of exploitation.

In arid and semiarid regions, extensive plant communities sometimes can be found along ephemeral stream channels and in expansive floodplains, which have shallow water tables. The plants in these communities, called *phreatophytes,* have extensive rooting systems that allow them to extract water from the water table or from the capillary fringe. Extensive stands of saltcedar occur in floodplains throughout the southwestern United States. Tree species such as ash, willow, cottonwood, and alder are indicators of shallow water tables and potable water in North America. The presence of such species does not mean that the shallow groundwater is necessarily recoverable, because plants can extract water from fine silts and clays that may not yield water to a well. Under conditions of high potential evapotranspiration demands, large quantities of groundwater can be transpired annually by phreatophytes (see Table 6.3).

Wetlands

Wetlands usually are low-lying areas that are connected with the groundwater system. Wetlands occur where there is an excess of water, either as a result of drainage to a depression in the landscape or where annual precipitation exceeds potential evapotranspiration over a large area with little topographic relief. The water table is at or near the ground surface throughout the year; therefore, wetlands exhibit high rates of evapotranspiration. Vegetation on wetlands can be forest, shrubs, mosses, grasses, and sedges. Although wetlands normally occur in lowland and coastal areas, they frequently form the headwater areas for streams and lakes.

The hydrologic behavior of any wetland is dependent largely on whether it is fed by regional groundwater. The water table of some wetlands is an expression of regional groundwater. Such wetlands exhibit a relatively stable water table and an even pattern of streamflow throughout wet and dry seasons. Wetlands that have perched water tables, or otherwise are separated from regional groundwater, exhibit greater seasonal fluctuations in both the water table and streamflow discharge. In either case, the association between wetlands and groundwater requires that the water budget of wetlands must explicitly account for groundwater inputs, outputs, and changes in storage.

The depth of the water table governs how wetlands respond to either rainfall or snowmelt. Wetlands normally yield high amounts of runoff only when the water table is at or above the soil surface. The percentage of rainfall that becomes streamflow is usually small except during the wet season (or snowmelt season in temperate climates) and when plants are relatively dormant. High evapotranspiration rates during the summer lower the water table; this creates considerable storage that must be satisfied before water tables rise and subsequently discharge increases. In the case of perched wetlands, it is not uncommon for streamflow to cease during the plant-growing season or extended dry periods.

Peatlands are examples of vast wetland areas and cover over 165 million ha globally. The extensive peatlands of North America and Europe are examples of wetlands where development in many forms is being planned or undertaken. Peatlands cover approximately 21 and 14 million ha in the United States and Canada, respectively, and are considered important for potential energy production, agriculture, wood products, and other purposes. The USSR and Finland, with 92 and 14 million ha of peatlands, respectively, have extensively developed their peatlands for peat production, wood products, and agriculture. Peatlands have been drained to enhance the productivity of forests, and peat has been extracted for energy and for horticultural purposes. Most peatlands have limited agricultural value because of low productivity and a short growing season in the northern latitudes.

The development of peatlands usually requires some combination of forest (vegetation) clearing, drainage, and peat extraction. These activities can alter the hydrologic response of a watershed. For example, deforestation and drainage by ditches can lead to higher volumes of snowmelt runoff, which can aggravate flooding in localized areas. Changes in water quality can take place as well. Concerning impacts on groundwater, however, there are some common misconceptions.

Peatlands, like many other wetlands, often are mistaken as important recharge areas for groundwater aquifers. Isolated wetlands can recharge groundwater by lateral seepage (Kleinberg 1984). In some instances, they can be important, if only because they are found in areas of high precipitation and, thus, are source areas for surface water systems. In general, wetlands are the result of an impeding layer that restricts the downward percolation of water, hence the shallow water table. As indicated earlier, wetlands actually can be isolated from the regional groundwater system and can prevent or impede groundwater recharge. Therefore, being able to predict the effects of wetland alterations on groundwater requires knowledge of the surface-groundwater linkages as well as an understanding of the hydrologic processes that are affected.

Problems associated with the development and use of wetlands usually are associated with those of too much water. Impacts of drainage, forest clearing, and other developments must be assessed in terms of changes in storage and routing within watersheds to understand possible impacts on flooding.

The hydrologic characteristics of wetlands can be summarized as follows:

1. Shallow water tables and flat topography are dominant features of most wetlands.

2. The depth of the water table governs evapotranspiration and streamflow discharge from wetlands—the deeper the water table, the lower the evapotranspiration and discharge.

3. Annual evapotranspiration far exceeds annual discharge for most wetlands.

4. Wetlands tend to be groundwater discharge areas more often than groundwater recharge areas.

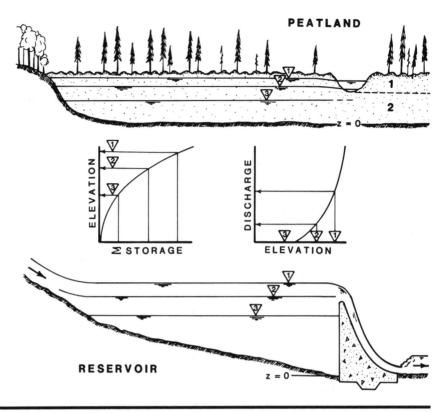

5.5. Streamflow from a peatland is governed by water table elevation similar to the way that discharge from a reservoir is governed by pool elevation (Guertin et al. 1987). Point 1 = high storage and elevation (peatland) corresponds to high discharges (reservoir); point 2 = as water table (peatland) or pool (reservoir) drops, discharge decreases; point 3 = when respective elevations drop below the outlet (peatland) or spillway (reservoir), discharge ceases; Z = datum.

5. Largely because of flat topography, wetlands function much like simple reservoirs (see Chapter 15); they attenuate flood peaks by temporarily storing or detaining water (Fig. 5.5).

6. Wetlands that are linked to regional groundwater systems exhibit less seasonal fluctuations in water table and streamflow discharge than do wetlands that are perched or otherwise isolated from regional groundwater.

◼ GROUNDWATER QUALITY

The usefulness of groundwater for drinking or irrigation depends on its quality, which is related to the type and location of the aquifer. Water from igneous and metamorphic rocks generally is of excellent quality for drinking. Exceptions occur in arid areas, where recharge water has high concentrations of salts because of high evaporation rates. The quality of water in sedimentary rocks varies; deep marine deposits can yield saline water, but shallow sandstones can have good-quality water. Unconsolidated deposits and other aquifers with high hydraulic conductivities, such as limestone caverns and lava tubes, can become contaminated from biological sources if they are close to surface sources of pollution. Human garbage, sewage, and livestock wastes can contaminate such aquifers readily.

Groundwater generally is of higher quality than surface water. Because it is in direct contact with rocks and soil material longer than most surface water, groundwater usually is higher in dissolved mineral salts (such as sodium, calcium, magnesium, and potassium cations with anions of chloride, sulfate, and bicarbonate). If such salts exceed 1000 ppm (or mg/1), the water is considered *saline*.

Groundwater that contains high amounts of calcium and magnesium salts is considered *hard* water. The hardness is determined by the concentration of calcium carbonate or its equivalent, as follows: soft water, 0–60 mg/l; moderately hard, 61–120 mg/l; hard, 121–180 mg/l; very hard, more than 180 mg/l. Although hard water leaves scaly mineral deposits inside pipes, boilers, and tanks, and hampers washing because soap does not lather easily in hard water, it does not represent health hazards. In fact, hard water is considered to be generally better for human health than soft water.

An issue of major concern for groundwater quality is contamination by chemicals, particularly hazardous wastes. Because of the slow movement of groundwater, the uncertainty of the location of all recharge areas, and the vastness of some aquifers, groundwater contamination represents long-term problems that are not easily or cheaply remedied.

Sources of groundwater contamination include waste disposal sites such as sewage, landfills, mine wastes, deep-well disposal of liquid wastes, and animal feedlots. Nonpoint contamination can result from widespread use of fertilizers and pesticides on agricultural, forest, and grazing lands. Once groundwater becomes contaminated, the rate and pathway of flow determine the severity of impacts and affect the ability to identify the source of contamination. Once a problem is identified, needed remedial actions can be expensive, time consuming, and often not feasible. The length of time that contamination has occurred, the type and behavior of contaminants, and the aquifer characteristics all affect the ability to correct groundwater pollution problems. Sometimes, we simply do not have adequate information concerning the aquifers that are being affected.

■ SUMMARY

A basic understanding of groundwater storage and flow characteristics, as well as knowledge of land use impacts on groundwater are important to watershed management. At this point in the text, you should be able to:

1. Define and illustrate a regional water table, perched groundwater, piezometric (potentiometric) surface, water table well, artesian and unconfined aquifer, capillary fringe, spring, and cone of depression.

2. Explain the components of a water budget for a groundwater aquifer; contrast a groundwater budget with a water budget for a watershed.

3. Explain the important factors that govern groundwater flow, using Darcy's equation as a point of reference.

4. Describe characteristics of an aquifer that would yield high quantities of groundwater on a sustainable basis.

5. Describe and explain how different land use activities, including changes in vegetative cover and soil characteristics, can affect groundwater storage.

CHAPTER 6

Vegetation Management, Water Yield, and Streamflow Pattern

■ INTRODUCTION

Land use activities that alter the type or extent of vegetative cover on a watershed frequently will change water yield and, in some cases, maximum and minimum streamflow. Changes in vegetative cover occur as a normal part of natural resource management and rural development. Commercial logging, shifting cultivation in developing countries, and conversions of forest or brushlands to croplands or pastures are examples of changes that can alter streamflow response. The hydrologic implications of extensive and long-term changes in vegetative cover are controversial. Extensive deforestation in the tropics, for example, has fostered widespread debate about possible changes in regional and global climate and precipitation.

The purpose of this discussion is to examine vegetation–water yield relationships and to point out the implications to water resource development and management. This chapter addresses such questions as, What are the real or anticipated effects of forest removal on the amount and distribution of precipitation? To what degree can water yield be manipulated by altering vegetative cover? Can vegetation be manipulated to complement water resource management objectives? To what extent are seasonal streamflow patterns altered by changing vegetative cover?

■ VEGETATION MANAGEMENT FOR WATER YIELD

Studies conducted throughout the world have demonstrated that annual water yields change when vegetation amount or type is substantially altered on a watershed. In general, changes that reduce evapotranspiration (*ET*) increase water yield. Evapotranspiration can be reduced by changes in the structure and composition of vegetation on the watershed.

Evaporative processes generally account for most of the annual precipitation on watersheds, consequently, the potential to increase water yield by decreasing *ET* is attractive. For example, 85–95% of the annual precipitation is evaporated or consumptively used by plants on many watersheds in arid and semiarid regions, leaving only 5–15% available for streamflow runoff. High-elevation mountain watersheds in the snow zones of the world yield as high as 50% of annual precipitation, but *ET* still remains significant and potentially subject to reduction through vegetative management.

Water yield usually increases when (1) forests are clearcut or thinned, (2) vegetation on a watershed is converted from deep-rooted species to shallow-rooted species, and (3) vegetative cover is changed from plant species with high interception capacities to species with lower interception capacities.

The amount of water yield change depends, in large part, upon the soil and climatic conditions and the percentage of the watershed that is affected. The largest increases in water yield often result from clearcutting forests. The length of time that water yields continue to exceed precutting levels depends on the type of vegetation that regrows on the site and the rate of regrowth. Higher water yield responses would be expected in regions with deep soils and high annual precipitation, whereas responses would be lower in magnitude in dry climates. Nevertheless, improving water yields has been emphasized in many semiarid regions, where small increases in water yield can be important for human and livestock needs.

The general relationships indicated in Table 6.1 can be used to determine approximate changes in water yield. Regionalized relationships and exceptions to the rule will be examined in the following paragraphs.

Table 6.1. Increases in water yield associated with reductions in vegetative cover, for noncloud or coastal forest conditions

Vegetative Cover Type	Increase in Water Yield per 10% Reduction in Cover		
	Average (mm)	Maximum (mm)	Minimum (mm)
Conifer and Eucalypt[a]	40	65	20
Deciduous Hardwood	25	40	6
Shrub	10	20	1

Source: Adapted from Bosch and Hewlett (1982), as reported by Gregersen et al. (1987).

[a]Pilgrim et al. (1982) indicated that in Australia, pine used more water than eucalypts. Dunin and Mackay (1982) also indicated that interception losses of *Pinus radiata* were 10% more than eucalypt forests on an annual basis; in Australia annual differences between pine and eucalypt forests were estimated at 35–100 mm/yr.

Humid-Temperate Regions
FORESTED UPLANDS

Paired catchment experiments in the eastern United States indicate a consistent relationship between water yield and forest cover. For example, water yield responses to the cutting of eastern hardwood forests have been summarized by Douglas (1983) as follows:

$$Y_H = 0.00224 \left(\frac{BA}{PI}\right)^{1.4462} \tag{6.1}$$

$$D_H = 1.57\, Y_{H_1} \tag{6.2}$$

$$Y_{H_i} = Y_H + b\log(i) \tag{6.3}$$

where Y_H = first year increase in water yield (in.) after cutting hardwoods (H); BA = percent basal area cut; PI = annual potential solar radiation in cal/cm²x 10^{-6} for the watershed; D_H = duration of the increase in water yield (years); Y_{H_i} = increase in water yield for the ith year after cutting (in.); and b = coefficient derived by solving equation 6.3 when $i = D_H$ and $Y_{H_i} = 0$.

For conifers, the relationships were:

$$Y_C = Y_H + (I_C - I_H) \tag{6.4}$$
$$D_C = 12 \tag{6.5}$$
$$Y_{C_i} = Y_C + b \log (i) \tag{6.6}$$

where $(I_C - I_H)$ is the difference in interception between conifers and hardwoods (in.).

The above relationships apply for conditions where annual precipitation exceeds 1015 mm and is uniformly distributed, and with solar radiation indices (defined by Lee 1964) of 0.2–0.34.

Humid forest areas of the Pacific Northwest of the United States also show potential for augmenting water yield by manipulating forest cover. The climatic regime is different from that of the humid East. Annual precipitation can exceed 4000 mm at the higher elevations on the windward side of the Cascade Mountains. Much of this precipitation falls during the winter months and occurs as snow in the higher elevations. Distinctive dry periods usually occur during July through September.

Clearcutting Douglas-fir forests has increased annual water yield 360–540 mm/yr compared to 100–200 mm/yr increases from partial clearcuts. Increases in yield diminish as forest vegetation grows back on the site. The water yield increase expected for any year following clearcutting on one Douglas-fir watershed in Oregon was calculated as (Harr 1983):

$$Y = 308.4 - 18.1 (X_1) + 0.087 (X_2) \tag{6.7}$$

where Y = annual water yield increase (mm); X_1 = number of years after clearcutting; and X_2 = annual precipitation (mm).

The above relationship would not apply for Douglas-fir forests in areas with persistent fog and long periods of low clouds; such situations exist in the coastal areas of the same region and show quite opposite responses to clearcutting. These so called "cloud forests" exhibit a reduction in water yield following clearcutting and will be discussed later.

WETLANDS

Wetlands cover vast areas in the humid-temperate regions of North America and Europe. Resource management on wetlands pose different hydrologic questions from those related to mineral soil watersheds previously discussed. Because wetlands occur as a result of excess water, their management to enhance water yield is a moot point. However, the water yield implications of widespread commercial peat extraction and forest harvesting are of interest, as they pertain to flooding and low streamflow re-gimes.

Clearcutting black spruce in a northern Minnesota peatland, for example, resulted in little change in annual water yield (Verry 1986). However, water tables in the clear-cut peatland rose as much as 10 cm higher during wet periods and dropped during dry periods to a level 19 cm lower than those of a mature forested peatland (control). Differences in interception explain the wet period response, whereas differences in transpiration explain the dry period response. The sedge understory apparently re-sponded to overstory removal with equal or higher transpiration rates than the original forest stand. This response likely would not have been predicted from models that ignore the physiological response of plant species on the watershed.

Semiarid and Arid Regions

Opportunities for increasing water yield by manipulating vegetative cover are limited in semiarid and arid watersheds. Unfortunately, these are areas where water is usually in short supply.

FORESTED UPLANDS

Watersheds in mountainous regions exhibit a variety of soils, vegetation, and climate, which are accentuated by differences in elevation, slope, and aspect. As a general rule, precipitation and water yield increase with elevation; therefore, the great-est potential for increasing water yield usually lies in the mid- to upper-elevation watersheds. The proximity of many such watersheds to agricultural and urban centers in drier valleys downstream makes water yield enhancement opportunities attractive to water resource managers. As a result, numerous catchment experiments have been conducted in the mountainous western United States to develop vegetative manage-ment schemes that increase water yield.

Opportunities for increasing water yield in the mountainous western United States depend on snow management as well as reducing *ET*. Much of the watershed research in this region has concentrated on timber-harvesting alternatives that redistribute the snowpack to achieve more runoff from snowmelt (Chap. 14). The reduced transpira-tion associated with timber harvesting increases runoff efficiency by leaving more water in the soil. Higher soil water content during the fall and winter months results in a greater percentage of snowmelt ending up as streamflow, rather than being stored in the soil.

Streamflow from high-elevation watersheds in the Rocky Mountains exceeds 1000 mm/yr. The region as a whole, however, yields less than 30 mm of streamflow per year, with less than 15% of the land area contributing the majority of streamflow. Water yield from these watersheds can be increased 20–60 mm/yr by harvesting co-niferous forests in small patches. Although increases diminish with the regrowth of vegetation, water yield in excess of precutting conditions can persist for 60–80 yr.

In the Sierra Nevada mountain range of the western United States, annual water yields vary from 350 to 1000 mm/yr, with the higher-elevation watersheds exhibiting the highest yields. If large forested watersheds were managed exclusively for water yield improvement, water yields could be increased from 2 to 6% by annual harvesting schedules (Kattelmann et al. 1983). Under multiple use and sustained-yield harvesting schedules, annual water yield increases of less than 20 mm would be expected.

The potential for increasing water yield from ponderosa pine forests in the southwestern United States has been of interest because of the scarcity of water and a rapidly expanding population. Depending on the percent of forest cover removed and annual precipitation, water yield increases of 25–165 mm/yr have been reported (Baker 1986). The effects normally persist for only 3–7 yr because of vegetative regrowth.

RANGELANDS

Most rangelands in the western United States are arid or semiarid ecosystems with little potential for water yield improvement. However, as pointed out by Hibbert (1983), water yield can be increased from watersheds that receive over 450 mm of precipitation per year and where deep-rooted shrubs can be replaced with shallow-rooted species such as grasses. Based on studies in Arizona and California, annual water yield increases (Q) from such conversions can be estimated by:

$$Q = -100 + 0.26P \qquad (6.8)$$

where P = mean annual precipitation (mm). Other vegetative management opportunities for increasing water yield are summarized in Table 6.2.

Table 6.2. Potential water yield increases by vegetative management on forested uplands and rangelands in the western United States

Vegetative Type	Annual Water Yield Increases Water Yield (mm)
Forest	
Aspen (*Populus tremuloides*)	100–150
Ponderosa Pine (*Pinus ponderosa*)	25–165
Pinyon Juniper (*Pinus*, spp., *Juniperus* spp.)	0–10
Rangeland	
Sagebrush (*Artemisia* spp.)	0–12
Semidesert shrublands	negligible

Source: Adapted from Hibbert (1983) and Baker (1986).

Domestic livestock graze on many rangelands in the western United States and generally are considered a natural component of these ecosystems. Most studies indicate that grazing has little effect on water yield.

RIPARIAN AND PHREATOPHYTE COMMUNITIES

Vegetation that occurs along stream channels and deep-rooted vegetation on floodplains, called *riparian* and *phreatophyte* communities respectively, consume large quantities of water. Annual consumption by such plant communities represents significant losses of subsurface water supplies, including groundwater (Table 6.3).

Table 6.3. Annual estimates of evapotranspiration from phreatophytes in the southwestern U.S.

Species	Water Table Depth (m)	Annual evapotranspiration (m)	Reference
Saltcedar (*Tamarix* spp.)	1.5	2.2	Van Hylckama (1970)
	2.1	1.5	
	2.7	1.0	
Mesquite (*Prosopis* spp.)		0.3–0.5	Horton and Campbell (1974)
Cottonwood (*Populus* spp.)		1.1	Horton and Campbell (1974)

Generally, the higher evapotranspiration losses occur when the water table is shallow.

The removal of phreatophyte and riparian vegetation in water-short areas such as the southwestern United States can result in groundwater savings. The removal of cottonwood along a stream channel in northwestern Arizona salvaged about 0.5 m of water over 8.9 ha (Bowie and Kam 1968, as reported by Horton and Campbell 1974). One of the most troublesome phreatophytes in the southwestern United States, salt-cedar (*Tamarix* spp.), has been the object of eradication efforts aimed at salvaging groundwater supplies. By significantly reducing or eradicating saltcedar transpiration over an area of 200 ha, for example, between 2 million and 4 million m^3 of water could be saved per year. This savings represents enough water to supply municipal needs for a small village. Mechanical and chemical measures to eradicate saltcedar communities have met with opposition, even in locales where water is in short supply, because of the wildlife habitat and aesthetic values of saltcedar communities. This opposition is an example of a multiple use conflict that can arise when vegetation is being manipulated for some specific purpose, in this case, increasing water supplies (see Chapter 11 for discussion on multiple use).

Tropical Regions

Relatively little is known about forest–water yield relationships in the tropics. One reason for this void is that few controlled catchment experiments have been con-ducted in tropical ecosystems. This lack of research is surprising because of the claims by some people that tropical forests exert a strong influence on regional precipitation, climate, and global weather systems. Large-scale and complex studies would be needed to understand and quantify such influences. As a result, questions dealing with regional or global implications of vegetative changes in tropical forest ecosystems have been addressed more with conjecture than with fact (Ex. 6.1).

The few controlled catchment experiments in the tropics show results in forest cover–water yield similar to those in temperate climates. For example, rain forests that were logged and cleared for pasture in North Queensland, Australia, resulted in a 10%, or 293 mm, increase in water yield over 2 yr (Gilmour et al. 1982). Weekly comparisons indicated that minimum discharges increased from 14 to 60% following land clearing and pasture development. These hydrologic responses were similar to those reported for cleared temperate-zone forests during the wet season.

The replacement of rain forest with tea plantations in Kenya, East Africa, showed

EXAMPLE 6.1

Deforestation in the Amazon Basin—evapotranspiration and rainfall implications

Although convincing evidence has been presented by Lee (1980) and others that removing forest cover has little effect on precipitation in temperate regions, the issue has been controversial concerning tropical forests. Salati and Vose (1984) suggest that in the humid tropics, and particularly the Amazon Basin, deforestation effects on atmospheric moisture can change the climate drastically and reduce rainfall. The following examines the possible changes in *ET* and rainfall that might result from deforestation in the Amazon Basin and considers whether such changes might be expected in other tropical forests.

The Amazon Basin, an area of about 5,800,000 km², is one of the largest river basins in the world. The Amazon River yields between 15 and 20% of the total freshwater flow in the world, which amounts to about 950 mm when expressed as a depth over the basin (Salati and Vose 1984). Assuming annual rainfall averages 2000 mm over the basin, *ET* is 1050 mm/yr (2000 mm − 950 mm). Marques et al. (1977) estimated that 48% of annual rainfall, or 960 mm, in the eastern central part of the basin is derived from *ET* within the basin itself. If we assume that this holds for the basin as a whole, then 91% (960/1050) of the basin *ET* is recycled back to the basin as rainfall. The amount of rainfall that originates from moisture outside the basin, therefore, would be 1040 mm.

Maximum reductions in *ET* due to clearcutting forest vegetation could vary from 40 to 65 mm/yr for each 10% of the area clearcut (Bosch and Hewlett 1982; Gilmour et al. 1982). If we assume a maximum reduction of 65 mm per 10% cleared and that crops or shrub-type vegetation occupy the cleared sites, the net reduction in *ET* would be offset by about 25 mm/yr per 10% of the area affected. Deforestation followed by conversion to crops of 30% of the Amazon Basin would result in:

ET reduction = (65 − 25) mm/10% × 30% = 120 mm/yr
New basin *ET* = 1050 mm − 120 mm = 930 mm/yr
Amount of *ET* contributing to *P* = 0.91 (930 mm/yr) = 846 mm/yr
Atmospheric moisture for *P* = 846 mm + 1040 mm = 1886 mm/yr
Annual water yield = 1886 mm − 930 mm = 956 mm/yr

Therefore, a 30% conversion of the Amazon would result in a 6% reduction of annual rainfall. Water yield would be increased by about 1%.

The above exercise could be repeated for a variety of different changes in vegetative cover, but the likelihood of major changes in rainfall over the Amazon Basin due to realistic projections in land use change is minimal (see table and figure). The clearcut conditions under A in the table represent the first year or maximum changes in *ET* following clearing.

Conditions under B would approximate those of conversion to crops or shrub lands. Salati and Vose (1984) suggest that changes in annual rainfall of 10–20% would be detrimental to the ecosystem; to achieve such changes, over 35% of the basin would have to be denuded, or over 60% clearcut and converted to crops or shrublands.

Estimated effects of clearcutting forest vegetation in the Amazon Basin on evapotranspiration, precipitation, and streamflow

Forest Vegetation Cleared (%)	Basin Evapotran-spiration (mm)	Average Annual Rainfall (mm)	Average Annual Streamflow (mm)	Reduction in Average Annual Rainfall (%)
A. No regrowth				
0	1050	2000	950	0
10	985	1936	951	3
20	920	1877	957	6
40	790	1759	969	12
60	660	1641	981	18
B. Followed by conversion to crops/shrubs				
10	1010	1959	949	2
20	970	1923	953	4
40	890	1850	960	6
60	810	1777	967	11
80	730	1704	974	15

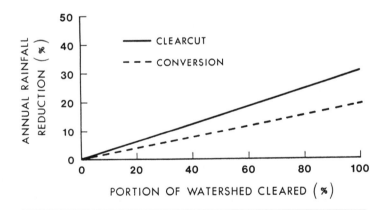

Estimated changes in annual rainfall (average) due to clearing forest cover in the Amazon Basin.

The possible effects of deforestation in other tropical areas would be expected to be smaller than the above because of the proximity of most tropical forests to large bodies of water. Atmospheric moisture likely would not be limiting to most of the humid tropics.

little effect on annual water yields, surface runoff, or sediment loss (Edwards and Blackie 1981). Clearing a bamboo forest in the same area, but followed by the establishment of a pine (*Pinus patula*) plantation, resulted in an initial increase in water yield. However, once the pine canopy closed, there was no difference in water yield from the original bamboo forest. Cultivation of small areas in evergreen forests increased water yield (expressed as a percent of annual rainfall) by 12%.

The effects of forest removal on water yield normally would be of shorter duration in the tropics than in temperate climates because of rapid regrowth of vegetation. Most forest management and logging activities would not be expected to influence water yield for more than a few years. When forests are converted to croplands or pastures, however, long-term and substantial increases in water yield can result. The larger the percentage of a watershed affected, the greater the increase in yield.

Cloud Forests—A Special Case

Forests that occur along coastal areas or on mountainous islands sometimes "produce" more moisture for a watershed than they consume by transpiration. In areas with frequent and persistent low clouds or fog, forests can intercept large amounts of atmospheric moisture, which condenses and drips from the foliage or runs down the stems. Although not precipitation, this process adds additional water to the soil that would not be added if the area were devoid of vegetation or contained low-growing vegetation.

The importance of fog drip has been suggested by many, but only quantified in a few catchment studies. Fog drip from mature Douglas-fir forests near Portland, Oregon, has been observed to add nearly 880 mm of water each year (Harr 1983). Cloud forests in the tropics, which occur primarily on old volcanoes or high mountains, have been reported to add significant amounts of water to local watersheds (Zadroga 1981).

Cloud forests usually are localized and do not cover vast areas of land. Their contributions to the annual water budget of a watershed depend on the density of trees, the total surface area of foliage, and the exposure of trees to wind-blown fog. Cloud forests can be important when they occur on municipal watersheds. In such instances, forests should be managed to sustain vigorous growth on mature stands for purposes of sustaining water yield.

Cloud forests that occur in narrow bands along the Pacific Ocean in northern Chile, though limited in extent, can contribute significantly to the annual water budget in this arid region. For example, in a region where the annual moisture input approximates 200 mm, measurements indicate that two-thirds of this amount is attributed to the interception of atmospheric moisture that flows inward from the Pacific Ocean and subsequently condenses. To further increase the amount of available moisture, artificial barriers have been constructed to intercept the movement of atmospheric moisture.

Estimating Changes in Water Yield

Changes in water yield that accompany changes in vegetative cover on a watershed can be estimated by several methods. A discussion of three general approaches follows.

REGIONAL RELATIONSHIPS

Mathematical relationships have been developed to predict water yield response to vegetative changes. Such expressions often are the result of regression relationships or localized experiments and should be used only in the region or area from which they were developed. Relationships can be used as approximations if climate, soils, topography, and vegetative types are similar in the area of application to the area for which they were developed (Ex. 6.2). Previously discussed methods by Douglas (1983) and Hibbert (1983) are examples of regional relationships.

WATER BUDGET APPROACH

The water budget approach, such as that of the U.S. Soil Conservation Service, can be used to estimate water yield for watersheds with deep soils and high infiltration capacities. Water yield from such watersheds is governed primarily by soil moisture storage characteristics. Water yield changes associated with changes in types of vegetative cover can be estimated by water budget analyses using different effective rooting depths (Ex. 6.3).

The basic method can be modified at the discretion of the user and as more detailed information becomes available. For example, the resolution can be reduced from monthly to daily accounting. If seasonal *ET* relationships are known, the *ET-PET* relationship can be modified, accordingly. Edwards and Blackie (1981) reported several *ET:PET* ratios for different plant-soil systems in East Africa; these ratios could be used in that region to improve estimates of *ET* changes. Likewise, functions like Equation 3.22 ($ET = [PET]f[AW/AWC]$) can be used. The *AW* and *AWC* terms are related to the effective rooting depth of the respective vegetation types. Knowledge of transpiration response to soil moisture conditions is assumed.

COMPUTER SIMULATION MODELS

Computer models for hydrologic simulation include simplified empirical relationships at one extreme and detailed process-oriented models at the other extreme. Models can contain derivations or elements of the previously discussed methods. More intricate and complex relationships can be considered and sensitivity analyses performed where data or assumptions are weak. Nevertheless, we often are constrained by a lack of basic knowledge relating vegetation and other land use changes to hydrologic response. Further discussion of simulation models is found in Chapter 17.

Upstream-Downstream Considerations

Increasing water yield from upland watersheds does not necessarily result in a significant increase in water yield at downstream reservoir sites. If a small portion of the watershed is clearcut, there generally will be little effect on streamflow. As the distance increases between treated watersheds and the storage reservoir, opportunities for water losses increase. Riparian or phreatophyte vegetation along stream courses can transpire large amounts of water. Likewise, channel infiltration losses, called *transmission losses,* can exceed any water yield increases from upstream areas, particularly in the case of ephemeral streams.

Transmission losses can be estimated by (1) estimating the hydraulic conductivity

EXAMPLE 6.2

Estimating water yield changes associated with the conversion from aspen to red pine in the Lake States

The expanding paper industry in the Lake States in the 1980s required softwood species for making high-quality paper. Mixed stands of conifers (softwood) and hardwoods and extensive aspen (*Populus* spp.) forests occur in the region. As a result, many stands of aspen have been converted to conifers in the region. The implications of widespread conversion on water yield can be approximated with the method by Verry (1976). Differences in interception of aspen forests and red pine forests, including overstory and understory species, were estimated and transformed into a gross precipitation–net precipitation relationship (see figure). With this relationship, changes in net precipitation caused by changes in forest type can be approximated. For example, if annual gross precipitation is 756 mm, the conversion of an aspen stand (23.0 m²/ha) to a red pine (*Pinus resinosa*) stand of the same basal area would decrease net precipitation by 66 mm/yr (633 mm − 567 mm). Because transpiration differences are not included in the method, the changes in net precipitation would provide conservative estimates of water yield changes. Annual streamflow for north-central Minnesota averages about 190 mm; for the area in which a conversion took place, annual streamflow would be reduced 35%. If only a portion of a watershed undergoes conversion, the changes in annual streamflow would be proportional to the percentage of the watershed affected. If 20% of a watershed was converted as explained above, annual water yield would be reduced to about 175 mm or 7%. The utility of this method is its simplicity and application with data that normally are available to resource managers.

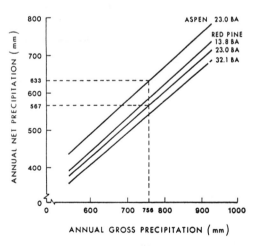

Relationship between net and gross annual precipitation for aspen and red pine (from Verry 1976).

EXAMPLE 6.3

Application of water budget method to estimate changes in water yield due to clearcutting a mature hardwood forest

A clearcut of 190 ha of mixed hardwoods is to be considered on a watershed that drains into a water supply reservoir. The city receiving water from this reservoir wants to determine how much water yield increase can be expected from such a cut. If sufficient water yield increases can be expected, the city may implement a sustainable forest management operation in which portions of their municipal watershed are maintained in clearcut or young-growth conditions.

To provide a conservative estimate of water yield expectations, precipitation and temperature records corresponding to a relatively dry 14-mo period were used to perform a water budget analysis for existing conditions—a mature, mixed hardwood forest (Table A). Soils were clay-loam

A. Water budget for a hardwood-covered watershed before clearcutting

| | Year 1 | | | | | | | | | Year 2 | | | | |
	Apr	May	Jun	Jul	Aug	Sep	Oct	Nov	Dec	Jan	Feb	Mar	Apr	May
						(mm)								
Average precipitation[a]	27	4	31	42	36	12	50	120	140	105	90	95	65	20
Initial soil moisture[b]	279	248	163	67	0	0	0	0	100	240	279	279	279	279
Total available moisture	306	252	194	109	36	12	50	120	240	345	369	374	344	299
Potential ET[c]	58	89	127	173	157	107	57	20	0	0	3	13	58	89
Actual ET[d]	58	89	127	109	36	12	50	20	0	0	3	13	58	89
Remaining available moisture	248	163	67	0	0	0	0	100	240	345	366	361	286	210
Final soil moisture[e]	248	163	67	0	0	0	0	100	240	279	279	279	279	210
Water yield[f]	0	0	0	0	0	0	0	0	0	66	87	82	7	0

[a]Average over the watershed for each month of record.
[b]At start of each month. Same as "final soil moisture" of previous month.
[c]Average annual values for the month, as estimated by Thornthwaite's method.
[d]Total available moisture, or potential ET, whichever is smaller.
[e]At end of month. Same as "initial soil moisture" for next month. This value cannot be larger than the available soil water-holding capacity determined for the watershed, for this watershed 279 mm.
[f]Water is yielded when the remaining available moisture exceeds the water holding capacity for the soil in the watershed (279 mm).

textured with a plant available soil moisture content of 164 mm/m. Plot studies indicated that the mature forest had an effective rooting depth of 1.7 m, which means that 279 mm of soil moisture could be used to satisfy evapotranspiration demands (1.7 m × 164 mm/m). Based on this water budget analysis, the 14-mo water yield was 242 mm.

To estimate the effects of clearcutting, the same initial conditions were used, but the effective rooting depth of the remaining plants was assumed to be 0.8 m, which corresponds to a herbaceous-shrub plant cover, a condition similar to that of a clearcut. The resulting available soil moisture capacity for the clearcut condition was 131 mm (0.8 m × 164 mm/m). Water yield for the clearcut condition (Table B) was 390 mm for

▶

EXAMPLE 6.3

B. Water budget for a clearcut hardwood forest

	Year 1									Year 2				
	Apr	May	Jun	Jul	Aug	Sep	Oct	Nov	Dec	Jan	Feb	Mar	Apr	May
							(mm)							
Average precipitation	27	4	31	42	36	12	50	120	140	105	90	95	65	20
Initial soil moisture	279	248	163	148	148	148	148	148	248	279	279	279	279	279
Total available moisture	306	252	194	190	184	160	198	268	388	384	369	374	344	299
Potential *ET*	58	89	127	173	157	107	57	20	0	0	3	13	58	89
Actual *ET*	58	89	46[a]	42	36	12	50	20	0	0	3	13	58	89
Remaining available moisture	248	163	148[a]	148	148	148	148	248	388	384	366	361	286	210
Final soil moisture	248	163	148	148	148	148	148	248	279	279	279	279	279	210
Water yield	0	0	0	0	0	0	0	0	109	105	87	82	7	0

[a]Actual *ET* is restricted by the available soil water capacity of the reduced rooting zone (279 mm − 131 mm = 148 mm); the final soil water content must still exceed 279 mm before any water is yielded.

the same 14-mo period. Water yield, therefore, was increased by 148 mm, or 273,600 m³. Of course, one must recognize that the 148 mm increase would be expected at the clearcut site and water can be lost before reaching the reservoir site.

of stream bottom material, (2) applying the hydraulic conductivity to the total area that is wetted by flow, and (3) applying the above for the duration of flow.

Clean gravel and coarse sand bed materials can have hydraulic conductivities in excess of 127 mm/hr. On the other extreme, consolidated bed material with a high silt-clay content can have hydraulic conductivities of 0.03 mm/hr. Transmission losses as high as 62,060 m³/km have been reported for channels in the southwestern United States (Lane 1983).

Water yield improvement schemes also should take into account the evaporative losses from the reservoir pool. In arid regions, reservoir evaporation can represent a large percentage of annual streamflow at the site. Todd (1970) reports annual lake evaporation to vary from 405 mm/yr in Maine to 2500 mm/yr in Arizona. The relationship between incremental increases in storage and corresponding increases in surface area of the reservoir pool determines, to a large extent, whether water yields increased by clearcutting will be available for later use.

Several methods are available to estimate lake evaporation. One of the simplest and most widely used is the pan evaporation method. Lake evaporation can be estimated by multiplying pan evaporation (E_p) by a pan coefficient (C_e) (see Equation 3.17).

Another consideration is that of the timing of the increased water yield. For example, if such increases in water yield occur during the season when the reservoir is normally full, any additional water supply will be of little value.

Although many studies have quantified the effects of vegetation changes on streamflow at upland watersheds, few have determined the net effects in downstream "user" areas. An Arizona study estimated that less than one-half of the streamflow increase attributed to vegetation management in the Verde River Basin would reach water users in Phoenix, approximately 150 km downstream (Brown and Fogel 1987).

■ VEGETATION MANAGEMENT AND STREAMFLOW PATTERN

Many water resource problems are related to the timing of water yield. Droughts and floods are the two extremes of streamflow that result from meteorological events. Solving problems of such streamflow extremes involves a variety of nonstructural and structural engineering approaches, as well as "people management." For example, reservoirs can be used to augment streamflow during droughts, and vegetation manipulation can either increase or decrease flows into the reservoir, thus affecting reservoir management (Ex. 6.4). But, water conservation measures by consumers and agricultural enterprises requires sociopolitical approaches or economic incentives.

EXAMPLE 6.4

> ### Water resource problems resulting from vegetation changes
>
> To develop a wood-based industry on the Fiji Islands, 60,000 ha of *Pinus caribaea* were planted on the country's two largest islands, Viti Levu and Vanua Levu. Plantations were established on the dry, leeward zones of both islands. On Viti Levu, a water supply dam with hydro-electric power stations was developed coincident with afforestation. The project was intended to supply water to the two largest "dry zone" towns on the island for 30 yr. Although annual rainfall on the windward sides of the mountains can exceed 4800 mm/yr, rainfall during the dry season (May through October) on the leeward slopes varies from 300 to 500 mm, with prolonged dry periods. As forest cover replaced mission grass cover, dry-season streamflow diminished, a cause for concern to the water supply project. Streamflow reductions of 50–60% were observed from water-sheds that had 6-yr-old pine stands. Greater reductions were expected once pine forests became mature. In this instance, the afforestation project was at cross purposes with the water resource project (Drysdale 1981).

In the case of flooding, several approaches can be taken to either minimize the effects of floods or to avoid them. Structural solutions include reservoirs and levees. Floodplain management and zoning represent a nonstructural alternative. Vegetation management of upland watersheds and along stream channels should be included as part of either approach.

Forest vegetation has long been thought to strongly influence the timing of streamflow by storing water during wet periods and releasing water during dry periods.

Such relationships are based largely on myth but have provided the impetus for forest conservation movements in Europe and the United States. By not properly accounting for the effects of forest vegetation on the amount and timing of water yield, water resource management objectives can become compromised (Ex. 6.4).

The following sections examine the extent to which watersheds can be managed to help solve problems of flooding and droughts.

Stormflow-Flooding Relationships

Questions dealing with the influence of vegetation and land use activities on flooding must be addressed with precise and consistent terminology. As pointed out by Hewlett (1982a), some confusion and misconceptions have arisen because of terminology problems. In popular usage, *flooding* usually means a high flow of water that causes economic loss or loss of life. A technical definition of flooding, and the one used here, is that streamflow rises above the streambanks and exceeds the capacity of the channel. A second point of confusion arises from streamflow-frequency analyses in which the annual maximum discharge is commonly called the *annual flood*. In many cases, the annual maximum discharge may not exceed the streambanks and thus technically is not a flood. Nevertheless, one often will encounter discussions of annual floods, 5-yr-recurrence interval floods, etc., when only some are truly floods.

To be more precise, streamflow events should be defined in terms of probability and in terms of hydrographic characteristics. For example, events should be described in terms such as the maximum annual peak discharge, the 0.02 probability or 50-yr-recurrence interval peak discharge, the 0.05 probability or 20-yr-recurrence interval stormflow volume, etc. By using this awkward terminology, we are accurately defining the event. The question of flooding then must be determined by subsequent study.

Determining the effects of upstream watershed disturbances on flooding requires that the on-site effects on hydrographic characteristics be determined and that these effects be viewed within the context of a watershed. Determining the impacts on flooding is difficult because of the routing and combining of all flows to downstream points of interest. Most catchment studies consider the impacts of land use on stormflow events only at the watershed outlet. However, the effects of land use on the magnitude and timing of peak discharges can be diminished and lengthened, respectively, as the event moves downstream. To better understand the flooding implications of watershed changes, consider first the stormflow response of first-order, or headwater, watersheds.

Stormflow-flooding analyses are facilitated by studying the streamflow hydrograph and relating the factors that govern its makeup. A streamflow hydrograph represents the integrated hydrologic response of a watershed to a given sequence of precipitation. Hydrographic characteristics of interest include stormflow volume and the magnitude and timing of peak discharge.

Watershed size, shape, land slope, channel slope, pond storage, and stream density are characteristics that remain relatively constant in time; each influences the stormflow response for a given precipitation event. The soil-plant system is the dynamic component of a watershed that, when altered, can affect the streamflow response to precipitation.

Land use activities affect stormflow response and flooding in the following ways:

1. Removal of vegetation or conversion from plants with high to low annual

transpiration and interception losses can increase stormflow volumes and the magnitude of peakflows. Such practices also can expand the source areas of flow. After a given precipitation event, antecedent soil moisture and water tables will tend to be higher; consequently less storage is available to hold precipitation of the next event, and source areas are expanded.

2. Activities that reduce the infiltration capacity of soils, such as intensive grazing, road construction, and logging, can increase surface runoff. As the proportion of precipitation that occurs as surface runoff increases, streamflow responds more quickly to precipitation events, resulting in higher peak discharges. Activities that promote infiltration would be expected to have the opposite effect.

3. The development of roads, drainage ditches, skidding trails, and alterations of the stream channel can change the overall conveyance system in a watershed. The effect usually is an increase in peak discharge caused by a shortened travel time of flow to the watershed outlet.

4. Increased erosion and sedimentation can reduce the capacity of stream channels at both upstream and downstream locations. Flows that would have remained within the streambanks previously may now flood.

The above impacts can have a noticeable effect on stormflow volume, peak magnitude, and timing of the peak for precipitation events that are not extreme in terms of amount and duration. As the amount and duration of precipitation increases, the influence of the soil-plant system on stormflow diminishes. Therefore, the influence of vegetative cover is minimal for extremely large precipitation events that usually are associated with major floods.

For events other than the extreme, stormflow characteristics change in relation to the severity of disturbance of the soil-plant system and to the percentage of watershed area affected. The percentage of area of large watersheds or river basins that is disturbed severely by fires, timber harvesting, road construction, etc., normally is small. Changes in streamflow that are detected in first-order watersheds become less evident downstream and can become confounded and difficult to predict because of the combined changes in volume, peak, and timing at different locations in the watershed. For example, stormflow volume can increase as a result of watershed disturbance, but the magnitude of the peak discharge downstream can be reduced if upstream peakflows are desynchronized (Fig. 6.1). It is not surprising, therefore, that reports of stormflow response to land treatments are variable with little general consensus. A few stormflow–land treatment studies of rainfall and stormflow events are examined in the following paragraphs to illustrate some of the points made above.

RAINFALL EVENTS

Several watershed experiments have shown increases in rainfall-caused stormflow volume and peak discharge following forest cutting. Some controlled experiments indicated little effect or even reductions in stormflow characteristics, which prevents generalizations (Table 6.4). Although many studies indicate that the greatest increases in peaks and stormflow volumes occur under wet antecedent conditions, a tropical rainforest example in Australia indicated little effect of forest clearing on stormflow parameters, but an annual water yield increase of 10% following forest clearing (Gilmour et al. 1982). The mechanism of stormflow production helps explain this discrep-

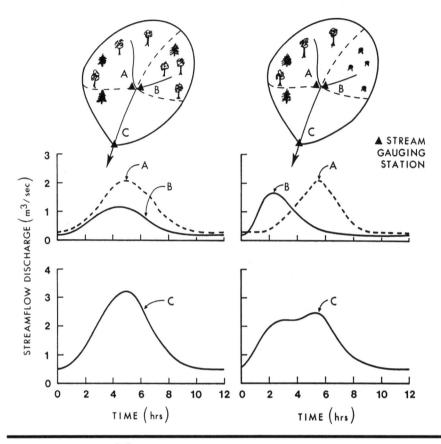

6.1. Effects of forest removal on upstream and downstream stormflow hydrographs where desynchronization of stormflow hydrographs occur.

ancy. Soils in the watershed have a hardpan with a marked reduction in hydraulic conductivity at depths from 0.2 to 0.5 m, restricting rapid percolation. The zone of low permeability in the soil, not vegetative cover, dominates the stormflow process during wet seasons. During the monsoon or postmonsoon seasons, widespread surface runoff occurs from undisturbed forests as well as from cleared areas.

A study indicating a reduction in peak discharge following forest clearcutting in British Columbia, Canada (Table 6.4), also showed that peak discharges were delayed by several hours (Cheng et al. 1975). The delayed peaks were attributed to soil disturbance that resulted in a rough surface with greater retention storage. Velocities of flow also were reduced by debris in the channel following logging.

The previous experiments clearly show the need to understand all factors governing the rainfall-stormflow process. The more important factors that should be considered in evaluating impacts of land disturbance on stormflow include:

1. The extent of the change in vegetative cover, particularly as it relates to changes in interception and antecedent soil moisture condition.

2. The soil moisture storage and hydraulic properties, the presence of water-impeding layers in the soil, and the changes in soil properties.

3. The mechanisms of stormflow production and the extent of changes in infiltration capacities or the variable source area.

Table 6.4. Changes in rainfall-produced stormflow following forest cover removal

Location, Climate, Zone	Vegetation and Soils	Treatment and Percent of Area Affected	Changes in Stormflow			References
			Peak (%)	Volume (%)	Timing (%)	
North Carolina, U.S.A., humid, temperate	Mixed hardwood, moderately deep soils gravelly loam	Clearcut, 100% (no log removal)	+6	+11	0	Hewlett and Helvey (1970)
New Hampshire, U.S.A., humid, temperate	Mixed hardwood, sandy loam soils, average depth o.s.m.	Clearcut, 100% Regrowth prevented by herbicides for 3 yr (no log removal)	+100 to +200	+30	0	Hornbeck (1973)
Oregon, U.S.A., humid, coastal	Conifers, shallow to deep, sandy soils	Commercial clearcut, 100% (logging, road construction)	+100 or less	+10 or less	0	Harr et al. (1975)
Minnesota, U.S.A., cold, continental	Mixed hardwood, glacial till soils, medium depth	Commercial clearcut, 70%	+170	+200	0	Verry et al. (1983)
British Columbia, Canada, humid, temperate	Conifers, gravelly sandy loam soils from glacial till	Commercial clearcut, 100% (logging)	−22	NR[a]	delayed	Cheng et al. (1975)
North Queensland, Australia, humid, tropics	Rainforest, deep clay soils, shallow hardpan	Clearcut, 100% (pasture development)	0	0	0	Gilmour et al. (1982)

[a]NR means not reported.

4. The changes in detention and retention storage associated with channels, ponds, and reservoirs.

5. The changes in the conveyance system of the watershed that affect the time of concentration of flow; roads and skid trails and their orientation with respect to land slope and proximity to stream channels.

6. The extent of surface erosion, gully erosion, and mass movements (mud slides, land slides, etc.) in relation to detention storage on the watershed and in the conveyance system.

SNOWMELT EVENTS

Forest removal affects streamflow from snowmelt by changing the spatial deposition of snow and changing the energy budget at the snowpack surface. Changes in snowmelt runoff often are attributed to changes in the *timing* of snowmelt; this led to the idea that the timing of snowmelt runoff can be managed by manipulating forest cover to desynchronize snowmelt from different parts of a watershed. This effect was observed in Minnesota, where a watershed was cleared partially in two successive years (see Chapter 14).

Clearing patches of forest cover in mountainous areas would not be as effective in reducing peak discharges as in flat terrain. Snowmelt runoff from mountainous watersheds normally is desynchronized as a result of differences in elevation, slope, and aspect. However, for relatively flat topography, there is some ability to change snowmelt rates and thus influence snowmelt peak discharges by manipulating forest cover. As with rainfall runoff, the influence of vegetative changes diminishes as the magnitude of precipitation (snowmelt) increases.

In cold continental climates, such as the northern United States, Canada, and northern Europe, changes in forest cover also can affect snowmelt runoff by altering soil frost. Soils usually are wetter in the fall after clearcutting, and they tend to freeze deeper with a greater occurrence of "concrete" frost. Snowmelt on frozen soil runs off rapidly. If large areas within a watershed are cleared at any point in time or are converted to croplands, higher peak discharges and volumes of runoff over frozen soil can lead to more frequent flooding. Rain or snow events, particularly when the soil is frozen, can cause severe flooding.

CONCLUDING THOUGHTS ON FLOODING

Flooding concerns are often downstream, far removed from upland watersheds where vegetative cover is undergoing change. Peak discharges and associated flood stages along major streams and rivers represent the accumulated flows from many watersheds of diverse topography, vegetation, soils, and land use. Increases in peak discharges from any headwater watershed can have little effect on downstream peaks because of the routing and desynchronization that normally occurs. However, when stormflow volumes are increased from upland watersheds, they are not damped to the extent that peaks are and result in an accumulative effect on downstream volumes and peak discharges. The combination of increased stormflow volumes and increased amounts of sediment deposited in channels can increase the frequency in which streamflow exceeds channel capacity.

Changes in land use, particularly changes in forest cover, more likely will affect smaller floods associated with return periods of from 5 to 20 yr, for example, than major floods associated with return periods of 50 yr or greater. Roads and culverts in rural areas, campgrounds, and small upland communities generally will be impacted by watershed changes more than large urban centers and agricultural areas along major rivers (Ex. 6.5). Floods of major rivers are affected more by meteorological factors than by land use activities in upland watersheds. Therefore, watershed management should be viewed in terms of complementing other means of achieving flood control or protection and not as a means by itself.

EXAMPLE 6.5

Determining effect of watershed changes on stormflow peak and culvert design for small catchments

Several upland forested watersheds were cleared and converted to pastures. The original forest roads in the area were designed on the basis of a 10% risk of failure over a 5-yr design life (thus, culverts were sized to accommodate the 50 yr return period peakflow). After the vegetation conversion, are the culverts now underdesigned?

For a 60-ha watershed that has been cleared, estimate the change, if any, that might be expected in the magnitude of the design stormflow peak, that is, the adequacy of the existing culvert system. Soils are medium heavy clays with good structure, and the 50-yr rainfall for a 12-min storm over 60 ha is 74 mm/hr.

Using the rational method (see Chapter 17):

$$Q_p = \frac{CP_g A}{360}$$

where Q_p = peak discharge in m³/sec; C = runoff constant (0.3); P_g = rainfall intensity (74 mm/hr); and A = area of watershed (60 ha).

$$Q_p = \frac{(0.3)(74)(60)}{360} = 3.70 \text{ m}^3/\text{sec}$$

Under a pasture condition, the C value is estimated to be 0.4; thus the peak associated with the above design criteria is now equal to:

$$Q_p = \frac{(0.4)(74)(60)}{360} = 4.93 \text{ m}^3/\text{sec}$$

In this example, the existing culverts are now underdesigned and the risk of having roads wash out is greater than 10% over the 5-yr period. An economic analysis would be needed to evaluate the benefits and costs of putting a new culvert system in place.

Low Streamflow

Dry-season streamflow is a concern to water resource managers because it often coincides with periods of greatest need. When precipitation is lacking, groundwater and reservoir storage are needed to provide water for irrigation and municipal requirements. Low streamflows can concentrate pollutants and streams become more sensitive to perturbations and temperature fluctuations. Consequently, low flows can place aquatic ecosystems under considerable stress. Because of the consequences of low flows, water resource management can be aimed at increasing streamflows during dry periods, or at least not diminishing low flows further.

Early conservationists pointed to the apparent relationships between forest cover and high streamflow and arid nonforested areas and low streamflow, as evidence that forests promote streamflow (Ex. 6.6). Forests were thought of as reservoirs that could store water during wet periods and release water during dry periods. Our present knowledge about vegetation-evapotranspiration-water yield relationships conflicts with this notion.

Most experimental evidence in rainfall-dominated regimes suggests that forest removal, or conversion from plants that are high users of water to plants that are low users of water, increases recession flow and sometimes dry-season flows. Wetter soil

---

EXAMPLE 6.6

Vegetation, land use, and hydrologic response

A multiple regression analysis was performed to evaluate the influence of forest cover, soils, climatic variables, and physical watershed features on flood peaks in West Virginia (Frye and Runner 1970). The following relationship was developed for flood peaks:

$$Q_p = aK_iF^b$$

where Q_p = peak discharge (m³/sec); a, b = constants for a given flood frequency; F = percent forest cover; and K_i = influence of all other factors.

This relationship shows that the magnitude of flood peaks increases with forest cover. How can you explain this finding?

Lee (1980) uses this example to show the types of problems one can encounter when using regression analyses to explain cause and effect relationships. The regression was developed for a large enough area to include forested, mountainous watershed with shallow soils, high precipitation, and steep topography in contrast to the nonforested watersheds with lower precipitation and streamflow. A valid comparison should have included watersheds that differed only in forest cover and that were under similar precipitation regimes.

conditions resulting from reduced evapotranspiration make the watershed system more responsive to small rainfall amounts and apparently lead to a longer period of soil water drainage and subsurface flow; continued precipitation inputs are needed, however, to sustain flow. Factors such as topography and geologic strata also can influence the time response of subsurface flow to rainfall events. Streamflow during droughts is sustained primarily by groundwater flow; therefore, any effects that changes in vegetative cover and soils have on streamflow during droughts would be attributed to changes in groundwater. In any case, low flows resulting from *extended* dry periods or droughts will not be substantially altered by changes in vegetative cover.

Streamflow that is influenced strongly by snowmelt usually is characterized by a long period of recession flows. Since forest cover can be manipulated to affect snow accumulation and melt, it has been suggested that snowpacks can be managed to enhance dry-season flows. Kattelmann et al. (1983) stated that the greatest contribution watershed management can make to meeting future water demands in California is by manipulating forest cover to delay snowmelt runoff. Any significant delay in streamflow response would be beneficial for the operation of reservoirs. As in rain-dominated regions, delayed and increased flows caused by vegetative manipulation would normally extend over short periods of time and would not affect flows during lengthy droughts.

Although early conservationists may not have recognized the correct cause-and-effect relationships of rainfall-runoff processes, they did observe that forest cover generally promotes high-quality water that flows in a less erratic manner than that from most other watershed cover conditions.

■ SUMMARY

The relationship of forests to water supply has been subject to considerable controversy, partly due to early misconceptions about the role of forests and vegetation in the hydrologic cycle. Verry (1986, p. 1039) responded to earlier "facts" that were "established with certainty" by Zon (1927) in light of existing information as follows:

1. The forest lowers air temperature inside and above it. [TRUE]
2. Forests increase the abundance and frequency of precipitation. [usually FALSE]
3. The destruction of forests affects the climate. [FALSE, but TRUE for microclimates]
4. On level terrain, forest transpiration drains marshy land. [mostly FALSE]
5. In hill and mountain country, forests conserve water for streamflow. [usually FALSE, sometimes TRUE]
6. Forests retard snowmelt. [usually TRUE, sometimes FALSE]
7. Forests prevent erosion. [TRUE, to a point]
8. Forests regulate the flow of springs . . . [usually FALSE, sometimes TRUE]
9. The total discharge of large rivers depends on climate. [TRUE]
10. Forests tend to equalize streamflow throughout the year by making the low stages higher and the high stages lower. [sometimes FALSE, sometimes TRUE]
11. Forests cannot prevent floods produced by exceptional precipitation, but they can mitigate their destructiveness. [TRUE]

Notice that most of the above answers are qualified—there are exceptions to most of the rules. An understanding of the cause-and-effect relationships and basic hydrologic principles help to explain such exceptions.

Key points that you should be able to explain after completing this chapter are phrased in the following questions:

1. What changes in vegetative cover usually result in an increase in the quantity of water yield?
2. What are the exceptions to the above?
3. What methods are available to estimate changes in water yield caused by changes in vegetative cover?
4. What factors are important in determining how much of a given change in water yield from upstream catchments becomes realized downstream?
5. How can land use practices affect streamflow during periods of high flows and of low flows? Give examples of changes in a watershed that can result in:
   - higher flows during the dry season
   - higher flows during the wet season
   - lower flows during both the dry and wet season
6. Does clearcutting of forests cause flooding to increase? If so, explain.

PART 2

Erosion, Sedimentation, Water Quality, and Land Use

■ The hydrologic processes discussed in Part 1 directly and indirectly affect soil erosion; the transport of eroded sediments; the deposition of sediments downstream; and the physical, chemical, and biological characteristics that collectively determine the quality of streamflow and groundwater. Land use and watershed management practices also directly affect erosion, sedimentation, and water quality via changes in the hydrologic processes. These topics are the subject of Part 2.

Soil erosion affects the productivity of upland watersheds and can adversely impact downstream areas. A basic understanding of erosion processes and the factors affecting erosion and downstream sedimentation is needed by members of many professions. A thorough working knowledge of erosion processes and their control probably is not reasonable for all resource managers and engineers, but they should at least be aware of the principal causes of erosion.

Soil erosion is the process of dislodgement and transport of soil particles by wind and water. Climate, topography, soil characteristics, vegetative cover, and land use all affect soil erosion. The downstream impacts

Measuring suspended sediment from a stream flowing through a rectangular weir.

of erosion depend on the factors that govern sediment transport from watershed surfaces and through the stream channel.

Chapter 7 is concerned with surface erosion from water or wind and methods of control. Wind erosion is included because of its importance in the management of watersheds in arid, semiarid, and coastal areas. Gully erosion and control and mass movement of soil, including sand dune formation, are discussed in Chapter 8. Sediment transport and deposition are the focus of Chapter 9. Collectively, these chapters address the general topics of erosion processes, erosion control, and sedimentation. Sediment transport and deposition impacts the quality of receiving waters and their use by downstream communities. Many other factors affect the quality of water flowing from upland watersheds; an understanding of these factors and processes is critical to the development of appropriate watershed management. Water quality is the subject of Chapter 10.

CHAPTER 7

Surface Erosion and Control of Erosion on Upland Watersheds

INTRODUCTION

In general, there are three erosion processes on upland watersheds: surface erosion, gully erosion, and soil mass movement. *Surface erosion* involves the detachment and subsequent removal of soil particles and small aggregates from land surfaces by wind or water. This type of erosion is caused by the action of raindrops, thin film flows, concentrated overland flows, or by wind. While less serious in forested environments, surface erosion can be an important source of sediment from rangelands and cultivated agricultural lands. *Gully erosion* is the detachment and movement of material, either individual soil particles or large aggregates, in a well-defined channel. This kind of erosion is a major form of geologic erosion that can be accelerated greatly under poor land management. *Soil mass movement* includes erosion in which cohesive masses of soil are displaced. Movement can be rapid, as with landslides, or it can be quite slow, as with soil creep and certain soil slumps. All of the above erosion processes can occur singly or in combination. Human activities, such as construction, road building, forest removal, intensive livestock grazing, and agriculture, can accelerate these processes. At times, it is difficult to distinguish or separate the basic types of erosion and whether they are natural geologic processes or have been accelerated by poor land use practices. Factors that affect soil erosion and sediment movement from a watershed are summarized in Figure 7.1.

THE EROSION PROCESS

Soil erosion is the process of dislodgement and transport of soil particles from the surface by water and wind. The soil particles can be dislodged by the energies expended at the soil surface by raindrops or by the eddies in surface runoff and wind, and then transported by wind or water or by the force of gravity. Therefore, erosion is a process in the physical sense that work requires the expenditure of energy. The energy is imparted to the soil surface by forces resulting from impulses produced by the momentum (mass × velocity) of falling raindrops or by the momentum of eddies in the turbulent flows of runoff or wind. It is these forces that cause work to be done in both the dislodgement and transport phases of the process.

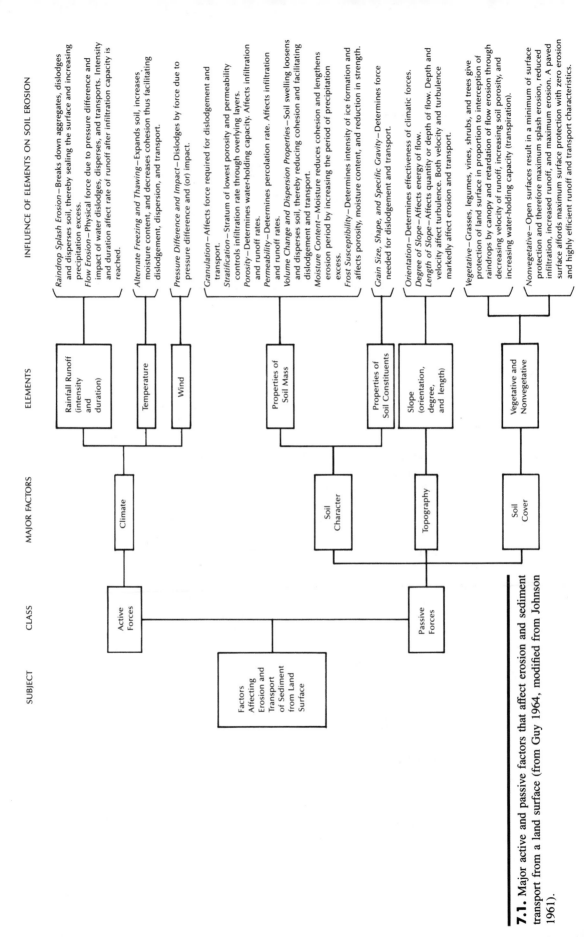

7.1. Major active and passive factors that affect erosion and sediment transport from a land surface (from Guy 1964, modified from Johnson 1961).

Water Erosion

The dislodgement of soil particles at the soil surface by energy imparted to the surface by falling raindrops is a primary agent of erosion, particularly on soils with sparse vegetative cover (Table 7.1). The energy released at the surface during a large storm is sufficient to splash over 200 metric tons of soil into the air on a single hectare of bare and loose soil. Individual soil particles can be splashed more than 0.5 m in height and 1.5 m meters sideways.

Table 7.1. Kinetic energy (K_e) associated with different intensities of rainfall, and illustration of soil displacement due to rainfall impact

	Rainfall Intensity (mm/hr)	Kinetic Energy[a] (Mj/ha·mm)[b]
Drizzle	1	0.12
Rain	15	0.22
Cloudburst	75	0.28

Source: Calculated from Dissmeyer and Foster (1980).
[a]$K_e = \frac{1}{2}$ (mass)(velocity)^2.
[b]Units are megajoules per hectare millimeter.

It often has been reported that the energy released at the soil surface by a rainstorm is greater than that released by the runoff produced. However, these calculations did not take into account the energy of turbulent eddies in runoff (Fig. 7.2). Furthermore, rainfall often is distributed more or less uniformly over an area, whereas runoff quickly becomes concentrated in rills and channels where its erosive power becomes magnified.

The major result of the impulses imparted to the soil surface by raindrops is the deterioration of soil structure by breaking down soil aggregates. The subsequent splashing of finer soil particles tends to puddle and close the soil surface and thereby increase surface runoff.

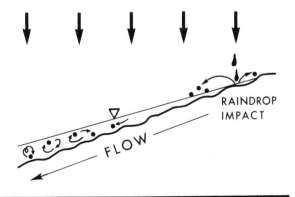

RAINDROP IMPACT

FLOW

7.2. Surface soil erosion as a result of raindrop impact and turbulent surface runoff.

Surface runoff takes place when the rate of rainfall exceeds the infiltration rate on slopes. Just as with rainfall, the kinetic energy of surface runoff required to dislodge, entrain, and transport soil particles depends upon the mass (depth) of water and its velocity. In addition, surface runoff is turbulent, that is, eddies in the flow make up the turbulence. These eddies are random in size, orientation, and velocity and provide the impulses to dislodge and entrain soil particles. The intensity of the turbulence in surface runoff depends upon the velocity and depth of runoff and the roughness of the surface over which water flows.

Surface runoff combined with the beating action of raindrops causes rills to be formed in the soil surface. *Rill erosion* is the form of erosion that produces the greatest amount of soil loss world wide. Sheet erosion takes place between rills, where it is termed *inter-rill erosion*. Sheet erosion is the movement of a semisuspended layer of soil particles over the land surface. However, minute rills are formed almost simultaneously with the first detachment and movement of particles. The constant meanders and changes in position of these small rills obscure their presence from normal observation, hence, the concept of *sheet erosion*.

As runoff becomes concentrated in rills and small channels and moves downslope, the velocity and mass of the suspension as well as the intensity of the turbulence in the flow increases. When the depth of runoff is shallow, raindrops striking the water surface can add to the turbulence. This increase of kinetic energy results in an even greater increase in the ability of the flow to dislodge and transport larger soil particles. If the flow carries a large load of sediment, the abrasive action of the load adds to the erosive power of the runoff. On steep, unobstructed slopes and with heavy rains, soil lost in this manner can be dramatic; it also is a common occurrence on drylands, where the normally sparse vegetative cover has been disturbed by poor land use practices.

The momentum that can be gained by surface runoff on a sloping area and, consequently, the amount of soil that can be lost from the area depends upon both the inclination and the length of unobstructed slope. As the length of the slope increases, soil loss per unit length initially is accelerated, but then approaches a constant rate. However, as the inclination of the slope increases, soil loss increases. Slope angle and slope length that allow the build-up in momentum in flowing water are major factors in accelerating rill erosion; the steeper and longer the slope, the greater become the problems of control. Once it becomes channelized, uncontrolled surface runoff is capable of creating the more spectacular gully erosion (see Chapter 8). Gullies are common features of sparcely vegetated lands.

Wind Erosion

In dry regions, erosion by both wind and water is a natural feature. Such erosion is an inevitable consequence of the environment, largely because rainfall is inadequate to support a protective cover of vegetation. Any use of drylands that further reduces the cover of vegetation tends to accelerate erosion beyond that which is a natural consequence of the environment. As a rule, watersheds that have natural vegetative cover and that receive precipitation of over 400 mm/yr experience little wind erosion. When soils are exposed, excessive wind erosion can occur, even in regions with over 800 mm/yr annual precipitation. In either case, wind erosion diminishes with increasing annual precipitation.

The action of wind and water often are complementary in their roles of removing soil in dry regions. For example, a soil stripped of vegetation by the abrasive action of wind-blown sand is rendered vulnerable to erosion by water, or a barren outwash sediment deposit is subject to erosion by wind. Sometimes, it is difficult to determine which is the dominant agent on a particular site; generally wind erosion is a long-term process of gradual removal, and water erosion is shorter term and can be very rapid. The conservation of soil and water in arid zones often must address both processes simultaneously. Fortunately, many of the principles of the erosion process and most of the methods of controlling erosion apply to either process.

The action of wind on the soil surface is analogous to the action of flowing water. Wind also exhibits turbulent flow, having a net velocity in the horizontal direction but with strong eddying in both the upward and downward direction. The air is compressed randomly by this turbulence, which produces gusts. Hot desert soils create thermal updrafts, which increase the turbulence. By their great velocity and upward eddies, gusty winds are able to dislodge small soil particles, lift them upward, and carry them away, much like suspended sediment in flowing water.

Wind can move larger soil particles by making them "jump" along the ground. The jumping particles also apply energy to the soil surface each time they hit the ground and, in doing so, dislodge other particles so that they too can be moved by the wind. This process is called *saltation,* which is also a major process in the movement of bed load, the larger particles that move along the bottom of a stream channel.

The largest soil particles that can be moved to any extent by wind are about 1 mm, thus, where the size of the soil particles extends over a wide range, wind has a sorting effect on the soil. Very fine clay and silt particles (less than 0.02 mm) are lifted into the air and carried away as wind-blown dust. Sand-size particles are carried along in the air layer near the ground by saltation until they reach an obstruction, where they can pile up into drifts and (under extreme conditions) into dunes. Just as gullies are advanced stages of water erosion, sand dunes are severe stages of wind erosion.

The erosive power of wind, as that of water, increases exponentially with velocity; but, unlike water, it is not affected by the force of gravity. Therefore, slope inclination is not a factor in wind erosion, except where sloping or hilly terrain forms barriers or influences wind direction. However, similar to the effect on the erosive power of water, the length of unobstructed terrain (fetch) over which the wind flows is important in allowing the wind to gain momentum and to increase its erosive power. Winds with velocities less than about 12–19 km/hr at 1 m above the ground seldom impart sufficient energy at the soil surface to dislodge and put into motion sand-size particles.

■ PREVENTING SOIL EROSION

Avoiding erosion-susceptible situations and inappropriate land uses is the most economical and effective means to combat soil erosion and to maintain the productivity of watersheds. The guiding rule is that the land user should consider carefully the principles of water and wind action in relation to each management decision, whether this concerns soil conservation techniques, water resource development, range management, forest management, or agriculture.

Situations that are particularly susceptible to soil loss include (1) sloping ground, particularly hills with shallow soils; (2) soils with inherently low permeabilities; and

(3) sites where denudation of vegetation is likely.

Maintaining a vegetative cover is the best means of reducing erosion hazard, but the occurrence of an adequate cover cannot be relied upon in drylands. Instead, the importance of reducing the energy of wind and flowing water suggests preventive measures that can be applied using simple land use practices. In preventing water erosion, the key is to maintain the surface soil in a condition that readily accepts water; the more water that infiltrates, the better the chance of sustaining plant growth and reducing the erosive effects of surface runoff. Guidelines for preventing water and wind erosion are outlined in Table 7.2.

Table 7.2. Guidelines for preventing water and wind erosion

Water Erosion
  Avoid land use practices that reduce infiltration capacity and soil permeability
  Encourage grass and herbaceous cover of the soil for as long as possible each year
  Locate livestock-watering facilities to minimize runoff production to water bodies
  Avoid logging and heavy grazing on steep slopes
  Conduct any skidding of logs on steep slopes in upward directions to counteract drainage concentration patterns
  Lay out roads and trails so that runoff is not channelized on steep, susceptible areas
  Apply erosion control techniques on agricultural fields, and promote infiltration
  Remember that the more water that goes into the soil, the better the chance of sustaining plant growth and reducing the erosive effects of surface runoff
Wind Erosion
  Avoid uses that will lead to the elimination of shrubs and trees over large areas
  Avoid locating livestock-watering facilities on erodible soils
  Protect agricultural fields and heavy-use areas with shelterbelts
  Manage animals and plants in your area to maintain a good balance between range plants, woody trees, and shrubs
  When planting shrubs and trees on grazing lands, locate and space them to reduce wind velocity

In areas where accelerated erosion is occurring, remedial soil conservation techniques will be necessary. These techniques should be designed to reduce the impact of the erosion processes and be applied first to those areas that have the highest production potential.

■ CONTROLLING SOIL EROSION

An understanding of the erosion processes suggests several broad actions that can be undertaken to control accelerated surface soil erosion. Actions that protect the soil surface against the energy of rainfall impact and increase the roughness of the surface, and thus the tortuosity of the flow path, reduce the energy of rainfall and surface runoff. Mechanical treatments that shorten the slope length and reduce the slope inclination lessen the energy of overland flow and can reduce the quantity and velocity of surface runoff. Any actions that prevent the channelization of surface runoff will reduce the opportunity for gully formation. Often, strips of vegetation perpendicular to the slope can slow and reduce surface runoff.

When controlling wind erosion, actions should be taken that reduce the length of fetch to reduce the momentum of wind and increase soil cohesiveness or armor the soil surface to prevent the lifting of soil particles by wind. The key is to reduce wind velocity near the ground, and to deflect the wind direction.

The most effective techniques are those that combine several of these actions. For example, nearly all the actions can be accomplished with an effective vegetation cover. In addition to reducing rainfall impact, increasing surface roughness, and thus reducing the velocity of surface runoff, maintaining vegetation cover can improve infiltration rates. Soil erodibility is decreased by the activity of roots and the improvement of soil structure by the addition of organic matter. Also, evapotranspiration by vegetation reduces soil water content between rainfall events and, consequently, provides more storage for rainfall and lessens runoff.

Surface Erosion Control on Forestlands

A minimal amount of surface erosion is expected in natural forests (Fig. 7.3). Undisturbed forests rarely experience erosion rates in excess of 0.04 t/ha/yr. Activities that remove vegetative cover and, most importantly, expose mineral soil lead to high rates of surface erosion. Silvicultural treatments in which the destruction of lesser vegetation and litter accumulations is minimized will help to control erosion by reducing the raindrop impact on a soil surface and by maintaining high infiltration rates. Residual strips of vegetation alternated with clearcuts and aligned perpendicularly to the slope can function as barriers to flowing water and the downslope movement of soil particles. Retaining strips of vegetation also can be employed to protect channel banks and streambeds during timber-harvesting operations. However, leaving residual

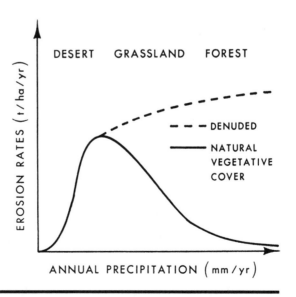

7.3. Relationship between erosion rates and annual precipitation for vegetation types and watershed cover conditions (modified from Hudson 1981 and others).

strips of vegetation is usually of little value in controlling erosion in mountainous watersheds because of rapid channeling of surface runoff.

The nature of the logging operation used in timber harvesting can affect the magnitude of surface erosion on a watershed. Watersheds undergoing logging operations and associated road development often result in erosion rates in excess of 15 t/ha/yr. Logging operations that generally reduce the compaction and disturbance of surface soils should be favored. Small cable systems can be used to remove felled timber on sites where tractors would cause excessive soil disturbance, for example, on slopes over 30–35%. Other methods, such as cable systems with intermediate supports to attain the necessary lift and extend the yarding distance, can be utilized on flatter terrain. Also, double-tired low ground-pressure vehicles with torsion suspension might replace crawler tractors. Keying the timber-harvesting operations to the dry season, the soil type, and minimizing the disturbance to the litter layer will lessen soil compaction and consequent surface erosion.

Establishing and maintaining a vegetative cover to protect cut banks and fill slopes along roads, on landings in timber-harvesting operations, and in other "critical" areas of exposed mineral soil will, in many instances, help to control surface erosion. Individual plant species have different values for erosion control, different site requirements, and different cultural requirements. Therefore, knowledge of available plant species for erosion control is important. Guides that specify plant species, site preparation, and seeding or planting techniques for local areas in the United States are available from federal and state land management agencies.

Most erosion problems on forestlands are attributed to improper road and skid trail design, location, and layout. Roads and trails are necessary for many activities on watersheds, but their potential impacts upon erosion usually exceed that of all other management activities considered. Erosion rates from road construction sites commonly exceed 95 t/ha/yr. No other activity results in such intensive and concentrated soil disturbance.

Many potential erosion problems can be eliminated in the planning stage, before road or trail construction. Emphasis should be placed on the development of a *system*, not a randomly located network. Through the consideration of a system of all feeder and hauling roads, the amount of mineral soil exposed is minimized. It also minimizes the investment in, and maintenance of, the system. One of the more important decisions to be made in planning is the width and allowable grade of the system, as these standards will affect the area of disturbance within a watershed.

Some erosion will result from roads and trails no matter how careful the layout, therefore, the objective is to minimize the magnitude of this erosion. To do so, a road or trail system should be located to minimize the extent of exposed soil and disturbed, unstable areas on a watershed; also, the system should be kept away from stream channels to the extent possible. A satisfactory location is the product of both considerations. Steep gradients should be avoided because roads or trails located on these sites often are less stable than on lesser slopes, and they expose more soil due to excessive cut and fill requirements. Also, steeper slopes concentrate water more quickly and impart a higher velocity to the flow than on less steep slopes. However, sufficient slope is needed at each location to facilitate drainage.

Other factors to consider in road construction are culvert size, spacing, and maintenance; adequate compaction of fill materials; and minimizing the amount of side-cast materials. Roadside ditch turnouts interrupt flow and divert runoff onto adjacent land. Temporary roads and trails should be stabilized immediately after use by seeding grasses or herbaceous cover mixtures and appropriate follow-up management. The USDA Forest Service and others have established construction guidelines, which when followed, should reduce the chances of serious erosion problems.

Megahan (1977, p. 239) summarized four basic principles that, if followed, would lead to reduced impacts of road construction on erosion and sedimentation:

(1) keep the area of roads on a watershed to a minimum by minimizing mileage and disturbance,
(2) do not locate roads in high erosion hazard areas,
(3) apply erosion control measures in areas that are disturbed by road construction, and
(4) reduce sediment delivery from roads to stream channels.

Surface Erosion Control on Rangelands

The greatest amount of erosion worldwide occurs in dry regions (Fig. 7.3). These regions are generally too dry for productive rain-fed agriculture; commonly, grazing is the only economical use of the land. In many developing countries, grazing is uncontrolled and excessive. The establishment of appropriate range management practices must be a first priority under these conditions, otherwise, any other soil conservation practice will fail. Often, simply controlling livestock density and the grazing practice is sufficient to restore depleted and eroding rangelands. The key is to maintain good vegetative cover and not to reduce infiltration capacities of rangelands which if overgrazed, are characterized by low plant density, compacted soils, surface runoff, and excessive erosion.

Fire is commonly used as a management tool to increase forage production of rangelands by removing woody vegetation. Controlled burns, if properly managed, should not adversely impact the hydraulic properties of soils. Uncontrolled fires can reach temperatures that are high enough to reduce infiltration capacities. In any event, fires leave large areas of exposed mineral soil, areas that are vulnerable to rainfall impact, surface runoff, and erosion.

If rangelands are in poor condition, reseeding and other measures may be necessary. Reseeding may require temporary mechanical treatments to conserve water and, thereby, aid vegetation establishment. Control of weed species may also be necessary.

VEGETATIVE MEASURES

Reseeding is expensive and can be justified economically only if it provides returns in forage and erosion protection over many years. Successful reseeding efforts depend upon rainfall patterns and site conditions. Successful seeding requires the following conditions:

1. Soils and precipitation must be adequate to provide a reasonable probability for success. Higher precipitation usually is required to establish plants on clay soils than on more sandy soils.

2. Indigenous or site-adapted species must be used. Selecting adapted ecotypes within a species also can provide an extra measure of success on some sites.

3. Seedbeds should be prepared to control unwanted vegetation and provide rapid infiltration. A loose, irregular surface seedbed is often desirable.

4. An adequate quantity of seed is needed to insure a successful stand of vegetation but not to the point of being wasteful. Seeding approximately 2–3 million viable seeds per hectare is a rough estimate of seeding intensity.

5. Seeds must be planted at the proper depth. The smaller the seed, the shallower it should be seeded. Broadcasting small seed on loose seedbeds frequently is adequate, but drilling is recommended for large seeds and on crusted seedbeds.

6. Seeding should occur when favorable moisture and temperature combine to give the longest possible period for germination and early growth.

7. Seedlings should be protected from grazing until they have become well established; this can require three or more growing seasons on dry sites.

8. Site preparation by mechanical techniques may be needed to prepare seedbeds and conserve water. These techniques seldom are justified economically.

MECHANICAL TECHNIQUES

Because they are expensive, mechanical treatments to improve rangelands can be justified only if runoff and sediment from the watershed threatens important downstream developments, reclamation is essential to the survival of people in the area who have no alternative means of livelihood, or the value of the increased production equals or exceeds the cost of treatment.

The purpose of mechanical treatments is to reduce surface runoff and soil loss by retaining water on-site until a vegetative cover can become established. Some of the more common treatments include contour furrows, contour trenches, fallow strips, pits, and basins. The type of treatment chosen depends upon the runoff potential of the site. Often, a combination of treatments may be desired, but planting should follow treatment as soon as possible.

Mechanical treatments have a limited life expectancy depending upon the amount of runoff and sediment produced on-site. Therefore, it is important to evaluate the site for its potential for maintaining a vegetative cover after the treatment has lost its effectiveness. A livestock management strategy usually must be formulated and enforced if the treatment is to have a lasting effect.

Contour Furrows. Contour furrows are constructed to break slope length and provide depression storage for surface runoff. They are small ditches 20–30 cm deep that follow the contour; they usually are constructed with a single blade, furrowed plow that forms a berm on the downslope side. Furrows form miniature terraces that hold the water in place until it infiltrates into the soil, are suitable for plant establishment, and usually are seeded after construction. Studies indicate that furrows are effective if the spacing between them is less than 2 m. At greater spacings, there is little effect except along the furrows.

A number of early trials with furrows failed because of the difficulty of following the contour and the lack of seeding and follow-up maintenance. If not placed along contours, furrows become drainage ditches that concentrate runoff and can accelerate erosion rather than prevent it. Following the contour is a difficult process and one of the disadvantages of the method. The effectiveness of furrows can be increased and the misalignment of furrows with the contours can be corrected somewhat by constructing crossbars across the furrows at intervals of 1.5–10 m. The furrows then become small basins and water from adjacent sections will be held in place if one section should break.

Contour Trenches. Trenches are nothing more than large furrows and usually are required on slopes too steep for contour furrows. There are two types: a shallow outside type (for slopes up to 70%) where the excavated material forms the barrier to overland flow; and the deeper inside type where the excavation retains most of the overland flow. Both types are expensive, usually require machinery, and must be designed to handle large stormflows. The failure of an upper trench could result in a domino effect on trenches downslope. If such a situation occurs, the resulting erosion can be much greater than that which would have occurred in the first place.

Fallow Strips. Revegetated strips have proven successful on level to gently rolling land to break the slope length until desirable vegetation can become established. The strips usually are about 1 m wide and parallel to the contour. Initially the strips are cultivated to destroy unwanted vegetation, loosen the soil surface, and prepare a seedbed. The original vegetation is left between the strips until the newly planted vegetation has become established. New strips then are tilled and planted and the process continued until the range has been rehabilitated. Conventional tillage equipment can be used for this technique.

Pitting. Pitting is a technique of digging or gouging shallow depressions into the soil surface to create depression storage for surface runoff. The treatment of extensive areas requires a tractor and pitter. A conventional disk plow can be modified into a pitter although a special disk plow is made for range use. Every alternate disk can be removed and the axle holes of the remaining disks offset from the center. Alternatively, rather than offsetting, a "half-moon" section can be cut from each of the remaining disks. The disks are arranged to strike the surface at different times, creating an alternate pattern of pits as the plow is pulled across the surface. The furrow is broken by the missing disk or by the missing section of the cut disk, which then forms a discontinuous furrow. A standard heavy 51-cm-disk plow with holes 8 cm off-center will produce pits about 20–30 cm wide by 45–60 cm long, 15 cm deep, and 40 cm apart. Under favorable conditions of soil type, soil moisture, and machine weight, the pits will have a storage capacity of about 0.013 m^3. The number of pits required per hectare can be estimated by dividing the estimated runoff produced from a design storm by the storage capacity per pit. Pitting is effective on slopes up to 30%, and it has been estimated that the technique can produce as much as four times the amount of forage as produced on untreated areas.

Basins. Basins are larger pits, usually about 2 m long, 1.8 m wide and 15–20 cm deep. They store a greater amount of water and can help create pockets of lush vegetation. Basins generally are more costly to construct and are not as widely used as pitting methods.

■ MEASUREMENT OF SURFACE EROSION

Surface erosion rates can be measured or approximated by several field methods. The most common methods include the use of plots, stakes or pins, and measurements of natural landscape features such as pedestals.

Erosion Plots

The most widely used method of quantifying surface erosion rates is to measure the amount of soil that washes from plots. Collecting troughs are sunk along the width of the bottom of the plots. Walls made of plastic, sheet metal, plywood, or concrete are inserted at least 10 cm into the soil surface and form the boundaries of the plot. The collecting trough empties into a container, or tank, in which both sediment and runoff are measured. Sometimes, these tanks are designed with recording instruments so that rates of flow can be measured. In other cases, the total volume of sediment and water are measured after a rainfall event.

Plots can vary in size from microplots of 1–2 m², to the standard plot of 6 ft × 72.6 ft (approximately 2 m × 22 m), which is the 0.01-acre (0.004-ha) plot used for the Universal Soil Loss Equation discussed later. The techniques used and the objectives of the experiment dictate the size of the plot. For multiple comparisons of vegetation, soils, and land use practices, the microplots are less expensive and are more practical for experiments that use rainfall simulators. Larger plots provide more realistic estimates of erosion because they better represent the cumulative effect of increasing runoff and velocity downslope. Plots larger than the standard can produce large volumes of runoff and sediment that are difficult to store. In such cases, devices that split or sample a portion of total water and sediment flow are preferred. Such fractioning devices allow larger plots to be used to quantify the effects of larger scale land use practices.

Erosion Stakes and Other Methods

The insertion of stakes or pins into the soil can be used to estimate soil losses and sediment deposition that occur along hillslopes. Commonly, a long metal nail with a washer is inserted into the soil and the distance between the head of the nail and the washer is measured. This distance increases as erosion occurs because the soil that supports the washer is washed away. If the washer causes a pedestal to form immediately beneath the washer (because of protection from rainfall impact), measurements should be made from the nail head to the bottom of the pedestal. A benchmark should be established in close proximity to the stakes as a point of reference and stakes should be clearly marked for relocation.

Normally erosion stakes are arranged in a grid pattern along hillslopes. Repeated measurements of stakes over time provide information on the changes in soil surface that result from soil losses and deposition. This method is inexpensive compared to the plot method, but presents more difficulty in converting observations into actual soil losses in tons per hectare.

Using the same principles of the stake method, erosion estimates sometimes can be made from natural landscape features. Pedestals often form beneath clumps of bunchgrass, dense shrubs, stones, or other areas that are protected from rainfall. As erosion removes soil from around them, the distance between pedestal top and bottom increases. Repeated measurements of the height of residual soil pedestals provide estimates as described above. The key is to relate measurements to a common point of reference or benchmark. Sometimes, soil that has eroded away from the base of trees can be estimated with repeated measurements of soil surface and a point on exposed tree roots or from a nail driven into the tree trunk.

■ PREDICTION OF SOIL LOSS

Because land management practices create a variety of conditions that influence the magnitude of surface erosion, land managers frequently want to predict the amount of soil loss by surface erosion. Of the methods available, the Universal Soil Loss Equation (USLE), in both its original and modified forms, is perhaps the most widely applied of the empirical approaches in which predictive equations are developed from analyses of source data. Process models structured through evaluations of cause-and-effect relationships sometimes are employed to estimate surface soil loss. In this discussion, however, emphasis is placed on the empirical approach.

Universal Soil Loss Equation

Prior to the development of the USLE, estimates of erosion rates were made from site-specific data on soil losses. As a result, these estimates were limited to particular regions and soils. However, the need for a more widely applicable erosion-prediction technique led to the development of the USLE by the USDA Agricultural Research Service. The original USLE of 1965 was based on the analysis of 10,000 plot-years of source data, mostly collected from agricultural plots under natural rainfall. Subsequently, because of the high costs of collecting data from plots under natural rainfall, erosion research has been conducted on plots with simulated rainfall. Rainfall-simulator data are employed in the revised USLE of 1978 to describe soil erodibility and to provide values for the effectiveness of conservation tillage and construction practices for controlling soil erosion.

In the following description of the USLE, the English units employed in its original development are used in the presentation rather than corresponding metric units. The basic USLE equation (Wischmeier and Smith 1965, 1978) is:

$$A = R\,K\,(LS)\,C\,P \tag{7.1}$$

where A = computed soil loss in tons per unit area; R = a rainfall erosivity factor for a specific area, usually expressed in terms of average erosion index (EI) units; K = a soil erodibility factor for a specific soil horizon; LS = topographic factor, a combined dimensionless factor for slope length and slope gradient, where L is expressed as the ratio of soil loss from a given slope length to soil loss from a 72.6-ft length under the same conditions (it is not the actual slope length), and S is expressed as the ratio of soil loss from a given slope steepness to soil loss from a 9% slope under the same conditions (it is not the actual slope steepness); C = a dimensionless cropping management factor, expressed as a ratio of soil loss from the condition of interest to soil loss from tilled continuous fallow (condition under which K is determined); and P = an erosion control practice factor, expressed as a ratio of the soil loss with the practices (for example, contouring, strip cropping, or terracing) to soil loss with farming up and down the slope.

Equation 7.1 provides an estimate of sheet and rill erosion from rainfall events on upland areas. It does not include erosion from streambanks, snowmelt, or wind, and it does not include eroded sediment that is deposited at the base of slopes and at other reduced-flow locations before runoff reaches the streams or reservoirs.

The term "universal" was given to the USLE to indicate that, in contrast to earlier erosion prediction equations that applied only to specific regions, the USLE applied initially in 1965 to the area of the United States east of the Rocky Mountains, and with the 1978 revision, to all of the United States.

By 1970, the USLE also was being applied to nonagricultural situations, such as construction sites and undisturbed lands including forests and rangelands. However, as extensive baseline data were not available for these applications, a subfactor method was developed to estimate values for the C factor. In essence, the subfactor method employs a set of relationships for canopy cover, ground cover, and internal soil effects to estimate a composite value for C. This development allows the use of source data collected from more basic studies to be utilized in applications of the USLE.

RAINFALL EROSIVITY FACTOR

The rainfall erosivity factor (R) is an index that characterizes the effect of raindrop impact and rate of runoff associated with the rainstorm. It is determined by calculating the EI for a specified time period, usually one year or one season within the year. The EI averaged over a number of these time periods (n) equals R:

$$R = \frac{\sum_{i}^{n} EI_i}{n} \tag{7.2}$$

The energy of a rainstorm depends on the amount of rain and all the component rainfall intensities of the storm. For any given mass in motion, the energy is proportional to velocity squared, therefore, rainfall energy is related directly to rain intensity by the relationship:

$$E = 916 + 331 \ (\log I_i) \tag{7.3}$$

where E = kinetic energy per inch of rainfall in ft-tons/acre; and I = rainfall intensity in each rainfall intensity period of the storm (in./hr). The total kinetic energy of a storm (k_e) is obtained by multiplying E by the inches depth of rainfall in each intensity period (n), and summing:

$$k_e = \sum_{i}^{n} [916 + 331 \ (\log I_i)] \tag{7.4}$$

The *EI* for an individual storm is calculated by multiplying the total kinetic energy (k_e) of the storm by the maximum amount of rain falling within 30 consecutive minutes (I_{30}), multiplying by 2 to obtain in./hr, and dividing the result by 100 (to convert from hundreds of ft-tons/acre to ft-tons/acre):

$$EI \text{ (storm)} = \frac{2 (k_e) I_{30}}{100} \qquad \textbf{(7.5)}$$

The *EI* for a specific time period (year or season) is the sum of the individual storms' *EI* values computed for all significant storms during that time period. Usually, only storms greater than 0.5 in. are selected. The *R* is then determined as the sum of the *EI* values for all such storms that occurred during a 20–25 yr period, divided by the number of years (Eq. 7.2).

Studies conducted on rangelands in the southwestern United States have shown that storm runoff is correlated highly with the *R* value for the storm. Therefore, although runoff could have been a parameter for inclusion in the USLE, the use of *R* is considered to be a better index for runoff and precipitation-induced erosion.

Runoff events associated with snowmelt and thawing soils are common on many watersheds. Erosion during these events can be appreciable. Therefore, to apply the USLE to these situations, a use for which it was not originally intended, the *R* factor must be adjusted. This adjustment, which is based on only limited data and general in nature, is one and a half times the winter precipitation (measured in inches of water), a value that is added to the *R* erosivity values for winter storms. Additional research is necessary to further verify and, if required, modify this adjustment procedure for wider use.

SOIL ERODIBILITY FACTOR

The soil erodibility factor (*K*) indicates the susceptibility of soil to erosion and is expressed as soil loss per unit of area per unit of *R* for a unit plot. By definition, a unit plot is 72.6 ft long, on a uniform 9% slope, maintained in continuous fallow, with tillage when necessary to break surface crusts and to control weeds. These dimensions are selected because they coincide with the erosion research plots used in early work in the United States. Continuous fallow is selected as a base because no single cropping system is common to all agricultural areas, and soil loss from any other plot conditions would be influenced, to a large extent, by residual and current crop and management effects, both of which vary from one location to another. The *K* value can be determined as the slope of a regression line through the origin for source data on soil loss (*A*) and erosivity (*R*), once the ratios for *L*, *S*, *C*, and *P* have been adjusted to those of unit conditions. When the *K* value was originally determined with natural rainfall data, it covered a range of storm sizes and antecedent soil moisture conditions. Results of later studies conducted with rainfall simulators were used to produce a soil erodibility nomograph based on soil texture and structure (Wischmeier et al. 1971). This nomograph, illustrated in Figure 7.4, is now used to obtain the *K* factor.

SLOPE LENGTH FACTOR AND SLOPE GRADIENT FACTOR

The topographic factors *L* and *S* indicate the effects of slope length and steepness,

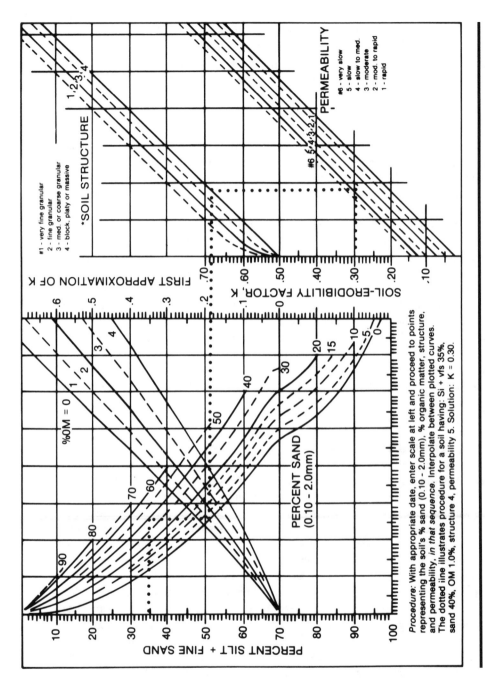

7.4. Nomograph for determining the soil erodibility factor, K, in English units (from U.S. Forest Service 1980, adapted from Wischmeier et al. 1971).

respectively, on erosion. Slope length refers to overland flow, from where it originates to where runoff reaches a defined channel or to where deposition begins. In general, slopes are treated as uniform profiles. Maximum slope lengths are seldom longer than 600 ft or shorter than 15–20 ft. Selection of a slope length requires on-site inspection and judgment.

The slope length factor (L) is defined as:

$$L = (\lambda/72.6)^m \tag{7.6}$$

where λ = field slope length (ft); and m = exponent, affected by the interaction of slope length with gradient, soil properties, type of vegetation, etc. The exponent value ranges from 0.3 for long slopes with gradients less than 5% to 0.6 for slopes over 10%. The average value of 0.5 is applicable to most cases.

The maximum steepness of cropland plots used to derive the S factor was 25%, which is less than many forested and rangeland watershed slopes. Recent investigations on rangelands suggest that the USLE can overestimate the effect of slope on noncrop situations. Consequently, the S factor likely will be adjusted downward in future revisions of the USLE.

The slope gradient factor (S) is defined as:

$$S = \frac{0.43 + 0.30s + 0.043s^2}{6.613} \tag{7.7}$$

where s = slope gradient (in percent).

Foster and Wischmeier (1973) adapted the LS factors for use on irregular slopes; this is especially useful on wildland sites, which rarely have uniform slopes. They describe the combined factor as:

$$LS = \frac{1}{\lambda_e} \sum_{j=1}^{n} \left[\left(\frac{S_j \lambda_j^{m+1}}{(72.6)^m} - \frac{S_j \lambda_{j-1}^{m+1}}{(72.6)^m} \right) \left(\frac{10,000}{10,000 + s_j^2} \right) \right] \tag{7.8}$$

where λ_e = overall slope length; j = sequence number of segment from top to bottom; n = number of segments; λ_j = length (ft) from the top to the lower end of the jth slope segment; λ_{j-1} = the slope length above segment j; S_j = S factor for segment j (Eq. 7.7); and s_j = slope (%) for segment j.

For uniform slopes, LS is determined as:

$$LS = \left(\frac{\lambda_e}{72.6} \right)^m S \left(\frac{10,000}{10,000 + s^2} \right) \tag{7.9}$$

CROPPING MANAGEMENT FACTOR

The cropping management factor (C) of the USLE represents an integration of several factors that affect erosion, including vegetation cover, plant litter, soil surface, and land management. Imbedded in the term is a reflection of how intercepted raindrops that are re-formed on a plant canopy affect splash erosion. Also, the binding effect of plant roots on erosion and how the properties of soil change as it lies idle are considered. Unfortunately, the manner by which grazing animals and other plant cover manipulations change the magnitude of C is not well defined. Studies to define these cause-and-effect relationships are needed to better understand the role of the C factor in calculating annual erosion rates.

In most cases, the value of C is not constant over the year. Although treated as an independent variable in the equation, the "true" value of this factor probably is dependent upon all other factors. Therefore, the value of C should be established experimentally. Runoff plots and fabric dams (filter fences) are useful for this purpose. One simple procedure is:

1. Install runoff plots on the cover complexes of interest, measure soil loss with fabric dams for each storm event, and record rainfall intensity and amount for at least a 2-yr calibration period.
2. Identify rainfall events with a threshold storm size great enough to produce soil loss.
3. Calculate the R value for each storm greater than the threshold storm (usually greater than 0.5 in.) for each year of record.
4. Determine the K and LS factors from the nomographs and equations given in the text.
5. Solve the USLE for C for each year of record; that is, $C = A/RK(LS)$, and calculate an average value for C.

Because of the variability in storms from year to year, an average value or an expected range in R values is useful. Such estimates can be made by developing a regression relationship between the calculated R values and storm amounts measured during the calibration period. Using a historical record of daily rainfall from the nearest weather station, the R value can be determined for each storm on record, and the average R for the watershed can be calculated.

In areas of the world for which there are no guidelines for the establishment of C values for field crops, it is easiest to correlate soil loss ratio with the amount of dry organic matter per unit area or with percent ground cover. For permanent pasture, rangelands, idle lands, and woodlands, C values can be estimated from published tables.

Nine elements or subfactors should be considered when developing this factor for forest conditions: soil consolidation, surface residue, canopy, fine roots, residual effect of fine roots after tillage, contour effect, roughness, weeds and grasses, and steps. Surface residue, the effect on the area covered by litter, slash, and live vegetation, is the predominant element. Tables and nomographs for estimating the C factor for forestry practices are given in Dissmeyer and Foster (1985).

EROSION CONTROL PRACTICE FACTOR

The effect of erosion control practice (P) measures is considered an independent variable; therefore, it has not been included in the cropping management factor. The soil loss ratios for erosion control practices vary with slope gradient. Practices characterized by P, including strip cropping and terraces, are not applicable to most forested and rangeland watersheds. Experimental data to quantify the P factor for non-crop management practices on forested and rangeland watersheds are not available.

Modifications of the Universal Soil Loss Equation

The USLE has been modified for use in rangeland and forest environments. The cropping management (*C*) factor and the erosion control practice (*P*) factor used in the USLE have been replaced by a vegetation management (*VM*) factor to form the Modified Soil Loss Equation (MSLE):

$$A = R\ K(LS)(VM) \tag{7.10}$$

where *VM* = the vegetation management factor, the ratio of soil loss from land managed under specified conditions of vegetative cover to that from the fallow condition on which the *K* factor is evaluated.

Vegetative cover and soil surface conditions of natural ecosystems, whether undisturbed or disturbed, are accounted for with the *VM* factor. Three different kinds of effects are considered as subfactors: (1) canopy cover effects; (2) effects of low-growing vegetative cover, mulch, and litter; and (3) land use effects. Relationships have been developed for each of the three subfactors (Fig. 7.5). The three subfactors

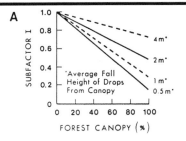

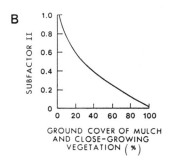

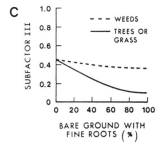

7.5. Relationships of forest canopy cover (A), ground cover (B), and fine roots in the topsoil (C) used to determine subfactors I, II, and III, respectively, for the *VM* factor (from Wischmeier 1975).

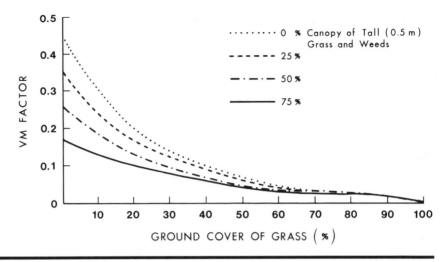

7.6. Relationship between ground cover conditions and the *VM* factor for the modified Universal Soil Loss Equation (adapted from Clyde et al. 1976).

are multiplied together to obtain the *VM* value. When a forest canopy is not present, for example with many rangeland conditions, relationships such as the one illustrated in Figure 7.6 can be used directly. The MSLE procedure is applied in Example 7.1.

More work has been carried out determining *C* values for the USLE than for *VM* factors, thus, there are more numerous tables of relationships for *C* than *VM* factors. Published values of *C* can be used as a substitute for *VM* if they account for the three effects described in Tables 7.3 and 7.4.

The MSLE procedure can be used as a guide for quantifying the potential erosion of different land use and land management strategies *only* if the principal interactions on which the equation is based are thoroughly understood. Failure to understand the

Table 7.3. C factors for undisturbed woodlands

Effective Canopy[a] (% of area)	Forest Litter[b] (% of area)	*C* Factor[c]
100–75	100–90	0.0001–0.001
70–40	85–75	0.002–0.004
35–20	70–40	0.003–0.009

Source: From U.S. Soil Conservation Service (1977).

[a]When effective canopy is less than 20%, the area will be considered as grassland or idle land for estimating soil loss. Where woodlands are being harvested or grazed, use table 7.4.

[b]Forest litter is assumed to be at least 5 cm deep over the percent ground surface area covered.

[c]The range in *C* values is due in part to the range in the percent area covered. In addition, the percent of effective canopy and its height has an effect. Low canopy is effective in reducing raindrop impact and in lowering the *C* factor. High canopy, over 13 m, is not effective in reducing raindrop impact and will have no effect on the *C* value.

EXAMPLE 7.1

Existing surface erosion rates (sheet and rill erosion) were estimated for a 12,000-ha watershed in the Loukos Basin, northern Morocco by applying the Modified Universal Soil Loss Equation (MSLE). Based on previous studies in the area, the values determined were R = 400, K = 0.15, LS = 10, and VM = 0.13 (based on a 30% ground cover of grass with a 25% canopy of tall weeds)

$$A = RK(LS)(VM)$$

$$A = (400)(0.15)(10)(0.13) = 78 \text{ tonnes/ha/yr (estimated annual soil loss)}$$

The total erosion rate from the watershed was 936,000 tonnes/yr. Revegetation measures, as part of a watershed rehabilitation project, are anticipated to result in the following:

½ watershed area = 25% forest canopy with a 60% ground cover of grass

½ watershed area = 80% grass cover with a 25% short shrub cover

These changes in vegetation cover would be expected to reduce the surface erosion (estimated by the MSLE with the modified VM factors determined from Table 7.4) as follows:

$$A \text{ (½ area)} = (400)(0.15)(10)(0.041) = 24.6 \text{ tonnes/ha}$$

$$A \text{ (½ area)} = (400)(0.15)(10)(0.012) = 7.2 \text{ tonnes/ha}$$

The erosion rate for the rehabilitated watershed would be 190,800 tonnes/yr.

equation can lead to invalid interpretations. If the underlying assumptions do not represent the actual processes in the forest environment, then predicted erosion values can be far different from actual erosion.

Both the USLE and MSLE require an estimated value for the R factor. General estimates can be obtained for the United States from publications by the U.S. Soil Conservation Service. For other parts of the world (and for specific conditions in the United States) long-term rainfall-intensity records must be analyzed. Often, these records are not available.

Williams (1975) modified the USLE by replacing the R factor with a runoff factor. The modification is based on the assumption that the total discharge and peak discharge rate resulting from a storm on the watershed depends upon the duration, amount, and intensity of the storm. The modified equation is:

$$Y_s = 95q_pQK(LS)CP \tag{7.11}$$

where Y_s = sediment yield in (tons); Q = volume of storm runoff (acre-ft); q_p = peak discharge (ft³/sec); and $K(LS)CP$ = as defined in the USLE.

The equation was developed to estimate sediment yield at the outlet of a watershed directly, rather than soil loss, on a storm by storm basis. Peak and total discharge can be estimated by the methods described in Chapter 17, if runoff data are not available. Satisfactory results have been obtained with Equation 7.11 when tested for a wide range of watershed sizes and slopes. However, it tends to overestimate sediment yield from small storms and to underestimate sediment yield for large storms.

Table 7.4. C or VM factors for permanent pasture, rangeland, idle land, and grazed woodland

Type and Height of Raised Canopy[a]	Canopy Cover[b] (%)	Type[c]	Cover that Contacts the Surface (% ground cover)					
			0	20	40	60	80	95–100
No appreciable		G	.45	.20	.10	.042	.013	.003
canopy		W	.45	.24	.15	.090	.043	.011
Canopy of tall weeds	25	G	.36	.17	.09	.038	.012	.003
or short brush (0.5		W	.36	.20	.13	.082	.041	.011
m fall ht)	50	G	.26	.13	.07	.035	.012	.003
		W	.26	.16	.11	.075	.039	.011
	75	G	.17	.10	.06	.031	.011	.003
		W	.17	.12	.09	.067	.038	.011
Appreciable brush or	25	G	.40	.18	.09	.040	.013	.003
bushes (2 m fall ht)		W	.40	.22	.14	.085	.042	.011
	50	G	.34	.16	.085	.038	.012	.003
		W	.34	.19	.13	.081	.041	.011
	75	G	.28	.14	.08	.036	.012	.003
		W	.28	.17	.12	.077	.040	.011
Trees but no	25	G	.42	.19	.10	.041	.013	.003
appreciable low		W	.42	.23	.14	.087	.042	.011
brush (4 m fall ht)	50	G	.39	.18	.09	.040	.013	.003
		W	.39	.21	.14	.085	.042	.011
	75	G	.36	.17	.09	.039	.012	.003
		W	.36	.20	.13	.083	.041	.011

Source: From U.S. Soil Conservation Service (1977).

Note: All values assume (1) random distribution of mulch or vegetation, and (2) mulch of appreciable depth where it exists. Idle land refers to land with undisturbed profiles for at least a period of three consecutive years. Also to be used for burned forest land and forest land that has been harvested less than 3 years ago.

[a]Average fall height of water drops from canopy to soil surface.

[b]Portion of total area surface that would be hidden from view by canopy in a vertical projection (a bird's-eye view).

[c]G = cover at surface is grass, grasslike plants, decaying compacted duff, or litter at least 2 in. deep; W = cover at surface is mostly broadleaf herbaceous plants (as weeds with little lateral-root network near the surface), and/or undecayed residue.

Soil Loss and Conservation Planning

For conservation planning, the *soil loss tolerance* needs to be established. Soil loss tolerance, sometimes called *permissible soil loss,* is the maximum rate of soil erosion that will still permit a high level of crop productivity to be sustained economically and ecologically. Soil loss tolerance (T_e) values of 2.5–12.5 tons/ha/yr often are used. The numbers represent the permissible soil loss where food, forage, and fiber plants are to be grown. Values are not applicable to construction sites but can be used for forest and other wildland sites.

A single T_e value normally is assigned to each soil series. A second T_e value can be assigned to certain kinds of soil where erosion has reduced the thickness of the effective root zone significantly, diminishing the potential of the soil to produce biomass over an extended period of time. The following criteria are used to assign T_e values to a soil series:

1. An adequate rooting depth must be maintained in the soil for plant growth. For shallow soils overlying rock or other restrictive layers, it is important to retain the remaining soil; little soil loss is tolerated. The T_e should be less on shallow soils or those with impervious layers than for soils with good soil depth or for soils with underlying soil materials that can be improved by management practices.

2. Soils that have significant yield reductions when the surface layer is removed by erosion are given lower T_e values than those where erosion has little impact on yield.

A T_e of 11.2 tons/ha/yr has been used for agricultural soils in much of the United States. This maximum value has been selected for the following reasons:

1. Soil losses in excess of 11.2 tons/ha/yr affect the maintenance, cost, and effectiveness of water control structures, such as open ditches, ponds, and other structures affected by sediment.

2. Excessive surface erosion is accompanied by gully formation in many places, causing added problems to tillage operations and to sedimentation of ditches, streams, and waterways.

3. Plant nutrients are lost; the average value of nitrogen and phosphorus in a ton of soil is about \$5 to \$10. Plant nutrient losses of more than \$25/ha/yr are considered to be excessive.

4. Numerous practices are known that can be used successfully to keep soil losses below this maximum tolerable level.

After having established the soil loss tolerance, the USLE can be written as:

$$CP = \frac{T_e}{R\,K(LS)} \tag{7.12}$$

By choosing the right cropping management system and appropriate conservation practices, a value for the combined effect of C and P (or VM) can be established that fits the equation. To do so, it is helpful to consult the erosion index distribution curve of the area to select the most critical stages as far as rainfall erosivity is concerned.

■ SUMMARY

Erosion of the soil by water can occur as surface erosion, gully erosion, and mass soil movement from upland watersheds. After completing this chapter, you should have a basic understanding of soil surface erosion and should be able to:

1. Describe the process of detachment of soil particles by raindrops and transport by surface runoff; how does this differ for wind erosion?

2. Explain how land use practices and changes in vegetative cover influence the processes of soil detachment described above.

3. Explain and apply the Modified Universal Soil Loss Equation (MSLE) in estimating soil erosion under different land use and vegetative cover conditions.

4. Explain how surface erosion can be controlled, or at least maintained at acceptable levels; what types of watershed management practices and guidelines are appropriate?

CHAPTER 8

Gully Erosion, Sand Dunes, and Soil Mass Movement

■ INTRODUCTION

This chapter discusses the processes and control of *gully erosion,* the control of wind transported sands, and the recognition of hazardous situations that can create massive earth movements. A fluvial system, of which a gully is a special case, is the product of interaction among many variables: relief above a base level, climate, lithology, the area and shape of the drainage basin, hillslope morphology, soils, vegetation, human and animal activity, the slope of a channel, channel pattern and roughness, the bed load it moves, and its discharge of water and sediment. Whenever any of these variables are changed, the others (with the exception of such independent variables as climate and lithology) also shift in response to the altered system. Basically, gully erosion occurs when the force of concentrated flowing water exceeds the resistance of the soil over which it is flowing. The process of gully stabilization is that which is followed by a natural system moving toward a state of dynamic equilibrium.

Gullies are severe stages of water erosion; sand dunes are the result of severe wind erosion and deposition. Steep mountain watersheds are particularly prone to *mass wasting* and gully cutting. Gravity is the primary agent of massive earth movements, and all of these processes are natural phenomena that have occurred to greater or lesser extent long before the advent of humans. However, poor land use practices and poorly planned development activities can accelerate erosion processes. Gullies, for example, can be created within a small badly managed farm unit, but the formation of inland sand dunes requires the denudation of extensive areas, such as can occur by excessive livestock grazing. Development activities, such as road building, often trigger massive earth movements. The greatest economic loss from these processes frequently does not occur in the area of origin but downstream, downwind, or downslope from the problem area. Sediment from severely gullied uplands can bury fertile bottomland soils, sand dune migration can cover more productive lands or human developments, and massive earth movements can create destruction, the cost of which sometimes is measured in terms of human life.

■ GULLY EROSION

A *gully* is a relatively deep, recently formed channel on valley sides and floors where no well-defined channel previously existed. The flow in these channels is almost always ephemeral. Gully development can be triggered by mass wasting or tectonic movements causing a change in base level. More often, gullies occur on areas that have a low-density vegetative cover and highly erodible soils. Development of new gullies or the rapid rate of expansion and deepening of older gullies often can be traced to removal of vegetative cover through some human activity.

A gully develops when surface runoff is concentrated at a *nickpoint* where there is an abrupt change of elevation and slope gradient and a lack of protective vegetation (Fig. 8.1). The fall of water over this nickpoint causes it to be undermined and to migrate uphill (headcuts). Simultaneously, the force of the falling water dislodges sediment below the fall and transports it downhill, lengthening and deepening the gully in the downhill direction (downcuts). In a *discontinuous gully,* where both of these processes are of equal importance, the gully bed has a stairstep configuration. A *continuous gully* generally gains depth rapidly from the headcut and then maintains a relatively constant gradient to the mouth, where the most active changes are taking place. Frequently, a series of discontinuous gullies will coalesce into a continuous gully (Ex. 8.1).

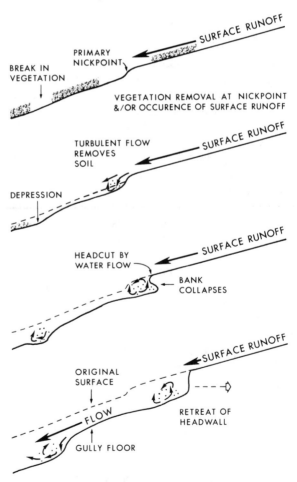

8.1. Illustration of gully formation and headwall retreat over time (adapted from Heede 1967 and Harvey, et al. 1985).

EXAMPLE 8.1

Use of field survey and air-photo interpretation to estimate gully erosion and sources of sediment (from Stromquist et al. 1985)

Air-photo interpretation at a 1:30,000 scale and field surveys were used to identify sediment sources, transport mechanisms, and storage elements to help estimate erosion rates from a 6.15-km^2 watershed in SW Lesotho. Gully-eroded areas increased by 200,000 m^2 and produced about 300,000 tons of sediment from 1951 to 1961. From 1961 to 1980, gully-eroded area increased by 60,000 m^2 and contributed about 90,000 tons of sediment.

Gully and sheet erosion over time in a 6.15 km^2 catchment in SW Lesotho (Stromquist et al. 1985, © S. African Geo. J., by permission).

Sediment production at the reservoir was estimated to be 300,000 tons from gully erosion and about 80,000 tons from surface erosion. The volume of sediment at the reservoir at full-supply level was 267,000 m^3, which corresponds to 360,000 tons of trapped sediment.

In SW Lesotho from 1951 to 1961 many of the discontinuous gullies became continuous gullies. This rapid gully expansion was explained partly by unusually high rainfall rates from 1953 to 1961, which averaged 100 mm/yr more than normal. This period was preceded by an extreme drought beginning in 1944, throughout which the loss of vegetative cover made the area susceptible to erosion during the high rainfall period of 1953 to 1961.

The use of aerial photography helped quantify both the loss of productive area and, as used in this study, helped identify sources of sediment. In this case, only a fraction of the watershed contributed the bulk of sediments to the reservoir site.

If conditions on a watershed are not improved, the gully will continue to deepen, widen, and lengthen until a new equilibrium is reached. Then, the process of deposition can begin at the gully mouth and proceed upstream until the slope of the gully sides and bottom is shallow enough to permit vegetation to become established. Plants growing in a gully signal the end of its active phase—barring disequilibration of its downcutting and depositional forces.

Gully erosion is most prevalent in drylands or in disturbed humid areas where soil compaction and vegetation removal have resulted in surface runoff. However, subsurface flow also can dissolve, dislodge, and transport soil particles. When large subterranean voids are present in the soil, no matric flow can occur. When such flow becomes turbulent (as opposed to laminar, matric flow), it is called *pipe flow*. Although common in humid, deep soil areas, particularly in old tree root cavities, animal burrows, etc., pipe flow also is common in dryland areas. In some cases, pipes can reach diameters of over 1 m. Soil pipes can form and grow in diameter until the soil above them collapses. This can lead to the formation of gullies, which most likely results in greater soil erosion than the actual pipe flow itself.

Discontinuous and Continuous Gullies

Gullies can be classified as *discontinuous* or *continuous*. As described by Heede (1976, p. 4), "Discontinuous gullies can be found at any location on a hillslope. Their start is signified by an abrupt headcut. Normally, gully depth decreases rapidly downstream. A fan forms where the gully intersects the valley." Discontinuous gullies can occur singly or in a system of downslope steps in which one gully follows the next. A continuous system can be formed by fusion with a tributary. Gullies also can become "captured" by a continuous stream when shifts of streamflow on an alluvial fan divert flow from a discontinuous gully into a parallel secondary gully. At the point of overflow, a headcut that advances upstream into the discontinuous channel will develop. Here, it will form a nickpoint and intercept all flow; the gully deepens with the upstream advance of the nickpoint.

Heede (1976, p. 8) describes the formation of continuous gullies as beginning "with many fingerlike extensions into the headwater area. It gains depth rapidly in the downstream direction and maintains approximately this depth to the gully mouth. Continuous gullies nearly always form systems (stream nets)." Continuous gullies are found in different vegetation types but are prominent in dryland regions. Removal of any vegetative cover can lead to gully and gully stream net formation if topography and soils are conducive to gully initiation.

At an early stage, gully processes proceed toward the attainment of dynamic equilibrium. As gullies become older they become more like a river or normal stream. Active gully development can be re-initiated by changes in runoff, vegetative cover, and physical changes in the landscape such as land uplift. Gully development is not necessarily an "orderly" process, proceeding from one condition to the next "advanced" one.

Gully Control

Gully erosion is the result of two main processes: *downcutting* and *headcutting*. Downcutting is the vertical lowering of the gully bottom and leads to gully deepening and widening. Headcutting is the upslope movement that extends the gully into headwater areas and increases the number of tributaries. To be effective, gully control must stabilize both the channel gradient and channel nickpoints.

Once it has been allowed to develop, gully erosion is difficult and expensive to control. However, severely gullied lands can threaten valuable on-site agricultural fields or cultural improvements, such as buildings or roads. Gullied watersheds also can be a source of sediment and flood water that threatens the production of valley farmland or the lifetime of irrigation works and reservoirs. In cases such as these, extensive gully control projects should be undertaken. Even then, the costs of control should be weighed carefully against probable benefits.

Permanent gully control can be obtained only by returning the site to a good hydrologic condition. This usually means the establishment and maintenance of an adequate cover of vegetation and plant litter, not only on the eroding site but also on the area where runoff originates. Expensive mechanical structures in the form of check dams and lined waterways may be necessary to temporarily stabilize a gully channel to allow vegetation to become established. The time varies from 1 to 2 yr in humid areas and up to 20–25 yr in dry regions; therefore, the structures have to be built accordingly. In no case should mechanical structures be considered as an end in themselves or as a permanent solution, regardless of how well they are constructed.

LONG-TERM OBJECTIVE OF CONTROLS—VEGETATION ESTABLISHMENT

The long- and short-term objectives of gully control must be recognized because sometimes it is difficult to reach the long-term goal of revegetation directly, particularly in areas of low rainfall. Stabilization of the gully channel is the first objective.

Where vegetation cover can be established, channel gradients sometimes can be stabilized without resorting to mechanical or engineering measures, however, vegetation alone can rarely stabilize headcuts because of concentrated flow at these locations. Rapidly growing vegetation that occurs with a high plant density and deep, dense root systems is most effective. Tall grasses that lie down on the gully bottom under flow conditions provide a smooth interface between flow and original bed and can increase flow velocities; such plants are not suitable for gully stabilization. The higher flow velocities with such plant cover can widen the gully even though the gully bottom is protected. Trees can restrict high-flow volumes and velocities and cause diversion against the bank. Where such restrictions are concentrated, new gullies can develop and new headcuts can form where the flow reenters the original channel. However, on low gradients and in wide gullies, especially at the mouth of such gullies, trees can be planted to form "live dams" to build up sediment deposits by reducing flow velocities.

If climate or site conditions do not permit the establishment of vegetation, mechanical measures or control structures will be required. Structures usually are required at critical locations along a gully channel such as nickpoints on the gully bed, headcuts, and gully reaches close to the gully mouth. At the gully mouth, changes in flow cause frequent changes in deepening, widening, and deposition. Normally, critical locations are identified in the field.

An effective control structure design must help vegetation to become established and to survive. Once the gully gradient is stabilized, vegetation can become established on the gully bottom; stabilized gully bottoms will then lead to the stabilization of banks because "the toe of the gully side slopes is at rest" (Heede 1976). Gully banks that are too steep for vegetation establishment can be stabilized more quickly by physical sloughing. The gully bottom should be stable before banks are sloughed.

Vegetation can be established more quickly if substantial deposits of sediment accumulate in the gully above control structures. Such deposits can store soil moisture and decrease channel gradients. The net effect of vegetation establishment in the channel and the reduced channel gradient is a decrease in peak discharge.

IMMEDIATE OBJECTIVES OF GULLY CONTROL

Gullies that are undergoing active headcutting and downcutting are difficult to stabilize and revegetate. Therefore, mechanical treatments often are needed to provide the short-term stability needed for vegetation establishment.

Other considerations such as soil type, rate of sedimentation, hydraulics, and the logistics needed to manage a watershed also come into the development of a solution. For example, if gullies are wide and deep, it may be necessary to construct large dams across the gullies to accumulate sufficient sediment for gully crossings. Large check dams may be undesirable or uneconomical. Other alternatives such as mechanical or structural controls then must be considered.

Check Dams. A check dam is a barrier placed in an actively eroding gully, the purpose of which is to trap sediment that is carried down the gully during periodic flow events. Sediment that is backed up behind the check dam (1) develops a new channel bottom with a gentler gradient than the original gully bottom, hence, reducing the velocity and the erosive force of gully flow; (2) stabilizes the side slopes of the gully and encourages their adjustment to their natural angle of repose, reducing further erosion of the channel banks; (3) promotes the establishment of vegetation on the gully slopes and bottom; and (4) stores soil water such that the water table can be raised, enhancing vegetative growth outside of the gully.

There are three types of check dams: nonporous dams (without weep holes); earth dams; and porous dams, which release part of the flow through the structure.

Nonporous dams, such as those built from concrete, sheet metal, wet masonry, or earth, receive heavy impact from the hydrostatic forces of gully flow. These forces require strong anchoring of the dam into the gully banks where most of the pressure is transmitted. Earthen check dams should be used for gully control only in exceptional cases, for it generally was the failure of the earth material in the first place that caused the gully. However, earthen dams constructed at the mouth of gullies (gully plugs) can be effective in regions where the watershed can be revegetated quickly and where the storage upstream from the plug is adequate to contain the larger storm flows. The plug may have no central reinforced spillway, but must have an emergency spillway to discharge water from extreme flow events. The flow released by the emergency spillway should not be concentrated but should spread out over an area stabilized by an effective vegetation cover or by some other type of protection such as a gravel field.

Porous dams transmit less pressure to the banks of gullies than do nonporous dams. Because gullies generally form in erodible, soft soils, it is easier, cheaper, and often more effective to construct porous dams. Loose rocks, rough stone masonry, gabions, old car tires, logs, and brush have all been used successfully to construct porous dams. Rocks, which are abundant in many areas, are superior to most other materials for constructing inexpensive but durable porous check dams; it is important not to have large voids that allow jetting through the structure and subsequent loss of effectiveness in trapping sediment. For loose rock dams, a range of rock sizes can be used to avoid this.

With the exception of gully plugs, an effective dam has three essential elements, the omission of any one of which will cause the structure to fail. The elements are (1) a spillway adequate to carry a selected design flow, (2) a key that anchors the structure into the bottom and sides of the gully, and (3) an apron that absorbs the impact of water from the spillway to prevent undercutting the structure.

Two additional components help to insure the life of the structure. A sill at the lower end of the apron provides a hydraulic jump that reduces the impact of falling water on the unprotected gully bottom (Fig. 8.2). Protective armoring on the gully banks on the downstream side of the structure can prevent undercutting on the sides of the dam.

The purpose of the spillway is to direct the flow of water to the center of the channel and, thereby, prevent cutting around the ends of the dam. Spillways of check dams can be considered broad-crested weirs with the discharge relationship (Heede 1976):

$$Q_p = C_f L H^{3/2} \tag{8.1}$$

where Q_p = the peak discharge of the design flow (m³/sec), C_f = the coefficient of the spillway; L = the effective length of the spillway (m); and H = the total depth of flow above the spillway crest (m).

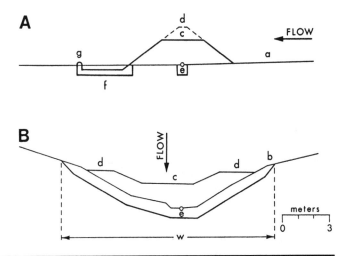

8.2. Cross sections of a check dam. A: Section of the dam parallel to the centerline of the gully; B: Section of the dam at the cross section of the gully. a = original gully bottom, b = original gully cross section, c = spillway, d = crest of freeboard, e = excavation for anchoring key, f = apron, g = end sill, w = width of bank (Heede 1976, p. 14).

The value of C_f varies with the roughness, breadth, and shape of the spillway. Because check dams are not constructed to precise engineering standards, a mean value of 1.65 for C_f is acceptable. Generally, trapezoidal spillways are preferred, since the effective length of the spillway becomes larger with increasing depth of flow.

Where vegetation is slow to establish, spillways should be designed to carry the peak discharge of the 20- or 25-yr-recurrence interval peak discharge. The length of the spillway relative to the width of the gully bottom is important for the protection of the channel and the structure. Normally, it is desirable to design spillways with a length not greater than the gully bottom to minimize splashing of water against the sides of the gully.

Most gullies have either trapezoidal, rectangular, or V-shaped channels. For broad rectangular and trapezoidal channels, Equation 8.1 can be used to determine spillway depth (H):

$$H = \left(\frac{Q_p}{C_f L}\right)^{2/3} \tag{8.2}$$

where L can be any length that does not exceed the width of the gully bottom.

In narrow rectangular and V-shaped gullies, the length of the spillway must be adjusted to prevent the water overfall from striking the gully sides. Heede and Mulfich (1973) developed the following equations for calculating spillway dimensions for these gully shapes:

$$H_v = \left(\frac{Q_p}{C_f Las}\right)^{2/3} \tag{8.3}$$

where:

$$Las = \frac{W}{D}\left(H_e - f_b\right) \tag{8.4}$$

where H_e = effective dam height (m); H_v = spillway depth (m); Las = spillway length (m); w = bank width of the gully measured from brink to brink (m); D = depth of the gully (m); and f_b = a constant referring to the length of the freeboard. In gullies with a depth of 1.5 m or less, the f value should not be less than 0.15; in gullies deeper than 1.5 m, the maximum value should be at least 0.30.

The stability of a check dam is increased by keying the dam into the bottom and sides of the gully. The purpose of extending the key into the gully sides is to prevent water from flowing around the dam, thus making the structure ineffective. Keying the dam into the gully bottom also prevents undercutting at the downstream side.

Dam construction begins with filling the key trench with loose rock, the size distribution of which should prevent large voids that allow flow to reach velocities that can lead to washouts. It generally is recommended that smaller materials be used, with 80% of material smaller than 14 cm.

Aprons are installed on the gully bottom to prevent flows from undercutting the structures at the downstream side. A general rule of thumb is that the length of apron should be about 1.5 times the height of the structure in channels with gradients less than 15% and 1.75 times with gradients steeper than 15% (Heede 1976). These lengths prevent the waterfall from the spillway from hitting the unprotected gully bottom.

The apron should be embedded in the gully bottom so that its surface is roughly level at about 0.3 m below the original gully bottom. Where flows are high, aprons are endangered by the so-called *ground roller* that develops where the hydraulic jump hits the gully bottom. These rollers rotate upstream, and if the hydraulic jump is too near the apron, they can undermine the apron. Therefore, at the downstream end of the apron, a loose rock sill should be built about 0.15 m in height above the gully bottom. A pool is created by the sill, which cushions the impact of the waterfall.

Check dams will fail if flows in the channel scour the gully side slopes below the structures, creating a gap between the dam and the bank. Turbulent flow below a check dam creates eddies that move upstream along the gully sides and erode the bank. Loose rock is effective for bank protection but should be reinforced with wire mesh secured to posts on all slopes steeper than 80–100%.

Channel banks should be protected along the entire length of the apron, and banks should be protected to the height of the dam if the channel bottom is sufficiently wide so that waterfall from the spillway strikes only on the channel floor. This height can be reduced away from the structure. If the waterfall strikes against the sides of a narrow gully, the height of bank protection should extend the entire length of the apron.

Headcut Control. Different types of structures can be used to stabilize headcuts. All should be designed with sufficient porosity to avoid excessive pressures; this eliminates the need for large structural foundations. Also, some type of "reverse filter" is needed to promote gradual seepage from smaller to larger openings in the structure. Reverse filters can be constructed if there is sufficient slope of the headcut wall so that material can be layered, beginning with fine to coarse sand, and on to fine and coarse gravel. Erosion cloth also can be effective.

Loose rock can provide effective headcut control, but flow through the structure must be controlled. The size, shape (preferably angular), and size distribution of the rock must again be selected to avoid large openings that allow flow velocity to become too great. Care must be taken to stabilize the toe of the rock fill to prevent the fill from being eroded. Loose-rock dams can dissipate energy from chuting flows and can trap sediment, which can facilitate vegetation establishment, thus helping to stabilize the toe of the rock fill.

Spacing between Dams. The purpose of check dams is to stabilize the gully bottom to prevent further downcutting and subsequent headcutting and extension of the gully. Therefore, each dam should be spaced upstream at the toe of the expected sediment wedge formed by the dam below. The first dam should be constructed in the gully where downcutting does not occur (e.g., where sediment has been deposited at the mouth of the gully, where there may be a rock outcrop or a maintained road crossing, or where the gully enters a stream system). The spacing of subsequent dams constructed upstream from the base dam depends upon the gradient of the gully floor, the gradient of the sediment wedges deposited in back of the dams, and the effective height of the dams as measured from the gully floor to the bottom of the spillway.

Sediment will be deposited behind a dam on a gradient less than the gradient of the gully bottom. The gradient of the deposit depends upon the velocity of the flows

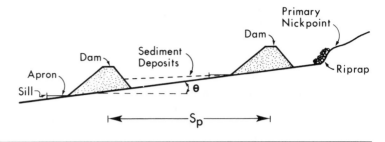

8.3. Diagram of placement of a check dam. S_p = spacing, θ = angle of gully gradient.

and the size of the sediment particles (Fig. 8.3). The ratio of the gradient of sediment deposits to the gradient of the original gully bottom has been estimated at between 0.3 and 0.6 for sandy soils and 0.6 to 0.7 for fine-textured soils; the steeper the original gully gradient, the smaller will be the ratio of aggraded slope to original slope. Head-cut areas above the uppermost dam should be stabilized with loose rock or riprap material (Fig. 8.3).

A calculation for the spacing of check dams was developed by Heede and Mufich (1973):

$$S_p = \frac{H_e}{K_c G \cos \theta} \tag{8.5}$$

where S_p = spacing; H_e = effective height of the dam, from gully bottom to spillway crest; θ = angle corresponding to gully gradient; G = gully gradient as a ratio ($G = \tan \theta$); and K_c = a constant, related to the gradient of the sediment deposits (s_s), which is assumed to be $(1 - K_c)G$.

Sample values of K_c for clay-rich soils in Colorado are $K_c = 0.3$ for $G \leq 0.2$ and $K_c = 0.5$ for $G > 0.2$. A K_c value can be determined for a particular area by measuring sediment deposits backed up behind 10-yr-old structures, and solving for K_c:

$$K_c = 1 - \left(\frac{s_s}{G}\right) \tag{8.6}$$

Spacing of dams calculated by the above formula is only a guide. The choice of actual sites should be made in the field and should take into consideration local topography and other conditions such as (1) placing the dam at a constriction in the channel rather than at a widened point, if there is a choice of one or the other within a short distance of the calculated position; (2) where a tributary gully enters the main gully, placing the dam such that it does not receive the impact of flow of the tributary; and (3) where the flow in the gully has meandered within the channel, placing the dam below the meander.

The spacing and effective height chosen for the dams depend not only on the gradient and local conditions in the gully but on the principal objective of the gully control. When the intention is to achieve the greatest possible deposition, the dams should have a relatively greater effective height and be spaced further apart. If the main concern is to stabilize the gully gradient and sediment deposits are not of interest, they could be lower and closer together.

VEGETATION-LINED WATERWAYS

The gully control measures described above are designed to reduce flow velocity within the channel and aid in the establishment of vegetation. Waterways are designed to reduce the flow in the gully by modifying the topography; to lengthen the watercourse, resulting in a gentler bed gradient; and to increase the cross section of flow, resulting in gentle channel side slopes. Shallow flows over a rough surface with a large wetted perimeter reduce the erosive power of flowing water.

The quick establishment of vegetation lining the waterway is essential for successful erosion control. Adequate precipitation and favorable temperature and soil fertility are all necessary for quick plant growth. Other requisites include (Heede 1976, p. 34):

(1) size of gully should not be larger than the available fill volumes;
(2) width of valley bottom must be sufficient for the placement of a waterway with greater length than that of the gully;
(3) depth of soil mantle must be adequate to permit shaping of the topography; and
(4) depth of topsoil must be sufficient to permit later spreading on all disturbed areas.

Waterways are more susceptible to erosion immediately following construction than are check dams, and vegetation-lined waterways require careful attention and maintenance during the first years after construction.

■ SAND DUNES

Just as gullies are severe stages of water erosion, sand dunes are severe stages of wind erosion. Sand dunes have been prevalent in the dryland regions of the world throughout geological history; however, some human activities have and are presently turning potentially productive areas into deserts. This process of *desertification* is the direct result of destroying the vegetative cover with no provisions for replacement or substitution. Poor land use practices increase the already heavy sediment load of aridland streams and indirectly provide additional material for dune building.

Types of Sand Dunes

The term *dune* often is restricted to those mounds of eolian material that exist independently of any fixed surface feature and are capable of movement from place to place. Dunes can be considered any extensive deposit of wind-blown sandy material, either along coastlines or deep inland. *Inland dunes* originate from sand produced by the weathering of rocks, mainly sandstone. They include crescentic accumulations (barchans), swordlike ridges (longitudinal dunes), large seas of sand (transverse dunes), turret-shaped mounds (shadow dunes), and shallow sheets of sand. *Coastal dunes* originate from sand deposited on the shore by waves. With low tide, the sand dries and is blown away. Coastal dunes include sand ridges parallel to the beach with toes at the high watermark (foredunes), dune fields (frontal dunes) along the leeward side of foredunes, or parabolic mounds aligned with the direction of the prevailing wind (blowouts). Both inland and coastal dunes are in areas where seasonal or perennial winds of more or less constant direction blow for extended periods and have a source of noncohesive sand grains that can be dislodged and transported by wind. Coastal dunes differ from inland dunes in that the upper few centimeters generally contain chlorides from salt spray and wind-blown salt.

Of greatest importance to the formation of both inland and coastal dunes is a source of loose sandy material, which furnishes the building material. The sources of material for inland dunes are most often of fluvial origin, including flood plains, active alluvial deposits, and the terminal basins of ephemeral drainage systems. These source areas undergo long dry periods between periodic or episodic sediment-laden flows that rework and expose existing grain size mixtures, as well as supply fresh material to be picked up and transported by the wind.

The sea at the coastline creates the source of material for coastal dunes, that is, a beach, which is the natural response of coasts to marine erosion. A beach absorbs energy and prevents access by the sea to the dunes behind it. A low coast is best defended by consolidated sand dunes. Therefore, methods that help to maintain a wide, high beach, backed by stable dunes, is desirable. Techniques available to build and widen beaches are structures that trap littoral drift, rock mounds that check wave action, sea walls used to protect areas behind the beach from heavy wave action, and artificial replacement of the beach. All of these methods are expensive and require detailed engineering and heavy equipment.

Dune Stabilization

Once dunes have formed, permanent stabilization can be achieved only by a well-developed vegetative cover. However, there are some areas where the site conditions are so severe that establishing a reasonable cover is not possible. There also are many areas that appear hopeless, but can be reclaimed through natural regeneration simply by protecting the area against livestock grazing, all-terrain vehicles, and foot traffic.

STABILIZATION WITH VEGETATION

The primary role of vegetation in dune stabilization is to decrease wind speed near the ground. Over the longer term, vegetation can increase the cohesiveness of the sandy material by the binding action of roots and by the addition of organic colloids. Plants trap wind-blown dust particles, which help improve soil texture, and they can improve the microclimate, the general ecology, and the economy of an area.

Success of permanently stabilizing sand dunes is dependent upon the selection of plant species that can survive and develop under the climatic and physical constraints of the site. Important site constraints include:

1. Climate—Temperature, humidity, potential evapotranspiration, and the amount and frequency of precipitation are of primary importance in plant selection. Long dry periods during times of high potential evapotranspiration are more important than monthly or seasonal averages. Plants must be selected that can survive the extreme drought periods of record.

2. Soil moisture—Soil moisture that is available for plant growth is tied closely to the climatic regime, but it is also dependent upon evapotranspiration rates. Sandy soil releases water readily to plants, but its capacity for storing water against gravity is low. Infiltration and percolation of water in sand dunes is high. Although the surface and near-surface soil material may be dry, water can be in sufficient quantities at deeper depths to support deep-rooted vegetation once such vegetation becomes established.

3. Quantity of available water—The composition of dune soil material is mainly quartz sand. Other common minerals that could affect plant growth are sodium chloride, calcium chloride, and carbonate salts. Furthermore, saline ground water is a common feature of drylands, thus, salt-tolerant species may have to be considered for some sites.

4. Nutrient deficiencies—Nearly all dunes are deficient in nitrogen and phosphorus. Although these nutrients can be added by commercial organic fertilizers, leaching is severe. Thus, nitrogen-fixing plants can be an essential choice for many sites.

5. Mobility of the surface—Unvegetated sand dunes can become unstable at any time. The sand is fine, loose, easily moved by the wind, and abrasive and destructive to plants when it moves. Preplanting mechanical stabilization with two or more stages of planting may be required. The crests of dunes are particularly harsh sites for establishing vegetation; species must thrive in shifting sand, survive inundation, and have growth rates that exceed sand deposition.

6. Exposure to wind—Exposure is important to the stabilization of coastal dunes. Plant species selected for stabilization must be able to tolerate salt-laden winds. South and west aspects of inland dunes may require plants that can resist high heat loads due to solar radiation and reflectance.

No single plant species will have all of the characteristics desired for the wide range of constraints encountered on sand dune sites. Dunes are extreme cases of land depletion, and the first priority is to establish vegetation. In some cases, this may mean choosing a species lacking in all other desirable characteristics except the ability to survive.

Plants should have sufficient height and a growth form dense enough to reduce the velocity of the wind high above the ground. Uniformity in growth between plants also is important. In most dune plantings, there will be a relatively wide spacing between plants. Variation in the height within the rows will force the wind currents through lower sections, which in turn will increase the velocity and carrying capacity of the wind at these points. Rooting characteristics also are important. Plants that develop dense, widely spreading root systems that take advantage of any soil moisture at some distance from the plant are desirable for stabilizing the soil. Plants whose root systems can withstand deep inundation by sand are an important consideration. Plants that produce large quantities of litter are desirable to provide soil-building organic matter and additional surface cover.

Plants that will reproduce or regenerate naturally on the site are desirable, otherwise, continuous maintenance and replanting will be necessary. If nonnative, or introduced, plants are used, they should have adaptive characteristics similar to those of local plant communities. Indigenous plants are often the best and safest choice. Plants that provide useful products to local inhabitants generally are most acceptable; species not desirable may fail. The challenge is to find species that are acceptable and that can survive in sand dune environments.

MECHANICAL METHODS OF STABILIZATION

In cases where site constraints do not allow for vegetative stabilization, mechanical methods must be used to stabilize a site temporarily until vegetation can become established. But, mechanical methods can seldom be justified unless valuable property is seriously threatened. In general, five actions can be taken singly or in combination:

1. Reshape the landscape—In some cases, partial or complete removal of the dune may be required before revegetation. Sometimes, less dramatic and less expensive regrading of the landscape to smooth the contours, cut down steep slopes, and fill depressions are required; often, this is necessary for coastal dunes where the foredune must be smoothed to allow more uniform wind flow.

2. Improve cohesiveness—The cohesiveness of the surface sands of dunes can be improved with water, oils, bitumen emulsions, chemical stabilizers, or clay. Unfortunately, these methods require expensive materials and equipment and are effective for only a short time period.

3. Improve soil fertility—Nearly all dunes are deficient in phosphorus and nitrogen. Commercial fertilizers, organic wastes, and sewage sludge all have been used successfully; but, they all are expensive.

4. Armor the surface—Most of the materials used to improve cohesiveness also armor the surface by consolidating a layer of soil material at or near the surface. Additionally, dunes can be protected during vegetative establishment by applying materials directly on the surface. Asphalt, hydroseeding, jute mats, mulch, and brush layering have all been used.

5. Modify velocity and direction of wind—Sand fences are commonly used to reduce wind velocity near the ground. The most satisfactory sand fences are those composed of living plants, provided the plants have uniform height and are planted at close spacings. However, artificial fences of nonliving materials (fences of native plant materials, palisade fences, snow fences, and mesh fences) may be necessary where the sand is too mobile for the establishment of live fences.

Fences may be constructed in parallel rows across the prevailing wind direction or on square or rectangular grids where wind direction varies during the year. Two factors important in spacing are the zone of influence both upwind and downwind of the fence, and the magnitude of the reduction in velocity within this zone. The zone of influence is greater for highly permeable fences, but the amount of reduction in wind speed is lower. The zone of influence and the magnitude of wind speed reduction increases with fence height and decreases with increasing distance both upwind and downwind from the fence.

■ SOIL MASS MOVEMENT

Soil mass movement refers to the instantaneous downslope movement of finite masses of soil, rock, and debris that is driven by gravity. Examples of these movements include landslides, debris avalanches, slumps and earthflows, creep, and debris torrents (Fig. 8.4). Such movement occurs at specific sites where hillslopes (and alterations to hillslopes) experience conditions in which *shear-stress* factors become large compared to *shear-strength* factors. These conditions are pronounced in steep, mountainous areas, particularly in humid zones that experience high-intensity rain-

WEATHERED
BEDROCK,
SOIL, ETC.

BEDROCK →

VERY RAPID TO
EXTREMELY RAPID

DEBRIS AVALANCHE

SAND

CLAY

SLUMP

SLOW TO RAPID

EARTHFLOW

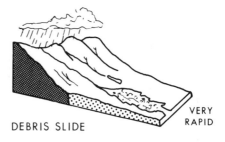

VERY
RAPID

DEBRIS SLIDE

8.4. Illustrations of soil mass movements (adapted from Varnes 1958, and Swanston and Swanson 1980).

fall or rapid snowmelt. A general classification of hillslope failures is presented in Table 8.1.

Processes of Movement

The stability of soils on hillslopes often is expressed in terms of a safety factor (F):

$$F = \frac{\text{resistance of the soil to failure (shear strength)}}{\text{forces promoting failure (shear stress)}} \qquad (8.7)$$

A value of $F = 1$ indicates imminent failure; large values indicate little risk of failure. The factors affecting shear strength and shear stress are illustrated in Figure 8.5.

Shear stress increases as the inclination (slope) increases or as the weight of the soil mass increases. The presence of bedding planes and fractures in underlying bed-

Table 8.1. Classification of hillslope failures

Kind	Description	Favored by	Cause
Falls	Movement through air; bouncing, rolling, falling; very rapid	Scarps or steep slopes, badly fractured rock, lack of retaining vegetation	Removal of support, wedging and prying, quakes, overloading
Slides (Avalanches)	Material in motion not greatly deformed, movement along a plane; slow to rapid	Massive over weak zone, presence of permeable or incompetent beds, poorly cemented or unconsolidated sediments	Oversteepening, reduction of internal friction
Flows	Moves as viscous fluid (continuous internal deformation); slow to rapid	Unconsolidated material, alternate permeable, impermeable fine sediment on bedrock	Reduction of internal friction due to water content
Creep	Slow downhill movement, up to several cm per year	High daily temperature ranges, alternate rain and dry periods, frequent freeze and thaw cycles	Swaying of trees, wedging and prying, undercutting or gullying
Debris, torrents	Rapid movement of water-charged soil, rock and organic material in stream channels	Steep channels, thin layer of unconsolidated material over bedrock within channel; layered clay particles (lacustrine clays) form slippage plane when wet	High streamflow discharge; saturated soils, often triggered by debris avalanches; deforestation accelerates occurrence

Source: From Swanston and Swanson (1980).

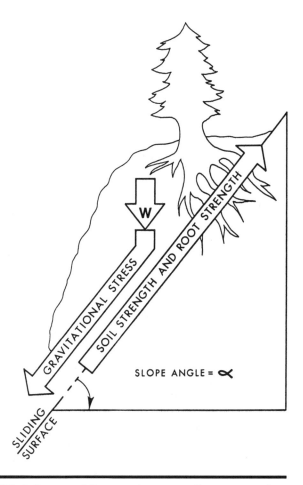

8.5. Simplified diagram of forces acting on a soil mass on a slope (adapted from Swanston 1974).

rock can result in zones of weakness. Earthquakes or blasting for construction can augment stress. The addition of large amounts of water to the soil mantle and the removal of downslope material by undercutting (for road construction, for example) are common causes of movement due to increased stress.

Shear strength is determined by complex relationships between the soil and slope and the strength and structure of the underlying rock. Cohesion of soil particles and frictional resistance between the soil mass and the underlying sliding surface are major factors affecting shear strength. Frictional resistance is a function of the angle of internal friction of the soil and the effective weight of the soil mass. Pore water pressure in saturated soil tends to reduce the frictional resistance of the soil. Rock strength is affected by structural characteristics such as cleavage planes, fractures, jointing, bedding planes, and strata of weaker rocks.

Plants exert a pronounced influence on many types of soil mass movement. The removal of soil water by transpiration results in lower pore water pressures, reduced chemical weathering, and reduced weight of the soil mass. Tree roots, which add to the frictional resistance of a sloping soil mass, can effectively stabilize thin soils, generally up to 1 m in depth, by vertically anchoring into a stable substrate. Medium to fine root systems can provide lateral strength and also improve slope stability.

Evaluating the Stability of Hillslopes

Detailed procedures have been developed to assess soil mass movement hazards and the potential for sediment delivery to channels. A discussion of such methods is beyond the scope of this book; however, the key factors that must be considered for hazard assessment are identified in Example 8.2.

EXAMPLE 8.2

Outline of factors to be considered when making hazard assessments of hillslope failures (from Swanston and Swanson 1980)

The stability of hillslopes can be judged by evaluating the following:
Land features
1. Landforms—qualitative indicator of potentially unstable land forms, e.g., fracturing and bedding planes parallel to slopes, steep U-shaped valleys, etc.
2. Slope configuration—convex or concave
3. Slope gradient

Soil characteristics
1. Present soil mass movement and rate
2. Parent material—cohesive characteristics, e.g., colluvium, tills, and pumice soils possess little cohesion
3. Occurrence of cemented, compacted, or impermeable subsoil layer—identify principal planes of failure
4. Evidence of concentrated subsurface drainage—indications of local zones of high soil moisture, springs, seeps, etc.
5. Soil characteristics—depth, texture, clay mineralogy, angle of internal friction, cohesion

Bedrock lithology and structure
1. Rock type—volcanic ash, breccias, and silty sandstone are susceptible to earthflows, etc.
2. Degree of weathering
3. Bedding planes or dips parallel to slope
4. Jointing and fracturing—locations, directions, and relationship to slope

Vegetative characteristics
1. Root distribution and degree of root penetration in the subsoil
2. Vegetation type and distribution—cover density, age, etc.

Hydrologic characteristics
1. Saturated hydraulic conductivity
2. Pore water pressure

Climate
1. Precipitation occurrence and distribution
2. Temperature fluctuations—frost heaving, etc.

Land Use Impacts

Modification of the vegetative cover, the soil system, or the inclination of a hillslope can affect soil mass movement. The impacts of land use can be estimated by relating them to factors affecting shear strength and shear resistance. Most commonly, road construction and forest removal activities have the greatest effect on soil mass movement. Undercutting a slope and improper drainage are major factors that accelerate mass movement. Proper road layout, design and control of drainage, and minimizing cut-and-fill (earthwork) can help to avoid problems. Areas that are naturally susceptible to mass movement should simply be avoided. In terms of logging practices on steep slopes, full-suspension yarding, cable yarding, balloon logging, and other alternatives to skid roads should be used.

The removal of trees from steep slopes, and particularly the "permanent" conversion from forest to pasture or crops, can result in accelerated mass movement. The reduced evapotranspiration with such activities can lead to wetter soils. Shear resistance is reduced by the loss and deterioration of tree roots, particularly in areas where roots penetrate and are anchored into the subsoil. Examples of accelerated soil mass movement following conversion from forest to pasture have been pronounced in steep, mountainous areas of New Zealand (Trustrum et al. 1984). In many instances, it is desirable to maintain tree cover on steep slopes to reduce the hazard of soil mass movement.

Normal forest harvesting and regeneration practices periodically can leave hillslopes susceptible to mass movement. Root strength deteriorates rapidly as roots decay following timber harvesting (Fig. 8.6). In the Pacific Northwest, several years are required before the regrowing forest exhibits root strength that is equivalent to that of mature forests (Sidle 1985). As a result, there generally is a 3- to 8-yr period when net root strength is at a minimum. The first several years after harvesting also coincide with the period of maximum water yield increases caused by reduced evapotranspira-

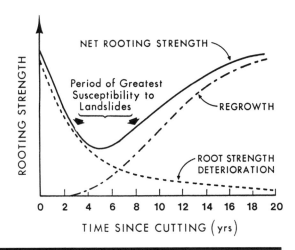

8.6. Hypothetical relationship of root-strength deterioration after timber harvesting and root-strength improvement with regenerating forest (from Sidle 1985).

tion (see Chapter 6). The result is more frequent occurrences of shallow landslides on steep slopes for several years following logging. The period of susceptibility is somewhat species dependent, that is, it is affected by the rate of root decay and the rate of regrowth of the tree species being managed.

■ SUMMARY

Gully erosion and soil movement can reduce the productive area (and productive capacity) of a watershed and can cause large quantities of sediment to be moved from the uplands to downstream channels (or downwind areas). A basic understanding of the processes involved and the factors that affect gully erosion, soil mass movement, and sand dune formation should be gained after reading this chapter. Specifically, you should be able to:

1. Describe and explain how gullies are formed.

2. Explain the role of structural and vegetative measures to control gully and wind erosion and dune stabilization.

3. Describe the different types of soil mass movement and explain the causes of each.

4. Explain shear resistance and shear strength as they pertain to soil mass movement.

5. Explain how different land use impacts, including road construction, forest harvesting, and conversion from deep rooted to shallow-rooted plants, affect both gully erosion and soil mass movement.

CHAPTER 9

Sediment Yield

■ INTRODUCTION

Sediment is the product of erosion, whether it occurred as surface, gully, or soil mass erosion. Only a portion of the soil eroded is passed through and out of a watershed during a storm event. Most sediment is deposited at the base of hillslopes, in flood plains following high flows or flood events, and within river channels. The rate at which sediment is discharged into the ocean is less than 25% the rate of upland erosion.

Sediment yield is the total sediment outflow from a watershed or drainage basin as measured for a specific period of time and at a defined point in the channel. Sediment yield normally is determined by sediment sampling and relating it to streamflow discharge, or by performing sediment deposit surveys in reservoirs. Estimated sediment yields from major river basins in the world are presented in Table 9.1.

Table 9.1. Average annual sediment yield from selected river basins that are among the 21 largest sediment-yielding rivers in the world

River, Country	Drainage Area ($\times 10^6$ km²)	Average Annual Streamflow Discharge ($\times 10^9$ m³/yr)	Average Annual Sediment Yield (10^6 tonnes/yr)[a]
Ganges/Brahmaputra, India	1.48	971	1670
Yellow (Huangho), China	0.77	49	1080
Amazon, Brazil	6.15	6300	900
Mississippi, United States	3.27	580	210
Mekong, Vietnam	0.79	470	160
Nile, Egypt	2.96	30	110
La Plata, Argentina	2.83	470	92
Danube, Romania	0.81	206	67
Yukon, United States	0.84	195	60

Source: From Milliman and Meade (1983), by permission.
[a]Metric tons per year.

Table 9.2. Sediment yield from small forested watersheds and larger watersheds of mixed land use in the United States

Region	Number of Watersheds	Sediment Yield (tonnes/ha/yr)[a]	
		Mean	Range
East			
Forested	65	0.17	0.02–2.44
Mixed use	226	0.35	0.02–4.42
West			
Forested	80	0.16	0.02–1.17
Mixed use	312	0.42	0.02–13.38
Pacific Coast			
Forested	26	3.93	0.04–43.56
Mixed use	103	10.37	0.13–111.86

Source: From Patric et al. (1984).
[a]Metric tons per hectare per year.

Streams discharging large quantities of sediment on an annual basis are those draining areas undergoing active geologic erosion or being subjected to improper land use. The degree of aridity also affects sediment yields. Because of lower vegetation densities on arid watersheds, sediment yields in relation to streamflow discharge generally are higher. For example, the Mississippi River watershed is 4 times larger than that of the Yellow River and the annual discharge is 12 times greater. The ratio of sediment load to discharge for the Yellow River is 22.04 as compared to 0.36 for the Mississippi (Table 9.1). The Mississippi traverses a humid zone, much of the watershed is vegetated, and soil conservation is practiced over extensive farm areas. In contrast, the Yellow River traverses a semiarid region of north-central China. It drains an area of deep loess, highly susceptible to geologic erosion, that also has been denuded by centuries of primitive agriculture. Examples of annual sediment yields in the United States for forested watersheds compared to mixed land use are presented in Table 9.2.

The relationship between upland erosion and downstream sedimentation involves complex processes, many of which are poorly understood. This chapter discusses the processes affecting sediment transport and deposition. The importance of land use and resource management actions are discussed as they directly and indirectly affect sedimentation.

■ SEDIMENT MOVEMENT AND MEASUREMENT

The *sediment discharge* of a stream is defined as the mass rate of transport through a given cross section of the stream and is usually measured as milligrams per liter (mg/l) or parts per million (ppm). The part of the sediment discharge consisting of fine particles, such as silt and clay, that is supported by the moving water and transported in suspension is called the *suspended load* or *wash load*. The *bed load* consists of sand, gravel, or rocks and is transported along the stream bottom by traction, rolling, sliding, or saltation (Fig. 9.1). Particles are moved when eddies formed

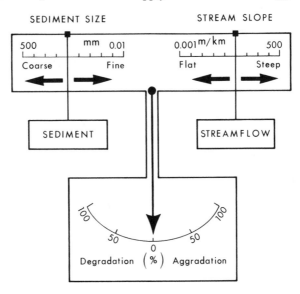

WATER SURFACE

CURRENT

SUSPENSION
(SILT & CLAY SIZE)

SALTATION
(SAND SIZE)

BEDLOAD   (ROCKS, GRAVEL)

9.1. Transportation of particles of sediment in running water.

by turbulent flow dissipate part of their kinetic energy into mechanical work.

The amount of sediment carried by a stream depends upon the interrelationships between the supply of material to the channel, characteristics of the channel, the rate and amount of streamflow discharge, and the physical characteristics of the sediment. The supply of material and streamflow depends upon the climate, topography, geology, soils, vegetation, and land use practices on the watershed. Channel characteristics of importance are the morphological stage of the channel, roughness of the channel bed, and steepness of the channel slope. Soils and geological materials of the watershed and the state of their weathering largely determine the physical characteristics of the sediment particles.

The interrelationships of these factors determine both the amount and type of sediment and the amount of energy available for the stream to entrain and transport the particles. When stream energy exceeds the sediment supply, channel degradation occurs (Fig. 9.2). On the other hand, when sediment supply exceeds stream energy,

SEDIMENT SIZE   STREAM SLOPE

500   mm 0.01   0.001 m/km   500

Coarse   Fine   Flat   Steep

SEDIMENT   STREAMFLOW

Degradation (%) Aggradation

9.2. Diagrammatic relationship of a stable channel balance (adapted from Lane 1955).

aggradation occurs within the channel. For a particular stream and flow condition a relationship between transport capability and supply can be developed (Fig. 9.3). Wash load consists of silts and clays, generally 0.0625 mm or smaller; sediment supply generally limits total sediment transport for smaller particles. As material gets larger, total sediment transport is more likely to be limited by transport capability.

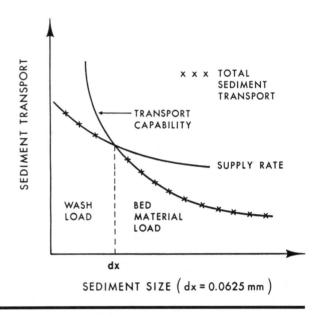

9.3. Rate of sedimentation as affected by transport capability and supply rate for different-size particles for a particular stream and flow condition (from Shen and Li 1976, as presented in Rosgen 1980).

Suspended Load

Particles can be transported as suspended load if their settling velocity is less than the buoyant velocity of the turbulent eddies and vortices of the water. Settling velocity primarily depends upon the size and density of the grain. In general, the settling velocity of particles less than 0.1 mm in diameter is proportional to the square of the grain diameter, while the settling velocity of particles larger than 0.1 mm is proportional to the square root of the particle diameter. Once particles are in suspension, little energy is needed for transport. A heavy suspended load decreases turbulence and makes the stream more efficient. Concentrations are highest in shallow streams where velocities are high.

As one would suspect, the concentration of sediment in a stream is lowest near the water surface and increases with depth. Silt and clay particles less than 0.005 mm in diameter generally are dispersed uniformly throughout the depth, but large grains are more concentrated near the bottom.

For most streams there is a correlation between suspended load and stream discharge. During stormflow events, the rising limb of the hydrograph is associated with higher rates of sediment transport and degradation (Fig. 9.4). As the flood peak passes

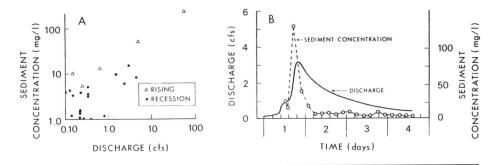

9.4. Example of the relationship between streamflow discharge and suspended sediment for a small stream in northeastern Minnesota. A: The relationships for several storm events; B: A single storm event (included in A).

and the rate of discharge drops, the amount of sediment in suspension also diminishes rapidly and aggradation occurs. If sufficient measurements of discharge and sedimentation are available, a relationship can be developed for use as a *sediment rating curve*. The relationship will most often take a power function form, such as:

$$SS = kq^m \tag{9.1}$$

where SS = suspended sediment load (mg/1); q = daily rate of stream discharge (m³/sec); and k and m = constants for a particular stream.

The amount of variability in the suspended sediment–discharge relationship for a given stream relates to channel stability and sources of sediment. Streams draining undisturbed forested watersheds are characteristically stable, with low levels of suspended sediment. However, suspended sediment is the major component of the annual total sediment that is discharged from streams draining forested watersheds. As either the magnitude of sediment contributed from the watershed changes or the stream channel itself becomes altered, the suspended sediment–discharge relationship changes. For example, forest fires can temporarily cause increases in suspended sediment downstream; the increase in the amount of sediment and any increase in streamflow associated with the fire can shift the relationship (Fig. 9.2). Floods likewise can change the relationship by bank overflow and the cutting of new channel segments that provide new sources of sediment. Newly cut stream channels have suspended sediment relationships different from those of a well-armored, stable stream. Studies have shown that in most instances, the suspended sediment relationships following such disturbances will eventually (sometimes several years) adjust back to the original sediment rating curve.

The rating curve relationship such as Equation 9.1 has been suggested as a method for estimating the effects of land use and management activities on suspended sediment. To use such an equation, stable relationships must be developed from field data, and any changes in the relationship caused by natural phenomena must be taken into account. Any significant shift in the relationship following some action such as logging, or conversion of vegetative cover on a watershed, then could be quantified.

The major difficulty, however, is separating changes in sediment rating curves that are caused by natural phenomena from those that are human caused. And, obtaining a representative sample of suspended sediment for measurement also is difficult, for concentrations can vary considerably with time and within a cross section of a stream.

Various techniques are available to estimate suspended sediment. The collection of grab samples is a common procedure, especially in small streams. However, this method may not be reliable because of the variability in sediment concentrations. Single-stage samplers consisting of a container with an inflow and outflow tube at the top are used on small, fast-rising streams. A single-stage sampler begins its intake when the water level exceeds the height of the lower inflow tube and continues until the container is full. Therefore, only the rising stage of the hydrograph is sampled, which can limit the use of the data.

Depth-integrating samplers minimize the sampling bias involved with single-stage samplers. A depth-integrating sampler (such as the DH-48) has a container that allows water to enter as the sampler is lowered and raised at a constant rate. Consequently, a relatively uniform sample for a given vertical section of a stream is obtained. Depending upon the size of the stream, a number of these samples can be taken at selected intervals across the channel. Each suspended sediment measurement should be accompanied with a measurement of streamflow discharge through the channel cross section.

After a suspended sediment sample is obtained, the liquid portion is removed by evaporating, filtering, or centrifuging, and the amount of sediment is weighed. The dry weight of suspended sediment usually is expressed as a concentration in milligrams per litter or in parts per million. Usually, measurements of suspended sediment and bedload are made separately because of differences in sizes of particles and in the distribution of particles in a stream.

Bed Load

Bed load particles can be transported in groups or singly and can be entrained if the vertical velocity of eddies creates sufficient suction to lift the grain from the bottom. They also can be started in motion if the force exerted by the water is greater on the top of the grain than on the lower part. Particles can move by saltation if the hydrodynamic lift exceeds the weight of the particle. They will be redeposited downstream if not reentrained. Large as well as small particles can be rolled or slid along the stream bottom; the more rounded particles, of course, are more easily moved.

The largest size of grain that a stream can move as bed load is called *stream competence*. The competency of a stream varies greatly throughout its length, and with time at any given point along its length. Stream competence is increased during high peak discharges and flood events.

The force required to entrain a given grain size is called the *critical tractive force*. The velocity at which entrainment takes place is called the *erosion velocity*. DuBoy's equation generally is used to calculate the tractive force for low velocities and small grains as a function of stream depth and gradient, and is written as:

$$T_f = W_w \, DS \tag{9.2}$$

where T_f = tractive force; W_w = specific weight of water; D = depth of water; and S = stream gradient.

For high velocities and large particles, stream velocity is more important than depth and slope; this has given rise to the sixth-power law:

$$competence = C\ V^6 \tag{9.3}$$

where C is a constant.

Doubling the stream velocity means that particles 64 times larger can be moved. However, the exponent is only approximate and varies with other conditions of flow.

Stream power, the rate of doing work, is used to express the ability of a stream to transport bed load particles. It is the product of streamflow discharge, water surface slope, and the specific weight of water. Relationships can be developed between unit stream power and unit bed load transport rate for a given stream, similar to the sediment rating curve discussed previously.

Another important concept in sediment transport is *stream capacity,* which is the minimum amount of sediment of a given size that a stream can carry as bed load. Increased channel gradient and discharge rate result in increased stream capacity. It has been found that if small particles are added to predominantly coarse streambed material, the stream capacity for both large and small particles is increased; but, if large particles are added to small-size grain material, the stream capacity is reduced. Small particles increase the density of the suspension and, therefore, the carrying capacity. Capacity also decreases with increasing grain size.

All of the variables affecting stream capacity are interrelated and vary with channel geometry. Streams that carry large bed loads (such as found in dryland regions where sediment sources are great) have shallow, rectangular or trapezoidal cross sections, because there is a steep velocity gradient near the streambed in such cross sections (Morisawa 1968). The typically parabolic cross sections of channels in humid regions, where sediment loads are relatively small, do not have steep velocity gradients near the streambed.

Bed load is more difficult to measure than suspended loads. No single device for measuring bed load is reliable, economical, and easy to use. While a number of bed load samplers exist, none are widely used. Instead, estimates can be obtained by measuring the amount of material deposited in sediment traps, reservoirs, settling basins, or upstream of porous sediment dams. These volumetric measurements can be partitioned into sands, gravels, and cobbles to determine the contributions by particle size.

■ SEDIMENT BUDGETS

As suggested earlier, the transport or routing of sediment from source areas where active erosion takes place to downstream channels involves many complex processes. A *sediment budget* is a simplification of these processes and includes consideration of (1) the rate of movement from one temporary storage to another, (2) the amount of sediment and time in residence in each storage site, (3) linkages among the processes of transfer and storage sites, and (4) any changes in material as it moves through the system—in essence, a quantitative statement of rates of production, transport, and discharge of soil material. To properly account for the spatial and temporal variations of transport and storage requires rather sophisticated models. A discussion of such models is beyond the scope of this chapter.

■ SEDIMENT DELIVERY RATIO

A commonly used method for relating erosion rates to sediment transport is the *sediment delivery ratio* (D_r), defined as:

$$D_r = \frac{Y_s}{T_e}$$ (9.4)

where Y_s = sediment yield at a point (wt/area/yr); and T_e = total erosion from the watershed above the point at which sediment yield is measured (wt/area/yr).

The sediment delivery ratio is affected by the texture of eroded material, land use conditions, climate, local stream environment, and general physiographic position. Generally, as the size of the drainage area increases, the sediment delivery ratio decreases (Fig. 9.5). Such relationships should only be used to provide rough approximations. As discussed previously, erosion and sediment concentrations can vary greatly for any given watershed.

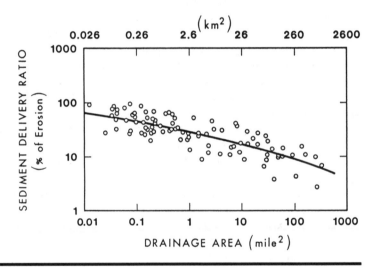

9.5. Sediment delivery ratio determined from watershed size (from Roehl 1962).

Before sediment delivery ratios or more detailed sediment routing models can be developed, erosion and sediment data must be collected. Often, these data are not available for upland watersheds.

■ SUMMARY

Surface erosion, gully erosion, soil mass movement, and channel scour combine to produce sediment in stream channels. Streams transport sediment as suspended sediment and bed load. The processes involved in sediment transport and deposition are complex. To obtain a detailed and thorough understanding of these processes would require a separate text by itself. Therefore, the purpose of this chapter was to introduce the subject and to provide sufficient information so that you should be able to:

1. Describe the different types of sediment transport.
2. Explain the relationships between stream capacity and sedimentation.
3. Explain the conditions under which aggradation and degradation occur in a stream channel.
4. Discuss the relationships that are normally found when the hydrograph characteristics of stormflow events are compared to the corresponding suspended sediment loads.
5. Explain the relationships between upland erosion and downstream sediment delivery; what are the factors that affect the sediment delivery ratio?

CHAPTER 10

Water Quality

◼ INTRODUCTION

The use of water, either actual or probable, must be defined before we can intelligently discuss the quality of water. A *water quality standard* refers to the physical, chemical, or biological characteristics in reference to a particular use. For example, water quality standards for irrigation are not necessarily acceptable for drinking water. Furthermore, certain changes in water quality due to watershed use can make water unusable for drinking but can be acceptable for fisheries, irrigation, or other uses. In some instances, we may be required by law to prevent water quality characteristics from being degraded from natural or "background" conditions. The objective of such laws or regulations is to maintain the quality of water for some possible unforeseen future use. The term *pollution* means that water has been degraded or "defiled" in some way that leaves an undesirable change. Again, this term must be related to the use of water.

This chapter reviews water quality characteristics of naturally occurring water, identifies some of the important land use impacts on water quality, and discusses monitoring methods. Recognizing that water quality discussions can include characteristics such as sediment, nutrients, pesticides, heavy metals, toxic chemicals, heated water, oxygen-demanding wastes, disease-causing organisms, and radioactive materials, we will concentrate only on those constituents commonly encountered in wildland settings. Furthermore, our discussion focuses on *nonpoint pollution* rather than *point-source pollution*. Point-source pollution is associated with industries or municipalities, whereby pollutants are discharged to natural waters through a pipe or ditch and can be measured and treated at a point. Nonpoint pollution refers to pollution that occurs over a wide area and is usually associated with land use activities such as agricultural cultivation, grazing, and forest management practices. Urban runoff represents an important source of nonpoint pollution, but will not be discussed in this book.

Nonpoint pollution presents problems to resource managers from the standpoint of processes involved and in developing procedures to eliminate or to minimize impacts. Vignon (1985) points out that a major difficulty is understanding and analyzing the mode of conveyance; for point sources, more conventional hydraulic methods can be used, that is, monitoring and analyzing discharge through pipes. Other characteristics that challenge the analyst are the intermittent nature and areal extent of nonpoint pollution. Identifying and quantifying the problem and then finding solutions are difficult. *Best Management Practices* (BMP) has been selected as an approach to control nonpoint pollution. The BMP approach involves the identification and implementation of land use practices in rural areas that prevent or reduce nonpoint pollution. In the case of erosion-sedimentation, many such practices are well known for agricultural, forestry, and road construction activities. For some types of pollutants, the BMP may not be known. In such instances, research that relates land use to water quality is needed.

PHYSICAL CHARACTERISTICS

Among the more important physical characteristics of surface water are suspended sediment concentrations, the level of thermal pollution, and the level of dissolved oxygen. Suspended sediments, which consist largely of silts and colloids of various materials, affect water quality in terms of domestic and industrial uses and can adversely affect aquatic organisms. Thermal pollution also has many direct and indirect impacts on aquatic organisms and water quality. Dissolved oxygen is an index of the sanitary quality of water.

Suspended Sediment

The physical quality of naturally occurring streamflow is determined, in large part, by the amount of sediment that it carries. As discussed in Chapter 9, the total sediment load in streamflow comprises bed load and suspended sediment. In terms of water quality, suspended sediment is more important because it restricts sunlight from reaching photosynthetic plants (measured as *turbidity*) and can affect aquatic ecosystems adversely by smothering benthic communities and by covering gravels that are often important spawning habitat for fish. Also, sediment carries many nutrients and metals that affect water quality.

SOURCES

Surface water from undisturbed forested upland watersheds have relatively low suspended sediment concentrations (10–20 ppm). Much of this sediment comes from the stream channel itself, although limited amounts can be contributed from surface runoff during large storm events. Where organic soils are prevalent, much of suspended material in streams is organic particles rather than mineral particles. Higher concentrations of suspended sediment often are the result of accelerated erosion caused by disturbances in drainage areas, such as road construction, logging operations, or natural catastrophes (including large floods, landslides, or fires). This problem is compounded when these disturbances take place on steep terrain and in close proximity to stream channels.

NUTRIENT AND HEAVY METAL TRANSPORT CAPABILITIES OF SEDIMENT

Nutrient and heavy metal losses from upland watersheds typically are measured by dissolved ion concentrations. However, a potentially important source of nutrient and heavy metal loss, and one that often is ignored, is that transported by sediment. This capacity is basically a function of the weathering forces of the physical and biological environment, the latter represented by the vegetation type on the watershed acting upon the parent bedrock. Also, pesticides (such as atrazine) are known to adsorb to soil particles and can be transported by the water system in this manner.

Transported sediment from drainages composed of different bedrock and vegetation combinations can carry high levels of nutrients and heavy metals. Sediment from upland watersheds with limestone, granite, basalt, and sandstone geologies in the southwestern United States show that, in general, limestone is high in calcium (Ca) and potassium (K), while basalt is high in sodium (Na). Magnesium (Mg) is highest in the sand fraction (0.061–2.0 mm) of basalt and the clay-silt fraction (less than 0.061 mm) of limestone. Often, sandstone has the lowest concentration of these elements, and granite is frequently intermediate. Nutrients adsorbed to sediment particles can be indicative of the type of geologic formation in an area. Vegetation types on a watershed of a given geology primarily affect the organic matter content, total phosphorus, and levels of extractable nutrients of the sediments.

Sediment transport of phosphorus can reduce the chemical quality of surface waters and thus result in substantial changes in aquatic ecosystems. Phosphorus is limited in many streams and lakes. When phosphorus loading increases in such systems, *eutrophication* (the process of nutrient enrichment leading to dense algae growth) can be accelerated. The resulting increase in algae and biomass in water systems can cause dramatic changes in water quality. For example, small pine-covered watersheds in Mississippi yielded less than 60 mg/l of suspended sediment, but the phosphorus (P) concentration averaged from 329 to 515 μg/g of sediment (Duffy et al. 1986). These concentrations of P were from 2 to 3.5 times greater than the concentration found in the soils of the watersheds. Most of the sediment was transported during stormflow events, accounting for 70% or more of total P export and over 40% of the total nitrogen (N) export, illustrating the importance of maintaining low sediment yields with respect to the chemical quality of water.

In many instances, variations in heavy metal (zinc [Zn], iron [Fe], copper [Cu], manganese [Mn], lead [Pb], and cadmium [Cd]) levels in a stream are correlated with variations in sediment concentrations. In the southwestern United States, sediment from different geologic strata has different heavy metal concentrations increasing in the following ascending order: sandstone, granite, limestone, and basalt (Gosz et al. 1980). From the standpoint of watershed management, land use practices that increase sediment production can increase nutrient and heavy metal loss transported by suspended sediment as well.

EFFECTS OF LAND MANAGEMENT PRACTICES

Suspended sediment concentrations often are increased following road construction, logging operations, heavy grazing, and other actions that disturb soil. Likewise, fire and floods can increase suspended sediment concentrations; these can be natural occurrences but sometimes are affected by land use. In many cases, the effects of individual activities cannot be isolated.

Roads, road construction, and maintenance are considered to be the principle sources of sediment from many upland watersheds (as discussed in chapters 7 and 8).

A number of studies and observations indicate that as much as 90% of the sediment produced from timber-harvesting operations in the United States originates from roads.

Mechanical timber-harvesting activities can increase sediment levels in streamflow, but the contributions from manual felling, limbing, and bucking of trees usually are negligible. Skidding and yarding operations with concentrated vehicular traffic often cause accelerated erosion, which can lead to downstream sedimentation. Fortunately, skidding and yarding techniques and machines are available that can minimize damage to the soil and limit sedimentation from many sites. A general rule of thumb is, the less compacting and disturbance of the forest floor, the less watershed damage will result from skidding and yarding activities.

Harvested areas on upland watersheds are subject to erosion processes until new vegetation is established, since the exposed mineral soil on these sites is the major source of suspended sediment. Furthermore, varying degrees of damage to the protective forest floor, which often provides protection against erosion processes, can occur with many timber-harvesting and log transport systems.

Fire also can be a contributor to accelerated erosion because of the loss of protective vegetation and litter and some physical changes of the soil surface. On many watersheds, combined logging and burning activities have produced increases in mass soil movements, which generally are attributed to the loss of mechanical support by the root system of trees and herbaceous vegetation. Various studies have demonstrated the effect of fire, timber harvesting, and road building on accelerated mass movements of soil and resulting sedimentation in streams (Chapter 8). Annual total sediment yields increased from 100 to 3,800 kg/ha following wild fires in ponderosa pine and Douglas-fir forests in the eastern Cascade Range of Washington (Helvey et al. 1985). This increased sediment loading increased nutrient losses of N, P, Ca, Mg, K, and Na, largely from the riparian zone where plant growth could be affected. Total N increased from 0.004 to 0.16 kg/ha/yr; available P increased from 0.001 to 0.014 kg/ha/yr; Ca, Mg, K, and Na increased from an average of 1.98–54.3 kg/ha/yr. When such increases are observed, the impacts on soil productivity can be of concern as well as the impacts on water quality. The authors of the above felt that the losses reported should not affect soil productivity.

Grazing by domestic livestock under properly specified conditions normally does not increase the amount of suspended sediment in streams. But, intensive grazing pressures on steep terrain and fragile soils can create problems. Sediment levels increase when livestock are allowed to overgraze riparian plant communities; this leads to streambank erosion and sediment deposition directly into stream channels.

Thermal Pollution

Water temperature can be a critical water quality characteristic in many streams. The temperature of water, particularly temperature extremes, can control the survival of certain flora and fauna residing in a body of water. The type, quantity, and well-being of flora and fauna frequently will change with a change in water temperature. Of particular concern is a temperature increase due to land use practices. In general, an increase in water temperature causes an increase in the biological activity, which in turn, places a greater demand on the dissolved oxygen in a stream. This effect is compounded by the fact that the solubility of oxygen in water is related inversely to temperature (Table 10.1). Changes in water temperature can result in the replacement

Table 10.1. Relationship between the saturated solubility of oxygen in water and water temperature

Water Temperature (°C)	Solubility of O_2 (mg/l)
5	12.8
10	11.3
20	9.0
25	8.2

of existing species, such as cold-water trout being replaced by warm-water bass or walleyes.

Clearing of vegetative overstories adjacent to a stream channel is one way in which water temperature can be increased. Removal of trees along a streambank increases the exposure to solar radiation, and the rise in water temperature can be predicted if one considers an energy budget for the water in the stream. If trees are removed from the streambanks the only change in the energy budget is an increase in solar energy entering the system, which will effect a rise in water temperature for there are no new outlets of energy from the system. Increases in stream temperature can range from fractions of a degree centigrade for slight openings in the forest overstory to over 10°C for a complete removal of trees along the streambank. Studies in the northeastern and northwestern United States have reported annual maximum stream temperatures to rise as much as 4°C and 15°C when riparian vegetation was removed from small streams.

Brown (1980) determined that the potential change in daily temperature due to streambank vegetation removal could be estimated from the following:

$$\Delta T = \frac{AR_n}{Q} 0.000267 \tag{10.1}$$

where ΔT = maximum potential daily temperature change due to exposure of a section of stream to direct solar radiation, in °F; A = surface area of stream newly exposed to direct radiation (ft²); Q = streamflow discharge (cubic feet per second, cfs); and R_n = net solar radiation received by water surface that is newly exposed (BTU/ft² [min]).

Mathematical models developed for application on upland watersheds in the western United States have been used to predict stream temperatures following modifications in the vegetative cover that shades a stream. In general, the models describe the physical situation of a stream, including the vegetation bordering it. Changes in these variables, as might occur through implementation of land management practices, often will result in corresponding changes in water temperature. Variables can be repeatedly changed to determine the possible effects of different methods of timber harvesting. Predicting water temperature changes also can be used to estimate corresponding changes in dissolved oxygen and subsequent impacts on aquatic flora and fauna. By doing so, a more complete understanding of the water quality consequences of changing riparian vegetation can be attained.

Dissolved Oxygen

The dissolved oxygen content in water has a pronounced effect on the aquatic organisms and chemical reactions that occur. The dissolved oxygen concentration of a water body is determined by the solubility of oxygen, which is inversely related to water temperature (Table 10.1), pressure, and biological activity. The solubility of oxygen in water can be estimated from the equation by Churchill et al. (1962):

$$O_s = 14.652 - 0.41022T + 0.0079910T^2 - 0.000077774T^3 \tag{10.2}$$

where O_s = solubility of oxygen (mg/l); and T = temperature of water (°C).

Dissolved oxygen is a transient property that can fluctuate rapidly in time and space. From a biological perspective, it is one of the most important water quality characteristics in the aquatic environment.

Dissolved oxygen concentration represents the status of the water system at a particular point and time of sampling. The decomposition of organic debris in water is a slow process, therefore, the resulting changes in oxygen status respond slowly as well. Methods have been developed that estimate the demand or requirement of a given water body for oxygen. In essence, this is an indication of the pollutant load with respect to oxygen requirements and includes measurement of *biochemical oxygen demand* or *chemical oxygen demand*.

Biochemical and Chemical Oxygen Demand

The biochemical oxygen demand (BOD) is an index of the oxygen-demanding properties of biodegradable material in water. Samples of water are taken from the field and incubated in the laboratory at 20°C, after which the residual dissolved oxygen is measured. The BOD curve in Figure 10.1 illustrates the two-stage characteristic that is typical; the first stage is related to carbonaceous demand, and the second stage to

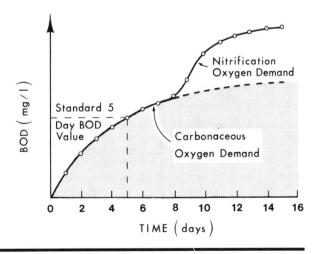

10.1. Example of a biochemical oxygen demand (BOD) curve illustrating the carbonaceous demand phase and nitrification phase.

nitrification. These two stages refer to the oxygen required to oxidize carbon compounds and nitrogen compounds, respectively. Unless specified otherwise, BOD values usually refer to the standard 5-day value, which is the carbonaceous stage. Such values are useful in assessing stream pollution loads and for comparison purposes (Table 10.2).

Table 10.2. Examples of biochemical oxygen demand (BOD) values for different conditions

	BOD (mg/l)	
Condition	5-day	90-day
Clean, undisturbed natural stream	< 4	. . .
Effluent		
Pulp and paper processing	20–20,000	. . .
Feedlots	400–2,000	. . .
Untreated sewage	100–400	. . .
Logging residue (needles, twigs, and leaves)	36–80	115–287

Source: Adapted from Ponce (1974), Dunne and Leopold (1978), and others.

Chemical oxygen demand (COD) is a measure of the pollutant loading in terms of complete chemical oxidation using strong oxidizing agents. It can be determined quickly because it does not rely on bacteriological action as with BOD. However, COD does not necessarily provide a good index of the oxygen-demanding properties of materials in natural waters. Therefore, BOD normally is used instead of COD.

When organic material such as human sewage, livestock wastes, or logging debris is added to a water body, bacteria and other organisms begin to break down that material to more stable compounds. If oxygen is readily available and mixed in and the organic loading is not too great, oxidation can proceed without any detrimental reduction in dissolved oxygen. When oxygen is limiting or loading is too great, anaerobic processes can occur, which result in a less efficient oxidation process with undesirable by-products in the water (Table 10.3).

A hypothetical sequence of changes that occurs downstream of heavy pollutant

Table 10.3. Examples of end products from organic loading in water bodies under aerobic and anaerobic conditions

Types of Compounds in Organic Load	End Products	
	Aerobic	Anaerobic
Carbonaceous (cellulose, sugars, etc.)	CO_2, energy, water	Organic acids, ethyl alcohol, methane (CH_4)
Nitrogenous (proteins, amino acids)	NO_3^{--} (in presence of N-bacteria)	NH_4^+, OH^- (NO_2^- temporary)
Sulfurous	SO_4^{--}	H_2S

loading of biodegradable material is illustrated in Figures 10.2 through 10.4. These figures show schematically the effects of discharging raw domestic sewage, from a community of about 40,000 people, into a stream with a flow of 100 cfs (2.8m³/sec).

The BOD increases instantly at the point of discharge, which is followed downstream (or in time) with a reduction in dissolved oxygen (DO) concentrations (Fig. 10.2). The reduction in DO steepens the gradient of oxygen between the atmosphere and the water body, increasing the reaeration rate. The DO reduction curve is at a minimum in the area undergoing active decomposition. As reaeration takes place, DO concentrations increase and eventually reach DO levels prior to pollution.

Bacterial growth proceeds exponentially in the degradation and active decomposition zones; the corresponding decomposition of nitrogenous organic matter takes place according to oxygen levels in the stream (Fig. 10.3). Other organisms respond to the modified environment, particularly those organisms adapted to conditions of low oxygen, low levels of light, and high concentrations of organic material. Although many organism populations return to prepollution levels, some do not. Because of the

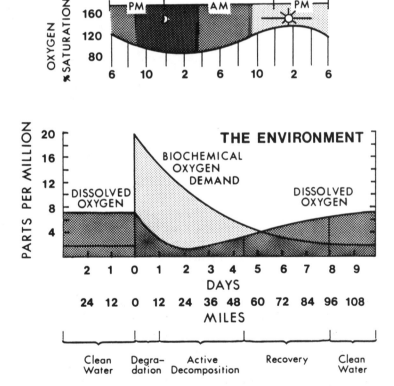

10.2. Effects of disposal of raw sewage in a stream on the dissolved oxygen and biochemical oxygen demand of stream water, either in time or downstream. The effects of reaeration rate and the diurnal characteristics of dissolved oxygen are also shown (from Bartsch and Ingram 1959, © Publ. Works J. Corp., by permission).

THE ENVIRONMENT

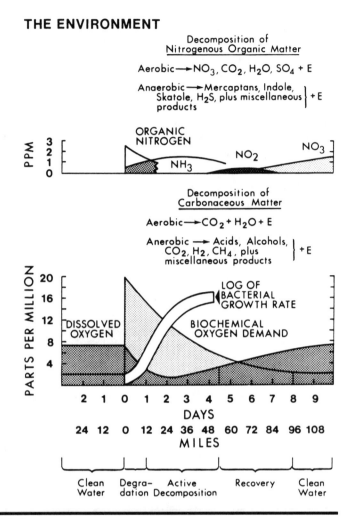

10.3. The relationship of accelerated bacterial growth with changes in dissolved oxygen and biochemical oxygen demand due to disposal of raw sewage in a stream (from Bartsch and Ingram 1959, © Publ. Works J. Corp., by permission).

higher nutrient levels in the recovery and downstream clean water zone, algae populations can flourish. As a result, the habitat for higher organisms is modified to the extent that species diversity does not fully recover to the upstream, prepollution conditions (Fig. 10.4). Notice also that population levels of certain adapted species increase in the active decomposition and recovery zones because of limited competition. As water quality conditions improve, the diversity of species recovers and populations of individuals within species drop to prepollution levels.

Other Characteristics

The physical condition of water often is described by several characteristics in-

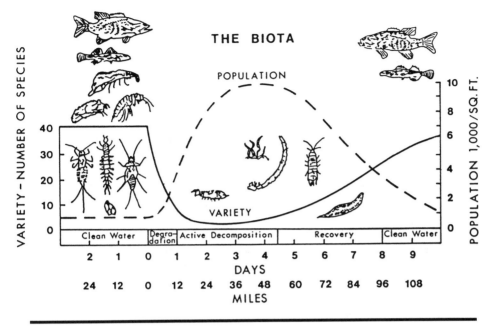

10.4. Effects of sewage disposal on species composition and populations of higher aquatic life forms in a stream (from Bartsch and Ingram 1959, © Publ. Works J. Corp., by permission).

cluding acidity, pH, alkalinity, specific conductance, and turbidity. These can be important indicators of water quality and can directly affect the chemical and biological condition of natural waters.

pH

The *pH* of water is the negative log, base 10, of the hydrogen ion (H^+) activity in moles per liter: a pH of 7 is neutral; a pH greater than 7 indicates alkaline water that normally occurs when carbonate or bicarbonate ions are present; a pH less than 7 represents acidic water. In natural waters, carbon dioxide reactions are some of the most important in establishing pH. When carbon dioxide (CO_2) enters water either from the atmosphere or by respiration of plants, carbonic acid is formed, which dissociates into bicarbonate; carbonate and H^+ ions then are liberated, influencing pH:

$$CO_2 + H_2O \rightleftharpoons H_2CO_3 \rightleftharpoons H^+ + HCO_3^- \rightleftharpoons 2H^+ + CO_3^{--} \tag{10.3}$$

The pH at any one time is an indication of the balance of chemical equilibria in water and affects the availability of certain chemicals or nutrients in water for uptake by plants.

The pH of water directly affects fish and other aquatic life. Generally, toxic limits are pH values less than 4.8 and greater than 9.2. Most freshwater fish seem to tolerate pH values from 6.5 to 8.4; most algae cannot survive pH values greater than 8.5.

ACIDITY

Acidity and pH are closely related indicators of H^+ ion activity in water. *Acidity of water is its capacity to neutralize a strong base to a designated pH.* Linked to pH, acidity is caused by the presence of free H^+ ions from carbonic, organic, sulfuric, nitric, and phosphoric acids. Acidity is important because it affects chemical and biological reactions and can contribute to the corrosiveness of water. The acidity of rainfall emerged as one of the prominent environmental issues concerning water quality and the environment in the 1980s (Ex. 10.1).

ALKALINITY

Alkalinity, the opposite of acidity, is the capacity of water to neutralize acid. Alkalinity also is linked to pH and is caused by the presence of carbonate, bicarbonate, and hydroxide, which are formed when carbon dioxide is dissolved. A high alkalinity is associated with a high pH and excessive dissolved solids. When water is high in alkalinity, it is considered to be well buffered, that is, large amounts of acid are required to change the pH.

Most streams have alkalinities of less than 200 mg/l, but some ground water can exceed 1000 mg/l when calcium and magnesium concentrations are high. Ranges of alkalinity of 100–120 mg/l seem to support a well-diversified aquatic life.

SPECIFIC CONDUCTANCE

Specific conductance is the ability of water to conduct electrical current through a cube of water 1 cm on a side, expressed as micromhos per centimeter at 25°C, or as microsiemens per centimeter (older instruments used the former units). By itself, this measure has little meaning in terms of water quality, except that specific conductance increases with dissolved solids. Its measurement is quick and inexpensive, and can be used to approximate total dissolved solids (*TDS*) as follows (Hem 1970):

$$TDS \text{ (ppm)} = A_o \times \text{Specific Conductance (micromhos/cm)} \tag{10.4}$$

where A_o = a conversion factor ranging from 0.55 to 0.75, with higher values associated with water high in sulfate concentration.

Specific conductivities in excess of 2000 μmhos/cm indicate a *TDS* level too high for most freshwater fish.

TURBIDITY

The clarity of water is an important indicator of water quality that relates to the ability of photosynthetic light to penetrate. *Turbidity* is an indicator of the property of water that causes light to become scattered or absorbed. The lower the turbidity, the deeper light can penetrate into a body of water and, hence, the greater the opportunity for photosynthesis and higher oxygen levels. Turbidity is caused by suspended clays, silts, organic matter, plankton, and other inorganic and organic particles. Standard instruments, called *turbidimeters*, are used to measure light penetration through a fixed water sample. Turbidity measurements, like specific conductance, can be used as an indicator of certain water quality constituents. For example, the more easily measured turbidity sometimes can be used to predict suspended sediment concentrations. Correlations between the two parameters is necessary, however.

EXAMPLE 10.1

Acid precipitation—what is it and what are the effects on aquatic systems? (From EPA 1980 and Postel 1984)

Acid precipitation became a major environmental issue in the late 1970s and early 1980s in the industrial countries of the northern hemisphere. The increasing acidity of precipitation is caused by the atmospheric inputs of sulfur oxides and nitrogen oxides from the burning of fossil fuels, such as coal, gas, and oil. Of concern to natural resource managers are the impacts of acid deposition (both liquid and solid atmospheric particulates) on aquatic and terrestrial ecosystems.

Even without air pollutants, naturally occurring precipitation is slightly acidic (pH of 5.6–5.7) because of the reaction of water with normal levels of atmospheric carbon dioxide. The industrial northeastern United States has experienced increasing acidity, with large areas experiencing rainfall pH values of 4.5 and below. In northern Europe, pH values as low as 2.4 have been reported—this is close to the acidity of lemon juice. The effects of acid deposition are widespread because of the long-range transport of acid by the atmosphere.

The impacts of acid deposition on streams and lakes are largely a function of the buffering capacity of soil surrounding them and the size of the watershed. If soils are alkaline or contain sufficient calcium, acids become neutralized and waters become acidified slowly, if at all. However, lakes and streams that occur on infertile, shallow soils over dense bedrock and have a low ratio of watershed area to water surface area are susceptible to acidification. Once the pH of such streams and lakes begins to drop much below 6.0, fish-food organisms and fish fauna become impacted. In Sweden, 50% of the lakes have a pH of 6.0 or less; half of those are below pH 5.0. When lakes reach a pH of less than 4.5, they are considered to be critically acid and cannot support fish life. Also of importance to watershed management is the impact of acid deposition on forest and other vegetation. Atmospheric pollution can inhibit nitrogen fixation in the soil; cause calcium, magnesium, and potassium to be leached from the soil; and can inhibit bacterial decomposition. Air pollutants, including acid deposition, caused a $1.2-billion loss of trees in West Germany during the summer of 1983 alone (Postel 1984). Under severe cases around smelters, forests can become nonproductive, and a loss of plant cover can lead to the same serious hydrologic problems encountered with other barren landscapes.

Even though acid deposition is not affected by watershed boundaries, by using the watershed as a unit for study, the direct and indirect effects on aquatic and terrestrial ecosystems can be more clearly identified. The solution to this problem, however, is not within the realm of watershed management.

■ DISSOLVED CHEMICAL CONSTITUENTS

One must realize that natural streams are not separate or distinct from the areas that they drain, but instead are an integral part of the ecosystem. Water is an effective solvent and as it comes into contact with each part of the system, the chemical characteristics of the water adjust accordingly. Chemical reactions and physical processes occur, often simultaneously, as the water contacts the atmosphere, soil, and biota. It is these reactions and processes, and the condition of each compartment of the ecosystem, that determine the kind and amount of chemical constituents in solution.

Streams that flow from undisturbed forested watersheds generally exhibit very low concentrations of dissolved nutrients. Because of this, the biological productivity in most such streams also is low and the water is generally of sufficient quality to be used for many purposes.

Sources of Nutrients

The major sources of dissolved chemical constituents in water that drains upland watersheds are geologic weathering of parent rock, biological inputs, and meteorological events. The cohesive properties of the dipolar water molecule allow it to wet mineral surfaces and to penetrate into the smallest of openings. Chemical and physical weathering converts rock minerals into soluble or transportable forms that can be introduced into streams and lakes. Biological inputs to water systems are primarily the photosynthetic production of organic materials from inorganic substances. Additional inputs are the breakdown of organic into inorganic compounds and the materials gathered elsewhere and subsequently deposited in the ecosystem by animals (including humans). Leaf fall into streams is an important source of organic matter and can result in periodic changes in nutrient concentrations. Some plants, particularly legumes, can add nitrogen to the soil by fixing free atmospheric nitrogen. Dissolved matter, including organic compounds and mineral ions, are added to the ecosystem by precipitation, dust, and other aerosols. Appreciable quantities of nitrogen, sulfur, and other elements often occur in precipitation and in dust and dry fallout from the atmosphere between precipitation events. However, the soil of natural ecosystems is considered to be the greatest contributor of dissolved chemical constituents to runoff. Land use activities that affect soil properties and processes, therefore, can affect the chemistry of streamflow.

In undisturbed ecosystems, the rock substrate and soil generally will control the relative concentrations of metallic ions (cations, such as Ca^+, Mg^{++}, K^+, and Na^+), while relationships between the biological and biochemical processes in the soil and precipitation events rarely govern the anionic (HCO_3^-, NO_3^-, and PO_4^{--}) yield. Anions, such as chloride (Cl^-), nitrate (NO_3^-), and sulfate (SO_4^{--}), originate from the atmosphere, at least in the absence of abundant sulfide minerals. The additions of these latter ions to streamflow, however, is largely regulated by various soil processes.

Some of the more important dissolved chemicals or nutrients that occur in undisturbed waters are described in the following paragraphs to help better understand the impacts of land use.

NITROGEN

Sources of nitrogen include the fixation of nitrogen gas by certain bacteria and plants, additions of organic matter to water bodies, and small amounts from the weathering of rocks. Nitrogen occurs in several forms, including ammonia, gaseous N, nitrite-N, and nitrate-N. Organic N breaks down into ammonia, which eventually becomes oxidized to nitrate-N, a form available to plants. In the absence of oxygen, nitrate can be converted back to ammonia and nitrogen gas by the process of denitrification.

High concentrations of nitrate-N in water can stimulate growth of algae and other aquatic plants, but if phosphorus (P) is present, only about 0.30 mg/l of nitrate-N is needed for algal blooms. Some fish life can be affected when nitrate-N exceeds 4.2 mg/l. When nitrate-N levels exceed 45 mg/l in drinking water, human health can be affected—in particular, the "blue baby" disease. Drinking water standards in the United States limit nitrate-N concentrations to 10 mg/l (EPA 1976).

Streamflow from undisturbed forestlands usually contain lower concentrations of nitrogen and nitrate-N than watersheds with other land uses (Table 10.4). Urban and agricultural development frequently increases nitrate-N and total N concentrations in streamflow.

Table 10.4. Mean concentrations of nitrogen and phosphorus for different land uses in the eastern United States

Land Use	Total N	Nitrate-N	Total P	Ortho-P
		(mg/l)		
Forest	0.95	0.23	0.014	0.006
Mostly forest	0.88	0.35	0.035	0.014
Mixed use	1.28	0.68	0.040	0.017
Mostly urban	1.29	1.25	0.066	0.033
Mostly agriculture	1.81	1.05	0.066	0.027
Agriculture	4.17	3.19	0.135	0.058

Source: From Omernik (1976).

PHOSPHORUS

Phosphorus originates from the weathering of igneous rocks, soil leaching, and organic matter. Less is known about the phosphorus cycle than the nitrogen cycle. The common forms of phosphorus essentially are defined by the analytical technique used to quantify them rather than by natural processes. In an aquatic environment, phosphorus becomes available to plants by weathering and is taken up and converted into organic phosphorus. Upon decay, the process is reversed.

Phosphorus concentrations in streamflow are affected by land use just as in the case of nitrogen (Table 10.4). Problems of eutrophication often are associated with accelerated loading of phosphorus to waters that are naturally deficient in phosphorus. Urbanization and agricultural land use represent the greatest problems of phosphorus loading to water bodies.

CALCIUM

Calcium is abundant in most waters because it is a major constituent of many rock types, especially limestone. Exceptions are acid peat and swamp waters. Soluble calcium occurs as long as CO_2 is present in the water and when pH values are less than 7–8. Calcium is one of the major ions contributing to hardness of water, total dissolved solids, and specific conductance. High calcium concentrations do not appear to be harmful to fish and other aquatic life.

MAGNESIUM

Magnesium is abundant in igneous and carbonate rocks, such as limestone and dolomite. Its solubility increases with greater concentrations of CO_2 or lower pH. If found in concentrations greater than 100–400 mg/l, magnesium can be toxic to some fish. When concentrations are less than 14 mg/l, waters generally support fish fauna.

SODIUM

Abundant in both igneous and sedimentary rocks, sodium is leached readily into surface and groundwater systems and remains in solution. However, it does not usually have any adverse impacts on fish fauna unless both sodium and potassium concentrations exceed 85 mg/l. Some levels of sodium have beneficial effects by reducing the toxicity of aluminum and potassium salts to fish.

POTASSIUM

Sources of potassium include igneous rocks, clays, and glacial material. It is usually less abundant than sodium, but it is essential to plant growth and is recycled by aquatic vegetation. Pristine waters generally contain less than 1.5 mg/l of K, but nutrient-enriched or eutrophic waters can contain over 5 mg/l. When K levels exceed 400 mg/l, some fish kills occur; levels greater than 700 mg/l can kill invertebrates as well.

MANGANESE

Manganese, found in igneous rocks, is leached from the soil. It is essential to plant metabolism and is circulated organically, becoming soluble upon decay. At pH levels of 7 or less, the most dominant form is Mn^{++}. Concentrations of manganese rarely exceed 1 mg/l in undisturbed waters. The drinking water standard for manganese is 0.05 mg/l.

SULFUR

Sulfur occurs naturally in water from the leaching of gypsum and other common igneous and sedimentary rocks. Weathering processes yield oxidized sulfate (SO_4^{--}) ions that are soluble in water. Sulfate also is found in rainfall at concentrations frequently exceeding 1 mg/l and sometimes greater than 10 mg/l. The higher concentrations of atmospheric sulfate are largely the result of air pollution, and are the main contributors to acid precipitation (Ex. 10.1).

Under reducing conditions, organic sulfur can be converted to sulfides. Metal sulfides occur with H_2S being present below pH 7 and HS^- ions occurring in alkaline waters. The sulfide H_2S produces a rotten-egg smell.

Generally, waters with a desirable fish faunae contain less than 90 mg/l sulfate; waters with less than 0.5 mg/l will not support algal growth. Drinking water standards are 250 mg/l for sulfate.

Transport Processes

Dissolved chemical constituents can leave a terrestrial system by subsurface flow through the soil, surface runoff, or groundwater. These processes are part of the "nutrient cycling," which consists of inputs, outputs, and movement of dissolved solids and gases within the system (Fig. 10.5). Frequently there is concern with outputs, that is, the streamflow from upland watersheds and the various factors that influence the chemistry of this runoff. This concern stems from the nutrient losses from forestlands, which causes water pollution for downstream uses.

Movement of water through soil, along with the associated biological activity, controls the ionic composition of water leaving upland watersheds as streamflow. The most chemically active components in soil are the clays and organic colloids. Clays have high exchange capacities in comparison to most other minerals in soil because of their large surface areas per unit of volume and their negative electrical charge. Organic colloids also have a large capacity to exchange ions in solutions for those absorbed on their surface.

A simplified concept of the exchange processes of clays and organic colloids is

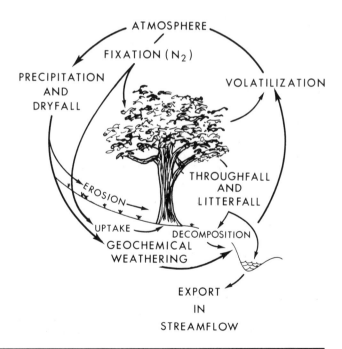

10.5. Example of a nutrient cycle for a forested watershed; some of the gaseous phases are not important for certain nutrients (adapted from Brown 1980).

that adsorbed cations are exchanged selectively for hydrogen ions from the soil water. The hydrogen ions, in turn, come principally from the solution of carbon dioxide in water and the dissociation of the resulting H_2CO_3 molecule into a hydrogen and a bicarbonate ion. Dissolved carbon dioxide originates mainly from the metabolism of microorganisms and plant roots in the soil. Only water that remains for some time in the interstices among soil particles is likely to accumulate an appreciable load of dissolved carbon dioxide and, consequently, be effective in leaching mineral ions. It is the flushing of these accumulations that creates the initially high levels during a storm-flow event.

Studies have shown that the ionic concentrations and their relationships to stream-flow discharge are variable. For example, a positive relationship exists between H^+ and NO_3^{--} concentrations and streamflow discharge from forested watersheds in New England, but no relationship exists between discharge and Mg^{++}, Ca^{++}, SO_4^{--}, and K^+. Individual cation concentrations, when considered on an annual basis, appear to be independent of discharge rate on watersheds in the Appalachian Mountains of the eastern United States. Inverse relationships between ionic concentrations and discharge have been reported in selected streams of the Rocky Mountains and in California. In large streams, ionic concentrations are commonly lower at times of high discharge than at low discharge, due in large part to the "residence time" of water in the soil. During periods of dry weather and low streamflow the slow movement of water through soils enhances the opportunity for chemical reactions. Dilution occurs when large volumes of water move through soils.

Effects of Land Management Practices

Land management practices can affect ionic balances on upland watersheds and the streamflow originating from them. Typically, the dissolved chemical load of streams after various forest disturbances such as timber harvesting or fire are largely a function of several biotic and abiotic characteristics that describe a natural ecosystem. For example, leaching rates are influenced by the form, amount, and intensity of precipitation events. Vegetative characteristics, primarily the composition and density of the plant species, influence the rates of nutrient uptake. The speed at which revegetation occurs after a disturbance controls, to a large extent, the initiation of nutrient recycling following the disruption. Soil characteristics, including porosity and texture, determine the pathways and rates of water movement in or over the soil matrix. Therefore, generalization of the effects of land management practices on water quality in widely differing upland watershed ecosystems is precluded by the intricate relationships among these and other variables. Three of the more common practices of interest are timber harvesting, fire, and grazing by domestic livestock.

TIMBER HARVESTING

When a forest is harvested, a number of important changes occur on a watershed that can change the concentrations of dissolved chemical constituents in streamflow. Trees are no longer in place to take up nutrients from soil, and noncommercial parts of the trees left as logging residues increase the amount of decaying forest litter. In addition, the removal of forest canopies makes the site warmer, while reducing evapotranspiration. Less evapotranspiration increases the soil water content, which in turn, accelerates the activities of microorganisms that break down organic material, including the added slash.

The increased respiration of microorganisms raises the partial pressure of carbon dioxide in the soil atmosphere, which also increases the bicarbonate anion level and leaches more cations from the system. In addition, nitrogen losses (as nitrate) can occur when they are produced by the oxidation of organic material (that is, *nitrification*) but not utilized by the forest vegetation that has been removed by harvesting.

Studies throughout the world show that, following intensive timber harvesting on well-drained soils, there is usually an increased loss of nutrients (cations and nitrate) from the logged area. For example, clearcutting northern hardwood forests in New Hampshire resulted in increases of 57 kg/ha for inorganic N, 71 kg/ha for Ca, and 15 kg/ha for K for the first 4 yr following cutting (Martin et al. 1986). The largest increases were observed during the second year after clearcutting. Concentrations of most nutrients were back to preharvest conditions by the end of the fourth year. Such increases in nutrient export from clearcut watersheds are often, at least partly, the result of increases in water yield that usually accompany clearcutting (see Chapter 6). Even if concentrations of nutrients in streamflow do not increase much, the increase in runoff volume can increase the nutrient loading of streams and lakes. This loading rarely is significant when roads and logging operations are properly planned. In general, normal forest practices do not cause excessive nutrient export from watersheds (Ex. 10.2).

EXAMPLE 10.2

Effects of clearcutting pine and site preparation on nutrient export from small watersheds in southeastern United States

Clearcutting of loblolly pine followed by site preparation with roller-choppers and planting caused nutrient export to increase, but the increase was slight and did not last beyond 2 yr (Hewlett et al. 1984). The concentrations of nutrients in streamflow did not increase following clearcutting, but water yield increases of 10–20 mm over 2 yr flushed more nutrients from the watershed than a paired (uncut) control. Nitrate-N loading increased 0.3 kg/ha for 2 yr following harvesting. The maximum nutrient flushing following timber harvesting was less than 0.5 kg/ha/mo for P, K, Ca, Mg, and Na; these were short-lived and diminished as regrowth occurred. Such nutrient losses result in neither soil fertility losses nor stream eutrophication.

Experimental watersheds at the Coweeta Hydrologic Laboratory in North Carolina experienced larger nutrient losses following hardwood clearcutting than those reported above. Net losses of 6.2 kg/ha and 3.6 kg/ha of N were measured for the first and second years following clearcutting (Swank and Waide 1979). Again, the losses reported were not considered a threat to the quality of streamflow.

FIRE

Burning the residue left in a forest after harvesting produces an even greater increase in the release of ions from the forest litter and mineral soil than the harvesting operation itself. The increased release of ions is due, in large part, to the breakdown of organic materials into a soluble form, making them easily removable by leaching. Generally, this process can lead to an increase in the total loss of nutrients with streamflow; however, in many instances, this increase is only temporary. In addition, volatilization of nitrogen and sulfur by fire results in losses from the watershed.

It has been reported that moderately severe fires in coniferous watersheds of the western United States have no specific effect on the concentrations of Ca^{++}, Mg^{++}, Na^+, and HCO_3^- in streamflow (Helvey et al. 1985). It was postulated that the ash constituents were dissolved by light rainfall and leached into permeable soil before the first snowfall. Because of the acidic nature of the soils on these watersheds, the dissolved cations were adsorbed by the exchange complex instead of being washed directly into the stream.

Rainfall events of high intensities that follow severe fires can move large quantities of soluble ash compounds into streams. But, as a forest regenerates after the fire, the dissolved chemical load of the stream generally returns to the levels observed before the fire.

DOMESTIC LIVESTOCK GRAZING

On many upland watersheds, especially in the western United States, grazing by domestic livestock is a common land use practice. Except where overgrazing occurs, this grazing generally does not have a significant impact on the dissolved chemical constituents in streamflow. However, when animals become concentrated near water bodies, for example in feedlots, nutrient loading can be high. More often the bacteriological quality of water can be adversely affected by grazing, as described below in the section on "Bacteriological Quality."

CHEMICALS USED IN LAND MANAGEMENT

Management of watersheds can require the use of a variety of chemicals, including fertilizers, pesticides, and fire retardants. We will not delve into a thorough discussion of all possible chemicals, their effects, or detailed guidelines for their use. Rather, we briefly discuss some important considerations from the standpoint of watershed management.

Hazards and Toxicity of Chemicals. Chemicals are used to accomplish some management objectives by being applied to a specific target organism (pesticides) or location (fertilizers and fire retardants). Of concern to watershed management are chemicals that find their way into the water system and become transported to nontarget organisms. The risks or hazards to nontarget organisms are determined by the chance or likelihood that they will come in contact with the chemical (exposure) and the toxicity of the chemical to that organism.

Toxicity effects can be either acute or chronic, and are not necessarily lethal. *Acute* effects are those caused by exposure to large doses of a chemical over a short period of time, and *chronic* effects are those caused by exposure to relatively small doses of a chemical over a long period of time. One must realize that the characteristics of the chemical and organism, in addition to the size of the dose, frequency, and duration of contact, all affect toxicity.

Toxicity to nontarget organisms usually is determined with bioassay techniques in which organisms are subjected to increasing concentrations of chemicals and observed over time. The concentration at which 50% of the organisms are killed is the lethal concentration (LC_{50}) or the median tolerance limit (TL_M). Values of TL_M for aquatic organisms and for commonly used chemicals are presented in Table 10.5.

Table 10.5. Values of 48-hr median tolerance level (TL$_M$) for selected pesticides and aquatic organisms

Pesticide	Range of Concentrations (ppb)		
	Aquatic Insects	Crustacea	Fish
Insecticide			
DDT	10–100	1–10	1–10
Endrin	0.1–1.0	10–100	0.1–10
Aldrin	1–10	10–100	1–100
Malathion	1–10	1–10	100–1000
Dieldrin	1–10	100–1000	1–100
Herbicide			
2,4-D (BEE)	1000–10,000	100–1000	1000–10,000
2,4-D (amine salt)	. . .	. . .	100,000–1 $\times$ 10^6
Picloram	10,000–100,000	10,000–100,000	10,000–100,000

Source: Adapted from Brown (1980) after Thut and Haydu (1971).

Chemical Behavior and Aquatic Systems. The basic rule of thumb in applying chemicals, whether they be pesticides, fertilizers, or fire retardants, is to minimize their contact with nontarget areas and organisms and, most importantly, prevent direct application to streams and lakes. Developing guidelines for application and good field management and monitoring are all needed to minimize problems of chemical application. Wind conditions, temperature, and proximity of target areas to streams and lakes must all be considered.

Once chemicals are applied properly to forest or rangeland areas, the risk to aquatic systems is dependent upon the persistence characteristics of the chemical and the hydrologic processes and characteristics of the site. Following application, chemicals can be either leached into and through the soil or carried by surface runoff. Therefore, rainfall rates, soil infiltration and hydraulic properties, soil depth, slope of the landscape, and organic matter can all affect transport. Usually, a *buffer zone,* an area in which chemical application is prohibited, is designated adjacent to water bodies. The size of the buffer zone depends on the above factors.

■ BACTERIOLOGICAL QUALITY

Bacteriological indicators often are employed to determine if water is of sufficient quality for drinking or human contact recreation (swimming etc.). An estimate of the number of organisms is an index of bacteriological water quality. Bacteria counted in most investigations are coliform and total bacteria. Knowledge of the cycles and variability of bacteria in natural waters and the relationships of bacteria to environmental factors on disturbed watersheds is sparse. However, there have been some investigations of bacteria-environment relationships on relatively undisturbed areas that, fortunately, can provide baseline information.

Seasonal coliform trends have been related to certain environmental factors, including air temperature and streamflow characteristics. Fluctuations in bacterial numbers of small, unpolluted streams in the Rocky Mountains generally were caused by intense summer rains of relatively short duration that produced overland flow. During periods of no precipitation when streamflow levels are stable, bacterial numbers seem to be related to the size of the water-streambed contact surface. As streamflow increases after precipitation events, some bacteria are deposited into the groundwater associated with the stream and, subsequently, released into the stream as it recedes. Bacterial numbers also will fluctuate during winter periods, even when the water temperatures are near freezing.

Timber-harvesting activities and resultant increases in turbidity have not affected coliform densities. However, grazing can cause bacterial densities of streams to rise, particularly where domestic livestock graze in marshy areas adjacent to the streams. The importance of this observation in the management of upland watersheds is obvious—to minimize the impacts of grazing by domestic livestock on the bacteriological quality of water, intensive grazing on sensitive riparian areas should be avoided.

Bacterial groups in streams, such as coliform, fecal streptococcus, and fecal coliform bacteria, are often closely related to physical characteristics of the streams. In the Rocky Mountains, bacterial counts appear to be especially dependent upon the flushing effect of surface runoff from rain storms, snowmelt, and irrigation outwash. Seasonal trends for all of the bacteria groups are similar throughout the year. Low counts prevail when the temperature of water approaches freezing, and high counts appear during rising flows and peakflows resulting from late spring snowmelt and rain. A short "postflush" decrease in bacterial counts takes place as runoff recedes in late spring. High bacterial counts are found again in the summer period of warm temperatures, and finally, counts decline in autumn.

In certain situations, the accumulation of organic material on the ground can act as a bacterial filter. For example, it has been found that rainfall and snowmelt that percolates through a strip of organic material contains fewer bacteria than water that had not passed through the strip.

The major source of fluctuations in bacterial counts (especially fecal coliform) that in many cases can lead to unacceptable pollution levels in streams, is the concentration of warm-blooded animals (including domestic livestock, big game animals, and humans) near streams. Therefore, if bacteria in the streams are to be kept below pollution levels, strict attention must be directed toward the control of grazing and other activities in riparian systems.

■ WATER-QUALITY MONITORING

To evaluate the kinds and amounts of substances present in water, representative water-quality measurements are required. Usually, sampling is necessary because continuous measurements of water quality are difficult and costly. A good sampling or monitoring procedure is based on knowledge of the water system being sampled, an understanding of the time and space distribution patterns of the parameters being sampled, and, most importantly, the purpose for which monitoring is being done.

The "environmental era" of the 1970s in the United States led to widespread water-quality monitoring programs that ended up with computer data banks filled with much worthless data. Costly physical, chemical, and biological data were collected from streams and lakes with little regard to overall objectives and application to environmental problems. Subsequently, a greater emphasis has been placed on better designs of monitoring programs.

The first and most important step in developing a monitoring program is to define the problem and clearly define goals and objectives. These objectives must not be vague and should be stated in terms that are explicit and meaningful. Criteria must be established that can be used to determine if specific objectives are met. Then, a sampling scheme can be established in time and space to provide the required information.

Water-quality monitoring programs are established to answer specific questions and should be designed accordingly. In general, monitoring programs for water quality–natural resource management situations are largely nonpoint in nature and can be classified as one of the following (Ponce 1980):

1. Cause-and-effect monitoring is conducted to determine the effects of specific actions on water-quality constituents. For example, monitoring may be set up to determine the effect of timber harvesting on suspended sediment concentrations or, more commonly, on several different water-quality constituents.

2. Baseline monitoring is conducted to help resource managers determine if there are certain trends in water quality at a particular location. Are certain water-quality constituents changing over time?

3. Compliance monitoring is carried out to determine if water-quality standards are being met. For example, such monitoring could be used to determine whether streamflow at a particular location is suitable for drinking water.

4. Inventory monitoring is designed to indicate existing water-quality conditions. For example, planning may be carried out in which several sites are being considered for recreational development that includes swimming. Sites must be selected that are suitable for water contact recreation.

The specific location, time, and frequency of water-quality sampling are determined by the type of monitoring being done and the normal statistical considerations (variability, cost of samples, accuracy needed, etc.). Also, the water-quality characteristics to be measured should be explicitly stated, and they should relate directly to the objectives.

The design of a monitoring program must locate sampling stations that are appropriate for the objectives and the type of monitoring planned. Cause-and-effect monitoring of streamflow quality can be carried out with the paired watershed approach (see Chapter 3) or with an "above-and-below" approach (Fig. 10.6). With the former,

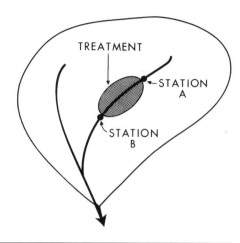

10.6. Example of station location for cause-and-effect monitoring study where the treatment can be readily isolated (from Ponce 1980).

water-quality measurements are taken at the outflow of a control watershed and one to be treated. Sampling is carried out for a sufficient period before treatment to establish regression relationships between the two watersheds. After the treatment, for example clearcutting a forest, sampling continues and changes in the regression relationship are tested statistically and these are used as an indicator of the effect of the treatment. With the second approach, sampling is done at station *A*, above the treated area, and at station *B*, downstream of the treated area (Fig. 10.6). The effect of the treatment can be determined by statistical methods that compare station means or that compare regression relationships at the two stations.

Compliance monitoring can use the same above-and-below approach discussed above, in which sampling stations are located to determine if a particular activity is causing water quality to exceed standards. For example, a forested area may be used as a disposal site for treated sewage from a recreational campsite. The water that is entering a stream channel must be monitored to determine if certain standards are being met.

Baseline and inventory monitoring require that sampling stations be located such that natural streams can be characterized. Multiple streams may be sampled concurrently, and over time the statistical distribution of water-quality characteristics compared to determine natural variability and to detect trends.

Much of the sampling done in the above monitoring approaches is with grab samples. Often, a grab sample obtained in a clean glass or plastic container is satisfactory, at least for preliminary analyses. However, a single grab sample is representative of the stream discharge only at the time of sampling. Some constituents, including suspended sediment, are affected by the magnitude of streamflow discharge (see Chapter 9). Discharge measurements should accompany all water-quality samples.

Once obtained, grab samples may have to be treated to protect against degradation of the contents. If the water samples are to be used later for organic analysis, the sample will have to be frozen or otherwise preserved. As a result, water-quality measurements in remote areas require careful planning and scheduling to ensure that the samples collected are handled correctly and that measurements are made promptly.

■ SUMMARY

The protection and maintenance of high-quality water is a fundamental goal of watershed management. This chapter introduces water-quality characteristics and describes the impacts of certain land use activities and disturbances on these characteristics and on the aquatic ecosystem. After completing this chapter you should be able to:

1. Define and explain the terms water quality and water pollution.

2. Identify and describe the different physical, chemical, and biological pollutants that are associated with different types of land use that can occur on upland watersheds.

3. Describe how nutrients and heavy metal concentrations and loadings to a stream can be accelerated above normal background levels, and discuss the implications.

4. Describe thermal pollution and explain its effects on an aquatic system.

5. Explain why dissolved oxygen is an important indicator of water quality, discuss what happens when DO levels are substantially reduced, and define BOD.

6. Describe and discuss the physical, chemical, and biological effects of introducing a biodegradable pollutant into a flowing stream.

7. Discuss how various silvicultural practices, range management practices, and associated activities can affect water quality; consider each major type of pollutant and indicate the kinds of management measures that are needed to correct or prevent water-quality problems.

8. Describe the different types of water-quality monitoring programs and discuss how to locate sampling stations for each.

Appropriate watershed management and planning are necessary to help sustain the functional life of reservoirs. The Tarbella Dam in north central Pakistan.

PART 3

Watershed Management and Planning

Earlier parts of this book deal with the technical aspects of hydrology and the effects of land use on streamflow quantity (Part 1) and quality and erosion-sedimentation (Part 2). Part 3 includes the topics of multiple use and planning and economics of watershed management. This part of the book emphasizes the interdisciplinary characteristics of watershed management, and the need to take into account hydrologic and socioeconomic factors when planning and implementing natural resource programs of many kinds. Here, we try to point out how the technical information can be put into use to help achieve sustainable, environmentally sound natural resource development.

CHAPTER 11

Watershed Management in the Multiple Use Concept

■ INTRODUCTION

The management of watershed resources to produce more than one product or amenity reflects the *multiple use* concept. In almost any discussion of natural resources management, multiple use is cited as a guiding principle. Although there has been little difficulty in gaining a general acceptance of the multiple use concept, it is not always easy to implement multiple use programs.

Most people concede that water or timber production is not necessarily the sole production function of a watershed, and that forage, wildlife, livestock, and recreation should be considered in management decisions. But, how much managerial effort should be allocated to each land use is a problem that decision makers and land managers have not been able to resolve. Reconciliation of conflicting interests is an important responsibility for all types of land managers.

A multiple use perspective is needed to achieve sustained, integrated watershed management, particularly in developing countries, where large rural populations depend upon a variety of resources that are produced in upland watersheds. It also is true that much of the intensive farming, grazing, and wood harvesting that takes place in these countries is leading to watershed degradation and adverse downstream impacts.

Programs aimed at increasing the productivity of watersheds cannot ignore the need to implement sound watershed management practices. On the other hand, watershed actions aimed at reducing erosion-sedimentation and other water-related problems cannot ignore the importance of upland watersheds in producing needed goods and services. The key is to design upland management strategies that diversify and increase income generation through the production of agricultural and natural resources, but under conditions that promote soil conservation and water resource objectives. To the extent that decision makers can incorporate a multiple use management philosophy into their planning, the level of income generated by a tract of watershed land and the sustained benefits downstream should both be enhanced.

Most watershed inhabitants in many countries practice, to some extent, multiple use, which involves the production of goods that they need, such as food, fiber, fuel, and fodder. Even though their emphasis may be to grow rice or corn, for example, they usually have some system of management or off-farm harvesting to provide fuelwood, construction wood, or fencing material. Most resource development activities also are tied closely to the development and distribution of water supplies. Therefore, multiple use is being practiced on many upland watersheds, but whether such multiple use is being properly managed for upland and downstream inhabitants alike is a point of concern.

■ MEANING OF MULTIPLE USE

The term multiple use may be applied either to areas of land or to particular natural resources. When applied to land areas, multiple use refers to the management of various natural resource products or product combinations on a particular watershed. The relationships of several natural resource products to one another can be complementary, supplementary, or competitive (Fig. 11.1). In a complementary relationship, the products increase together; a supplementary relationship is one where changes in one product have no influence on another; and a competitive relationship exists between products when one must be sacrificed to gain more of another. Conceivably, several products on a particular land management unit can be complementary, supplementary, and competitive with one another, depending upon the range of the production functions. It is imperative that the wildland administrator ascertain which relation confronts him before implementing a land management decision. In Figure 11.1, for example, the administrator will not be able to influence water production by altering timber production if operating in area *a* or *b*.

When applied to a particular natural resource, multiple use refers to the utilization of the resource for various purposes. Water can be used for irrigation, industrial op-

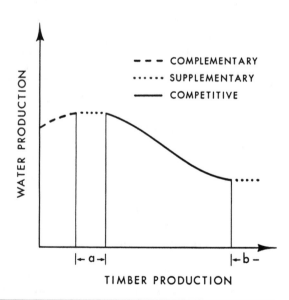

11.1. A hypothetical relationship between water and timber production on a land management unit, illustrating competitive, complementary, and supplementary relations.

erations, or recreation; timber can be utilized for lumber, pulpwood, or fuel; and forage can have value as feed for livestock or wildlife species, or for watershed stabilization. Here again, the utilization of the natural resource can be complementary, supplementary, or competitive.

In practice, the multiple use concept involves both the multiple use of lands and of particular natural resources on watersheds. Demands on particular natural resources (water) for specific uses (irrigation), in turn, place demands on the land where the natural resources are produced (watersheds).

■ OBJECTIVE OF MULTIPLE USE MANAGEMENT

The objective of multiple use management is to manage the natural resource mixture for the most beneficial combination of present and future uses. The general idea of maximizing benefits from a given natural resource base is not necessarily new, but it has become more important as competition for limited and interrelated natural resource products increases.

Every watershed does not necessarily have to be managed for all possible natural resource products simultaneously. Instead, most watersheds are utilized for a wide array of natural resource products in varying degrees, as dictated by relative levels of supplies and demands. Multiple use can be accomplished by one or more of the following options:

1. Concurrent and continuous use of several natural resource products obtainable on a particular watershed, requiring the production of several goods and services from the same area.

2. Alternating or rotating the use of the various natural resource products, or combinations thereof, on a watershed.

3. Geographic separation of uses or use combinations, so that multiple use is accomplished across a mosaic of land management units on a watershed, with any particular unit of land being put to the single use to which it is most suited.

All of these options are legitimate multiple use management practices and, therefore, should be applied in the most appropriate combinations. From society's point of view, multiple use involves a broader set of parameters than would be considered by a private investor. In general, society is more interested in "conserving" benefits for future generations, whereas the private investor is more apt to make decisions based, in large part, upon relatively short-term profit motives. To the extent possible, effective multiple use management should accommodate the full spectrum of today's needs while providing for tomorrow's requirements.

■ TYPES OF MULTIPLE USE MANAGEMENT

The two fundamental types of multiple use management are resource oriented and area oriented. *Resource-oriented multiple use management* refers to the alternative uses of one or more natural resources. For example, timber can be managed for lumber, fuelwood, or pulp. Such management is dependent upon knowledge of interrela-

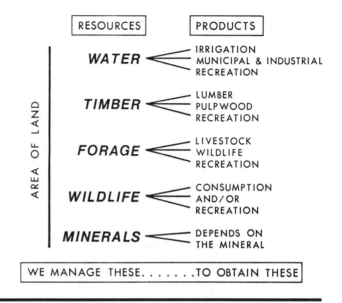

11.2. Multiple use is the management of multiple resources that results in several products.

tionships describing how the management of one natural resource affects the utilization of others, or how one use of a particular natural resource affects other uses of the same resource. Substitutions between and among natural resource products, and the associated benefit-cost comparisons of alternative production combinations, are taken into account.

Resource-oriented multiple use management requires an understanding of the production capacities of natural resources. However, to accomplish effective and efficient multiple use, natural resources must not only be related to each other but also related to the needs and wants of people.

Area-oriented multiple use management refers to the production of a mix of products and amenities from a given land area. Area-oriented multiple use must consider the physical, biologic, economic, and social factors relating to resource product development in a particular area. This provides a framework in which information concerning the management of land units can be arranged, analyzed, and evaluated. Area-oriented multiple use draws the information needed to describe resource potentials from resource-oriented multiple use, then relates this to the dynamics of local, regional, and national demands (Fig. 11.2). Area-oriented multiple use management is not necessarily intended to replace other forms of land management but to complement them.

■ INTEGRATING WATERSHED MANAGEMENT AND MULTIPLE USE

The problems of integrating watershed management within the multiple use concept are not always realized by the decision makers. Sometimes, management objectives are specifically resource oriented. However, decision makers must be aware of area-oriented multiple use management implications, especially when considering extensive watershed areas. Many land management considerations, policy formulations, and institutional conflicts, in general, are confronted when attempting to integrate the component parts of multiple use in watershed management.

Land Management Considerations

Multiple use management generally involves the development, application, and evaluation of land management systems that alter natural or agricultural resource production. However, the impact of a forest management system can extend to other products and amenities. In addition to wood and agricultural products, many other resources are usually in demand, and these products must be allocated in an efficient manner to maximize total benefits to society. Likewise, we should minimize adverse impacts such as flooding, water pollution, sedimentation, etc. on other resources.

Resource management systems designed to alter the production of commodity goods and amenities commonly are recommended by various interest groups. Furthermore, the implementation of these systems often requires sweeping modifications of vegetation on lands where the potential to alter production is the greatest. Also, some of these systems could jeopardize other land values and associated incomes. Furthermore, some are irrevocable, at least in the short run, in that they can easily be implemented but cannot be undone if they turn out to be mistakes.

To effectively incorporate multiple use into watershed management the following is needed:

1. On-site measurements of the yields of natural and agricultural resource products for the alternative multiple use management systems under consideration.

2. Knowledge of the benefits and costs associated with each alternative.

3. Recognition of the *externalities,* the off-site impacts that are related to each alternative; for example, the effects on downstream water quality or streamflow quantity.

From this information, decision makers can undertake economic evaluations of alternative multiple use systems to select the best course of action. Importantly, these economic evaluations must be tempered to satisfy the goals of multiple use, as stated by the societal groups that pay for and benefit from the implementation of the plan.

ESTIMATES OF NATURAL AND AGRICULTURAL RESOURCE PRODUCTION

On-site measurements of natural and agricultural resource product yields are required to determine their response to alternative management systems. These products include fuelwood, lumber, agricultural crops, forage for livestock and wildlife, water, and recreation. Consequently, estimates of wood production and agricultural crop production before and after a land management system has been imposed are desirable.

An example of production relationships of water, timber, and herbage yield with different levels of forest strip cutting in Arizona is presented in Figure 11.3. Such relationships allow resource managers to quantify the effects of management alterna-

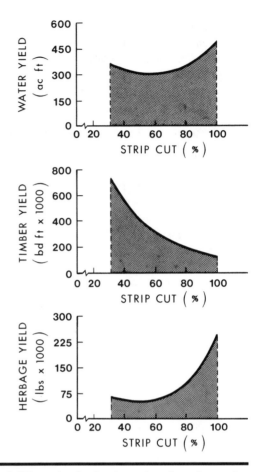

11.3. The effects of different levels of strip cutting of ponderosa pine on multiple resources in Arizona (from O'Connel and Brown 1972).

tives on products of interest. The management implications for other resources can be derived from such relationships. For example, predictions of herbage production and utilization subsequently can be translated into meat gains and wildlife habitat potential. Water yield and quality measurements should be estimated to represent the conditions before and after the land management system is put in place. On-site inventory programs aimed at providing adequate measurements of resource products and trade-offs among products are necessarily of high priority.

Measurements of natural and agricultural resource products can be represented as a product mix (Table 11.1). All resource products derived from a particular area or class of land can be described quantitatively in such a table. A product mix representing the existing situation (M_0) can be compared to alternative multiple use practices (M_1 and M_2). A set of comparisons form a basis for choosing a multiple use management system from a range of alternatives by appraising the impacts of the management redirections upon upland (on-site) productivity and externalities (downstream, etc.) as well.

Table 11.1. Framework of a hypothetical product mix for alternative multiple use management systems on a watershed

Item (annual production)	Management Alternatives		
	M_0 (existing situation)	M_1	M_2
Wood cut			
Fuel wood (m³)	X_{01}	X_{11}	X_{21}
Construction (m³)	X_{02}	X_{12}	X_{22}
Wood growth			
Fuelwood (m³)	X_{03}	X_{13}	X_{23}
Construction (m³)	. . .	. . .	. . .
Agricultural crops			
Maize (kg)	. . .	. . .	. . .
Potatoes (kg) etc.	. . .	. . .	. . .
Livestock			
Meat (kg)	. . .	. . .	. . .
Milk (kg)	. . .	. . .	. . .
Wool (kg)	. . .	. . .	. . .
Wildlife (number)	. . .	. . .	. . .
Water yield (m³)	. . .	. . .	. . .
Downstream irrigation			
Storage (m³)	X_{0n}	X_{1n}	X_{2n}

The product mix representation in Table 11.1 can be used to select the best course of action to meet an objective of management by assigning values and performing an economic analysis comparing the existing condition with various multiple use alternatives. Importantly, an analysis also should consider the changes in products and amenities over time. For example, under the existing condition (M_0), soil erosion may result in a decline in productivity over time. Alternatives that include soil conservation practices may show an increase in productivity over time as well as increases in usable downstream water yield. The true benefits of each alternative, compared to the existing conditions, are represented by differences in on-site productivity and externalities over time. Example 11.1 describes product mixes for different forest management alternatives in the southwestern United States. Multiple resource relationships associated with a particular forest management option and changes over time are discussed for the same forest type in Example 11.2.

BENEFITS

Determining the benefits and costs of implementing and maintaining an effective multiple use system is prerequisite to selecting the best alternative. Quantifying and valuing multiple goods and services represents a real challenge to the analyst. Often, estimates by experienced professionals are needed to offset the lack of quantitative data.

Direct benefits can be dependent on the sale of products removed in the initial establishment of a management system. The increase in a lumber-only market could become obsolete if a pulpwood mill were installed. The presence of additional outlets

EXAMPLE 11.1 —————————————————————————————————

Multiple use management of a ponderosa pine–forested watershed in the southwestern United States

A product mix for a southwestern ponderosa pine–forested watershed (adapted from McConnon et al. 1965)

Item (per hectare basis)	Management Alternatives			
	M_0 (as is)	M_1 (converted)	M_2 (uneven-aged)	M_3 (even-aged)
Timber cut (m³)	0.0	9.0	4.9	3.8
Timber growth (m³)	4.2	2.5	5.5	5.2
Livestock (kg gain)	0.068	0.48	0.0045	0.27
Wildlife (number of deer)	0.021	0.034	0.032	0.033
Water (cm)	15.0	22.0	16.0	18.0

The above table represents a comparison of product mixes for different management alternatives for a ponderosa pine watershed. These comparisons show what is gained and lost in multiple use terms, assuming that a response to management redirection can be accurately estimated. If things remain as they are, M_0, the annual outputs per hectare will be 4.2 m³ of timber growth, enough forage for 0.068 kg of livestock gain, 0.021 deer, and 15 cm of water. With conversion of moist sites to grass, M_1, the annual outputs will be 2.5 m³ of timber growth, forage for 0.48 kg of livestock gain, 0.034 deer, and 22 cm of water; 9 m³ of timber will be cut on each hectare. Columns M_2 and M_3 contain the response elements of uneven-aged and even-aged forest management, respectively. It is important to note that, if M_0 is the "best" as judged by an assessment of the gains and losses in natural resource products, the existing land management practice should be continued.

could alter the expected monetary returns by making previously unmerchantable wood material salable. Since market conditions can change quickly and affect returns significantly, the wood resource should be described in terms of multiproduct potentials (fuelwood, construction lumber, etc.) and provide timber-quality and yield information for management and utilization decisions on a continuing basis.

In terms of an increase in on-site agricultural production, direct benefits will require a level of production in excess of the subsistence level. When available, the commodity surplus can be sold locally or transported to regional markets. In the latter instance, revenues may flow into the local economy that, in all likelihood, would not otherwise be available. As with the sale of wood, market conditions for agricultural products can change through time. Consequently, the direct benefits derived from increased agricultural production should be evaluated over a range of alternative cropping strategies.

EXAMPLE 11.2

Multiple resource changes over time associated with strip cutting a ponderosa pine forest in Arizona (O'Connell and Brown 1972)

A one-third strip-cut treatment was applied to a 1267-acre watershed in north-central Arizona to increase water yield, while providing acceptable sediment concentrations and enhancing wood and herbage values at the same time. The treatment involved clearing one-third of the area in alternate, irregularly shaped strips that measured a width of approximately 60 ft. The strips were designed to trap and retain snow (see Chapter 14), and their margins were irregularly shaped to stimulate natural openings. Ponderosa pine seedlings were planted in the cut strips, and the trees were thinned to a basal area of 80 ft²/acre in the intervening forested strips.

A 90-yr rotation is proposed on the watershed with three cuttings at 30-yr intervals. By clearcutting an adjacent 60-ft strip at each cutting, a step-type forest is anticipated.

The dynamic nature of the expected production levels of water, wood, herbage, and sediment yields from the watersheds on this 90-yr rotation are illustrated below. Water yields are increased periodically because of redistribution of snow in a manner favorable to streamflow, reduced use of water by vegetation, and increased surface runoff following each strip-cutting operation. The exposure of bare soil and the reduction of tree cover at the time of strip cutting are responsible for the indicated increase in herbage and sediment yield. The yields of all three annual outputs, that is, water, herbage, and sediment, decline as the forest cover becomes reestablished.

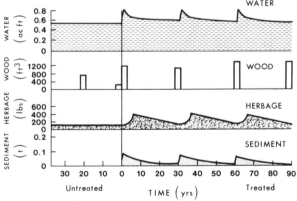

Changes in water, wood, herbage, and sediment yields associated with strip cutting of a ponderosa pine forest on a 90-yr rotation in Arizona (from O'Connel and Brown 1972).

Wood production is shown only in terms of the amount of sawtimber available for harvest at the time of each cut and is calculated on the basis of existing volume and known growth rates.

Conceivably, benefits derived from a change in the production of other resource products (for example, water for downstream irrigation, forage for livestock and wildlife, recreation, etc.) could be determined by comparable objective analyses, although these markets are generally more poorly defined than those for timber resources and agricultural products.

Direct benefits from combined production systems are evaluated in terms of the sale of agricultural crops, domestic livestock, and primary wood products. However, changes in the levels of output in combined production systems frequently are difficult to assess because of the "linkages" among products. Nevertheless, a measure of these changes is necessary to quantify direct benefits in a multiple use evaluation. Analytical techniques for obtaining these measures are not always adequate, however, and investigations to develop new methodologies are needed. Flexibility is important, as many of the benefits derived are utilized on-site and not necessarily sold in a marketplace.

COSTS

A relatively large body of information on the cost of watershed management practices is available in the literature. Unfortunately, these data normally reflect a particular economic situation and time, and cannot easily be adjusted to different conditions. To overcome this problem, the collection of "gross job time" cost data, in terms of physical input-output variables characterizing the management system and land area, frequently are prescribed.

As an illustration, inputs collected can include labor time, equipment time, direct supervision time, and materials. Outputs specify total production as units harvested, planted, etc. Costs then are determined by multiplying inputs by current wage rates, machine time, and material costs. The sum of costs divided by the number of production units accomplished gives an estimate of the average unit cost for a watershed management practice. Of course, other approaches can be followed, although once again, information on costs should not be site or date specific.

The flexibility derived from the collection of objective benefit-cost data will allow multiple use management systems to be reevaluated as economic conditions change through time. Consequently, a system initially considered economically impractical because of depressed market conditions or high implementation costs could become operational with increased market outlets, or a change in wage or machine rates.

EXTERNALITIES

Of great importance in integrating multiple use into watershed management is the ability to diversify and increase income and to properly assess externalities. In fact, consideration of externalities is the essence of integrating multiple use into a watershed management framework. In general, externalities are the effects of decisions made by one party on the gains or losses of other parties. However, these gains or losses do not necessarily enter into the decisions of the first party.

Two classes of externalities can be considered: technical and pecuniary. *Technical externalities* affect third parties through changes in production functions, while *pecuniary externalities* impact third parties through the market place. Furthermore, technical externalities are concerned with efficiencies of a system, whereas pecuniary externalities affect the distribution of income.

Serial technical externalities are those that trigger a chain reaction in a one-way direction. A classic illustration of a serial technical externality is when people on an upstream watershed impede the delivery of downstream irrigation water supplies due to their use of the land. Here, the upstream users of a watershed affect the downstream users, but the technical actions of downstream users cannot impact those upstream. *Reciprocal technical externalities* are presented by a complex web of spatial and temporal effects and interactions, both forward and backward, among parties. An example of a reciprocal technical externality is one that occurs when a user of a "community" pasture increases the number of animals that are grazed beyond the carrying capacity of the land. Not only is less forage available for the other users of the pasture, but less forage eventually will become available to the first party.

In making economic evaluations of multiple use management systems that are characterized by recognizable externalities, it becomes necessary to incorporate these externalities in the decision-making process. Models often are needed to perform such evaluations, particularly under circumstances of limited data and information. Therefore, research to assist in alleviating this deficiency is paramount to planning and evaluating multiple use management.

ECONOMIC EVALUATIONS

To make an economic evaluation of multiple use management systems, decision makers may select one or more of the following economic objectives: (1) to maximize benefits; (2) to maximize the returns on an investment; or (3) to achieve a specified production goal at least cost.

Source data required to satisfy the first two objectives include estimates of natural and agricultural resource product values and physical responses resulting from the management redirection, and costs of implementing the proposed forest management system. To satisfy the third objective, goals, which often are derived through the political process, must be established for various levels of production. In all instances, the outputs of multiple use of natural and agricultural resources play an important role.

Economic evaluations frequently consist of an array of pertinent economic analyses designed to help make a better decision. An individual analysis can yield a one-answer solution to the problem of selecting a land management system that maximizes the economic returns to a watershed. A group of such analyses based on different criteria will result in an array of items for decision makers that could include:

1. Estimates of multiple use production associated with the alternative land management systems.
2. Estimates of costs that are associated with the alternatives.
3. Least-cost solutions for different goals of multiple use production.
4. Gross and net benefits associated with a range of multiple use management alternatives.
5. Investment returns and benefit-cost ratios (see Chapter 13) associated with different multiple use management systems.

The above array is simply illustrative and, therefore, must be modified according to local, regional, and national economic philosophies and institutions. In fact, the selection of the appropriate criteria is the key to meaningful economic evaluations of multiple use.

Policy Formulations and Institutional Conflicts

Given the above array of economic relations, one should be able to choose the "best course of action," that is, implement a land management practice designed to achieve a specified goal. However, policy issues and institutional conflicts also must be resolved before multiple use becomes operational.

The question of who will pay for the implementation of a watershed management system designed to alter, for example, water production must be answered. The group of people or the land management agency that carries out the practice may not derive benefits from all of the natural resource products affected. It is questionable that the USDA Forest Service, which carries out many watershed management programs in the United States, will receive benefits that are commensurate with their costs. The role of downstream groups benefitting from altered water production on upstream lands will have to be established regarding the cost sharing.

Also, the benefits and costs of a watershed management practice designed to alter water production must be ascertained with respect to the needs of society as a whole. Different viewpoints must be presented, so people can determine how a management practice is going to affect them individually and collectively.

Local groups on or near the area that is directly affected by a watershed resources management practice, regardless of its intended purpose, will want to know how the management program may affect them personally. Their viewpoint often can be determined by an evaluation of on-site "raw," natural resource products or by the value added through manufacturing stages in the economic progression from watershed to consumer within the local area. A single economic solution may not be suitable, but analyses that reflect different viewpoints may furnish the required answer.

Regional interests, such as a state government, may bear a large portion of the investment for a watershed management practice. Determining the effects on the economy of a state seems appropriate to this viewpoint. In the United States, a nationwide viewpoint also must be the basis for some evaluations, primarily because many of the watersheds that may be subjected to land management practices are federally managed. Therefore, the federal government may contribute a portion of the investment.

Perhaps the greatest problem in pursuing the multiple use concept is developing an efficient institutional framework through which watersheds subjected to the multiple use management can be managed. A realistic multiple use management plan must either work within the existing institutional framework or, if necessary, modify that framework to be effective in attaining the watershed management goals. An assessment of the political and social organizations through which natural resources are currently administered could suggest the necessity for institutional reform.

Agroforestry and Multiple Use: Special Considerations

Within a watershed boundary, many land use systems can be spatially represented, including protection forestry, production forestry, agricultural cropping, grazing by domestic livestock, and agroforestry. In many countries, there is a mosaic of these and other land uses in upland watersheds. Although area-oriented multiple use is widely practiced in these countries, multiple use *management* is rare.

Some of the best opportunities to match appropriate land uses within watersheds to achieve both upland productivity and downstream protection involves the integration of *agroforestry* into watershed management. Agroforestry is a system of land use where woody perennials are grown on the same land unit as agricultural crops or animals, either sequentially or simultaneously (Fig. 11.4). As such, agroforestry practices represent *combined production systems*. Such practices represent area-oriented multiple use in the purest sense of the word, but they have a distinctive focus on the

AGROFORESTRY CROP ROTATION SYSTEMS

SHIFTING CULTIVATION

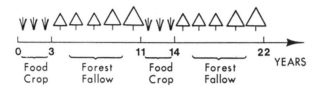

TAUNGYA SYSTEM

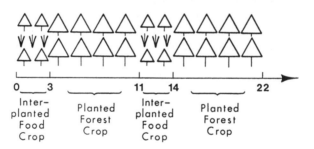

AGROFORESTRY INTERCROPPING STSTEMS

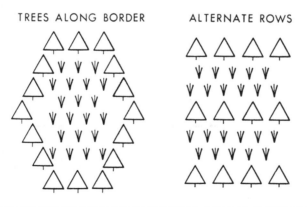

11.4. Examples of agroforestry systems in which woody perennials are grown sequentially or simultaneously with food crops (from Vergara 1985).

welfare of upland inhabitants. Swiddening, border tree-planting, alternative rows and strips, and random mixes represent viable land use options in the tropics. The key for managers and planners is to adopt appropriate agroforestry practices and to achieve watershed management objectives simultaneously. In critical areas, protection forests can be the only answer. With a multiple use objective and agroforestry practices as tools, a mix of goods and services can be obtained that not only meet management objectives but are accepted by upland inhabitants.

Many agroforestry practices are attractive means of integrating multiple-resource management with watershed management. Several reasons can be given:

1. Agroforestry practices have been used for centuries by indigenous forest-dwelling communities in countries such as India, the Philippines, Costa Rica, and Kenya and are, therefore, largely accepted by local people.

2. In areas where people have occupied the land for a sufficient time to observe the impacts of proper and improper swidden practices, the tendency has been to practice *sustainable* technologies.

3. A wide array of practices are available that can be adapted to different soils, topography, and climate that achieve productivity goals without sacrificing soil and water conservation.

4. Woody perennials as parts of well-planned agroforestry systems can serve as windbreaks (border planting in Figure 11.4), can help stabilize soil in steep topography (Fig. 11.5), and can help manage soil moisture conditions that are more favorable for watershed management purposes.

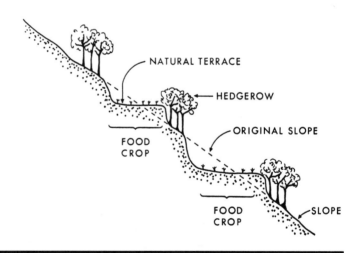

11.5. Example of natural terraces that form over time as a result of planting alternate rows of woody perennials with food crops along the contour of a slope (from Vergara 1982).

■ SUMMARY

The basic purpose of multiple use is to take advantage of the interrelationships between and among the natural and agricultural resources on a land unit so that, by the manipulation of one or a few of the resources, additional benefits may be derived from many of the related resources. In recognizing these multiple use potentials and incorporating them into comprehensive, integrated land management planning, more efficient utilization can be made of the resource base on the land unit. From a watershed management perspective, a multiple use approach directs planners and decision makers away from viewing watershed management as solely "rehabilitation" work, thus, planning can proceed with more of a sustainable approach to achieve both upstream and downstream objectives. The emphasis on integrating watershed management and multiple use becomes increasingly important in the future, as rural and urban development proceeds on the more fragile watershed lands throughout the world.

After completing this chapter, you should be able to:

1. Explain the concept and objectives of multiple use.
2. Identify and explain the different ways that multiple use can be implemented.
3. Develop and explain a relationship between two natural resource products of your choosing (like the one in Figure 11.1); indicate competitive, complementary, and supplementary relationships as they pertain to your figure.
4. Discuss the major constraints of implementing multiple use management.
5. Discuss how agroforestry practices help to achieve watershed management objectives.
6. Explain the role of multiple use in the planning and implementation of a watershed management program.

CHAPTER 12

Planning and Appraising Watershed Management

■ INTRODUCTION

As stressed throughout this book, land use activities on watersheds involve complex interactions, where an activity in one area impacts the activities in other areas. Most watershed management activities have impacts on a number of different people as well. Because of these interactions, it is critical that land use and management activities on a watershed be coordinated through a practical, integrative planning process.

■ THE PLANNING PROCESS: AN OVERVIEW

Planning for watershed management involves an integration of three major sets of elements. First, there are the *objectives* established on the basis of problem analysis in the watershed area and directives from higher level authorities. Second, there are the various *constraints*—budget, physical-biological, social, cultural, political—associated with the specific situation. Third, there are the *techniques* for carrying out alternative technical watershed management activities. Watershed management planning involves organizing, analyzing, and integrating the objectives, constraints, and techniques in such a way that decision making and implementation are more efficient and effective than if an unplanned approach is used.

Many of the constraints involved in watershed management are physical, such as climate, soil conditions, and land form. But just as many constraints are social, economic, and institutional in nature, for example, available budget, cultural limitations, political acceptability. The challenge for the manager and planner is to bring all these factors directly into the planning process, using accurate and detailed data where available, and using approximations and order of magnitude estimates in other cases.

In only a few instances will the manager have "enough" data and information to make risk-free decisions concerning actions and reactions. Planning, thus, requires a number of judgement calls and a great deal of flexibility. If we have learned one thing from the past, it is that watershed projects and programs seldom develop as planned. The manager who is ready to adjust to changes in basic conditions is farther ahead than one who sticks rigidly to an original plan despite changes in conditions. A major purpose of this chapter—and indeed the whole book—is to provide background and practical support for managers and planners so that they can be better prepared to anticipate these needed adjustments, identify critical information and concepts, and work more easily with the inevitable changes in constraints and opportunities that will take place as planning and implementation proceed.

In practice, the administrator of a watershed management program is a synthesizer and an integrator of many disciplines and fields. As such, this chapter attempts to keep in mind the need for synthesis—for blending social, physical, and biological sciences, and for blending science with art, since in the final analysis planning and management are as much art as science.

As discussed elsewhere in the book, each watershed-related problem has its own unique set of technical elements and characteristics. Thus, in terms of physical planning (such as the identification and design of needed physical structures, vegetative manipulation, etc.), each project requires a somewhat different technical approach. The same does not hold for the planning process itself. Regardless of the type of watershed program, the same planning process can be used. It is only the relative emphasis on each step in the process that will differ, not the nature of the steps themselves. This chapter lays out the basic steps and what they involve. The "fine tuning" of the planning process will be discussed in terms of adjustments in emphasis and content needed to deal with particular types of problems.

The Watershed Management Planning Context

In the final analysis, watershed management activities are undertaken to benefit humans. We do not undertake activities to reduce erosion as an end objective. Rather, we undertake them to avoid losses that have direct human value, such as reduced food production or loss of reservoir storage, which leads to reduced hydropower production. Figure 12.1 provides an overview of the watershed management system. Three major elements are considered in this framework. First, there are the watershed management practices (inputs) and the costs associated with them. Second, there are the physical effects and environmental changes associated with the management practices. Third, there are the economic changes (both benefits or costs) associated with the effects; these are the changes that can be associated with economic value to humans. The relationships between watershed management activities (inputs) and their physical effects (outputs) are discussed throughout the book. Valuation of inputs and outputs is discussed in Chapter 13.

The effects and benefits indicated in Figure 12.1 are defined as changes or differences "with and without" the watershed management project or activities being considered. For example, when we say "increase productivity" or "reduce sedimentation," we are referring to the differences in productivity or sedimentation with and without the project or activity. In any given case, productivity can still be declining with the project or activity, but at a slower rate than without the project; thus, there is a higher level of productivity (an increase) over what it would have been without the project (Fig. 12.2), and this represents a benefit.

The benefits of a hypothetical watershed project are illustrated in Figure 12.3A. In this instance, which is common for severely degraded watersheds, the initial phase of a project causes productivity to fall below levels of the without-project condition (*AG*). For example, certain critically disturbed areas are removed from cultivation and

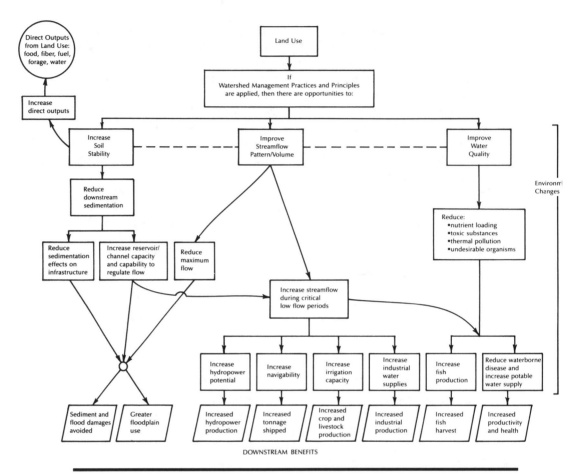

12.1. Physical effects and measures of benefits from watershed management (adapted from Gregersen et al. 1987).

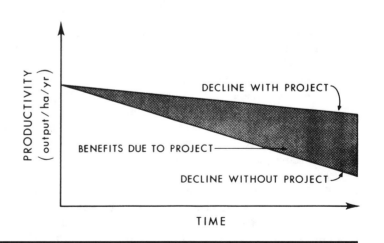

12.2. Productivity differences with and without a management project.

production is temporarily reduced on areas that are undergoing structural and revegetation measures. After some time, productivity increases and is maintained at a higher level (*BC*). The benefits of the project in upland productivity are represented by the area *GBCE* in Figure 12.3A. Benefits can sometimes be mistakenly identified as only FBCD if the with-and-without approach is not applied. In the example of sedimentation of a reservoir (Fig. 12.3B), the watershed management activity results in a slower rate of reservoir capacity reduction and the downstream benefits of the project would be area *ABC*. Note again that the project initially has little effect on the rate of loss of reservoir capacity. However, as structural and vegetative measures become effective, the rate of loss declines and eventually reaches a relatively stable condition. The reservoir capacity still declines with the project, but at a lower rate.

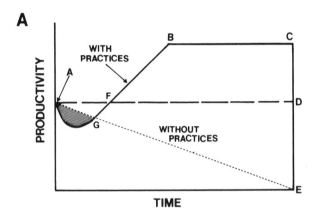

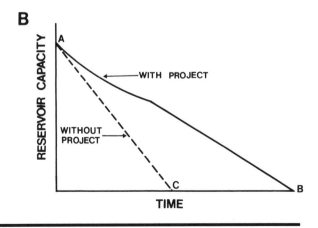

12.3. Relationships of upland productivity (A) and downstream sedimentation of a reservoir (B) under conditions "with" and "without" watershed management practices (from Gregersen et al. 1987, © FAO, by permission).

Steps in the Planning Process

The planning process involves the following steps:

1. Monitor and evaluate past activity and identify problems and opportunities.

2. Identify main characteristics of the problems/opportunities identified and define constraints and objectives (to overcome problems or take advantage of opportunities); develop strategies for action.

3. Identify alternative actions to implement strategies, given the constraints.

4. Appraise and evaluate the impacts of alternatives, including environmental, social, and economic effects; assess uncertainty associated with results.

5. Rank or otherwise prioritize alternatives and recommend action when recommendations are requested.

In other words, we deal with the questions—How do we decide that something needs to be done? What is it we want to do? What alternatives do we have available to do it? Which alternative(s) is (are) best, given the circumstances?

Planning as an Iterative Process

Project planning is an iterative process of successive approximations, where we learn from past experience and then incorporate that learning into the on-going planning process. Watershed management planning, thus, involves incremental learning. In practice, planners seldom go into a situation and immediately get down to the business of detailed (and often expensive) project design. Rather, the planners go through a series of iterations, from a quick, low-cost assessment of the situation through progressively more sophisticated and detailed design and appraisal stages until they have all the information that is needed, wanted, or affordable in order to make a decision.

This incremental process of successive approximations makes good sense, since a major purpose of planning is to help decision makers and resource managers reject unsuitable options at an early stage, before too much time and resources have been spent studying and developing them. With many years of experience, a planner can focus almost immediately on an appropriate strategy and a few viable and suitable options for dealing with a given situation. Of course, this is the objective—to be able to discard unsuitable alternatives with a minimum expenditure of time and effort and to spend more time on the few alternatives that experience has taught are the best in a given situation. Figure 12.4 provides a view of how the design and appraisal stages develop together, with appraisals being made at each stage to decide whether or not to continue, which alternative solutions to a problem should be rejected, and which should be looked at in more detail. There is nothing fixed about the number of stages involved; three shown in Figure 12.4 are for illustrative purposes only.

Of course, many persons will be quick to point out that, by following rules of thumb and past experience, we risk missing more efficient or effective solutions to a given watershed problem, ones that could be identified if more time and resources were devoted to the effort. This essentially is correct. However, funds, skills, and time are scarce in most situations, and most managers have stringent time constraints and limited resources to devote to problem analyses, project designs and evaluations, com-

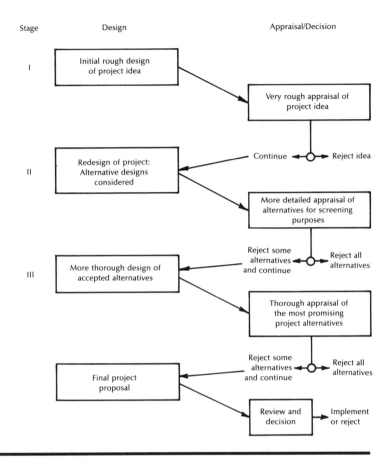

Stage   Design   Appraisal/Decision

12.4. Stages in the project-planning process (OECD 1986, by permission). The number of iterative stages can vary depending on the project situation.

parisons of alternatives, and so forth. The optimum solution is constrained by the availability of time and resources.

In the remainder of this chapter, each of the steps in the watershed management planning process is discussed in more detail. In keeping with our objective and orientation, we attempt to dwell on the practical solutions and to avoid the impractical ones, even though the latter may be theoretically more appealing than the former.

■ MONITORING AND PROBLEM IDENTIFICATION

The process of planning really has no beginning and no end in an ongoing or operating watershed management situation. However, for the purpose of exposition and explanation, the logical starting point is before a problem or opportunity is identified—with monitoring.

In almost every part of the world, someone is collecting data about land and water uses and abuses over time, for example, the changes that are taking place in the biological and physical environment. This information can be used to determine whether or not a watershed management problem exists and what could be done to resolve it.

The types of information needed to identify problems are many and diverse. Key information needed to describe the environment is found in the categories of hydrology, climatology, soils, and vegetation. In general, data are collected on both a long-term, continuing basis to define major problems, and on a short-term, sometimes intermittent basis to provide information to solve particular "crises." Ideally, long-term monitoring allows observation and analysis of resource responses over time to help identify problems. For example, precipitation and streamflow data need to be collected on a continuous basis for many years before we can characterize flooding, drought, and erosion conditions.

In addition to long-term continuous data acquisition and monitoring, data often are collected on a one-time basis to analyze a specific, known problem. This type of analysis may be performed to quantify the severity of a particular problem or to determine if corrective actions being taken on the watershed actually are solving the problem.

How data are generated by hydrologists, biologists, soil scientists, and so forth to meet these informational needs is discussed in specific chapters throughout this book. Different types and levels of detail and accuracy are needed in different situations, depending upon the intensity of land use, the rate at which problems appear to be developing, or the severity of an already identified problem. Thus, other things being equal, collection of more detailed information on sediment loads and siltation can be better justified for a watershed that drains into a multipurpose reservoir than for a relatively unpopulated watershed that drains directly into the ocean. Similarly, the monitoring of water quality in a river passing through large population centers normally should be much more intense than similar efforts for an isolated river that flows through wildlands.

Often, no formal measuring or monitoring system is used to produce the information that leads to identification of watershed management concerns and eventual action. Rather, problems are observed directly after they have occurred, for example, when it becomes increasingly apparent that a reservoir is silting up rapidly, when the scars of erosion begin to appear on the landscape, or when floods become more frequent and serious.

Regardless of how problems and opportunities are noticed, their definition becomes one of the first steps in watershed management planning. For the purpose of this book, we have broken down the types of problems commonly encountered into the categories discussed in Chapter 1. In many instances, more than one solution to a problem may be possible. For example, water supplies may be enhanced by developing reservoir projects and water-harvesting schemes for livestock on the range. In other cases, some solutions can be mutually exclusive. For example, increased cultivation or agroforestry activity to enhance food production may require that grazing by livestock be discontinued entirely.

Not explicitly discussed previously are other nonproduction-oriented objectives of watershed management, such as sustaining or enhancing wildlife habitat or providing scenic beauty. In many parts of the world, societies set aside watershed lands that have particular beauty, historical significance, or other amenities. These can be valid objectives and, therefore, must be considered in a planning effort together with adjacent or nearby lands that are managed for quite different purposes.

In sum, the types of problems that are of importance in watershed management are many and varied. In some cases, planning involves actions to prevent the problem from occurring; in other cases, the problem already exists and the planning involves development of a program to reduce the problem or (at least) ameliorate the conditions that caused it. While the specific actions taken in each case may differ, the planning process will be the same. The importance of monitoring and problem identification cannot be emphasized too much. The problem statement will set the focus and orientation for the rest of the planning activity.

IDENTIFYING CONSTRAINTS, SETTING OBJECTIVES, AND DEVELOPING STRATEGIES

The next stage in the planning process involves setting objectives and developing strategies to solve the problems or respond to the opportunities. The objectives generally flow directly from the problem analysis. In their most general form, statements of objectives merely indicate that there is a need to develop a cost-effective means of overcoming or preventing the identified problem or to ameliorate the conditions causing it, eventually leading to benefits such as identified in the bottom line of Figure 12.1. If flooding is the problem, the objective is to lessen floods so flood damage can be reduced. If poor-quality drinking water is the problem, the objective is to improve water quality and reduce health problems. With greater levels of specification, objectives can be translated into targets that are constrained, for example, in terms of the riskiness of approaches taken, level of cost applied, and level of achievement of other objectives.

Single vs. Multiple Objectives

Single objectives, even when constrained in a number of ways, are not too difficult to deal with in terms of the planning process. In most cases, where one is dealing with single constrained objectives, clear decision criteria can be developed for determining the extent to which alternative project designs (sets of activities) are acceptable and even how they rank relative to each other. As discussed earlier, ranking is a common step in the decision-making process.

Difficulties arise when more than one objective exist and, thus, multiple objectives have to be considered. Decision-making models have been developed to deal, in theory at least, with *multiple objectives.* In practice, however, the use of such models has not been widespread nor particularly successful. For decision-making purposes, it is easier to focus on one main objective, with other objectives expressed as constraints on the main one. For example, a major project objective can be reduction of sedimentation in a given reservoir. Additional objectives, such as better water quality or enhanced river transportation, then may be expressed as constraints on the main objective. With a given budget level, the objective may be to maximize reduction of sedimentation in the reservoir subject to an associated maximum permissible level of water pollution, a maximum allowable reduction in grazing herds in upland areas, and a minimum level of increase in agricultural productivity through intensification of land use with increased fertilizer and other inputs.

Some planners avoid the problem of dealing quantitatively with multiple objectives by developing an array of effects of alternative project designs for the various objectives. The decision maker then has to provide subjective weightings to compare different alternative combinations of outputs related to the various objectives.

Developing a Strategy to Achieve Objectives

Once objectives have been clearly established and agreed upon, a general strategy for action needs to be developed. The distinction between "strategy" and "plan" is subtle and probably more a matter of degree. Here, the term *strategy* is used to describe the general *direction* taken to achieve the objectives. A *plan* further includes the *magnitudes* or *targets* to be achieved and *timing* of the actions to be taken to achieve them.

A strategy to reduce erosion that is causing reduced agricultural productivity and downstream sedimentation might consist of the following:

1. Identify and define cost-effective land use practices that can decrease erosion.
2. Develop an extension system that will provide people with the information they need to choose the appropriate practices.
3. Develop incentive mechanisms to get local populations interested in using these land use practices.
4. Provide credit facilities to give people the ability to adopt the new methods.

The important thing here is not the strategy statement itself, but the process by which it was developed. If we just look at the problem statement, we could think of a number of alternative strategies to reduce erosion. For example, in an autocratic situation, we could suggest regulation against certain land uses with appropriate enforcement; in other cases, the best strategy might be to leave the situation alone because the fiercely independent nature of the local people would preclude any reasonable chance for success, thus, it would be better to spend our scarce resources and time elsewhere. There are many other scenarios that could be developed and transformed into strategy statements. So how do we decide on one specific strategy?

Considering Constraints

We arrive at a logical strategy by looking systematically at information on the constraints and conditions that surround the problem. Constraints that might have been considered in the above example include:

1. Literacy is low and mass communication facilities do not exist in the region; there is no current extension organization in operation.
2. Landforms and soils are such that only certain types of changes of land use practices would have a good chance of success in the area.
3. The political structure is such that effective regulation and enforcement would be difficult; an approach using incentives would be needed.
4. There do not appear to be cultural constraints that stand in the way of changing land use practices, although tradition is important to the locals; incentive mechanisms would have to be included, at least initially.

5. Currently, the financing mechanisms available for long-term crops and live-stock management are inadequate; since some tree crops will probably have to be established on steep slopes, the need for improved credit mechanisms, alternate incomes, and other ways to support tree crop establishment and other long-term activities would be needed.

Many preliminary questions would be asked during this strategy formation stage. The idea is not to formulate and quantify exact plans of action—that is, how many acres will have to be treated with a certain treatment; how much of an incentive payment and what kind will be needed, and so forth. Instead, in developing a strategy, we go rather quickly through the whole context of the project to (1) eliminate some approaches that obviously would not work, given the existing constraints, (2) determine which constraints need to be removed to have a reasonable chance for success, and (3) identify any obvious strong points that should be taken advantage of in project design and implementation.

■ IDENTIFYING ALTERNATIVE ACTION PLANS TO IMPLEMENT STRATEGY

Once an acceptable strategy has been developed, we get down to the details of design of alternatives to implement the strategy. The task becomes much more specific and more technical. The need is to identify the various actions that could be used to implement the strategy and produce desired results. This is where the technical expertise of the hydrologist, soil scientist, forester, engineer, and other technical specialists, as well as the expertise of social scientists, politicians, and others dealing with social, economic, and cultural elements, come into the picture.

Basically, the types of actions needed in different instances include physical/engineering actions (terraces, dams, gabions); biological actions (planting, cutting vegetation); regulatory measures to discourage or require certain actions (regulating grazing, timber harvest); actions to create incentives (provision of free goods and services, subsidies, credit, outright cost sharing, and so forth); and educational activities (information materials, demonstration).

The task at this stage is to identify the possibilities and the array of options that are available, given the constraints and circumstances surrounding the project. Much of this book is concerned centrally with the appropriate choice of such actions under different problem situations. The manager has to be familiar with a great number of different techniques and potential actions that are available to solve various types of problems, which, in turn, exist at different levels of development and with different degrees of severity.

■ APPRAISING ALTERNATIVES

While the alternatives are being developed, they also are being appraised or evaluated (Fig. 12.5); in most cases, appraisal is an ongoing activity. In its broadest meaning, "appraisal" refers to the process of identifying, defining, and quantifying the likely or expected impacts of an action (a practice) or closely related set of actions (a project). Some of these impacts will be positive and some will be negative.

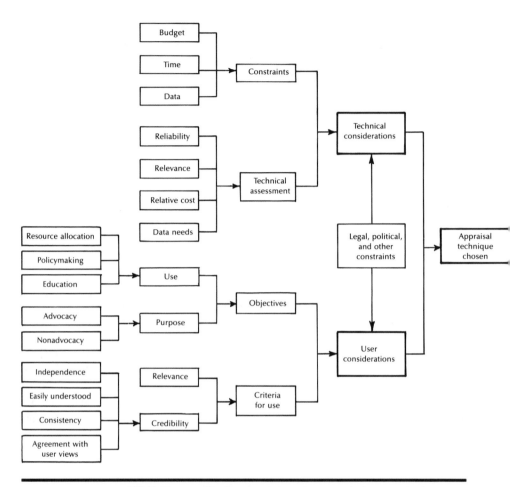

12.5. Factors affecting the choice of an appraisal approach (Gregersen and Lundgren 1986).

Nature of Impacts Being Appraised

A representative list of impacts or effects of watershed management activities, divided for the sake of convenience into economic and financial, environmental, and social effects, is presented in Table 12.1. Note here that the effects indicated in Table 12.1 relate to different views of the impacts of a given change.

For example, assume that a watershed management project results in 100 more people being employed as road workers, tree planters, and guards to prevent illegitimate woodcutting or grazing on certain critical watershed areas. This is an actual physical change due to the project; it is a fact. The economist looks at allocation of resources to these newly employed people, the redistribution of income that takes place, implications for public budgets, and the implications in terms of regional and national levels of production over time. The watershed management expert may look at the implications of increased forest protection on soil and water quality, ecological stability, water yield, and other physical-biological impacts. The social scientist, in

Table 12.1. Common effects of watershed management activities

Economic / financial effects on:
    Regional and national level of production
    Allocation of resources
    Regional and national income
    National balance of payment
    Stability of income over time
    Distribution of income (both interpersonal and intertemporal)
    Public Budgets
Environmental effects on:
    Ecological diversity
    Ecological stability
    Wildlife protection
    Soil protection
    Landscape aesthetics
    Water yield and timing
    Water quality
    National patrimony
Social effects on:
    Regional employment
    Working conditions
    Public participation
    Migration flows
    Cultural traditions
    National vulnerability
    Political stability

Source: Organization for Economic Cooperation and Development (1986), by permission.

Note: For convenience in exposition, we have divided the effects into three categories, namely, economic/financial, environmental, and social. Other categories could equally as well have been chosen.

turn, may look at regional employment changes in terms of effects on cultural systems, social cohesion, conflicts with previous institutional traditions, that is, informal tenure traditions, and so forth. The point is that the employment of the 100 additional persons due to the project can have a myriad of different so-called effects or impacts, depending on who is viewing the change.

Some worry about double counting of effects when, for instance, we say that the increase in employment increases income, ecological stability, community cohesion, and feelings of self-worth. These are merely different measures of concern related to the same physical change. They are complementary measures that relate to different decision criteria and describe different dimensions of the same physical change. All the impacts may be of interest to decision makers.

Making Appraisals Useful and Relevant

Project appraisals are useful only if they provide timely information of relevance to decision makers in such a way that the decision maker is comfortable with the information. This means that a clear distinction needs to be made between the technical analyst's considerations in choosing a "good" appraisal approach and the user's view of what characterizes a good, acceptable and usable appraisal. Figure 12.5 outlines the two points of view and the characteristics or criteria of relevance.

The task of a good planner or appraiser is to bring these two sets of criteria or considerations together into the final appraisal. This integrative point of view pervades throughout the present discussion. Integration of the perspectives of users and technical personnel is a key ingredient in successful planning.

Appraisals should support the objective of using the minimum amount of resources needed to reach an acceptable decision on how best to achieve an objective. In some cases, this point is reached after a "quick and dirty" appraisal—the evidence and political agreement are so clear concerning the best alternative that one need go no further to reach a clear decision. In other cases, a more detailed and thorough second-stage appraisal is needed—the evidence is not quite clear enough after the first-stage appraisal to make a judgement. Finally, in cases involving major commitments of resources, a formal feasibility study is needed to arrive at the point where a comfortable decision can be made. Sometimes, a formal appraisal (feasibility study) also is required by the institutions involved. Table 12.2 indicates considerations for each of three selected stages of appraisal.

It is important to pursue appraisal of projects at sequential levels, because both resources for appraisal are limited in most cases and it encourages initial consideration of a number of alternatives for achieving objectives. Starting out with only two alternatives—do nothing and option A—is being unduly restrictive. The preferable approach is to start with a number of alternatives and then to narrow them down systematically in stages (Fig. 12.3). This also insures that economics is integrated into planning and design, rather than being an afterthought or something tacked on at the very end of project planning. Such involvement at early stages is desirable.

A fundamental question in any evaluation is, "What criteria are we going to use?" The following chapter discusses some of the most common economic criteria used for watershed management decision making. Suffice it to say here that there are many different criteria that are used in most decisions.

The appraisal results can be presented in different ways depending on the nature of the planning situation. In general, it is preferable to present a ranked set of alternatives, or perhaps several rankings, utilizing different appraisal criteria. However, ultimately, the decision concerning which alternative is chosen can only be made by the responsible decision maker.

Dealing with Risk and Uncertainty in Appraisals

In most watershed projects, one faces a situation of uncertainty rather than *risk*. The distinction is simply that in the case of risk one can apply probabilities to various outcomes, while in the case of uncertainty, no such quantitative measures of probability of occurrance can be generated. In a situation of uncertainty, one can always develop some subjective probability estimates for different aspects of a project that are of interest. However, such estimates often do more harm than good, since subjectivity in the planning process should not be hidden. We suggest using a standard, straightforward sensitivity analysis, or an analysis of how the measures of project worth or desirability would change under different assumptions concerning the values of key parameters (Gregersen et al. 1987).

Table 12.2. Description of stages in the evaluation process

Stage I. Rough appraisal of the project idea

Make tentative calculation of the economic effects of the "most obvious" project alternative and the "without" alternative

Make quick assessment of financial, administrative, and political feasibility

Attempt to detect adverse environmental effects (i.e., long-term and system effects), social effects and effects on different groups concerned (i.e., distributional effects)

Consider means to mitigate negative effects

Outcome: recommendation on whether or not to continue with project idea

Performed by: project initiator, using existing available information

Stage II. More detailed appraisal for screening purposes, using the results of Stage I

Design several project alternatives that seem relevant in light of existing objectives and of the major problems arising in the environmental and social fields, as identified in Stage I

Acquire economic, financial, environmental and social expertise for the appraisal

Make calculations of the economic and financial effects of the alternatives, possibly improving upon existing forecasts and shadow prices

Identify and describe the major social effects, possibly with the help of a representative discussion group

Identify and describe the major environmental effects, particularly indirect and long-term effects

Sample public opinion on the project alternative

Exclude alternatives that are not feasible for administrative or political reasons

Establishing rankings of the remaining alternatives (as seen by various groups), possibly using the representative discussion group

Outcome: Identification of several promising project alternatives, elimination of alternatives with obvious flaws, decision on whether to continue the project

Performed by: Appraisal team in collaboration with external expertise and possibly a representative discussion group

Stage III. Thorough appraisal of the most promising project alternatives, given the results of Stage II

Redesign the project alternatives in the light of results obtained in Stages I and II

Complete the detailed analysis of economic/financial, environmental and social effects, collecting new data where necessary and utilizing the insights of a representative discussion group (Level of detail depends on the time and budget available, on the purpose of the appraisal and the nature of the project)

Complete an appraisal report on the most promising alternatives, in the form of a scenario of likely developments over time for each alternative, including the "without" alternative

Rank the most promising alternatives as seen by various groups, in collaboration with the representative discussion group, and possibly with input from local hearings

Prepare summary presentations of the scenarios and the ranking for the decision makers, public groups, financial institutions, and other authorities

Outcome: The necessary basis for choosing between project alternatives or terminating the project

Performed by: Appraisal team, in collaboration with the discussion group and whatever expertise is available given budgetary and time constraints

Source: Organization for Economic Cooperation and Development (1986), by permission.

■ RECOMMENDING ACTION

In some cases, the planner's task stops when he or she has evaluated the alternatives and the implications of risk and uncertainty for the different options. In other cases, however, the planner is asked for recommendations, both with regard to which alternative should be undertaken and to the timing and approach of implementation.

■ PLANNING AS A CONTINUOUS PROCESS

What has been described thus far is a simplified and idealized model of the watershed management planning process, where we move from problem identification through design to implementation. In fact, the planning process in most cases is an ongoing and a continuous process. As mentioned, it is an iterative process, with information concerning results of actions and emerging problems constantly being fed back into it. This information is used then to suggest incremental changes in the ongoing program or project. More formally, the process of collecting and disseminating information on ongoing operations is part of the monitoring and evaluation task referred to earlier. There is a constant feedback of information, which is synthesized and analyzed and then put into the development of alternative strategies and suggestions for action. This type of continuous process leads to a healthy interaction between planners, technical personnel, and managers of watershed management activities.

■ RESEARCH AND THE PLANNING PROCESS

Of course, one objective throughout this process is to improve our ability to respond to problems and to create and react to opportunities. There are always information gaps that hinder such improvement and which should trigger an investment in research.

To help decide what information is needed or what research should be undertaken, one can begin with a conceptual model (Fig. 12.6). That is, given the existing level of knowledge, develop a model that defines the system and specifies as output the information that is needed. After describing the conceptual model, one can then determine those processes that cannot be quantified with the existing information. This then points to gaps in knowledge and the need for research. The information that is needed to operate a predictive model that quantifies project impacts defines the monitoring or data collection needs.

Once research needs and data requirements are identified, the necessary work can be carried out. With research projects, field and other experimentation must be evaluated and used to transform the conceptual model into a workable model. The model development then must be followed with model testing and, once verified, application to actual projects. The data needed for application of the model, in turn, help to identify the type and resolution of data to be collected. Of course, more than one model normally is required to address all aspects of watershed projects, not only hydrologic data. Certainly, hydrologic models should be developed so that they can be interfaced, when necessary, with other resource and economic models.

■ SUMMARY

Planning is needed when we have to deal with interrelated events. Since land use activities on watersheds have interrelated impacts, both spatially and over time, planning of such activities and their coordination can be a productive and useful undertaking. Planning involves a number of steps, including monitoring and evaluating past activity to identify problems and opportunities; specification of objectives for overcoming problems or taking advantage of opportunities; identification of constraints;

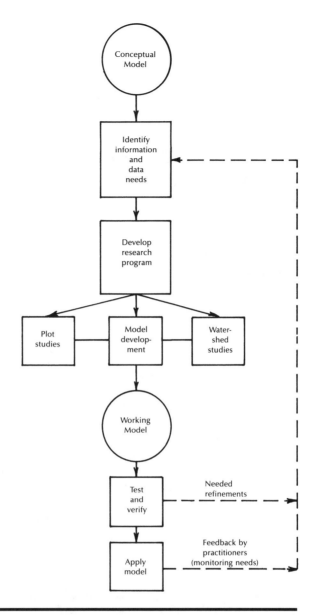

12.6. An approach for developing a watershed research program.

definition of alternative strategies to achieve objectives; identification of plans for implementing the strategies; evaluation of the likely impacts—environmental, social, and economic—of the different alternatives; and ranking of alternatives and formulation of recommendations.

At the end of this chapter, you should know:

1. Why planning is important.
2. What is involved in planning for watershed management.
3. What concrete steps need to be taken in the planning process.
4. In general, how one can go about appraising watershed management plans and projects.

CHAPTER 13

The Economics of Watershed Practices and Management

■ INTRODUCTION

While technical personnel in watershed management work predominantly with physical and biological processes, they also must have some understanding of the economic and financial implications of what they are doing. This understanding is important for those allocating budgets to watershed management activities; they want to know about the economic value of doing what is being proposed, how much it will cost, and what the cash flow (including recurrent costs) will be over time. Technical personnel also will want to understand economics so they can choose the most cost-effective or most economically efficient alternative for achieving a given purpose. This chapter explores the major economic aspects of watershed management. An overview of the ways in which economists go about valuing and analyzing the benefits and costs associated with watershed management activities is provided.

■ ECONOMIC AND FINANCIAL EFFECTS OF INTEREST TO DECISION MAKERS

Economic and financial appraisals of watershed management projects attempt to provide pertinent and timely answers to the following questions asked by decision makers:

1. Are economic benefits greater than costs for the entire project? How is that for each of its separate components?
2. What is the budget impact likely to be for the management agencies and for the private entities involved?
3. Will the project increase economic stability of the affected regions? Will it have balance-of-payments impacts?
4. Will the project be attractive to the various private entities (such as those upstream) who will have to put resources into the project to make it work? What will be the income redistribution impacts of the project?

Chapter adapted from Gregersen and Contreras (1979), Gregersen et al. (1987), and OECD (1986).

■ DISTINCTION BETWEEN ECONOMIC AND FINANCIAL APPRAISALS

The distinction between economic and financial appraisals needs to be kept in mind. The economic analysis evaluates whether or not a project yields net benefits to society as a whole. The financial analysis evaluates the actual expenditures and receipts associated with a project; it also deals with who pays and gains and, thus, with whether individuals are likely to be interested in cooperating in a project—a critical requirement to achieve sustainable projects.

The financial appraisal deals strictly with market-traded goods and services, actual money inflows and outflows, and who gets paid and who pays. Market-traded goods and services refer to those that are openly bought and sold and, therefore, have identified market prices attached to them. The economic appraisal also considers market-traded goods and services, but attempts to value them in terms of society's true willingness to pay for them. Sometimes, these values differ from market prices, as indicated later. In addition, the economic analysis includes the social benefits and costs of goods and services that are not traded in the market place; for example, it attempts to consider the values of such things as health effects, flood prevention, aesthetic benefits, wildlife preservation, etc. The major financial and economic components of an appraisal are summarized in Table 13.1.

Table 13.1. A comparison of financial and economic analysis

	Financial Analysis	Economic Analysis
Focus	Net returns to equity capital or to the private group or individual	Net returns to society
Purpose	Indication of incentive to adopt or implement	Determine if government investment is justified on economic-efficiency basis
Prices	Prices received or paid either from the market or administered	May require shadow prices, e.g., monopoly in markets, external effects, unemployed or underemployed factors, overvalued currency
Taxes	Cost of production	Transfer payment and not an economic cost
Subsidies	Source of revenue	Transfer payment and not an economic cost
Interest and loan repayment	A financial cost; decreases capital resources available	A transfer payment and not an economic cost[a]
Discount rate	Marginal cost of money; market borrowing rate; opportunities cost of funds to individual or firms	Opportunity cost of capital; social time preference rate
Income distribution	Can be measured re: net returns to individual factors of production such as land, labor, and capital but not included in financial analysis	Is not considered in economic efficiency analysis; can be done as separate analysis or weighted-efficiency analysis with multiple objectives

Source: From Gregerson et al. (1987), as adapted in part from F. J. Hitzhusen (1982).
[a]Unless external loan.

A few terms in Table 13.1 need definition. First, *economic efficiency* refers to the relationship between economic costs and benefits. Economists most often look at economic efficiency in terms of what they call "present value." This merely means that all costs and benefits are brought back to a common point in time, in this case the present, by discounting them, using an acceptable interest rate. The concept of "discounting" is discussed later in this chapter. The reader interested in more detailed discussion of economic-efficiency concepts and calculations can refer to Gregersen et al. (1987) or any standard text on economic analysis. If the present value of benefits is greater than the present value of costs for a project, and there is no cheaper way of achieving the objective being sought, then the project is considered to be an economically efficient use of resources.

A second term requiring explanation is *shadow price,* which also is discussed in greater detail later. It is a value (or "price") that is derived by economists to reflect society's true "willingness to pay" for a given good or service. *Transfer payment* refers to the fact that control over resources is transferred from one individual or group to another individual or group. Thus, a tax is a transfer payment—control over resources equal to the amount of the tax is transferred from the individual paying the tax to the government. Similarly, a subsidy is a transfer payment. Since the economic analysis looks at benefits and costs to society as a whole, without distinguishing between payments and receipts by individuals, taxes are not considered economic costs, but rather as transfer payments, which do not influence costs as such. On the other hand, in the financial analysis, a tax is a definite cost to the individual paying it and, thus, enters the calculations as such.

The *discount rate* is used to adjust or normalize costs and benefits that occur at different times so they all reflect value at the same point in time. Discounting assumes that society values a dollar of present cost or benefit more highly than a dollar of cost paid or benefit received sometime in the future. This assumption holds true in most societies. For example, when we lend money as a business, we expect to get interest as a payment for foregoing using the loaned money on consumption today. If we lend $100 at 8% interest, we expect 10 yr from now to get $100 × (1.08)^{10}, or $215—that is our original $100 plus $115 of interest. Similarly, if we borrow $100 at 8% interest, we expect to have to pay back $215, 10 yr from now. We could discount $215, 10 yr at 8% interest by using the discount formula and arrive back at $100 of present value. Present value is determined by:

$$V_p = \frac{V_f}{(1 + r)^t} \tag{13.1}$$

where V_p = present value; V_f = future value; r = discount rate; and t = time, year 1 to n.

For the above example, $215/(1.08)^{10} = $100.

We can take this discussion one step further to get to the idea of discounting as a means of equating payments (costs or benefits) occurring at different points in time. Suppose we are dealing with two projects and we can only pick one. Assume that there is one cost right now of $50 in both projects. The only other values involved are a net benefit of $180 in 5 yr for project A and a net benefit of $215 in 10 yr in project B. If time did not matter, we would pick B, since the benefit is higher. But, time does matter, so we need to compare the two benefits at some common point in time. To do this, we discount both values back to the present. We already saw that the present value of $215, 10 yr from now is $100. The present value of $180 5 yr from now is $180/(1.08)^5 = $122. So, project A turns out to be the best investment, if 8% is the relevant discount rate; it has a higher present value than B. A more detailed discussion of discounting is found in references on economic appraisals.

STEPS IN THE ECONOMIC ANALYSIS PROCESS

Economic appraisals of watershed management components or projects should include at least the following basic steps, once alternatives for achieving an objective have been identified in the planning process. For each alternative identified:

1. Define and quantify the physical inputs and outputs involved; develop tables that show inputs and outputs as they occur over time.

2. Determine unit values (both actual financial-market prices and economic values) for inputs and outputs, and develop judgements on likely changes in such values over time, for example, growth in wages or fuel costs.

3. Compare costs and benefits by calculating relevant measures of project worth and other indices and measures needed to answer relevant questions raised by decision makers; consider the implications of risk and uncertainty, for example, through a sensitivity analysis, which indicates how measures of project worth might change with changes in assumptions concerning input and/or output values.

The above steps relate to each other as shown in Figure 13.1, which outlines both

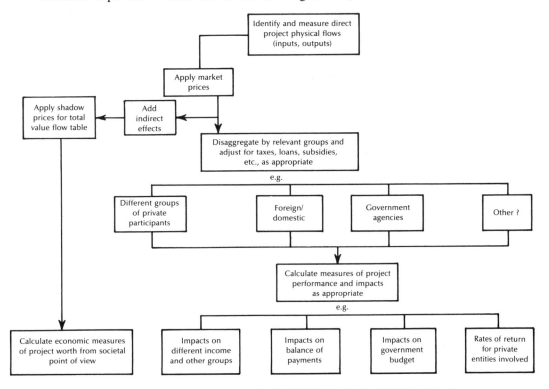

13.1. Overview of economic and financial assessment processes (OECD 1986, by permission).

the financial and the economic considerations involved in watershed management project appraisals designed to obtain the information indicated in the bottom row of the figure. The term "project" refers to both self-contained projects and watershed practices that are incorporated in other projects.

As indicated in Chapter 12, the appraisal process generally is an iterative one of successive approximations, as one passes through increasingly detailed and complex stages of evaluation. This also holds for economic and financial appraisals, which should be adapted to the stage in the planning process and the needs of the decision maker. We briefly explore each of the steps in an economic analysis of a watershed management project, and then apply the process to a case example in the following paragraphs.

■ IDENTIFYING AND QUANTIFYING PHYSICAL INPUTS AND OUTPUTS

Developing information on the relationships between inputs and outputs is one of the major tasks facing the watershed management specialists; it is also a major subject of this book. Such information, put in a specific project context, provides the basis for estimating and quantifying the inputs and outputs associated with the project being analyzed. As such, it is in this first step that the main interaction between economist and technical expert takes place.

Information Needed

In the process of identifying and defining the alternatives to be evaluated, the technical watershed management experts have to identify and quantify most of the inputs and associated outputs in physical terms. For an economic analysis, data on these inputs and outputs are needed in a form that includes information on the units in which the inputs and outputs are measured; the source of the inputs, for example, whether they are to be purchased or provided by project participants on a work-share or other basis; and the timing of when inputs are needed and outputs will occur. This information is provided in what generally is called a *physical-flow table*, which shows the flow of physical inputs and outputs over time.

The technical experts generally can meet these data needs if they are aware of them early enough in the planning process. Typical categories of inputs used are shown in Table 13.2. These inputs are used to produce various outputs related to water yield and streamflow benefits (Fig.13.2), to water-quality benefits (Fig. 13.3), and to soil-stabilization benefits (Fig. 13.4).

With-and-Without Principle

A point that has been emphasized previously and bears reemphasis here is that the input and output quantities included in a physical-flow table need to reflect the differences with and without the project. As an example, assume that two forest guards have been and will continue to be stationed on a given area to protect fragile areas from encroachment and deforestation (without project situation). With the project, the total number of guards will be increased to four. It is the additional two guards that

Table 13.2. Examples of inputs for watershed management projects

Category of Inputs	Examples—Description
Workforce	Resource managers—forest, range, watershed managers and planners
	Engineers and hydrologists—design of erosion-control structures, flood-plain analyses, water yield estimate, etc.
	Skilled labor—construction
	Unskilled labor
	Training/extension specialists to facilitate adoption of project
Equipment	Detailed listing of equipment needed for project construction and maintenance
	Schedule of needs and equipment maintenance, i.e., timing
Land	Land classified according to suitability for various uses
	Designate sensitive areas to be protected (benefits foregone)
	Areas to receive treatments followed by management
Raw materials	Utilities—energy, fuels, etc.
	Wood—construction, fence posts, etc.
	Other construction materials—concrete
	Water
Structures and civil works	Housing, roads, other facilities needed for project that are not part of project itself; if part of project, they are included in work force, materials, etc., listed above.

Source: From Gregerson et al. (1987), by permission.

should be included, not the total number of guards, since two would be there with or without the project.

Many outputs associated with watershed management projects also are in the form of losses avoided, for example, agricultural productivity losses avoided and flood or drought losses avoided. Even though these outputs often are difficult to define using the with-and-without principle, they have to be included, since they are as real and important in human value terms as increases in production.

Inputs and Outputs Related to Human Use and Value

Another point that needs to be stressed is that an economic analysis looks at inputs and outputs in relation to human value. Thus, tons of soil loss avoided is not an adequate output measure. People normally do not put value on soil loss as such; rather, such losses avoided have to be related to food losses avoided or other losses avoided that can be linked directly to human values. From the economist's point of view, discussion of input and output relationships is complete when it has established the relationship between inputs used and goods and services consumed by humans and valued by society (Figs. 13.2–13.4).

Dealing with Nonmarket, Nonquantifiable Outputs

There are some beneficial effects (or outputs) of watershed management projects that are not easily measured, such as health or aesthetic benefits. If they cannot be quantified and valued, they still should be mentioned explicitly and described to the extent possible in a final appraisal. Many of the nonquantifiable benefits relate to fundamental issues associated with the sustainability of human activity, including such

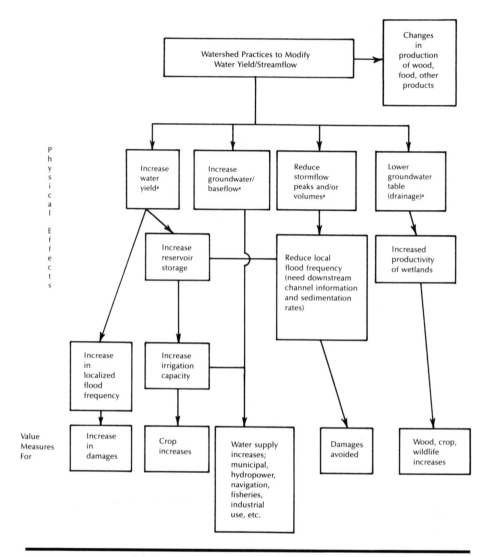

13.2. Examples of physical effects and measures of benefits from watershed practices that modify water yield and streamflow response; outputs are those "with" the project compared to "without" the project (Gregersen et al. 1987, © FAO, by permission).[a] Some practices can result in the opposite effects, resulting in different benefits or costs.

benefits as ecosystem preservation and gene pool maintenance. These relate to fundamental human needs that generally are thought to be important, but which cannot be quantified and valued, other than in an anecdotal or descriptive fashion.

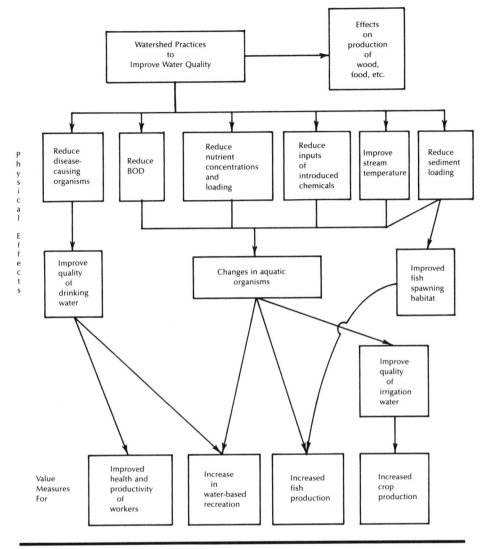

13.3. Examples of physical effects and measures of benefits from improvement of water quality; outputs are those "with" the project compared to "without" the project (Gregersen et al. 1987, © FAO, by permission).

■ VALUING INPUTS AND OUTPUTS

To answer the budget and other financial questions raised earlier, the valuation approach is straightforward: market prices are used for those inputs and outputs traded in the market. Nonmarket costs and benefits are not considered in financial analyses. Since market prices generally are determined straightforwardly, we will concentrate on the valuation of benefits and costs for the economic analysis.

Measures of Economic Value and Shadow Pricing

What is economic value in practical terms? The basic measure of value used is *willingness to pay* (WTP) (Gregersen and Contreras 1979). It is a measure that reflects society's willingness to pay for goods and services at the margin, that is, if another

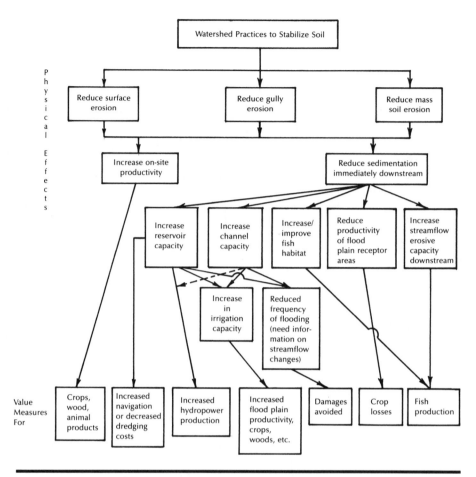

13.4. Examples of physical effects and measures of benefits from soil-stabilization practices; outputs are those "with" the project compared to "without" the project (Gregersen et al. 1987, © FAO, by permission).

unit were made available. It is a reflection of scarcity value in the sense that the more that is available, the less any individual generally is willing to pay for the good or service at the margin.

Another common measure used is *opportunity cost* (OC), which is a measure of value of the opportunity foregone when a resource is used for one thing rather than another. A typical example would be the OC of setting aside an area as a watershed protection area. The OC applied to the land set aside would be the value of the timber, minerals, grazing, and other benefits foregone. As another example, the OC of using labor to produce "X" is the value of the production foregone by not using that same labor in its next best use, producing "Y." For example, assume that a worker is producing one cord of firewood per day and selling it for $30. That worker then finds a job near home that will pay $40 a day. The wage is $40, but the OC—the value given up when the worker has to quit producing fuelwood—is only $30.

The relationship between WTP and OC is direct. The OC values are those used in measuring the WTP for the goods and services foregone. In the firewood example above, the OC was the willingness to pay for one cord of wood, assumed to be $30.

In a competitive economy with no constraints on the movement of prices, one can assume that market prices adequately reflect WTP at the margin. It is for this reason that market prices are widely used in economic as well as financial analyses. However, WTP and OC can diverge from market prices when there are price regulations, for example, price ceilings, minimum prices, or where prices are affected by subsidies or taxes (Gregersen and Contreras 1979).

When divergence between market prices and true WTP occurs, existing market prices are inadequate measures of economic value and, therefore, are "adjusted" to reflect true scarcity in the economy. These adjusted prices are called *shadow prices*. The adjustments frequently are based on observed market prices, but increase or decrease the price of the good or service to reflect true scarcity value. For example, the $30 OC from the woodcutter might be used as a shadow price for labor instead of the government set minimum daily wage of $40.

A second instance where shadow pricing is required is in the case of goods and services that do not have observable market prices. Many environmental services are of this type. In this case, the analyst attempts to derive shadow prices that reflect society's WTP for the good.

Developing Shadow Prices

A general classification of approaches to valuing inputs and outputs or deriving shadow prices or measures of WTP is shown in Figure 13.5. Most watershed management costs and benefits can be handled with one of these three approaches.

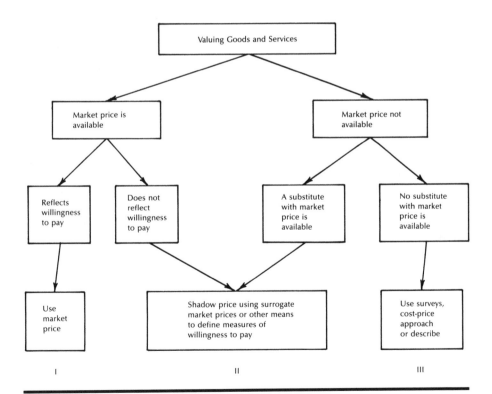

13.5. Valuation conditions and approaches (Gregersen et al. 1987, © FAO, by permission).

USING MARKET PRICES

In the case where a market price is considered to reflect adequately WTP for a good or service, the market price itself can be used in the economic analysis as a reflection of economic value at the margin (Gittinger 1982, Hufschmidt et al. 1983, Dixon and Hufschmidt 1986). A general guideline would be to use the market price for a good or service, unless there is an obvious reason to believe that it is significantly distorted. There are a number of reasons for this suggestion:

1. Market prices often are accepted more readily by decision makers than are artificial values derived by the analyst.
2. Market prices generally are easy to observe, both at a single point in time and over time.
3. Market prices reflect the decisions of many buyers, not just the judgement of one analyst or administrator (as in the case of subsidized prices).
4. The procedures for calculating shadow prices are imperfect and, therefore, estimates can (in certain cases) introduce larger discrepancies than the simple use of even imperfect market prices.

USING SURROGATE MARKET PRICES

In the case of costs and benefits not themselves valued in the market but for which clear substitutes exist in the market, one can use the market prices of the substitutes to develop surrogate or proxy values for the costs or benefits being valued.

For example, as mentioned earlier, there is no market for the soil eroded from uplands and the sediment deposited on lowlands. Values can be placed on these effects by several different means. One approach examines the market prices of eroded uplands or silted lowlands, and then compares them to market prices for other comparable land unaffected by erosion. In this with-and-without analysis, the difference in land values acts as a surrogate or proxy price for the damage caused by erosion. In another approach, the market value of crop losses due to erosion is used to value the cost of erosion, and the value of changes in production on the fields on which sediment is deposited is used to measure the value of the soil moved through the erosion process.

Surrogate market approaches also can be used to develop appropriate shadow prices when market prices are felt to be distorted. For example, a common shadow-pricing problem is that of labor for a development project in an area of high unemployment. If the project generates new employment and if there is a government-mandated minimum wage in the economy, then that minimum wage is not likely to reflect adequately opportunity cost for the use of the previously unemployed labor. The minimum wage will be higher than the true opportunity cost of employing additional workers. In such cases, one can make an estimate of what the unemployed were producing, such as home repairs, growing food for the family, taking odd jobs as they arise, while out of a fulltime job. The value of this production then is taken as the shadow price or measure of economic value for the labor, as in the woodcutter example above.

USING HYPOTHETICAL VALUATION APPROACHES

In some cases where there are no possibilities to derive acceptable market price measures of value, one can derive some value information through surveys or through expert judgement. Further, it is possible to derive minimum values for some benefits through analysis of the cost of producing or deriving them. This is commonly called a *cost-price analysis,* since it uses costs to derive some information on which to judge minimum value of benefits that would be required to break even with costs. It always should be borne in mind that such values represent only a lower boundary on the value of the good or service in question. In other words, the resulting value represents the minimum value the decision maker would have to place on the output to ensure a break-even relationship between economic costs and benefits.

Because either surrogate or hypothetical market prices do not rely on market prices, the results have to be interpreted carefully. For project analyses, these approaches should be used only when market-based approaches are impractical or impossible. Of course, this type of valuation approach is the ultimate basis for political decisions. The decision maker makes the judgement that the value of certain watershed management outputs is greater or less than the resources needed to produce them. This type of decision is made every day without any quantitative analysis of monetary values. Frequently, this form of valuation is implicit and never described explicitly.

One of the above three approaches provides a means of generating at least some information about the monetary value of the benefits listed in the bottom rows of Figures 13.2–13.4. Specific valuation methods and techniques appropriate for each category of watershed management costs and benefits are discussed by Gregersen et al. (1987) and others.

COMPARING COSTS AND BENEFITS: MEASURES OF PROJECT WORTH

Once the physical-flow tables and the unit-value assumptions are clearly formulated, then it generally is a straightforward task to bring the two together to develop two basic tables used in financial and economic analyses, namely, the *cash-flow table* for financial analyses and the *economic value–flow table* for the economic analyses. The cash-flow table shows the flows of actual money expenditures and receipts over the life of the project, generally by 1-yr intervals. The economic value–flow table shows the flows of economic costs and benefits (for example, shadow-priced market and nonmarket benefits and costs) over the life of the project.

The reason for developing the economic value-flow and cash-flow tables is to organize information so that it can be used to evaluate and compare project alternatives. At least two such evaluation questions are always of interest to decision makers. Is the proposed project worth doing? If so, is the project better than other alternative uses of available scarce resources?

Specific Questions of Interest

Five questions concerning costs and benefits generally are relevant in an appraisal of a watershed management project or set of activities. These questions, applied to each project alternative being evaluated, are as follows:

Questions to be answered using market prices only
1. What is the budget impact likely to be for the agencies and private entities involved?
2. Will the project be attractive to all the private entities (including upstream landowners) who will have to put resources into the project to make it work?
3. What are the income-distribution impacts of the watershed management activities proposed for the project?

Questions to be answered using both market and shadow prices
4. Are economic benefits greater than costs, that is, is the project an economically efficient use of resources?
5. Will the project increase economic stability of the affected region? Will it have balance-of-payments impacts?

Analyses Using Only Market Prices

Although market prices sometimes are distorted due to government interventions, monopoly elements, or other factors, they do affect various project decisions directly; thus, the appraisal of any watershed management project will require some analyses based strictly on actual prices paid or received for marketed goods and services.

BUDGET IMPLICATIONS OF PUBLIC SECTOR CASH FLOW

A treasury normally requires budget analyses using market prices. It will require an analysis of a proposed project in terms of what is taken into the treasury and what goes out as public expenditure. Since most watershed management projects (from the government perspective) mainly involve costs with few monetary returns, the budget analysis usually will show a negative cash flow. In some cases, various mitigation or preventive costs that are avoided because of the project (such as channel or canal dredging, water purification, or reconstruction of flood-damaged infrastructure) will be counted as "benefits."

The budget analysis using market prices is useful for indicating the financial resources required from the treasury to carry out the proposed project. Since it is not an economic analysis, it does not provide enough information on the benefit or value of the project for a decision maker to make an informed decision with regard to the merit of the project. This decision requires an economic analysis, described below.

FINANCIAL IMPLICATIONS FOR PRIVATE ENTITIES

A market-based, *discounted* cash-flow analysis provides enough information to private entities (for example, a farmer or a firm) to enable them to make decisions. Since private entities correctly are concerned with their actual costs and their returns, they should use market-based prices. Since they also are concerned with when costs and benefits occur, they should use discounting in their cash-flow analysis, so they can better compare alternatives in present value or comparable terms.

The results of the financial analyses are crucial for three main reasons: (1) the planner or analyst has to know whether or not the project or activities being proposed will be attractive to those private entities that will have to put resources into the project to make it work; (2) the information from the cash-flow analysis can be used to develop information needed to design appropriate incentive or tax packages to help ensure project implementation; and (3) the same information is needed for budgeting purposes.

In developing appropriate incentive packages, a number of institutional issues also need to be considered, including those related to land tenure and to distribution of costs among regions. The upstream land users generally incur the costs of watershed management, while the downstream population benefits; thus, some transfer mechanism may be needed. Absorptive capacity of government and local institutions to handle increases in investment also needs to be considered.

INCOME-REDISTRIBUTION IMPLICATIONS

Most watershed management projects have income-redistribution effects—hiring labor, buying inputs and land, and paying administrative expenses. In addition, if the project has important productivity effects, these also are translated into income when goods or services are bought, sold, or consumed.

Decision makers frequently are concerned with the income-redistribution effects of a project, especially if people living in the project area are poor or politically sensitive. The analyst can estimate the amount of new money going into a region because of the project; it also is possible to determine who likely will be the primary recipients of these new resources. Note that this analysis examines the benefits and costs of the project in market-price terms. These prices include subsidies (a return) and taxes (a cost). As an example, laborers get wages in money, not the shadow price of labor that may be used in the economic analysis. Since laborers also spend money, not "shadow money," it is appropriate to use market prices in analyzing income-redistribution implications.

As such, the market-based analyses describe the actual flows of money and market-traded goods and services in the economy and in the project area. They do not tell whether the project is economically efficient, equitable, or desirable, nor do they say anything about external effects of the actions of decision makers. That is the appropriate role for economic analyses and political considerations.

Questions Requiring Use of Both Market and Shadow Prices

Some of the questions of interest to decision makers take on a more social context that requires going beyond the mere consideration of market prices and market-traded goods and services. These questions relate to the basic economic efficiency of alternatives, for example, the relationship between the total costs to society and the total benefits it receives from investment in a given project or set of activities. They also relate to questions regarding economic stability and balance-of-payments effects.

ECONOMIC-EFFICIENCY ANALYSIS

Once the two value-flow tables have been set up, as discussed earlier, the streams of benefits and costs can be evaluated to compare alternative projects. Economic analysis is a systematic way to do this comparison. In practice, there are three principal value measures used, namely *net present worth, economic rate of return,* and *benefit-cost ratio;* all three are calculated using the same cost and benefit data and assumptions.

Net Present Worth (NPW). Also known as *net present value (NPV), NPW* is based on the desire to determine the present value of net benefits from a project. If the goal of the analysis is to determine the total *net* contribution (net benefits) of a project to society, the *NPW* criterion provides a consistent one for ranking alternatives. The formula for the *NPW* calculation is:

$$NPW = \sum_{t=1}^{n} \left[\frac{B_t - C_t}{(1 + r)^t} \right] \tag{13.2}$$

where B_t, C_t = benefit or cost in year t.

Economic Rate of Return (ERR). The *ERR* frequently is used to evaluate projects. Unlike the *NPW* or the benefit-cost ratio, the *ERR* does not use a predetermined discount rate. Rather, the *ERR* is the discount rate that sets the present value of benefits just equal to the present value of costs. That is, the *ERR* is the discount rate, r, such that:

$$\sum_{t=1}^{n} \left[\frac{B_t}{(1 + r)^t} \right] = \sum_{t=1}^{n} \left[\frac{C_t}{(1 + r)^t} \right] \tag{13.3}$$

or

$$\sum_{t=1}^{n} \left[\frac{B_t - C_t}{(1 + r)^t} \right] = 0 \tag{13.4}$$

The *ERR* calculation requires the same basic information as is used in a *NPW* calculation. Although the discount rate is not prescribed but is determined as a result of the calculation, this does not eliminate the use of a reference discount rate or financial interest rate. In an analysis using the *ERR* measure, the calculated *ERR* is compared to some reference discount rate to decide whether or not the project is economically efficient. For example, if the *ERR* calculated is 15% and the opportunity cost of project funds is 10%, the project would be economically attractive. However, if project funds "cost" 18%, the project would be financially unattractive.

Benefit-Cost Ratio (B/C Ratio). The ratio simply compares the present value of benefits to the present value of costs:

$$B/C \ Ratio = \frac{\sum_{t=1}^{n} \left[\frac{B_t}{(1 + r)^t} \right]}{\sum_{t=1}^{n} \left[\frac{C_t}{(1 + r)^t} \right]} \tag{13.5}$$

If the *B/C Ratio* is greater than 1, the present value of benefits are greater than the present value of costs and the project is an economically efficient use of resources, assuming there is no lower-cost means for achieving the same benefits.

As should be clear by now, these three measures of project worth are closely related; this is not surprising, since they use the same data. This relationship can be shown as follows (Gittenger 1982):

NPW = (Present Value of benefits) − (Present Value of costs)

The ERR is equal to that discount rate which results in:

(Present Value of benefits) = (Present Value of costs)

$$BC\ Ratio = \frac{\text{Present Value of benefits}}{\text{Present Value of costs}}$$

This symmetry naturally extends to the results of the calculations. The values of these three measures have the following relationships:

If $NPW > 0$, then $ERR \geq r$ and $B/C > 1$

If $NPW < 0$, then $ERR < r$ and $B/C < 1$

If $NPW = 0$, then $ERR = r$ and $B/C = 1$

In spite of the fact that all three measures use the same basic data and have a symmetry in their results, it is possible that when a set of alternative projects is examined, different evaluation criteria can give different project rankings. This raises the question of *which* criterion ($NPW, ERR,$ or B/C Ratio) to use.

Deciding Which Criterion to Use. Maximum total NPW is the *economic* objective (the "objective function") we seek for investment of available scarce resources. Accordingly, NPW always must be a part of any choice criterion or ranking scheme for accepting or rejecting projects or project increments (Dixon and Hufschmidt 1986).

The ERR and B/C Ratio measures give no indication of the magnitude of the net benefits. As a result, reliance on either ERR or B/C Ratio can result in total net benefits (and as a consequence, welfare) from the project or projects selected being smaller than by using the NPW criterion.

In cases where projects or project increments are not mutually exclusive and there are no constraints on costs, all projects (or increments) that yield positive NPW can be accepted. In cases where not all projects or increments can be selected because of a cost constraint, the goal is to select that set of projects or increments that yields the greatest *total NPW*.

Gittinger (1982) made a comparative analysis of these three measures of present value and presented the results in tabular form. In Table 13.3, an adaptation of the Gittinger table, we distinguish between project selection or ranking under three conditions: independent projects with no constraints on costs, independent projects with an overall constraint on costs, and mutually exclusive projects. For independent projects in the absence of cost constraints (highly unrealistic case), each of the three measures can be used to select or reject projects, because each distinguishes between efficient and inefficient use of resources (Table 13.3).

Table 13.3. Comparison of the three measures of present value

Selection or Ranking Rule for:	NPW	ERR	B/C Ratio
Independent Projects			
No constraint on costs	Select all projects with $NPW > 0$; project ranking not required	Select all projects with ERR greater than cut-off rate of return; project ranking not required	Select all projects with $B/C > 1$; project ranking not required
Constraint on costs	Not suitable for ranking projects	Ranking all projects by ERR may give incorrect solution	Ranking all projects by B/C Ratio where C is defined constrained cost, will always give correct ranking
Mutually Exclusive Projects (within a given budget)	Select alternative with largest NPW	Selection of alternative with highest ERR may give incorrect result	Selection of alternative with highest B/C Ratio may give incorrect ranking
Discount Rate	Appropriate discount rate must be adopted	No discount rate required, but reference rate of return must be adopted	Appropriate discount rate must be adopted

Source: Adapted from Gittinger (1982) and Dixon and Hufschmidt (1986).

However, when there is a constraint on costs for independent projects, such that not all economically justifiable projects can be selected, only the *B/C* measure can give correct rankings for project selection. Assume there are five (A–E) independent projects available, and assume a cost constraint of $300,000 (Table 13.4). Ranking by *NPW,* one would choose project A with the highest *NPW* and just use up the available budgeted cost. However, ranking on the basis of *B/C,* one would choose B, C, E, then D. The reason why *NPW* does not work for ranking projects when costs are constrained is that *NPW* says nothing about returns per unit of scarce factor, in this case cost or budget. For the *B/C* ranking to be correct, it must be formulated so that the costs that are constrained appear in the denominator of the ratio.

Table 13.4. Comparing use of NPW and B/C for ranking projects

	Cost	Benefit	*NPW*	*B/C*
A	300,000	310,000	10,000	1.03
B	100,000	108,000	8000	1.08
C	100,000	108,000	8000	1.08
D	50,000	52,000	2000	1.04
E	50,000	53,000	3000	1.06

For mutually exclusive projects (such as two or more projects that would use the same site), the *NPW* measure is the only one that will always lead to the correct selection. Again, assume that alternatives A–D (Table 13.4) are mutually exclusive alternatives and the only ones available for a given area; the budget constraint is still $300,000, which has to be spent in the area. It is evident in this case that choice A maximizes *NPW* on the area. If the budget were reduced to $100,000, then either B or C would be the logical choice; A is no longer an alternative, given the cost constraint. Now, suppose that all the *NPW*s in the table were calculated at a discount rate of 10% and assume that you could borrow funds up to $300,000 at 8%. Then project A would be chosen for this particular area. In all of the above cases, "correct" selection or ranking is defined as the one that yields the largest *NPW* when one uses up the constrained factor, that is, budget, land, and so forth.

Discount Rate for Public Evaluations. Whereas in financial analysis an interest rate that reflects market rates for investment and working capital usually is used and, hence, is sensitive to inflation rates, the discount rate used by governments in an economic analysis usually is not readily observable in the economy. Economists have developed a number of approaches for determining and justifying a discount rate for economic analysis. These include the opportunity cost of capital and the social rate of time preference (Baumol 1968, Gittinger 1982, Hufschmidt et al. 1983, Dixon and Hufschmidt 1986).

The actual rate used in an economic analysis will be country specific, and it should be established as a matter of government policy. Important factors governing the choice of rate will be the opportunity cost of capital, or the cost of money to the government, and the government's current view of the consumption and investment mix of the private sector in relation to its concerns for future generations. However, whatever rate is selected, it should be used to evaluate all projects on a relative basis. A comparison of projects evaluated with different discount rates is untenable logically.

Stability and Balance-of-Payments Assessments

One of the questions of relevance to decision makers concerns the effect of watershed management projects on regional economic stability and balance of payments. These concerns, while real enough, do not fit into a benefit-cost analysis. They are best answered separately and then presented along with the economic-efficiency analysis.

REGIONAL IMPACTS OF PROJECTS

Decision makers frequently are concerned about the regional economic impacts of projects, which are related to the income-distribution effects described earlier. Whenever there is a change because of a project (new jobs, new crop areas, increased crop yields), the analyst must determine what is the *incremental* net benefit of the project, not the gross benefit. For example, new jobs may be created by a hillside stabilization program. The appropriate measure of economic impact is not the total wages paid to laborers, but the total *minus* the amount they would have earned if the new jobs were not created (their opportunity cost). Similar care must be taken with the use of land or capital resources.

With watershed management projects, the following points illustrate the types of potential regional impacts:

1. Job creation in construction and maintenance of management structures and facilities.
2. Job creation through new or expanded production in agriculture, fisheries, or transportation.
3. Increased productivity of existing cultivated areas and fishery resources.
4. New production on previously unused fields or water resources.
5. Forestry or fuelwood-related job creation and increased production.
6. Secondary impacts of the previously listed changes (secondary impacts have to be handled very conservatively and carefully to avoid double counting).

While the actual elements in a regional-impact analysis will vary from case to case, such an analysis will be useful to decision makers when alternative projects are being considered.

On a larger scale, a regional analysis should address the question of economic stability and likely changes as a result of the project. One would expect that a successful watershed management project would help to stabilize production (agricultural, forestry, fishery) and, thus, incomes in the region. There also may be project-induced migration within the region and between regions. These effects are handled both quantitatively and qualitatively. Schuster (1980) discusses techniques for determining magnitudes of regional distributional impacts in the case of forestry projects.

BALANCE-OF-PAYMENTS EFFECTS

In general, an individual watershed management project would not be expected to have major balance-of-payments (BOP) effects. Other than imported inputs and their valuation, the most likely BOP effects will be through associated production activities. Taken together, a set of watershed management projects can have major BOP effects. For example, increased exports of agricultural, fish, and forestry products resulting from increased site productivity due to a watershed management project can affect the BOP, either through exports or substitution of domestic production for imports.

The two main concerns in valuing BOP effects are the correct determination of the actual effect of the project (using a with-and-without analysis in an opportunity cost framework), and the use of the correct shadow price for foreign exchange. For example, as a result of improved watershed management, land is shifted from production of cotton to rice. Both commodities presently are exported. The BOP effect, thus, is the value of increased rice exports less the value of decreased cotton exports, both valued using the correct shadow price for foreign exchange.

Assessment of Nonmonetary Benefits and Costs

In spite of all of the advances made in economic valuation of nonmarketed goods and services, there are always some effects of projects that are impossible to either quantify or value. For example, the construction of some capital infrastructure, such as a dam, a flume, or a power transmission line, may have a negative aesthetic impact on an upland area: the view is not as natural or pleasing as it previously was. This kind of *aesthetic* effect is almost impossible to quantify—there are no accepted units of measurement or value for scenic beauty. Similarly, a project that would require a change in the life-style of a traditional community will have a *cultural* impact. These impacts also are difficult to quantify.

In such cases, effects that cannot be quantified or monetized should still be recognized and described, kept within the analysis, included in a qualitative fashion, and presented to the decision maker. In this way, the effects will not be ignored, even though they cannot be entered directly into the economic analysis.

■ SUMMARY

Watershed management primarily involves physical activities—both structural and nonstructural; however, the impacts (both positive and negative) of such activities are felt in terms of economic and social welfare. For example, there could be an increase or decrease over time in agricultural and livestock production and, thus, food availability could increase or decline, lives could be saved by prevention of flooding, or spending scarce resources on dredging reservoirs and channels could be avoided. Therefore, it is necessary for those working in watershed management activities to understand the broad economic impacts associated with their activities and to understand how one goes about evaluating or appraising those impacts in economic terms, both in uplands and in downstream areas.

This chapter provides an overview of the economics of watershed management by introducing terms, concepts, and approaches used in analyzing the economics of watershed management projects and activities. The steps involved in an economic appraisal of a watershed management project include:

1. Identify and quantify the physical inputs and outputs involved.
2. Define the unit values that should be attached to those inputs and outputs.
3. Compare the costs and benefits involved.

These steps should provide answers to questions related to the soundness of a proposed project or set of activities from economic and financial points of view. Information is provided on the budget implications of the project; the impacts of the project on economic stability, foreign-exchange balances, and employment; and the attractiveness of the project to the public and private entities that will be involved.

When you are finished with this chapter you should understand:

1. The general nature of an economic analysis.
2. The specific ways in which this process is applied to watershed management activities and projects.
3. The ways in which economists go about the task of developing an economic evaluation.

PART 4

Special Topics

■ Part 4 supplements the earlier parts of the book with chapters 14, 15, 16, and 17, entitled Snow Hydrology, Watershed Management Considerations for Engineering Applications, Water Harvesting, and Hydrologic Methods, respectively. Chapters 14 and 16 are of interest for specific courses and geographic areas. Because many watershed management practices involve nonstructural (vegetative) and structural (engineering) measures, Chapter 15 was written to highlight some of the key interrelationships that are important for resource development. Particular emphasis is placed on watershed management–reservoir management relationships. Chapter 17 describes many of the analytical tools that are available to provide hydrologic information that is needed to plan and implement watershed management projects and programs. Chapter 18 presents basic statistical methods.

Snowmelt runoff from a ponderosa pine watershed in northern Arizona.

Table 14.1. Terminology used in snow hydrology

Term	Definition
Snowpack	Mixture of ice crystals, air, impurities, and liquid water if melting
Snowpack density	Weight per unit volume; for pure ice = 0.92 g/cm³, for a snowpack, it can vary from less than 0.10 g/cm³ to over 0.40 g/cm³
Snow water equivalent (*WE*)	The weight of snow expressed as the depth of liquid water over a unit of area = (density) × (depth)
Cold snow	Snow with a temperature below 0°C
Temperature deficit (T_s)	Snowpack temperature below 0°C
Thermal deficiency	Heat required to raise the temperature of 1 cm *WE* of cold snow by 1°C (the heat capacity of water is 1 cal/g/1°C, for ice it is 0.5 cal/g/1°C, and for air it is 0.24 cal/g/1°C)
Liquid water-holding capacity	Analogous to soil moisture; it is the water held against gravity on snow crystals and in capillary channels in the snowpack (*f*); it varies with density, crystal size and shape, and capillarity; $f = 0.03$ on average, generally less than 0.05; at 0°C, $f = 1 - B$ (*B* is thermal quality defined below)
Ripe snowpack	Snowpack that has reached its maximum liquid water-holding capacity against gravity; the snowpack temperature is isothermal at 0°C; it is primed to transmit liquid water
Cold content	Heat required to raise the temperature of a cold snow layer of depth *D* to 0°C, $= 0.5 \, \rho \, DT_s$
Latent heat of fusion	Heat required to change 1 g of dry snow at 0°C to a liquid state without changing the temperature, or changing from liquid to solid at 0°C = 80 Cal/g = 80 cal/cm³
Water equivalent of cold content (W_c)	$W_c = 0.5 \, (WE) \, T_s/80 = (WE) \, T_s/160$
Thermal quality (*B*)	The ratio of heat required to melt the snow to the heat required to melt an equal mass of pure ice at 0°C (*B*); for a wet, melting snow, $B < 1$; for a dry snow at 0°C, $B = 1$; for a cold dry snow, $B > 1$

Snow Hydrology

INTRODUCTION

Snowpacks represent major sources of fresh water for many regions in the world. Snowpacks that accumulate in mountains, particularly in semiarid or arid climates, are often the primary source of fresh water for downstream reservoirs. Runoff from snowmelt is not always beneficial to downstream communities, however, and can cause damaging floods when melt occurs too fast or when flood-level flows are sustained over long periods of time. One-third of the water used for irrigation in the world comes from snowpacks. It is not surprising then that water resource managers and hydrologists are interested in snow hydrology.

The distribution of snowfall and the ripening and melting processes of snow are particularly affected by forest vegetation. Changes in forest cover, therefore, can result in changes in the above processes. Some changes in forest cover occur inadvertently as a result of management activities; however, sometimes forest cover can be manipulated to achieve specific water resource objectives. Watershed managers in temperate climates, where snow is important, need to be able to recognize how their management affects snowpack accumulation and snowmelt runoff. Definitions of terminology in snow hydrology are given in Table 14.1

MEASUREMENT OF THE SNOW RESOURCE

Snowfall can be measured with the standard rain gauges discussed previously, but it is more difficult. With its low density and high surface area, snow is more susceptible to wind, which results in rain gauges catching less than the true snowfall. In addition, snow tends to cap or bridge over the orifice of rain gauges and clings to the sides of containers. Since it usually remains on the ground for some period of time, snow does not need to be measured as it falls. The most common method of determining the amount of snow is to measure its depth on the ground and, if possible, its weight. Such measurements can be made adjacent to standard rain gauges or they can be made in surveys over an area in which several measurements are taken over time.

Snow Surveys

Snow surveys are used to estimate the amount of water in the snowpack and the condition of the snowpack during periods of accumulation and melt on courses consisting of a few to 20 or more sampling points along a transect. These surveys are conducted during periods that normally have maximum snow accumulation (March 1 or 15 or April 1 in the western United States).

Snow depth and snow water equivalent are measured in a snow course using cylindrical tubes with a cutting edge. These tubes are graduated in inches or centimeters on the outside of the tube to measure depth. Large-diameter tubes (3 in.) are used in areas with shallow snowpacks. Smaller-diameter tubes, such as the Mount Rose sampler (1.49 in. diameter), are preferable for measuring snowpacks that exceed 3 ft in depth.

The manner in which a snow course is laid out depends on how the survey information is to be used. If snow surveys are to provide an index of snow water equivalent to predict snowmelt runoff volumes, they do not necessarily need to represent the average of the watershed in question. Instead, a snow course can be located in an accessible area that is flat, is protected from wind, and that has a deep snowpack even in the drier years. The volume of snowmelt runoff is then estimated with a regression relationship based on selected snow course data. The regression equations developed are of the general form:

$$\text{Spring snowmelt runoff volume} = PI - LI \tag{14.1}$$

where PI = indexes of precipitation inputs, such as snow water equivalent, spring rainfall, or fall rainfall; and LI = indexes of losses, for example, evapotranspiration estimates.

Often, multiple regression equations are developed that have the following components:

$$Y = a + b_1X_1 + b_2X_2 + b_3X_3 - b_4X_4 \ldots + b_nX_n \tag{14.2}$$

where Y = volume of snowmelt runoff; X_1 = maximum snow water equivalent (based on snow surveys data for April 1, for example); X_2 = fall precipitation (October–November rainfall); X_3 = spring rainfall (April), X_4 = pan evaporation for October–April; and b_i = regression coefficients.

This approach has been used widely by the U.S. Soil Conservation Service in the western United States.

If the purpose of a snow survey is to provide an estimate of the mean depth of snow water equivalent over a watershed (for example, as input data for a hydrologic model), the snow course should be designed differently than explained above. In this case, the snow course should represent the spatial distribution of snow over the watershed area. The same principles discussed in estimating the mean depth of rainfall for a watershed (see Chapter 2) should be applied in such instances.

Other Methods

The availability of telemetry and satellite systems has expanded the methods of measuring snowpacks. Telemetry has been particularly useful to transmit data collected by means of pressure, or snow, pillows located in remote sites. As the name implies, such pillows or metal plates measure the weight of snow, usually by means of pressure transducers. The weight of the snowpack is converted into units of snow water equivalent. A network called SNOTEL (*Sno*w Data *Tele*metry System), developed in the western United States, uses radio telemetry to transmit snow pillow data, temperature, and other climatological data from remote mountain areas. These data complement snow course data and have the advantage that they represent current conditions on the watershed. Hydrologists can retrieve data from the system any time they wish. For example, conditions that lead to rapid snowmelt may be detected as they occur. These often are called "real-time" predictions.

Satellite imagery can be useful to assess the extent of snow-covered areas, particularly for large river basins. Water resource managers sometimes develop relationships between the percentage of area in a watershed that is covered with snow and streamflow due to snowmelt. As satellite technology improves, there will be opportunities for relating many types of snowpack spectral characteristics with snowpack condition, melt, and other related processes.

■ SNOW ACCUMULATION AND MELT

Generally, the deposition of snow over a watershed is affected by the same factors affecting rainfall (see Chapter 2). On a microscale, snow accumulation can be quite variable as it is influenced by wind, local topography, forest vegetation, and other physical obstructions such as fences. Newly fallen snow usually has a low density, often assumed to be 0.1 g/cm³, which makes it susceptible to wind action; it also has a high albedo, ranging from 80 to 95%. Between snowfall and snowmelt, several changes take place within the snowpack. These changes, called *snowpack metamorphism,* are largely the result of energy exchange; are associated with the ripening process; and involve changes in the snow structure, density, temperature, albedo, and liquid water content.

Snowpack Metamorphism

A snowpack undergoes many changes from the time snow falls until snowmelt occurs. Snow particles, which are initially crystalline, become more granular as wind, energy, and liquid water affect the snowpack. Snow crystals become displaced and the snowpack settles, resulting in an increase in density. Alternate thawing and freezing at the snow surface, followed by periods of snowfall, can cause ice planes or lenses to form within a snowpack. In addition, the temperature of the snowpack changes in response to long-term sequences of either warm or cold weather. As warmer weather dominates, there is a progressive warming of the snowpack. Of course, the snow can never reach a temperature in excess of 0°C. The albedo of snow diminishes over the time that the pack is exposed to atmospheric deposition of forest litter, dust, and rain. As indicated earlier, a new snowpack can have an albedo in excess of 90%; an older, ripe snowpack can have an albedo value of less than 45%.

The above discussion gives a sense of what snowpack metamorphism entails. What is needed, however, is a way to quantify snowpack metamorphism so that we can determine when a snowpack is "ready" to yield liquid water. A snowpack is considered to be ripe when it is primed to produce runoff, that is, when the temperature of the snowpack is 0°C and the liquid water–holding capacity of the snowpack has been reached. Any additional input of either energy or liquid water will result in a corresponding amount of liquid water being released from the bottom of the pack.

COLD CONTENT

The energy needed to raise the temperature of a snowpack to 0°C per unit area is called the *cold content*. It is convenient to express the cold content in the equivalent depth of water entering the snowpack at the surface as rain, which upon freezing will raise the temperature of the pack to 0°C by releasing the heat of fusion (80 cal/g). Taking the specific heat of ice to be 0.5 cal/g/°C, the following relationship is obtained (Ex. 14.1):

$$W_c = \frac{\rho D T_s}{160} = \frac{(WE)T_s}{160} \tag{14.3}$$

where W_c = cold content in equivalent depth of liquid water (cm); ρ = density of snow (g/cm³); D = depth of snow (cm); WE = snow water equivalent (cm); and T_s = average temperature deficit of the snowpack below 0°C.

EXAMPLE 14.1

Cold content calculation for a snowpack where the snowpack depth = 100 cm, the snow density = 0.1 g/cc, and T_s = −10°C

Because the heat of fusion equals 80 cal/g and the specific heat of ice equals 0.5 cal/g/°C, the amount of energy required to bring the temperature of the snowpack up to 0°C can be determined by:

$$WE = (0.1 \text{ g/cm}^3)(100 \text{ cm}) = 10 \text{ g/cm}^2$$

To raise the temperature of the pack (which at −10°C would be solid ice) by just 1°C would require:

$$(10 \text{ g/cm}^2)(0.5 \text{ cal/g/°C}) = 5 \text{ cal/cm}^2/°C$$

To raise the temperature of the snowpack from −10°C to 0°C then would require:

$$[0°C - (-10°C)](5 \text{ cal/cm}^2/°C) = 50 \text{ cal/cm}^2$$

To express the energy requirement in terms of equivalent inches of snowmelt:

$$(50 \text{ cal/cm}^2)(1 \text{ g/80 cal})(1 \text{ cm}^3/\text{g}) = 0.63 \text{ cm}$$

Cold content could have been calculated directly by:

$$W_c = \frac{(0.1)(100)(10)}{160} = 0.63 \text{ cm}$$

LIQUID WATER–HOLDING CAPACITY

A snowpack can retain a certain amount of liquid water similar to a soil. This liquid water occurs as hygroscopic water, capillary water, and gravitational water. The *liquid water–holding capacity* of a snowpack (W_g) is calculated by:

$$W_g = f(WE + W_c) \tag{14.4}$$

where f = hygroscopic and capillary water held per unit mass of snow after gravity drainage, usually varying from 0.03 to 0.05 (g/g); WE = snow water equivalent (cm); and W_c = cold content (cm).

TOTAL RETENTION STORAGE

The total amount of melt or rain that must be added to a snowpack before liquid water is released is the *total retention storage* (S_f):

$$S_f = W_c + f(WE + W_c) \tag{14.5}$$

When the total retention storage is satisfied, the snowpack is said to be ripe.

Snowmelt

Once the snowpack is ripe, any additional input of energy will result in melt water being released from the bottom of the snowpack. The main sources of energy for snowmelt are essentially the same as those for evapotranspiration. To calculate snowmelt, therefore, requires either an energy budget approach or some empirical approximation of energy available for snowmelt.

ENERGY BUDGET OF A SNOWPACK

The energy that is available either to ripen a snowpack or to melt snow can be determined with an *energy budget* analysis. The energy budget can be used to determine the available energy for ripening or melt, as follows:

$$M = I_s(1 - \alpha) + I_a - I_g + H + G + LE + H_r \tag{14.6}$$

where M = energy available for snowmelt (cal/cm²); I_s = total incoming shortwave (solar) radiation (cal/cm²); α = albedo of snowpack (fraction); I_a = incoming longwave radiation (cal/cm²); I_g = outgoing longwave radiation (cal/cm²); H = convective transfer of sensible heat at the snowpack surface (cal/cm²), can be + or − as f (gradient); G = conduction at the snow-ground interface (cal/cm²); LE = flow of latent heat [condensation (+), evaporation or sublimation (−)] (cal/cm²); H_r = advected heat from rain or fog (cal/cm²).

If all the above energy components could be measured, snowmelt could be determined directly. The amount of snow that melts from a given quantity of heat energy depends on the condition of the snowpack, which can be expressed in terms of its thermal quality. *Thermal quality* is the ratio of heat energy required to melt 1 g of snow to that required to melt 1 g pure ice at 0°C, and is expressed as a percentage (Ex. 14.2). A thermal quality less than 100% indicates the snowpack is at 0°C and contains liquid water; conversely, a thermal quality greater than 100% indicates a snowpack at less than 0°C with no liquid water. Snowmelt, therefore, can be determined by:

$$M = \frac{\text{total energy (cal/cm}^2)}{B80 \text{ cal/g}} \tag{14.7}$$

where M = snowmelt (cm); and B = thermal quality, expressed as a fraction.

Under most conditions, total energy cannot be measured. Therefore, approximations, such as the generalized snowmelt equations or the Temperature Index Method (Degree-day Method) discussed later in the chapter, normally are used to estimate snowmelt.

EXAMPLE 14.2

Determining snow thermal quality by the calorimeter method, when the snow depth = 60 cm, the volume of snow sample taken = 15,000 cm³, and the weight of sample = 2000 g.

The above sample was placed in a thermos, which initially contained 7,000 g of water at 32°C. After adding the snow sample, and after all the snow melted, the temperature of the water in the thermos was 8°C. The following calculations were made:

$$\text{snow density} = \frac{2000 \text{ g}}{15,000 \text{ cm}^3} = 0.133 \text{ g/cm}^3$$

$$\text{snow water equivalent } (WE) = (0.133)(60 \text{ cm}) = 8.0 \text{ cm}$$

First, determine the heat energy needed to raise the temperature of the melted snow water from 0°C to 8°C:

$$(2000 \text{ g})(8°C)(1 \text{ cal/g/°C}) = 16,000 \text{ cal}$$

The heat energy available was:

$$(7000 \text{ g})(32 - 8°C)(1 \text{ cal/g/°C}) = 168,000 \text{ cal}$$

The heat available to melt ice would equal:

$$168,000 \text{ cal} - 16,000 \text{ cal} = 152,000 \text{ cal}$$

Therefore:

$$\text{ice content} = \frac{152,000 \text{ cal}}{80 \text{ cal/g}} = 1900 \text{ g}$$

$$\text{thermal quality } (B) = \frac{1900 \text{ g}}{2000 \text{ g}} = 0.95 = 95\%$$

The snowpack contained 5% liquid water and was at a temperature of 0°C.

The generalized snowmelt equations were developed from extensive field measurements at snow research laboratories in the western United States. All major energy components for forest cover conditions are considered. The following discussion develops the generalized snowmelt equations by considering each major source of energy separately.

Solar Radiation. The amount of solar radiation reaching a snowpack surface is dependent upon the slope and aspect of the surface, cloud cover, and forest cover. In the Northern Hemisphere, south-facing slopes receive more radiation than north-facing slopes. The more moderate the slope, the more moderate the effect that slope has on solar radiation. By determining the slope and aspect of an area, the corresponding solar radiation for a particular latitude can be determined.

The amount of solar radiation striking a snowpack surface in the open is a function of the percentage of cloud cover and the height of the clouds (Fig. 14.1). The corresponding melt that occurs from solar radiation is:

$$M = \frac{I_s (1 - \alpha)}{B80} \tag{14.8}$$

A ripe snowpack with a 3% liquid water content reduces the above relationship to:

$$M = 0.0129\, I_s(1 - \alpha) \tag{14.9}$$

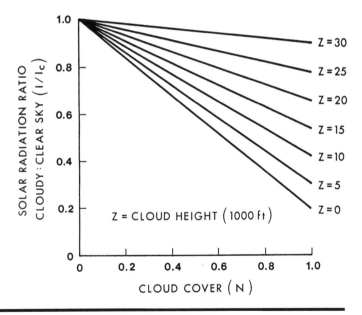

14.1. Relationship between solar radiation and cloud height and cover (from U.S. Army Corps of Engineers 1956).

The percentage of incoming solar radiation that reaches the snow surface depends primarily on the type of cover, density, and condition of the forest canopy. As the density of a forest canopy increases, incoming solar radiation decreases exponentially (Fig. 14.2). As a result, with dense canopies, the effect of forest cover overrides the effects of cloud cover previously discussed. Coniferous forest cover can reduce substantially the amount of solar radiation that reaches a snow surface. In contrast, deciduous forests have less of an effect on solar radiation.

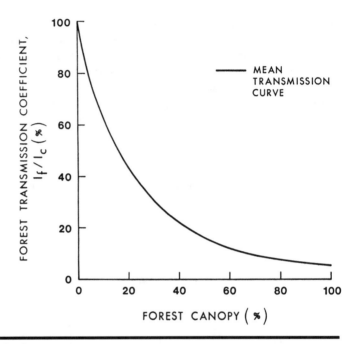

14.2. Relationship between conifer forest canopy density and transmission of solar radiation (from U.S. Army Corps of Engineers 1956).

Longwave Radiation. Snow absorbs and emits nearly all incident longwave or terrestrial radiation. The amount of radiation being emitted from a snowpack is limited by the narrow range of temperatures of snowpacks. Because a snowpack temperature cannot exceed 0°C, its maximum longwave radiation is 0.459 cal/cm²/min.

Net longwave radiation at a snow surface is determined largely by overhead back radiation from the earth's atmosphere, clouds, and forest canopies. Back radiation from the atmosphere is a function of the water content of air. Over snowpacks, the vapor pressure of air usually varies between 3 and 9 mb pressure, resulting in a fairly constant rate of longwave reradiation of 0.757 cal/cm²/min. Therefore, under clear skies, the net longwave radiation at a snow surface is approximately:

$$R_c = 0.757 \ \sigma \ (T_a)^4 - 0.459 \text{ under clear skies} \tag{14.10}$$

where R_c = net longwave radiation (cal/cm²/min); σ = Stefan-Boltzmann constant = 0.826×10^{-10} (cal/cm³/min/°K⁴); and T_a = air temperature (°K).

When clouds are present, the back radiation to the snow surface is determined by the temperature at the base of the clouds and the net longwave radiation becomes:

$$R_{cl} = \sigma \, (T_c^4 - T_s^4) \tag{14.11}$$

where R_{cl} = net longwave radiation (under cloudy skies); T_c = temperature at the base of clouds (°K); and T_s = snowpack temperature (°K).

Under partial cloud cover, the loss of longwave radiation from the snow pack is:

$$R_c \, (1 - K_c N) \tag{14.12}$$

where $K_c = f$ (cloud type and ceiling); and N = portion of the sky covered by clouds (fraction).

Similarly, for a snowpack beneath a dense conifer canopy, the net longwave radiation (R_f) is:

$$R_f = \sigma \, (T_f^4 - T_s^4) \tag{14.13}$$

where T_f = temperature of the underside of the forest canopy, (°K).

Because temperatures of the trees are rarely measured, T_f is often estimated from air temperature (T_a). Under clear sky conditions and a ripe snowpack, the net longwave radiation under a conifer canopy is:

$$R_{lw} = \sigma \, T_a^4 \, [F + 0.757(1 - F)] - 0.459 \tag{14.14}$$

where F = canopy density (decimal fraction).

Snowmelt that is caused by net longwave radiation under conditions of dense forest cover or low clouds can be approximated by:

$$M_{lw} = 0.142 \, T_a \tag{14.15}$$

where M_{lw} = snowmelt caused by longwave radiation (cm); and T_a = air temperature measured at 2 m above the snowpack (°C).

Net Radiation. The (all-wave) net radiation that is available for snowmelt is governed largely by forest cover conditions and cloud conditions. Because watershed management activities can affect forest cover density directly, we will focus on this aspect.

There is a trade-off between shortwave and longwave radiation at a snowpack surface as the forest cover changes. As forest cover increases, the solar radiation at the snowpack surface is reduced greatly; the longwave radiation loss from the snowpack is reduced; and the longwave gain component from the canopy increases (Fig. 14.3). Between 15 and 30% canopy cover, net all-wave radiation at the snowpack surface is at a minimum; net radiation is highest at 0% cover, but it also is relatively high at dense forest canopy conditions because of the much higher net longwave component. These relationships have significant implications for forest and snowpack management to be discussed later.

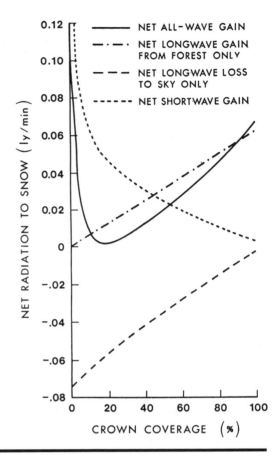

14.3. Net radiation of snowpack as related to forest canopy coverage (from Reifsnyder and Lull 1965).

Convection-Condensation Melt. Heat energy can be added to snowpack by the turbulent exchange of sensible heat from the overlying air and by direct condensation on the snow surface. In general terms, this energy exchange can be approximated by:

$$q_e = A_e \frac{dq}{dz} \tag{14.16}$$

where q_e = energy exchange (cal/cm²/time); A_e = exchange coefficient; and dq/dz = vertical gradient of temperature or water vapor.

For a ripe snowpack, the snow surface would have a temperature of 0°C, with a corresponding vapor pressure of 6.11 mb. Using these values for the snow surface and by determining air temperature and relative humidity measurements in the air above the snow surface allows us to estimate the energy exchange.

Snowmelt from convection can be estimated from:

$$M_c = 0.0005 \frac{P}{P_o} (z_a z_b)^{-0.167} T_a v \tag{14.17}$$

where M_c = convective snowmelt (cm); P, P_o = air pressures at the snow surface and at sea level (mb), respectively; z_a, z_b = heights (m) above the snow surface at which air temperature and wind speed are measured, respectively; and v = wind speed (km/day).

Snowmelt from condensation can be approximated from a similar relationship:

$$M_e = .0024 (z_a z_b)^{-0.167} (e_a - e_s) v \tag{14.18}$$

where M_e = condensation snowmelt (cm); e_a = vapor pressure of the air at height z_a (mb); and e_s = vapor pressure of the snow surface (6.11 mb for a melting snow surface).

The above equations can be combined and simplified to provide an estimate of melt due to convection-condensation. In doing so, the P/P_o ratio is assumed to be a constant that can have values from 0.7 to 1.0 (at sea level); 0.8 is assumed for mountainous areas. Also, dewpoint temperatures can be used to represent vapor pressures. Under these assumptions, and assuming a ripe snowpack ($T_s = 0°C$), the combined equation becomes:

$$M_{ce} = 0.00078 \, v \, (0.42 \, T_a + 1.51 \, T_d) \tag{14.19}$$

where M_{ce} = convection-condensation melt (cm/day); v = mean wind speed (km/day); T_a = mean air temperature (°C at 2 m above the snowpack); and T_d = mean dewpoint temperature (°C at 2 m above the snowpack).

Rain Melt. Snowmelt caused by the addition of sensible heat from rainfall is relatively small. It can be estimated from air temperature and rainfall measurements for a snowpack with a thermal quality of 100% as:

$$M_p = \frac{P_r T_a}{80 \text{ cal/g}} = 0.012 P_r T_a \tag{14.20}$$

where M_p = daily snowmelt (cm); P_r = daily rainfall (cm); and T_a = average daily air temperature (°C).

Again, the above relationship holds for a ripe snowpack. If the snowpack has a temperature below 0°C, additional energy can be released to the pack by virtue of the release of the heat of fusion (80 cal for every 1 cm of rain that freezes).

Conduction Melt. Heat energy can be added to the base of a snowpack by conduction from the underlying ground. For any given day, the amount of energy available by conduction and, hence, the amount of melt is relatively small. Daily values of 0.5 mm frequently are assumed, and sometimes this component is simply ignored if snowmelt is being estimated over a short period of time. For seasonal estimates of snowmelt, however, conduction melt can be significant. Ground melt, based on conduction measurements by the U.S. Army Corps of Engineers (1956), indicated that monthly totals in the Central Sierra Mountains in California ranged from 0.3 cm in January to 2.4 cm in May.

COMBINED GENERALIZED BASIN SNOWMELT EQUATIONS

The relationships developed in the preceding sections provide the foundation for a set of generalized equations that can be used to estimate snowmelt for a small watershed (U.S. Army Corps of Engineers 1960). Because of the influence of forest cover on energy exchange, the forest cover condition of a watershed determines which equation to use. For rain-free periods, the daily melt from a ripe snowpack (isothermal at 0°C, with a 3% liquid water content) is calculated by one of the following equations that are differentiated on the basis of forest canopy cover (F):

Heavily Forested Area ($F > 0.80$):

$$M = 0.19 \, T_a + 0.17 \, T_d \tag{14.21}$$

Forested Area ($F = 0.60$ to 0.80):

$$M = k \, 0.00078 \, v \, (0.42 \, T_a + 1.51 \, T_d) + 0.14 \, T_a \tag{14.22}$$

Partly Forested Area ($F = 0.10$ to 0.60):

$$M = k' \, (1 - F) \, .01 \, I_s(1 - \alpha) + k(0.00078v) \, (0.42 \, T_a \\ + 1.51 \, T_d) + F \, (0.14 \, T_a) \tag{14.23}$$

Open Area ($F < 0.10$):

$$M = k' \, (0.0125 \, I_s)(1 - \alpha) + (1 - N) \, (0.104 \, T_a - 2.13) \\ + N(0.013 \, T_c) + k(0.00078v) \, (0.42 \, T_a + 1.51 \, T_d) \tag{14.24}$$

where M = daily melt (cm); T_a = air temperature (°C) at 2 m above the snow surface; T_d = dewpoint temperature (°C) at 2 m above the snow surface; v = wind speed (km/day); I_s = observed or estimated solar radiation (cal/cm²/day); α = snow surface albedo (decimal fraction); k' = basin shortwave radiation melt factor, which depends on the average exposure of the open areas to solar radiation compared to an unshielded horizontal surface; F = average forest canopy cover for watershed (expressed as a decimal fraction); T_c = cloud-base temperature (°C); N = cloud cover (expressed as a decimal fraction); and k = basin convective-condensation melt factor, which depends on the relative exposure of the watershed to wind.

The only empirical "fitted parameters" in the above equations are k and k'. The basin shortwave radiation melt factor (k') can be estimated from solar radiation data for a given latitude, slope, and aspect. Because one has to average several slopes and aspects for a given watershed, the k' value represents an average for the watershed. In general, watersheds with a southern exposure would tend to have a $k' > 1$; those with northern exposures would have a $k' < 1$. A watershed that has a balance between north- and south-facing slopes would have a $k' = 1.0$. The basin convective-condensation melt factor (k) is similarly an average value for a particular watershed that indicates the exposure of the snowpack to wind; values range from $k = 1.0$ for open areas to $k = 0.8$ for dense forest cover.

TEMPERATURE INDEX METHOD

The data requirements for the generalized snowmelt equations restrict their use in many situations, particularly in remote areas and for day-to-day operational conditions. As a result, simplified methods that depend only on air temperature data have been developed to estimate snowmelt.

The temperature index method is an empirically derived equation of the form:

$$M = MR(T_a - T_b) \tag{14.25}$$

where M = daily snowmelt (cm); MR = melt-rate index or degree-day factor (cm/°C-day); T_a = daily air temperature value, usually either the average daily or maximum daily temperature (°C); and T_b = base temperature at which no snowmelt is observed (°C).

The difference, $T_a - T_b$, yields the degree-days of heat energy available for melt. The melt-rate index relates this heat energy to snowmelt that occurs on the watershed. Although we know that the air temperature is but one source of energy for snowmelt, it correlates well with radiation inputs, particularly during the snowmelt season, and it also is a reasonable index for forested conditions. The equation for the temperature index method (Eq. 14.25) is derived from regression analysis of daily melt versus air temperature (Fig. 14.4). The melt-rate index is the slope of the regression line, and the base temperature (T_b) is that air temperature at which no melt is observed. Examples of temperature index coefficients for three watersheds are presented in Table 14.2.

Because the temperature index method is developed for a particular watershed,

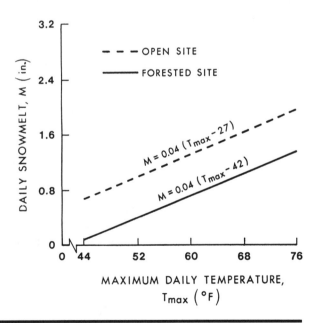

14.4. Temperature index relationships for maximum daily air temperatures (U.S. Army Corps of Engineers 1960).

Table 14.2. Base-temperature and melt-rate indices for three watersheds in the western United States

Watershed	Mean Temperature			Maximum Temperature		
	Base Temperature (°F)	Melt-rate Index		Base Temperature (°F)	Melt-rate Index	
		Apr	May		Apr	May
Central Sierra, Calif.	26	0.036	0.062	29	0.020	0.038
Upper Columbia, Mont.	32	0.037	0.072	42	0.109	0.064
Willamette, Ore.	32	0.039	0.042	42	0.046	0.046

Source: From U.S. Army Corps of Engineers (1956).

both the melt-rate index and base-temperature values can differ from one area to the next. The elevation difference and proximity of the air temperature station to the watershed will affect the values that are derived.

◾ FOREST MANAGEMENT–SNOWPACK MANAGEMENT RELATIONSHIPS

Because trees affect snow accumulation and melt, it follows that snow accumulation and melt patterns can be changed by manipulating forest density. Much of the snowmelt runoff in temperate regions of the world derives from high-elevation forested zones, which suggests even further the possibilities of using forest management practices to enhance snowmelt water yield. But can water yield be enhanced without increasing the potential for flooding from snowmelt runoff? Also, are snowpack management practices compatible with other forest uses?

Many studies have indicated that forest management affects snowpacks in ways that can produce greater snowmelt runoff and therefore flooding potential. Furthermore, thinning and clearing of forest overstories to increase water yield frequently can be made compatible with the demands for wood, forage, wildlife, and recreational use of forestlands.

The potential of increasing the water yield from forested watersheds appears to be greater for snow than for rainfall in many temperate areas. Snow generally accumulates on forested sites throughout winter, providing a large reservoir of stored water potentially available for use in the spring. For example, the Salt-Verde Basin in central Arizona often stores between 3 and 6 billion m^3 of water as snow prior to the beginning of snowmelt in the spring. If snowmelt water yields were increased by 10%, an additional 300 to 600 million m^3 of water could be captured annually.

Enhancing Water Yield

Forest cover can be altered in basically two different ways to increase recoverable water yield: reduce forest densities by thinning and remove forest overstories by clearcutting in different spatial arrangements. More snow accumulates in sparsely stocked forest stands and in small clearings in forest stands than in dense conifer stands (Table

14.3). These greater accumulations can contribute to increased runoff, particularly when such increases occur in areas that already have wetter soils. The problem is one of determining the most efficient method that is also compatible with other forest management objectives.

Table 14.3. Increase in maximum snow accumulation (water equivalent) after cutting in western conifer forest

Location and Forest Cover	Treatment	Maximum Increase in Snow Accumulation (in.)	(%)
Fraser Experimental Forest, Colo.	Uncut: 11,900 fbm	0.0	
	Cut (residual volume):		
Mature lodgepole pine	6000 fbm	0.81	12
	4000	1.01	15
	2000	1.49	21
	0	1.99	29
Young lodgepole pine	Heavy thinning (reduction from 4400 to 630 trees per acre)	2.3	23
	Light thinning (reduction from 4400 to 2000 trees per acre)	1.7	17
Mature Englemann spruce–subalpine fir	Removal of 60% of volume by strip cutting and group and single-tree selection	2.8	22
Front Range, Rocky Mountains, Colo.	Selection cut	0.45	6
Ponderosa Pine and Douglas-fir	Commercial clearcut	1.21	29
North Central Wyo. Lodgepole pine	Clearcut blocks	2.5	40
Willamette Pass, Ore. Mountain hemlock and true fir	Strip-cut, strips 2 chains wide	5	15
Central Sierra Snow Laboratory, Calif., (NE)	Clearcut	11	23
	East-west strip, 1 tree-height wide	12	26
Red fir	Block cutting, 1 tree-height wide	15	34
	Selective cutting; crown cover reduced from 90% to 50%	2	5
	90% to 35%	9	19
	Commercial selection cut	7	14
	Wall-and-step forest	19	25
Minnesota	Single-tree selection	0.1	4
Black spruce	Shelterwood	0.7	28
	Clearcut strip	1.5	60
	Clearcut patch	2.0	80

Source: From Anderson et al. (1976).

Thinning forest stands has been shown to increase snowpack accumulations. The stand structure following thinning usually is an irregular pattern of small, randomly spaced openings. Although snow water equivalents often are increased as a result of thinning, the resultant effects on water yield are usually slight. Creating small clearcuts in forest stands also has been shown to result in increased snowpack accumulations. Depending on the size, shape, and orientation of the openings, such clearings also can result in increased water yield.

Deposition and redistribution processes of snowpacks in and adjacent to forest openings involve at least three factors: (1) more snow can accumulate in openings than under forest overstories during snowfall events due to wind eddies in the openings; (2) snowpacks in openings may be augmented during and after storms by snow blown from surrounding forest canopies; (3) the snowpack can be greater in openings than under forest canopies, because there are no interception losses, although some investigators minimize the importance of snow interception losses.

Ablation (that is, melt and evaporation) factors affecting snowpack profiles involve variations in shortwave and longwave radiation fluxes. Shaded sides of openings receive less solar radiation than exposed sites. Observations suggest that the highest rate of ablation occurs along the north side of east-west clearcut strips. Exposure to more solar radiation explains such observations.

Rates of ablation also are influenced by spatial variations in longwave radiation emission from trees adjacent to an opening. Trees exposed to solar radiation are warmed and emit more longwave radiation than trees not warmed by solar radiation. A snowpack absorbs almost all of the longwave radiation striking it. Therefore, snow on the side of a forest opening exposed to solar radiation is likely to be exposed to more longwave radiation (emitted from adjacent, heated trees) than snow on the shaded side. Consequently, a combination of shortwave and longwave radiation causes, at least in part, the relatively high rates of ablation along exposed sides of forest openings.

It is difficult to isolate the effects that all the processes of deposition, redistribution, and ablation have on snowpack profiles extending through openings and into adjacent forests. The profiles represent the net result of all these processes prior to the time of observation. However, several studies have shown some consistent responses that have led to guidelines for enhancing water yield (Ex. 14.3).

Snowmelt-Runoff Efficiency

The amount of water derived from snowmelt depends on the dynamics of snowpack accumulation and melt and on snowmelt-runoff efficiency. *Snowmelt-runoff efficiency,* defined as the portion of the snowpack on-site that subsequently is converted into runoff, can be derived as:

$$SRE = \frac{Q}{P - SWE} \, 100 \qquad\qquad (14.26)$$

where SRE = snowmelt-runoff efficiency (%); Q = runoff (cm); P = precipitation input (cm); and SWE = change in snowpack water equivalent (cm), a decrease is negative.

Snowmelt-runoff efficiency can vary considerably from one watershed to the next or from year to year on a given watershed, due to climatic patterns and changes in watershed condition. Snowmelt-runoff efficiencies for watersheds in the southwestern United States have varied from 20 to 45% on a given watershed from peak snowpack

EXAMPLE 14.3

Effects of strip cutting forests on snowpacks and water yield

Strip cutting lodgepole pine forests in Colorado had been shown to affect wind patterns, snow accumulation, and melt (Gary 1975). When strips were cut at a width equal to from one to five times the height of surrounding trees, snow water equivalents were from 15 to 35% higher in the strips than in the adjacent forest. Nearly 30 yr after harvest, average peak snow water equivalent in the cut watershed still remains 9% above that of an uncut watershed (Troendle and King 1985). Increases in annual flows above predicted levels are decreasing slowly in response to the regrowth of forests. Apparently, one-third of the increase in annual flows is attributed to this net increase in snow water equivalent; two-thirds of the increase are largely due to reductions in evapotranspiration.

Similar results have been observed in ponderosa pine forests in Arizona. The snow water equivalent within the cut portion of a strip that was cut at a width equivalent to the height of the surrounding forest was increased 60%, or about 3 cm, compared to the uncut forest (Ffolliott and Thorud 1974). In the figure below, snowpack in the forest adjacent to the strip cut was reduced, resulting in a zone of influence that was much wider than the cut itself. Brown et al. (1974) cut a watershed of mature ponderosa pine in the same area in which strips one times the height of the trees were cut in between strips two times the height of the trees. They found that this treatment increased water yield by about 3 cm and the effect was sustained for at least 5 yr.

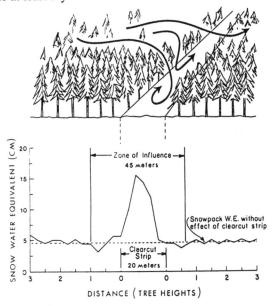

Effects of strip cutting a ponderosa pine forest in Arizona on wind patterns and snow deposition (adapted from Ffolliott and Thorud 1974).

accumulation to the end of snowmelt runoff. The amount of snowfall and the timing of snowmelt account for much of the variability. Within a given region, snowmelt-runoff efficiencies have ranged from 25 to 85%, with much of this difference being attributed to physiographic features.

In general, snowmelt-runoff efficiency depends on watershed slope, soil depth, soil type (texture and structure), vegetation characteristics, and climatic variables. The presence and type of soil frost that can occur has a pronounced effect on runoff efficiency in western mountains and the higher latitudes of North America. Other variables of importance include moisture conditions before the snow season, peak snowpack accumulation, and duration of snowmelt runoff. As a rule, high efficiencies occur on watersheds that experience concrete soil frost, heavy precipitation inputs prior to the start of snowpack accumulation, deep snowpacks at the peak of accumulation, or large amounts of rainfall (rain on snow) during the snowmelt season.

Effects of Forest Management on Flooding from Snowmelt

The earlier discussion concerned the effects of using different clearcutting configurations to augment water yield. In the process of increasing water yield from snowmelt, a concern for water resource managers is the potential for increased snowmelt flooding.

The results of controlled watershed experiments indicate that the effect of forest cutting on snowmelt streamflow peaks and volumes varies from one area to the next, and even from year to year. When small catchments are 100% clearcut, the odds are that snowmelt runoff will increase. Whether such increased runoff results in an increase in flooding downstream depends on many factors, including the condition of other parts of the basin that contribute flow to flood-prone areas, and the basin characteristics that affect timing and routing of flow.

In general, peak discharges from snowmelt have increased after forest removal. Exceptions have been observed in the coastal range of the Pacific Northwest. Harr and McCorison (1979) reported a 32% reduction in snowmelt peak size following clearcutting in Oregon, and suggest that condensation-convection melt occurring from snow on tree crowns is at a higher rate than that occurring at ground level (where the majority of the snow would be after clearcutting). But, their results have been altered by more recent work (Ex. 14.4).

Changes in snowmelt runoff often are attributed to changes in the timing of the melt, which can be managed by manipulating forest cover to alter the timing (or desynchronize) from different parts of a watershed or river basin. This effect has been observed in Minnesota where a mature aspen stand on a watershed was cleared only partially in two successive years (Verry et al. 1983). When forest cover from one-half of the watershed was cleared, the snowmelt runoff peak was reduced (1971 in Figure 14.5); when more than 70% of forest cover was cleared the next year, snowmelt peak discharge was nearly doubled (1972 in Figure 14.5). Open and forested sites experience snowmelt at such different rates and times that they contribute to streamflow at much different times. As the percent of a watershed that is clearcut exceeds 60%, snowmelt peak discharge will be expected to increase in Minnesota. Furthermore, the effects can persist for several years (through 1979 in Figure 14.5). Other areas with similar climate, vegetation, and topography might experience a similar response to forest clearing.

EXAMPLE 14.4

Rain-on-snow events and the affect of forest canopy

Some of the most severe flooding in areas that receive snowfall is attributed to rain-on-snow events. The combination of rainfall plus the large influxes of sensible heat that are associated with rainstorms can add large amounts of liquid water to the soil surface. Rain-on-snow floods have been frequent in areas that have a transient snowpack—areas where the air temperature frequently hovers around 0°C during the winter. Such is the case in the Pacific Northwest, where influxes of warm, moist air from the Pacific Ocean can result in high streamflows and saturated soils that led to frequent landslides.

Berris and Harr (1987) studied the influence of forest cover on snow accumulation and melt during rain-on-snow events in the western cascades of Oregon. Their work suggests:

1. If air temperature is near 0°C when snow falls or if snow is present on the forest canopy when rain occurs, higher outputs of water occur from forested areas than cleared areas. the snow covered canopy offers a greater surface area that is exposed to convection-condensation processes than the snowpack surface in a cleared area; more rapid melt occurs from the snow on the canopy.

2. If no snow is present on the forest canopy when rain occurs and rainfall rates exceed 5 mm/hr, clearcut areas yield more water than forested areas, once the snowpack is ripe. Wind accentuates these differences.

The dilemma posed by these apparently conflicting results is how to best manage forests that will not promote high streamflows and landslides. If a series of snowfalls are interspaced with a series of rainstorms, situation (1) above could lead to high streamflows and sufficient water input to saturate soils and promote landslides in forested areas. If snow accumulates over time without appreciable canopy-interception melt, then situation (2) can lead to similar problems from clearcut areas. Although management guidelines may be difficult to establish in such an instance, the most reasonable approach may be to maintain a diversity of cover conditions on a watershed—and restrict the percentage of a watershed that can be clearcut at any one point in time.

Clearing patches of forest cover in mountainous areas would not be as effective as the above example in reducing peak discharges. Runoff from mountainous watersheds already is more desynchronized than flat watersheds because of differences in elevation, slope, and aspect.

In cold continental climates, changes in forest cover also can affect snowmelt

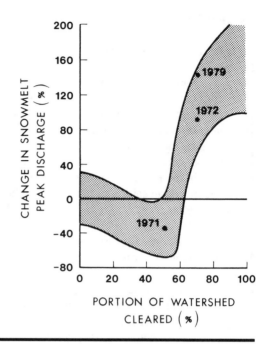

14.5. Relation between the portion of a watershed clearcut and the change in annual snowmelt peak discharge compared to a mature stand of hardwoods in the Lake States (from Verry et al. 1983).

runoff by altering soil frost conditions and, thereby, runoff efficiency. Snowmelt on frozen soil runs off the soil surface rapidly. Soils usually are wetter in the fall under clearcut conditions, and they tend to freeze deeper and have a more frequent occurrence of "concrete"-type frost. If large areas within a watershed are converted from forest cover to croplands or are under clearcut conditions, the combination of more rapid snowmelt and more rapid (and more efficient) runoff can lead to more frequent downstream flooding.

■ METHODS AND MODELS FOR PREDICTING SNOWPACK-SNOWMELT RELATIONSHIPS

The basic information and empirical studies discussed previously have been incorporated into methods ranging from simple regression equations to complex computer simulation models. Although a detailed discussion of all such models is beyond the scope of this book, examples are presented to illustrate the conceptual nature of existing methods and models.

Prediction of Snowmelt

As discussed earlier, several methods are available to estimate snowmelt, ranging from the simple temperature index method, to the generalized snowmelt equations, to detailed energy budget models. The first two have been used most frequently in practice (for example, the Hydrologic Engineering Center HEC-1 and *Streamflow Simulation And Reservoir Routing* (SSARR) models include both methods). Although these methods are used mostly for engineering design and streamflow forecasting, they also can be used to evaluate the effects of forest cover on snowmelt runoff. The principal components of a snow accumulation and melt model are illustrated in Figure 14.6.

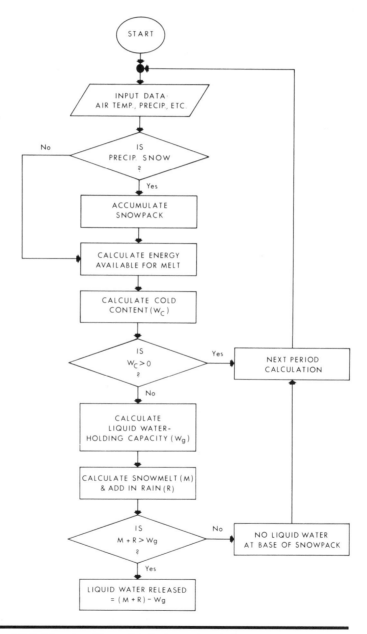

14.6. Flowchart illustrating the important relationships and components in a "typical" snow accumulation and ablation model.

Streamflow from Snowmelt

Modeling snowpack dynamics is but one part of predicting snowmelt runoff, as discussed in the section on snowmelt-runoff efficiency. The entire process, from snowfall to streamflow, requires that the components illustrated in Figure 14.7 be considered. All the processes need to be considered either explicitly or implicitly in a snowmelt-runoff model. The degree to which processes are simulated within a given model vary with the purpose of the model. The model presented by Anderson (1978), is a "point energy and mass balance" model of snow cover that is theoretically complete but also complex. In contrast, the SSARR model was developed for routine operational streamflow forecasting and, therefore, has minimal data and initialization requirements (U.S. Army Corps of Engineers 1972). Many of the energy budget relationships and snowpack condition characteristics must be simplified for operational use.

Some simplified relationships have been developed to estimate streamflow from snowmelt. For example, if watersheds have been studied during previous snow accu-

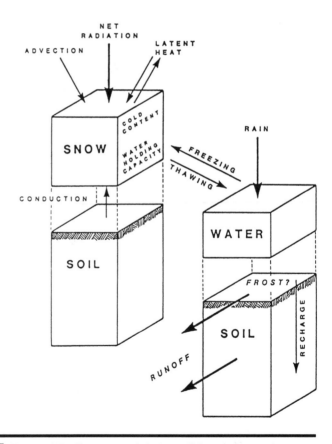

14.7. Factors that affect snowmelt and runoff from a snowpack.

mulation-melt seasons, one may be able to estimate the water available for streamflow runoff (Q_m) from:

$$Q_m = M_o A_s \ (SRE) \tag{14.27}$$

where M_o = daily snowmelt (cm/day); and A_s = snow covered area on the watershed (area units).

Snowmelt-runoff efficiency can be entered directly to solve the above if the appropriate values are known for the watershed. If not known, SRE values can be calculated for specific conditions from known relationships for the area.

Equation 14.27 could be used with the temperature index method to predict snowmelt on a given day. Equation 14.27 estimates the fraction of that melt water that appears as streamflow. Because snowmelt water yield is discharged from a watershed primarily as movement through the soil to the stream channel, all of the snowmelt from one day does not necessarily appear as streamflow on that same day. Instead, only a fraction can appear on that day, and the rest may be spread out over several days.

Approaches have been outlined to compute streamflow for a given day based on snowmelt from previous days and any existing channel flow (Rango and Martinec 1979). In essence, these methods compute a recession coefficient of streamflow from a watershed. This coefficient is calculated as the ratio of one day's streamflow divided by that of the previous day. It is used in relationships such as the following:

$$Q_n = J_n(1 - k_b) + Q_{n-1} k_b \tag{14.28}$$

where Q_n = streamflow on day n (m³); J_n = water released from the snowpack available for streamflow on day n (m³); Q_{n-1} = streamflow on previous day (m³); and k_b = recession coefficient.

A relationship of average daily discharge of streamflow can be derived from Equation 14.28 by dividing the daily volumes of streamflow by 86,400 (the number of seconds in a day). If the volumes of streamflow are expressed in cubic meters, average daily discharge can be given in cubic meters per second as follows:

$$Q_n = I_n(1 - k_b) + Q_{n-1}k_b \tag{14.29}$$

where Q_n = average daily discharge on day n (m³/sec); I_n = average discharge of snowmelt on day n (m³/sec); and Q_{n-1} = average daily discharge on previous day (m³/sec).

The recession coefficient (k_b) is assumed to be a function of discharge. In general, it is "set" to represent specific watershed conditions.

There are a number of methods and models developed from these methods that are used to predict snowpack dynamics, to describe these dynamics in relation to forest management activities, and to estimate the magnitude of the resulting snowmelt runoff. These analytical tools are valuable to watershed managers concerned with snow hydrology.

■ **SUMMARY**

Knowledge of snow hydrology is essential for the wise management of watersheds and water resources in many parts of the world. Snow accumulates, ripens, melts, and contributes to streamflow in response to climatological factors and the soil-vegetation system present on a watershed. We not only need to understand the hydrologic processes and factors involved in snow hydrology, but we also need methods to predict the streamflow response that results from a given set of climatic variables and vegetative cover conditions. After reading this chapter, you should be able to:

1. Explain the factors affecting snow accumulation, snow ripening, and snowmelt.

2. Explain and be able to quantify the snow ripening process of a snowpack; explain the effects of snowpack condition on spring snowmelt floods.

3. Describe the differences between snowmelt under a conifer forest and that in an open field using an energy budget approach.

4. Calculate snowmelt using either the temperature index method or the appropriate generalized snowmelt equation; discuss the advantages and disadvantages of the two methods.

5. Describe the conditions under which forest management can increase water yield due to changes in snowmelt runoff; what types of management activities are most effective? How can snowmelt flooding be moderated?

CHAPTER 15

Watershed Considerations for Engineering Applications

INTRODUCTION

Upland watersheds form the headwater areas of streams and rivers and are important recharge areas for many groundwater aquifers. As such, their management is an essential and integral part of any water resource development project or management plan. However, rarely are watersheds managed solely for water resource purposes. The exception would be municipal watersheds that are managed to provide municipal and industrial water supplies for local communities. As discussed earlier, upland watersheds usually are managed to provide many different resources besides water, including food, wood, fiber, minerals, and energy. As a result, the hydrologic importance of upland watersheds to downstream engineering works may be overlooked.

It should be emphasized early in this chapter that watershed management is not a panacea for all water resource problems. Likewise, engineering solutions, such as reservoirs, levees, or water diversion schemes, cannot by themselves solve water resource problems completely. Floods, droughts, landslides, and soil erosion are natural phenomena that occur no matter what types of management or engineering measures are instituted. However, by developing land use practices that are compatible with soil and water conservation principles and in concert with water resource development programs, the magnitude of many water resource problems can be reduced.

The purpose of this chapter is to demonstrate the importance of including watershed management considerations in water resource development programs and engineering solutions. Specifically, we intend to provide an understanding of the linkages between watershed management, land use practices, and some of the most common engineering works used in water resource development. As discussed in chapters 12 and 13, such linkages must be quantified before the value of watershed management can be quantified.

SURFACE WATER DEVELOPMENT

Surface water problems arise because of the variability in the timing, location, and quality of water yield. In terms of total quantity, we have no shortage of fresh liquid water on earth. Although nearly 98% of all fresh liquid water is groundwater, the remaining 160,000 km³ of surface water is more than sufficient to meet all human needs. This water is dispersed spatially and is in constant flux. Many watersheds on the earth's surface do not provide adequate surface water supplies to meet human demands on a dependable basis. Even in the humid tropics where annual rainfall can exceed 3000 mm, periodic droughts or annual dry spells can cause crop damage and losses of livestock and human lives. Conversely, damaging floods can occur periodically in the most arid regions where annual precipitation is less than 250 mm. It is not surprising, then, that nations, agencies, and even local communities make large investments in engineering projects to gain some measure of control over water resources.

Surface water development can involve a variety of structures and practices designed to alter the amount, timing, and quality of water yield. Benefits derived from such development include increased water supplies for municipal-industrial needs, irrigation, and livestock. Some projects are designed to modify the streamflow regimen to provide flood control, or to provide a more sustained flow during dry periods for navigation, hydroelectric power production, or to protect downstream fisheries.

Water yield from a watershed is the residual of precipitation minus evapotranspiration and some deep-seepage loss. Therefore, methods of increasing water supplies on-site logically would involve either increasing precipitation or reducing evapotranspiration. Many imaginative schemes have been devised over the years to alleviate water shortages, including:

1. Reservoir storage. Water is stored during wet periods and released during times of need, or can be transferred from areas with excess water to locations with water deficiencies.

2. Weather modification. The seeding of clouds has been tested and used successfully in only a few instances to increase localized precipitation and, in some instances, to dissipate thunderstorms or flash flood–producing clouds.

3. Desalinization of sea water. The technology now is available to take ocean water from along coastal areas and remove the salt so that water can be used for human and crop consumption.

4. Evaporation or transpiration suppression. Techniques that can reduce evaporation from small water bodies or can reduce transpiration losses are being tested and applied. Although some show promise, they are likely to be useful only on a limited scale.

5. Vegetation manipulation to reduce annual consumptive use. Water yield can be increased in many areas by converting from one species of vegetation to another, or by implementing forest cutting practices (chapters 6 and 14).

6. Towing icebergs. The transport of icebergs from polar regions to arid coastal areas has been suggested as a means of increasing water supplies; this has been suggested for coastal areas like southern California and countries in the Middle East.

Each of the above methods has some limitations, yet, they provide alternatives to more traditional methods of increasing water yield. For example, the development of a desalinization operation along the coast of an arid country may preclude the need for reservoir construction in upland areas. Agricultural and industrial growth that would likely follow in the coastal area could provide jobs for rural watershed inhabitants, which may be important in developing countries. The benefits to watershed lands can be a reduction in the intensity of land use, such as grazing and cropping practices, and enhanced opportunities to rehabilitate and properly manage upstream watersheds.

The methods discussed above are not the only alternatives to increasing water yield. Water reuse and conservation measures in households, industrial plants, and farms can reduce the demand for water. Activities that promote groundwater recharge during periods of abundant rainfall can be used to increase groundwater supplies that, in turn, can be used during periods of high demand. All possible options should be considered when water shortages are anticipated; by studying the alternatives and taking an integrated approach, less costly and more environmentally sound solutions may be gained.

Even though there appears to be many alternative means of increasing water yield, in practice, reservoirs and associated transport systems are by far the most common. Therefore, the following discussion centers on the linkages between reservoirs and upstream watersheds.

■ RESERVOIRS

From a historical perspective, reservoirs have been considered the main tool by which water resources are managed. As a rule, reservoirs represent large investments of capital, and they frequently are justified on the basis that they provide multiple benefits, such as increased water supplies, hydropower production, flood control, and maintenance of streamflow levels needed for dilution of pollutants or for navigation in downstream channels. Water-based outdoor recreation and fisheries industries also can benefit. Local and regional economic growth can be stimulated from the development of large reservoir projects, yet, critics of reservoirs point to their high economic and environmental impact costs and to the fact that many have been constructed regardless of adverse impacts—they sometimes are built to be political showcases.

The construction and operation of large reservoirs or reservoir systems, of course, are not without costs, and once constructed, reservoirs can cause dramatic changes in the types and patterns of land use, both in upstream and downstream areas. Rural inhabitants often must be relocated and productive bottomlands and valuable wildlife habitat can be lost. Altered land use can also change the hydrologic characteristics and erosion-sedimentation processes of upstream watersheds.

Without careful planning, design, and operation, the economic life of reservoirs may be shortened. The goods and services for which the project was constructed may not be sustained over the period for which the project was designed. The result of such a failure can impact local and regional economies and lead to considerable social disruption. Even when reservoir projects function according to plans, some unanticipated problems can arise. For example, people may encroach into flood-prone areas below reservoirs because of an unwarranted feeling of security. Floods, which inevitably occur, sometimes result in much greater economic loss than would have occurred prior to the construction of the project. Therefore, floodplain management and zoning, that is, keeping people and buildings out of flood hazard areas, and upstream watershed protection measures should be integral parts of any reservoir project.

Management of Reservoirs

Reservoirs that are designed, constructed, and operated in concert with upstream watershed management should be capable of achieving the goals for which they were built (Table 15.1). To a limited extent, the upstream vegetative cover can be manipulated to complement reservoir operations (see chapters 6 and 14). The type and extent of vegetative cover can influence the amount and timing of streamflow from a watershed. For example, water yield can be increased in many areas by converting from deep-rooted (trees) to shallow-rooted (grass) vegetation. Without a reservoir, much of the increased water yield likely would flow from the area during high-runoff periods and would be unavailable during drier periods when irrigation was needed. When flood control is an objective, watershed management practices designed to maintain high infiltration rates and low surface runoff are needed. Wetland areas in a watershed attenuate stormflow peaks, and if flooding is a concern, their preservation or protection should become part of the management program. Such practices can affect the magnitude and frequency of flooding, except for flooding associated with extremely large storms that occur infrequently.

Vegetation influences are minimal for major hydrologic events such as 100-yr-return-period floods, or severe droughts. On the other hand, reservoirs usually are designed to function during such extreme events. Whether or not a reservoir remains functional over time, however, depends largely on vegetation characteristics and the overall condition of upstream watersheds. Accelerated rates of sedimentation can cause a premature loss of reservoir storage and an inability to meet demands.

Determining Storage Requirements

Determining the storage capacity of a reservoir requires that water yield and rates of sediment deposition be estimated and balanced against projected demands for water. The total storage capacity of a reservoir is the sum of the active storage and dead storage. *Active storage* is that which is needed to meet all demands, that is, to prevent shortages and in some cases to provide flood control benefits. *Dead storage* is that part of the reservoir that is allocated to trap and hold sediment; it should be of sufficient volume to prevent sedimentation from affecting the active storage for a period of time equal to the economic design life of the reservoir. The gates in a dam that are used to release water in reservoir operations are located immediately above the upper level of the dead storage zone. The detailed procedures for determining reservoir storage needs can be found in most hydrologic engineering texts and therefore will only be briefly discussed here.

ACTIVE STORAGE

Two general approaches exist to estimate storage requirements, a simplified method for quick estimation or first approximations, and a detailed sequential analysis.

Simplified Methods. Simplified methods include the sequential mass curve, or Ripple, method and the nonsequential mass curve (U.S. Army Corps of Engineers 1977). Only the Ripple method, which involves the construction of a mass curve of

Table 15.1. Watershed and reservoir management as they relate to several water resource management goals

Water Resource Management Goals	Watershed Management Objectives/Activities[a]	Reservoir Management Objectives/Activities
Increase available water supplies for irrigation, municipal, supplies, etc.	Manipulate vegetative cover to increase water yield, (convert from deep-rooted to shallow-rooted species on watershed) Minimize or control erosion and sedimentation to maintain storage space in reservoir for the duration of design life; rehabilitate watersheds in poorly managed areas	Provide storage to accommodate increased water yield; to provide firm yield for demands
Reduce flood hazard	Maintain vegetation and soils in good condition through proper land management; maximize infiltration and minimize surface runoff; rehabilitate where necessary Minimize sedimentation of channels to maintain channel capacity Preserve and protect wetlands; minimize wetland drainage and development Construction of contour trenches and furrows to increase detention storage or lengthen infiltration time Enhance infiltration capacity of disturbed lands with mechanical treatments such as soil ripping or chisel plowing, followed by revegetation	Provide storage space for runoff during flooding; provide storage for high runoff to be released during dry periods
Maintain surface water supplies with a high quality for human consumption or fisheries resources	Restrict or carefully manage land use activities conducive to production of sediments, disease-carrying organisms, and excessive nutrient loading; maintain vegetation and soils in good condition Rehabilitate watersheds where needed	Regulate outflow to enhance desirable downstream water quality characteristics (dissolved oxygen and temperature)
Provide hydroelectric power	Manage watersheds to sustain life of reservoir as above	Maintain a dependable storage with sufficient head to generate enough electricity to meet demands

[a]Objectives and activities may not apply in every situation.

accumulated streamflow volumes over a critical period of time, is discussed here. This period of time corresponds to the duration of a drought of a magnitude for which the reservoir is designed (Fig. 15.1). The expected total demand for water (municipal, irrigation, hydroelectric power, etc.) is expressed as a constant rate over time, and

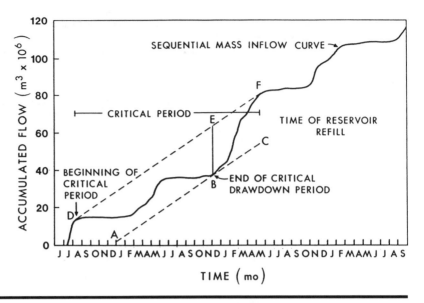

15.1. The sequential mass curve, or Ripple, method of determining reservoir storage (from U.S. Army Corps of Engineers 1977). Given: desired yield = 38 m³ × 10⁶/yr. Construct line *ABC* with slope = 38 m³ × 10⁶/yr tangent to mass curve at *B* (lowest possible point of tangency). Construct line *DEF* parallel to *ABC* and tangent to mass curve at *D* (highest point of tangency prior to *B*). Line *BE* represents the maximum storage requirement to produce the desired yield (about 26 m³ × 10⁶ is required).

then plotted as a straight line with the slope equal to the demand rate. This straight line (*DEF*) is constructed tangent to the mass curve at the beginning of the drought period. A second parallel line (*ABC*) is constructed tangent to the mass curve at the lowest point during the drought period. The vertical distance between these two lines (*BE*) represents the storage needed to meet the demand during the drought period.

Detailed Sequential Method. The detailed sequential method uses a water budget approach that involves tabulating the demands for water and all the inputs and outputs in the sequence for which they occur at the reservoir site. Tabulations can be made on a daily, weekly, or monthly basis and represent seasonal variability in inputs, outputs, and demands. Demands must represent *all* demands for water, both at the reservoir site and downstream. For example, municipal water supplies can be withdrawn directly from the reservoir, but irrigation water can be withdrawn downstream from the dam. There also can be minimum flow requirements immediately below the dam; such a demand must be added to the irrigation requirement but is complementary to releases from the reservoir for generating hydroelectric power. Thus, demands can be considered as competing or complementary. All competing demands must be totalled for each tabulation period. The storage required to meet all demands is determined by:

$$S_t = Q - E + P - D_m \tag{15.1}$$

S_t = storage required in units of volume; Q = inflow from streams and local areas (in units of volume); E = evaporation from the reservoir pool (in units of volume); P = precipitation on the reservoir pool (in units of volume); and D_m = demands for water (in units of volume).

This approach has several advantages over simplified methods: (1) demands can vary over time; (2) either observed or simulated water yield data can be examined; (3) changes in land use that affect water yield can be considered part of the analysis; and (4) the analysis is more amenable to a systems approach and computer simulation. The last point is important when more than one water resource development activity is being considered within a large watershed.

Historical streamflow records corresponding to a severe drought period usually are used in determining conservation storage requirements for a reservoir. An alternative to using historical streamflow data as input (Q) in Equation 15.1 is to use a *stochastic model* to generate streamflow. Such models predict streamflow events based upon the statistical characteristics of streamflow records, including the randomness of hydrologic events. A stochastic model generates streamflow records that follow a certain statistical pattern but that have a random component. As a result, each generated streamflow record is unique. For reservoir studies, one can generate several hundred years of records and then examine low-flow sequences that can be used to estimate conservation storage requirements. These sequences have a chance of occurring and, therefore, help to overcome the limitation of basing storage requirements only on observed historical records.

Any large-scale changes in the type or extent of vegetative cover on a watershed can lead to changes in inflow to the reservoir. If such changes occur after a reservoir has been designed, problems can result in meeting the projected demands (see Example 15.3).

DEAD STORAGE

The magnitude of dead storage space required for a reservoir depends upon the quantity of sediment flowing into the site, the percent of inflowing sediment that is trapped, and the density of the deposited sediment. The quantity of sediment flowing into the site depends on local and upstream surface erosion, mass soil erosion, and streamflow-channel erosion processes. The trap efficiency of a reservoir is considered to be a function of the ratio of reservoir storage capacity to annual inflow; as this ratio increases, the amout of sediment that becomes trapped increases. The density of sediment in the reservoir depends on the type of material—its specific weight and the amount of consolidation that takes place over time.

The quantity of sediment flowing into a reservoir can be estimated by several methods, including the detailed methods presented in chapters 7, 8, and 9 and those below:

1. Sediment surveys from nearby reservoirs or ponds, which provide the best information for existing land use conditions.

2. Erosion-sediment delivery ratio data for landscapes and channels similar to the watersheds in question and in the same climatic regime.

3. Application of locally derived equations or simulation models that have been

verified with data from similar watersheds.

Changes in land use, particularly those that affect the vegetative cover, litter, and soil surface of watersheds, can change sedimentation rates. The development of roads and the construction activities associated with the engineering projects themselves can lead to accelerated surface erosion, mass soil erosion, and channel erosion. Activities that result in higher stormflow peaks and volumes can accelerate channel scour, streambank erosion, and sedimentation. It is imperative, therefore, that anticipated changes in land use be evaluated in designing reservoirs.

Generalized equations or models are useful in examining the effects of several different land use activities on erosion and sedimentation. The results of modeling work can be helpful in pointing out needed land management constraints, protection measures, and erosion-sediment control. Options then can be developed to correct or reduce problems of sediment deposition at the dam site.

If erosion control practices are deemed necessary before or during dam construction, the effectiveness of alternatives must be evaluated carefully. Excessive levels of sedimentation can add significantly to the cost of a project (Ex. 15.1). Structural and nonstructural erosion control measures also are costly and should be aimed at the most critical sources of sediment. For example, if the main source of sediment at the site is derived from within the channel system, surface erosion control measures are not the answer. If surface and gully erosion are the main problems, structural and nonstructural solutions usually must be considered together. Structural solutions alone usually are not economically feasible, unless they are accompanied by appropriate land use practices that are compatible with soil conservation principles (see Chapter 8). In addition, all activities that are taking place on the watershed, and those anticipated,

EXAMPLE 15.1 ————————————————————————

Sediment and reservoir design (from Gregersen et al. 1987)

Sedimentation of reservoirs poses a serious threat to India's extensive irrigation system. Reducing sedimentation rates can significantly reduce the cost of dam construction (Sinha 1984). A 25% reduction in sediment export from a 629-km² watershed to one reservoir would allow the dam height to be constructed 0.53 m lower than the originally designed 36.6-m height. This translates into a savings of 4.5% in dam construction, not to mention the reduction in the number of hectares flooded by the reservoir pool. At another project, sedimentation from a 114-km² watershed would have to be reduced 75% to realize a 6% reduction in cost by reducing the height of the dam by 0.61 m. In the first project, a combination of watershed management and engineering measures may be capable of reducing sedimentation significantly. However, reductions of 75%, as required in the latter project, would be difficult to achieve. In either example, economic analysis with sound technical data (see Chapter 13) would be needed.

should be considered collectively. In other words, sedimentation from road construction and maintenance activities should be considered along with other sources such as surface, gully, and streambank erosion. Even if erosion can be reduced effectively, there already may be sufficient sediment within the channel system to continue sediment delivery at high levels over a long period of time (a method of evaluating changes in sedimentation at a reservoir site is outlined in Example 15.2).

Once a dam has been constructed and it is discovered that rates of sedimentation have been underestimated, the large investment of capital and human and land resources practically dictate some type of sediment control. Unfortunately, it can be too late to carry out effective erosion-sedimentation reduction after the dam has been constructed. Watershed management should be considered in the *early planning stages* of reservoir design.

Reservoir Operation

The effects of watershed use and management on reservoir operation can best be understood by considering an actual reservoir project, as illustrated in Figure 15.2. This multipurpose reservoir has storage space allocated for both conservation (water supply) purposes and flood control. Within the conservation storage is a buffer zone, the top of which is used as a threshold to allocate water releases from the reservoir for different demands during critical dry periods. Once the reservoir pool elevation drops to the top of the buffer zone, water can be released only for those purposes predetermined to be most important, such as providing municipal water supplies. Other, less essential needs will not be met until the pool elevation is higher than the top of the buffer pool. Several buffer zones can be used as a mechanism to allocate water on a priority basis during periods of shortages. If the project has a hydroelectric power–generating capacity, the amount of head required to drive the turbines—and the corresponding storage—would be an added operational zone in the reservoir. Once sediment begins to encroach into the various storage spaces, operating the reservoir to meet the respective demands becomes more difficult. As shown in Figure 15.2, sedi-

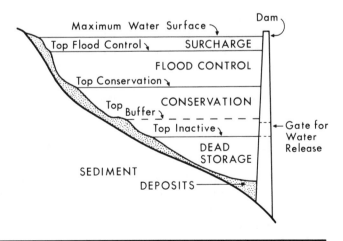

15.2. Storage allocation for a multipurpose reservoir with associated sedimentation.

EXAMPLE 15.2 _____

Method of evaluating current and projected land use impacts on reservoir life (adapted from Brooks et al. 1982)

Situation

A multipurpose reservoir will be constructed with a planned completion date 5 yr from the present. The design life of the project is 40 yr. The reservoir has the capacity to store 14 million m³ of sediment (once this storage is exceeded, the reservoir may be unable to meet all demands). The 18,200-ha watershed for the reservoir is in poor hydrologic condition; overgrazing and poor cultivation practices have resulted in high rates of soil erosion and downstream sedimentation. A watershed rehabilitation project, in which 50% of the uplands will be reforested and the remaining 50% will be reseeded with perennial grasses and forbs, is planned. For the project to be effective, only limited grazing will be allowed on the nonforested area; the forested area will be protected. This work, coupled with gully control structures in critical areas, is deemed necessary to reduce sedimentation rates at the reservoir site. The rehabilitation efforts should be in full effect in 8 yr.

Data

1. Existing rates of erosion (by Modified Universal Soil Loss Equation defined in Chapter 7):

$$A = RK(LS)(VM) = (80)(0.3)(10)(0.17)$$
$$= (40.8 \text{ tons/acre/yr})(2.23) = 91 \text{ tonnes/ha/yr}$$

2. Sediment density = 1.5 tonnes/m³
3. Sediment delivery ratio = 0.39
4. Total sediment deposited at reservoir site is estimated to be about 50% from surface erosion and 50% from channel erosion.

Assumptions Made

The watershed project likely will take 8 yr before it is in place and effective; after 8 yr, the soil condition should be improved (the soil erodibility factor $K = 0.28$) and the watershed vegetative cover will be:

½ watershed area = 50% forest canopy with a 60% ground cover (grass)

½ watershed area = 40% grass cover with 25% short shrub canopy

Gully control structures will be in place in headwater areas by the end of 3 yr following reservoir construction; assume all sediment delivered from upstream gullies will be negligible for 1 yr (that is, the structures are effective for only 1 yr); after that, consider the upstream erosion-sedimentation process to continue, but at the new rate.

Questions Posed

1. Under existing conditions, how many years will it take to exceed the designed reservoir sediment storage capacity?
2. If the watershed project is implemented, how many years will it take before the sediment storage capacity is exceeded?

Solution

1. Existing Rates of Erosion:

$$\frac{91 \text{ tonnes/ha/yr}}{1.5 \text{ tonnes/m}^3} = 60.7 \text{ or } 61 \text{ m}^3/\text{ha/yr}$$

For entire watershed:

$$(61 \text{ m}^3/\text{ha/yr})(18{,}200 \text{ ha}) = 1{,}110{,}200 \text{ m}^3/\text{yr}$$

Using a delivery ratio of 0.39, the amount of sediment delivered from upstream surface erosion is:

$$0.39(1{,}110{,}200 \text{ m}^3/\text{yr}) = 432{,}978 \text{ m}^3/\text{yr or } 433{,}000 \text{ m}^3/\text{yr}$$

If this is half of the total sediment that is delivered, total delivery is approximately:

$$(2)(433{,}000 \text{ m}^3\text{yr}) = 866{,}000 \text{ m}^3/\text{yr}$$

At this rate, the storage capacity will be exceeded:

$$\frac{14 \times 10^6 \text{ m}^3}{866{,}000 \text{m}^3/\text{yr}} = 16.2 \text{ yr after construction}$$

2. Since it will take 8 yr before the watershed practices are effective, the first 3 yr after the reservoir is constructed will have approximately the same rates of sedimentation.

On year 4, the sedimentation will be effectively controlled from upstream areas; the channel erosion will contribute 433,000 m³. By year 5, *K* will change from 0.3 to 0.28, and *VM* will change for the reforested and grassland areas and the new rates of surface erosion are:

Forested Area

$VM = 0.06$
$A = (80)(0.28)(10)(.06)$
   $= (13.4 \text{ tons/acre/yr})(2.23) = 29.97 \text{ tonnes/ha/yr or } 30 \text{ tonnes/ha/yr}$

This corresponds to 20 m³/ha/yr from half of the area, or 9100 ha, resulting in a total erosion of 182,000 m³/yr. With 0.39 sediment delivery ratio, this becomes 70,980 m³/yr sediment.

Grassland Area

> $VM = 0.09$
> $A = (80)(0.28)(10)(.09)$
> $= (20.2 \text{ tons/acre/yr})(2.23) = 45 \text{ tonnes/ha/yr}$
> $= 30 \text{ m}^3/\text{ha/yr}$ from the other half of the area or 9100 ha, with a total erosion of 273,000 m³/yr. With 0.39 sediment delivery ratio, this becomes 106,470 m³/yr

The total annual sediment delivery after watershed management practices are in place is:

> $70,980 \text{ m}^3 + 106,470 \text{ m}^3 = 177,450 \text{ m}^3$

Sedimentation after the reservoir project is completed
Years 1–3 at existing sediment rate $= (3)(866,000 \text{ m}^3/\text{yr})$
> $= 2,598,000 \text{ m}^3$

Year 4   only channel erosion $= 433,000 \text{ m}^3$

Year 5 $177,450 \text{ m}^3 + 433,000 \text{ m}^3 = 610,450 \text{ m}^3/\text{yr}$
and on

Years After Reservoir Completed	Sedimentation (m³/yr)	Remaining Sediment Storage (m³)
1	866,000	13,134,000
2	866,000	12,268,000
3	866,000	11,402,000
4	433,000	10,969,000
5	610,450	10,358,440
.	.	.
.	.	.
.	.	.
22	610,450	0

Therefore, with the project, the sediment storage capacity will be exceeded after 22 yr, in contrast to 16.2 yr without the project. To determine if the watershed project is feasible, an economic analysis would need to be performed (see Chapter 13).

ment typically does not settle out only in the dead storage space. Coarse materials are deposited at various inflow points in the upper reaches of the reservoir pool, whereas the finer sediments tend to settle out near the dam.

As sediment fills the active storage space, the capability of a reservoir to meet all demands becomes limited (Ex. 15.3). Storage volumes in the conservation pool can be inadequate to meet demands during periods of drought. Likewise, there may not be

EXAMPLE 15.3

Effects of land use on sedimentation levels in the Panama Canal watershed (from Larson and Albertin 1984)

The passing of each ship through the Panama Canal requires 197,000 m³ (52 million gal) of water to operate the locks. This freshwater is supplied from a 3339-km² watershed; water storage for operation is supplied by Gatun Lake, through which the canal passes, and Alhajuela Reservoir located at a higher elevation. Over 92% of the Alhajuela watershed has a slope exceeding 45%, of which 13,400 ha were cleared of forest and cultivated or pastured during the 1972–1973 period. Surface, gully, and mass soil erosion resulting from these land use practices have contributed sediment to the 800 million m³ of reservoir storage space. Sedimentation yields from the watershed before and after clearing were 10.5 and 29.1 tonnes/ha/yr, respectively. Sediment soundings made in Alhajuela Reservoir showed that deltas were filling the narrow and shallow parts near the mouths of tributaries. Sedimentation depths by 1978 averaged 1.7 m, ranging from 1m in deep areas to between 3 and 6 m in the delta areas. Sedimentation rates prior to land clearing and cultivation (1973) averaged 3.32 cm/yr, or 937,000 m³/yr. After clearing, sedimentation averaged 9.6 cm/yr or 2,595,000 m³/yr. This almost threefold increase in sedimentation was attributed to the clearing of only 18.2% of the watershed.

Because of the potential impacts of accelerated reservoir sedimentation on the operation of the canal, a watershed management plan was prepared in 1978. The program consisted of institution building, education and research, and implementation of watershed practices, including agroforestry, plantation forestry, forest reserves, pasture management, land use zoning, and soil conservation. More intensive sediment sampling of streams and the reservoir were accompanied by the establishment of three experimental watersheds to quantify the effects of forest-clearing practices on runoff, erosion, and sediment yield.

adequate storage space in the flood control pool to control major flood events. Some of these problems can be overcome, at least partly, by using an operational rule curve approach to reallocate storage space for different purposes on a seasonal basis, as illustrated in Figure 15.3. *Rule curves* provide target pool elevations that vary with the season; their purpose is to provide operational guidelines that allow the most efficient use of reservoir storage. Typically, the season in which irrigation supplies are needed is a period in which the threat of large floods is slight, therefore, the elevation of the conservation pool can be raised into the normal flood control pool during that time. When the flood season approaches, the conservation pool is then lowered to provide flood control space. Rule curves allow demands to be met with a smaller total storage capacity in the reservoir. But even rule curve operations may not suffice when sedimentation becomes excessive.

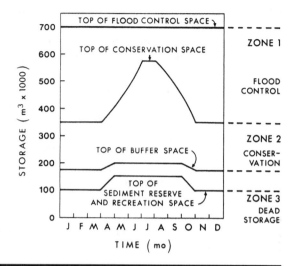

15.3. Operational rule curves illustrating seasonally varying storage requirements of a multipurpose reservoir (from U.S. Army Corps of Engineers 1977).

The development of rule curves involves considerable knowledge of the variability of inflow to the reservoir and a clear understanding of seasonal water demands, priorities, and the downstream channel capacity. Typically, high- and low-streamflow sequences observed in the past are used to develop and test rule curves to insure that water requirements and all constraints are met. When streamflow records are limited at the site, regional data can be used or streamflow records may be simulated with either deterministic or stochastic models.

Rule curves serve as guides in the operation of a reservoir, and the ability to adhere to these guides is improved by providing the reservoir manager with accurate, real-time forecasts of inflow. Many operating constraints must be considered along with the rule curves. For example, most reservoirs have restricted rates of change of outflow to prevent rapid surges of water downstream. In some cases, this can cause the reservoir pool elevation to deviate from the rule curve. Similarly, rule curves may occasionally be violated to accommodate temporary anomalies in the system. Examples would include changes in operation to accommodate the passage of migrating fish or to assist downstream efforts to remove a barge that has gone aground. However, such deviations in rule curve operations should not be allowed to adversely affect some other part of the system.

Although the focus of this discussion has been on reservoirs, it should be recognized that erosion and sedimentation can reduce the capacity of water conveyance systems that are needed to transport water from the reservoir to the locations where it is needed. Erosion control can be needed along with channel stabilization to keep conveyance systems operational.

Design Floods

Design floods (or design storms) are selected for reservoir studies as standards against which the performance of the facility can be evaluated. The design flood is simply the streamflow from a large storm and is defined by some selected criteria.

Design floods typically are referred to as spillway, reservoir, or project design floods. The spillway design flood is selected to determine the size of the spillway of the reservoir. The reservoir design flood, usually of a lesser magnitude, is used for sizing the flood control storage of a reservoir—the amount of space to be reserved for flood control.

There are several approaches for determining design floods. The *probable maximum flood* (PMF) is the flood that may be expected from the most severe combination of hydrometeorological conditions that are reasonably possible for an area. Typically, such a large event is used in the design of a spillway, particularly where failure would be disastrous in terms of loss of life. The *standard project flood* (SPF) is used as an upper limit design flood for major reservoirs or local protection projects. Often, a figure of 40–60% of the PMF rainfall is used to generate the SPF.

The estimated flood events are based on knowledge of the meteorological conditions in the region. A certain amount of judgement is used in determining both of these floods. An alternative approach is to determine floods with specific return intervals such as the 20-yr, 50-yr, or 100-yr event. A risk is associated with these design floods. Reservoir spillways probably should not be designed on the basis of recurrence intervals except where loss of life is not a factor or where the economic impacts of failure are insignificant. It must be realized, for example, that a reservoir designed on the basis of a 100-yr-recurrence-interval flood has associated with it a risk of failure of 67% over a 100-yr period (see Chapter 17). In the case of multiple projects, the design on the basis of the 100-yr event could be very misleading; if 100 reservoirs were designed in this manner, there is a 67% chance that one of those reservoirs will fail in any given year.

As with low-flow analyses used in conservation-storage studies, stochastic streamflow data can be generated for flood analyses. The concept of the design storm or design flood simply allows us to preselect the performance criteria that we wish to use for a particular water resource facility. Again, this performance criteria can be based on many factors other than hydrologic considerations. The economical, institutional, political, environmental, and social aspects also may be determining factors in the selection of performance criteria.

Selection criteria for design floods usually are established by an agency responsible for designing and operating the reservoir. If a project has a high dam with a large volume, and it is determined that the structure cannot be overtopped without disastrous consequences, an PMF likely would be chosen for spillway design. On the other hand, run-of-river hydroelectric power plants or diversion dams may be designed by means of an SPF or some historical flood event, in which case the structure could be overtopped without suffering serious damage. Small dams that impound 1–2 million m³ of water or less, or small recreational lakes and farm ponds, can be designed on the basis of floods with a specified recurrence interval. In such cases, where a dam is low enough and the storage small enough so that no serious hazard exists to downstream inhabitants if a failure occurs, an event such as the 50-yr recurrence interval flood may be selected.

Methods of simulating stormflow or flooding events are discussed in Chapter 17. For an SPF or PMF generation, one likely would select a model and use meteorological (rainfall) data to simulate streamflow. In the case of recurrence interval design floods, the study would involve a frequency analysis of existing streamflow records or the use of generalized criteria established by a governmental agency.

■ SMALL HYDROPOWER DEVELOPMENT

Since ancient times, the force of flowing water has been utilized as a source of motive power to drive pumps, grind grain, lift hoists, and by the 1880s, generate electric power. As technology in hydraulic turboelectric developments progressed, efforts were directed toward large-scale hydropower installations on large river systems and water bodies. This activity continued until the 1950s, when discoveries of extensive petroleum reserves pushed the prices of fossil fuels downward, to almost $1 a barrel, making oil-fired steam generation economically attractive.

Renewed interest in hydropower occurred in the early 1970s when fossil fuel prices rose to over $25 a barrel. Simultaneously, coal prices quadrupled to nearly $45 a metric ton, and the cost of nuclear fuel escalated to $42 a pound for yellow coke. Therefore, the change in the comparative economics of hydropower made potential installation sites more attractive. In addition, it indicated the economic feasibility of utilizing small water flows for small hydropower plants.

Small hydropower plants are hydraulic turboelectric plants whose capacity is 5000 w or below. Other definitions mention installation sites with flows less than a minimum discharge, for example, 1 m³/sec, regardless of the head. Being of small capacity, the plant machinery and auxiliaries generally are simple and inexpensive in design. In upland watersheds, the potential number of sites for such development is much greater than for large-scale hydropower dams.

Hydrologic Requirements

The *head* and *quantity* of water available must be known before a small hydropower installation is considered. For small plants, measures of streamflow in terms of annual mean, minimum, and maximum, and in some instances, flood flows over the previous 5 yr can be adequate. But, the hydrologic analysis becomes more detailed and involved as the size of the plant increases and the investment level grows.

Records of streamflow can be obtained by site measurements using flow meters or precalibrated control sections, or with hydrologic models. Upstream water sources also should be investigated for possible consolidation of diverted flows and leakages toward the main stream channel.

TOTAL HEAD

The *total head* (H) of a stream is the difference in elevation between the turbine of the hydropower system and the water level above the turbine, or the vertical distance between the turbine and the water level at the intake.

Frequently, a hydropower station will require a dam. With high-head turbines (discussed below), the dam may be located at a considerable distance upstream and the water conducted to the turbine through a pipe. When selecting a dam site, it should be remembered that the greater the vertical distance between the turbine and the water surface behind the dam, the greater the head will be. The greater the head, the more power a given amount of water will produce. Therefore, dam sites should be selected to obtain the highest possible head.

For preliminary work, the head can be estimated from topographic maps by measuring the differences in elevation between the turbine and the intake. Once a good intake point has been chosen, it is best to measure the vertical distance between the two by differential leveling.

NET HEAD

The *net head* (h) is the actual head or pressure available to drive the turbine when friction and other losses have been deducted from the total head. Friction losses vary with the type of pipe used, its diameter, and the length of pipe. Concrete and tile pipes have the highest losses, while PVC pipe has some of the lowest. The larger the diameter of pipe, the less the friction losses will be. Friction losses also increase with increasing length of pipe and with the number of bends or curves in the pipe. The choice of a hydropower installation site should be one where the highest head can be obtained in the straightest line and the shortest distance.

There are other losses in the total head at the turbine. In large part, these losses vary with the type of turbine utilized. Impulse turbines are commonly used in small hydropower installations that operate on a high head. The head loss for these turbines is across the gap between the nozzle and the tail water. Therefore, the net head (h) is the total head (H) less the friction losses in the pipe and the loss at the turbine:

$$h = H - \text{(pipe friction loss + loss at turbine)} \tag{15.2}$$

Friction losses in pipes can be read from standard tables obtained from the pipe manufacturers; head losses in turbines also can be obtained from the manufacturer of the turbine.

QUANTITY OF WATER

The quantity, or volume, of water flowing in the stream determines the amount of hydropower that can be developed at a site. Therefore, knowledge of streamflow is imperative.

In general, streamflow varies with the season of the year, and the minimum flow represents the amount of water that can be used to drive the turbines on a continuous basis. As the streamflow increases, the amount of power that can be developed also increases. Consequently, it is necessary that a stream be measured (see Chapter 4) at various times of the year or that streamflow sequences be simulated with models (see Chapter 17).

Topographic and Geologic Surveys

Topographic surveys complement the hydrologic measurements in the assessment of the water potential for small hydropower development. The size and contours of the watershed drainage and storage areas should be determined. Knowledge of the land to be submerged behind a dam, if a dam is to be built, is also important. Usually, the topography of the ground surface will suggest the appropriate location of an installation site and the necessity and location of a dam, although there are other factors to be taken into consideration, including the character of underlying rock strata, property lines, and pond area.

Geologic investigations frequently are undertaken to determine the structural strength of the areas where heavy loads are to be placed. Additionally, these investigations provide information on the water permeability of the soil and rock formations. Geologic studies also can indicate possible sources of quarry materials for the construction of dams.

Determination of Power Output

Having knowledge of the net head (h) and the streamflow (Q), the theoretical power (TKW) that a stream can produce is calculated by:

$$TKW = \frac{hQ}{102} \tag{15.3}$$

This equation gives the potential power that a stream can produce when the efficiencies of the turbines and generators in the system are 100%; however, this is seldom the case. In small hydropower plants, turbines usually drive the generators directly, either through a gear box or with belts. Manufacturers often claim an efficiency as high as 95% for gear boxes and 97% for single-belt drives. The best alternators, when DC current is generated, can have efficiencies of about 80%. A good turbine will operate at an efficiency of only 80%. Therefore, the overall efficiency for a gear box alternator system, for example, is calculated as:

$$\begin{aligned} \text{Efficiency} &= 0.95(\text{gear box})0.80(\text{alternator})0.80(\text{turbine}) \\ &= 0.60, \text{ or } 60\% \end{aligned} \tag{15.4}$$

This example is a relatively high efficiency that might be difficult to obtain in practice. Most systems operate at efficiencies less than this; to be on the safe side, it is better to assume an efficiency of about 50%. Therefore, the practical power (PKW) that can be generated by a stream is:

$$PKW = 0.50\left(\frac{hQ}{102}\right) \tag{15.5}$$

The above calculation should be made for the lowest and the highest seasonal flows, and the average dependable flow for a month. Once a practical power output that can be generated at a potential installation site has been determined, the work of the watershed resource manager may be completed. The task of actually designing the hydropower station to fit the situation usually is turned over to an electrical or mechanical engineer. The manufacturers of hydropower systems also provide this service. However, resource managers should be aware of some of the fundamentals.

Types of Hydropower Systems

Basically, there are two types of hydropower systems. *High-head systems* depend, in large part, upon the head of a stream, rather than the quantity of water available. These systems are best suited to locations where the power demand is not great. Many of these systems, with power outputs of 5–10 kw, have been installed throughout the world. *Low-head systems* depend on the quantity of water, not the head of the stream. These systems frequently are installed on relatively level terrain, but in streams and rivers with relatively high volumes of flow.

Turbines employed in the high-head systems are the impulse type, such as the Pelton or Tungo wheel. Turbines in low-head systems are usually of the reaction type, such as the old-fashioned waterwheel.

Environmental Considerations

Appraisals of small hydropower developments should include the nonenergy aspects of the water resource. For example, the quality of the water, in terms of acidity or alkalinity, and the type and density of the suspended sediments are important in selecting the turbine to be employed. The flow of water over spillways and outlets also can alter the water temperature, oxygen content, and in some cases, cause nitrogen oversaturation, which can be detrimental to downstream aquatic life. Such environmental concerns should be incorporated into the planning schemes by the energy sector.

Economics of Small Hydropower Developments

Small hydropower systems can be operated either as an isolated power source or tied into an existing electric power network or grid. In many instances, considerable savings in investments and social benefits can be realized with small systems. Rural inhabitants in remote areas can enjoy electricity for lighting, refrigeration, pumping power, and cottage industries, while at the same time, benefit from smaller investments in transmission lines, savings in reduced costs of maintenance, and simpler technology.

An economic evaluation of small hydropower developments should consider two principal costs: the capital expenditures of the investments and the annual operating costs. These costs then are compared with the values of benefits derived. Evaluation techniques include the calculation of the net present value, the benefit-cost ratio, and the internal rate of return (see Chapter 13). For most small developments, a benefit-cost analysis is performed in which the ratio of discounted benefits to discounted costs is determined.

In general, the observational experience is that the capital expenditures of small hydropower installations are two to five times that of an equivalently sized diesel or steam power plant, depending upon the size and layout. However, annual operating costs (labor, maintenance, repairs, etc.) of small stations are small. Therefore, the overall economic evaluation can yield favorable results for the small installation, although when the power output has to be transported to distant users, the costs of the transmission lines must be considered. Small hydropower developments commonly are most economical for remote and isolated areas, where the transmission investments are small and fuel transport is a problem. Furthermore, the relative simplicity of small hydropower equipment also makes it suitable for more isolated locations.

■ SUMMARY

Water resource development projects and programs usually include engineering structures, often reservoirs. To be successful, existing and future land use and management of upland watersheds must be considered in the planning, design, and implementation of such projects. After reading this chapter you should have some insight into how reservoirs and small hydropower plants are developed and managed, and how they are affected by land use and watershed management. Specifically, you should be able to:

1. Explain how different vegetation on a watershed can affect reservoir design and operation.
2. Answer the following questions:
   - what are the most critical factors that determine whether a reservoir will function as designed?
   - what can happen to the designed life of a reservoir when land use changes after the construction of a reservoir?
   - what role can small hydropower plants play in overall watershed development?
3. Discuss why and suggest how watershed management should become an integral part of reservoir, hydropower, and other water resource engineering development.

CHAPTER 16

Water Harvesting

■ INTRODUCTION

Water harvesting is a technique of developing surface water resources for the purpose of augmenting the quantity and quality of existing water supplies or for providing water where other sources are either not available or too costly. *Water-harvesting systems* can be defined as artificial methods for collecting and storing precipitation until it can be used for watering livestock, small-scale subsistence farming, and domestic use. These systems include a *catchment area,* usually prepared to improve runoff efficiency, and a *storage facility* for the harvested water, unless the water is to be immediately concentrated in the soil profile of a smaller area for growing drought-hardy plants. A water distribution scheme also is required for those systems devoted to irrigation. The technology of water harvesting can be applied to almost any dry region of the world (Ex. 16.1).

■ WATER-HARVESTING SYSTEMS
Configuration and Use

The geometric configuration of water-harvesting systems depends upon the topography, the type of catchment treatment, the intended use, and the personal preference of the designer. Microcatchments, strip harvesting, roaded catchments, and harvesting aprons are some of the more common types.

Microcatchments and strip harvesting can be successful in years of normal or above normal rainfall and are best suited for situations in which drought-resistant trees or other drought-hardy perennial species are grown (Ex. 16.2). The microcatchment procedure can be used in complex terrain or on steep slopes, where other water-harvesting techniques may be difficult to install. The collection area can range from 10 to 1000 m², depending upon the precipitation in the area and plant requirements; usually from one to several plants are grown on the low side.

Strip farming is a modification of the microcatchment method. Berms are erected on the contour, and the area between them is prepared to serve as the collection area. Runoff between the berms then is concentrated above the downslope berm to irrigate

EXAMPLE 16.1

Water-harvesting techniques applied in dry regions

Australia

Australia was among the first of the Western countries to install operational water-harvesting systems, which were designed to provide water for livestock and domestic needs. In 1948, the Public Works Department, western Australia, initiated a program of construction of roaded catchments. These catchments were made by clearing, shaping, and contouring to control length and degree of slope, and by compacting with the aid of pneumatic rollers. An estimated 2500 roaded catchments, with an averge size of approximately 1 ha, have been installed principally to supply water for livestock. Also, there are 21 roaded catchments totaling 706 ha, ranging in size from 12.1 to 70.8 ha presently being used to furnish domestic water for small towns in western Australia (Burdass 1975).

Israel

Researchers in Israel were the first to experiment in the application of new techniques to water harvesting. They have found various methods effective in increasing surface runoff, including land smoothing and compaction and the formation of sodic crusts by spraying applications of various asphaltic materials. Among the asphaltic formulations, heavy fuel oil diluted with kerosene proved to be both effective and economical. Ratios between contributing and receiving areas on the order of 3:1 to 6:1 were found to be effective in rainfall zones of 200–250 mm.

Unirrigated orchards provide a livelihood for an appreciable number of farmers (Hillel 1967). Water received in the planting zones of experimental plots provided soil moisture equivalent to the entire normal winter rainfall in the Mediterranean climatic zone of the country.

United States

The village of Shungopovi is built on top of a sandstone rock mesa on the Hopi Reservation in northeastern Arizona and had no source of water. From the time of first establishment, the villagers carried water up from the valley, initially on foot and later on the backs of burros. In the early 1930s, a small water-harvesting system was installed to partially relieve the water shortage. An area of approximately 0.33 ha was set aside and cleared, and the loose soil was removed to expose the sandstone bedrock. Below the area, a deep cistern was hewed into the rock and a concrete roof was constructed. This system was a functional part of the village water supply for about 30 yr, at which time, a community well and pump on the valley floor and uphill water-distribution system was installed (Chiarella and Beck 1975).

EXAMPLE 16.2

Experimental water-harvesting system in southern Arizona (Karpiscak et al. 1984)

A water-harvesting system consisting of a gravity-fed sump, a storage reservoir, sixteen catchments, and an irrigation system occupies nearly 2 ha of retired farmland near Tucson, Arizona. The combined designed capacity of the gravity-fed sump and the storage reservoir is approximately 2400 m³ of water. The sump and the storage reservoir were treated with sodium chloride (NaCl) to decrease infiltration, and the main reservoir was covered with 250,000 empty plastic film cans to decrease evaporation.

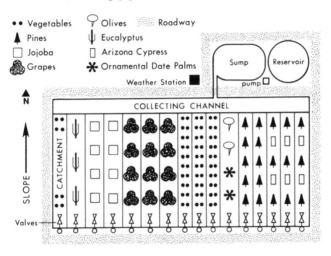

An example of a water-harvesting system as part of an agroforestry project in the Avra Valley, near Tucson, Arizona (from Karpiscak et al. 1984).

The 16 catchments, also treated with NaCl to decrease infiltration, have been used to concentrate rainfall runoff around planted agricultural crops and tree species in untreated planting areas at the base of the catchments. Excessive runoff flows directly into a collecting channel and then into the sump. Each catchment, about 1.5 ha in size, is approximately 90 m in length, varies from 6 to 18 m in width, and slopes about 0.5%.

The irrigation system consists of a 6000-w centrifugal pump, an 8-cm pipeline connecting the sump and the storage reservoir to the pump, two 5-cm PVC pipelines connecting the pump to the field plots, and 2-cm polyethylene driplines equipped with 0.01-m³/hr drip emitters. The valving system permits the movement of water from the sump to the storage reservoir, from the storage reservoir to the sump, and either the sump or the storage reservoir to the field. A water meter records the amount of water applied to the plants.

the vegetation planted there. Only drought-hardy plants should be grown with this type of system.

Apron-type water-harvesting systems, used primarily for livestock, wildlife, and domestic water supplies, are designed for minimum maintenance and must be fenced (Fig. 16.1). The catchment area (apron) is treated to obtain a high runoff efficiency, unless an existing impermeable surface is in place. Gravel-covered asphalt-impregnated fiberglass is a common treatment (Ex. 16.3). A storage tank with evaporation control is required with the necessary pipes and valves to conduct the water to drinking troughs or to households.

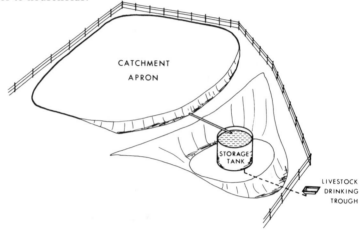

16.1. An example of simple water-harvesting system (from Frasier and Myers 1983).

The apron-type system is the simplest to design. As a first approximation for the size of apron required, the following equation is helpful:

$$A = b\frac{U}{P} \tag{16.1}$$

where A = catchment area (m²); b = 1.13, a constant; U = annual water requirement (l); and P = average annual precipitation (mm).

Roaded catchments are well suited to growing high-value horticultural crops such as fruit trees, nut trees, and grapes and for providing water for livestock. These catchments are best adapted to very gently sloping ground. A roaded catchment consists of parallel rows of drainages 100 m or less long and spaced 15–18 m apart. Trees or horticultural species are planted in the drainages. The areas between drainages are shaped much like high-crowned roads to serve as catchments. Side slopes of the catchment roads and longitudinal slopes of the drainages should be no more than about 2% to prevent erosion. The catchments are cleared of vegetation, smoothed, and treated (NaCl has been effective on expanding-clay soils) to reduce infiltration. If high-value horticultural crops are grown, water storage is necessary to provide supplemental irrigation water; this is accomplished easily by diverting excess water from the drainages into a storage facility.

EXAMPLE 16.3

Asphalt coverings for apron-type water-harvesting systems in Iran

Asphalt coverings were applied at a rate of 1 l/m^2 to slopes above the experimental runoff plots and terraces (2 m wide) on a hillside near Tehran, Iran, for harvesting rainwater for growing trees; rainfall runoff over a 5-yr period was substantial, *Robinia pseudocacia, Cupressus arizonica,* and *Fraxinus rotundifolia* were planted. There was a significant increase in height, stem diameter, and crown development of plants in asphalt-treated plots as compared to controls (Mehdizadeh et al. 1978).

Water harvesting for agriculture requires a more complex system than do the other systems. The size of the catchment area in relation to that of the agricultural area must be balanced against crop demands and water-storage capability. However, the systems can be readily adapted to existing topography, provided there is a level area to farm and care is taken with catchment construction to provide low slopes or, in steep terrain, short slopes broken by diversions. Compartmental reservoirs consisting of three storages are recommended. Electric, engine, or wind-driven pumps usually are necessary to transfer water between ponds and to drive the irrigation system, although gravity systems might be possible in steep terrain. Since relatively large quantities of irrigation water usually are required, efficient catchments are necessary, but treatments can be expensive. Sodium chloride, one of the least expensive treatments, is effective in locations where the soil has a sufficient quantity (about 10% or more) of expanding clays.

Water harvesting for subsistence farming has been successfully installed and shows great promise in alleviating the food and nutrition problems of arid lands. However, training in new techniques is necessary; more information is needed from around the world on crop phenology and water requirements; and additional demonstration projects under varying economic, social, and climatological conditions are needed to develop universal prescriptions (Ex. 16.4).

EXAMPLE 16.4

The use of furrows and ridges for water harvesting in India

Trials with okra were carried out to study the effects of different water conservation methods on plant growth and yield. Out of eight methods tried, the highest yield was obtained in furrows running east to west with plants in two rows 45 cm apart at the base of ridges 60 cm apart. The beneficial effect of this method was attributed to the rainwater drainage from the ridges to the plants (Vashistha et al. 1980).

Catchment Areas

The catchment area of a water-harvesting system is impermeable to water and can be used to produce runoff. Some examples of different catchment surfaces are:

1. Natural surfaces, such as rock outcrops.
2. Surfaces developed for other purposes, including paved highways, aircraft runways, or rooftops.
3. Surfaces prepared with minimal cost and effort, such as those cleared of vegetation or rocks and smoothed, or both smoothed and compacted.
4. Surfaces treated chemically with sodium salts, silicones, latex, or oils.
5. Surfaces covered with asphalt, concrete, butyl rubber, metal foil, plastic, tar-paper, or sheet metal.

The particular surface treatment selected will depend, in large part, upon the cost and availability of materials and labor. In general, the greater the runoff efficiency and life of treatment, the greater the cost. At one end of the scale, simple smoothing and compaction of nonporous soils is effective but requires annual maintenance. On the other end of the scale is asphalt-impregnated fiberglass covered with gravel, which can last 20 yr or more.

Desirable characteristics of catchment treatments include:

1. Runoff from the surface must be nontoxic to humans, plants, and animals.
2. The surface should be smooth and impermeable to water.
3. The surface material should have high resistance to weathering and should not deteriorate because of chemical or physical treatments.
4. The surface material need not have great mechanical strength, but it should be able to resist damage by hail or intense rainfall, wind, occasional animal traffic, moderate water flow, plant growth, insects, birds, and burrowing animals.
5. The surface material should be inexpensive and require minimum site preparation.
6. Maintenance should be simple.

Obviously, there is no single treatment that would have all of these characteristics. Some tradeoff is necessary, but lowest cost over the long term is often the overriding objective. Estimates of the costs of water harvesting using various catchment treatments in the United States are given in Table 16.1.

Selection only on the basis of cost can be a mistake, however. For example, simple, smoothed catchments produce water at low cost, but they do not provide runoff from small storms that characterize rainfall periods in many arid zones. A large, expensive structure might have to be built to store water for use during the period when no runoff occurs. The cost of a simple smoothed catchment plus the large storage required could be greater than the cost of a more expensive catchment that provides runoff from small storms.

There is no standard shape for a catchment surface. Flexibility is encouraged to utilize the natural topography to minimize the construction costs. The slope of the surface should be only as steep as necessary to cause runoff; ideally, the slopes should be less than 5%. The catchment surface must be cleared of vegetation, rocks, and

Table 16.1. Water costs for various water-harvesting treatments

Treatment	Runoff (%)	Estimated Life of Treatment (yr)	Initial Treatment Cost ($ US/ha)	Annual Amortized Cost[a] ($US/ha)	Water Cost in a 500-mm Rainfall Zone ($ US/ 1000m³)
Rock outcropping	20–40	20–30	< 120	< 240	58–119
Land clearing	20–30	5–10	120–230	< 120	79–119
Soil smoothing	25–35	5–10	600–840	120–240	66–188
Sodium dispersant	40–70	3–5	840–1440	120–240	34–119
Silicone water repellents	50–80	3–5	1440–2160	240–480	58–188
Paraffin wax	60–90	5–8	3600–4800	600–1200	132–394
Concrete	60–80	20	24,000–60,000	2040–5280	499–1725
Gravel-covered membranes	70–80	10–20	6000–8400	480–1200	119–335
Asphalt fiberglass	85–95	5–10	12,000–24,000	1680–5760	346–1321
Artificial rubber	90–100	10–15	24,000–36,000	2520–4920	494–1056
Sheet metal	90–100	20	24,000–36,000	2040–3120	399–679

Source: Modified from Fraiser (1975), by permission.
[a] Based on the life of the treatment at 6% interest.

other debris that might reduce the durability of a treated surface or retain water on the surface.

Water Storage

Basically, there are three types of storages: the soil profile, excavated ponds, and tank or cistern containers. Ancient water-harvesting systems were simple arrangements where water was directed from hillsides onto cultivated areas, with the idea of immediately storing the water in the soil for plant use. The problem with this arrangement was whether or not sufficient water could be stored to offset a prolonged drought. However, the method is still in use today and can be used to grow drought-resistant varieties of trees and other economic plants.

Excavated ponds are often the only economical means of storing the large quantities of water needed for farming, but evaporation and seepage are serious problems. Evaporation suppression on water impoundments is still in the experimental stage; surface-area reduction, reflective methods, surface films, mechanical covers, floating styrofoam balls, and empty plastic film canisters have all been used. Most have been somewhat effective, but a simple economical method has yet to be developed. Surface films generally are not economical on small impoundments. Reflective methods (beads or dyes floating on the surface) are ineffective in windy conditions. Some types of floating mechanical covers and floats have worked well in experimental situations, but most are short-lived and all are expensive.

Two relatively inexpensive methods for reducing evaporative surface area that have been effective in some situations are the compartmented reservoir system and sand- or rock-filled reservoirs. The compartmented reservoir is a system of pumping water between two or three ponds to minimize total surface area. Sand or rock reservoirs are structures either deliberately filled with rock or designed to capture gravel and sand alluvium, as well as water. However, about 50% of the capacity can be lost after filling. Sometimes, the dam is built in stages, so that only coarse sediments are deposited. A well is sunk behind or through the dam to draw out the stored water. After the water level has sunk to about 1 m below the surface of the fill, evaporation effectively ceases.

Seepage from ponds can account for 60–85% of the total annual water loss. Seepage control is simpler and less expensive than evaporation control. Chemical dispersing agents, bentonite, soil cement, membrane liners, asphalt, salt, and simple compaction have all been used successfully to seal impoundments. Treatment method and application rate is determined by soil type, purpose of the impoundment, severity of wetting and drying cycles, and economics.

Tanks or cisterns can be used effectively for livestock watering and domestic supplies. Seepage and evaporation are less difficult to control and are less expensive. Any container capable of holding water is a potential water-storage facility. External water storage, a necessary component for a drinking water supply system, also can be a part of a runoff-farming system, where the water is applied to the cropped area by some form of irrigation system. In many water-harvesting systems, the storage and water distribution facility is the most expensive single item, representing up to 50% of the total cost.

There is an almost infinite number of types, shapes, and sizes of wooden and reinforced plastic storages. Costs and availability are primary factors for determining the potential suitability of these storages. One common type of storage is a steel tank with vertical walls and a concrete or other type of impermeable bottom. Storages constructed from concrete and plaster are relatively inexpensive but require considerable hand labor. Roofs over the storages are a common technique for suppressing evaporation, although they are usually expensive. Floating covers of low-density synthetic foam rubber are an effective means of controlling evaporation from vertical-walled, open-topped storages, and they are not expensive.

■ CONSTRAINTS AND STRATEGIES

The strategy to be taken in developing a water-harvesting system depends upon a number of constraints. Some of the more important include:

1. The need for acceptance by the local community, whether the system is to be used for livestock, domestic purposes, agroforestry, or farming.
2. The quantity and quality of water required to meet the demand.
3. The availability of alternative, less expensive sources that could be developed.
4. The amount, seasonal distribution, and variability of rainfall.
5. The materials, labor, and machinery available and suitable for installing a water-harvesting system within budgetary limitations.
6. The provisions for maintenance.

Need for Acceptance

The need for water in arid and semiarid lands is common and must be reconciled with what can be accomplished. Furthermore, the user must be aware of the potential benefits as well as the limitations of a proposed water resource system. Rural people generally cannot take chances with unproven methods for their survival, but the ultimate success of a water-harvesting project depends on the full support of the user for proper operation and maintenance.

In areas where the concepts of water harvesting and runoff farming are not fully accepted, the first system installed must be constructed from materials that require minimum maintenance and have maximum effectiveness. It may be necessary to build a higher-cost system to insure acceptance of the concept by the user. Once the concepts are accepted, it often is possible to utilize lower-cost materials and techniques on subsequent units, even though these systems may have a greater chance of failure or require additional effort from the user. If users have been shown that the *ideas* are valid, they are more likely to expend the extra effort to operate and maintain the system properly.

Water Quantity and Quality

With some exceptions, such as microcatchments and strip catchments, most water-harvesting systems must have storage facilities to supply the quantity of water needed at the time it is needed. For livestock, the need depends on the grazing systems employed and the monthly distribution of rainfall. Many combinations of catchment and storage sizes will provide the desired quantities of water, but the problem is to find the most economical combination. For domestic supplies, people in the United States require from 20 to 40 l/day for cooking, drinking, and washing. The system should be designed to account for this minimum requirement, in addition to any losses that would occur by evaporation or seepage from storage.

Water-harvesting systems designed for agriculture are more difficult to design. There frequently is little information on the minimum total water requirements of agricultural crops, although consumptive use data are available for crops abundantly supplied with water. Of equal importance to the total water requirement is the timing of the water needs. The seasonal pattern of use from initial establishment of the crops to harvest must be satisfied by the design of the water-harvesting system. This type of information has been developed for many crops under intensive irrigation, although these values can be higher than needed for many runoff-farming applications. Relationships of this nature must be developed or estimated for proper design of agricultural water-harvesting systems and matched with the water supply to determine frequency and amount of irrigation.

Water collected from a catchment can contain organisms and water-soluble impurities from windblown dust deposited on the surface, chemical pollutants directly from the treatment (salt, silicone, tars, or oils), weathering by-products created by deterioration of the treatment materials such as asphalt and certain plastics, which deteriorate in sunlight and heat into water-soluble products. Animal feces can be a source of bacterial and viral contamination, if the area is not fenced and properly graded. However, the quality of water from most surface treatments usually is adequate for livestock, but filters are needed in most cases if the water is for human consumption. None of the surface treatments, even with sodium, appear to affect plant production.

Alternative Water Sources

Although water harvesting is not necessarily expensive, there may be other sources of water near a particular site that can be developed more cheaply or that would insure more reliable supplies. For instance, untapped springs, a shallow groundwater table that may receive reliable recharge along a mountain front, and perched water that might be tapped with horizontal wells offer possibilities. All potential sources should be thoroughly investigated and evaluated with respect to number, location, yield, dependability, and quality before embarking on a project. If there are other convenient sources that can be developed economically, but are deficient in yield or dependability, they may be used to supplement a system. When groundwater quality is poor (high salt content, for example), harvested rainwater might provide sufficient dilution for the intended use.

In some cases, incorporating intermittent water sources into the total water supply system can permit the installation of a smaller water-harvesting facility. The harvested water can be saved for periods when the ephemeral sources are insufficient or dry up entirely. This combination not only saves time and money but can be of major importance during extended drought periods.

Amount, Distribution, and Variability of Precipitation

The amount, distribution, and variability of seasonal or annual rainfall are the key factors that must be evaluated in designing a water-harvesting system. Long-term daily records of precipitation are the most desirable; in arid lands, at least 15–20 yr of record usually are needed. If there are large variations among years, data from the two wettest years should be eliminated. If sufficient long-term data are available, stochastic methods can be used to determine the probabilities of extreme periods. Mean annual rainfall is not a good indicator of available water because there will be more years with rainfall less than the mean than there will be years with rainfall greater than the mean.

To compensate for dry years, the size and efficiency of the catchment areas and storage can be increased. Regardless of the design, there will be risk involved because of the uncertainty of rainfall. The user must decide the amount of risk that can be accepted should there be insufficient rainfall during some periods.

In general, water harvesting likely will be uneconomical in locations with an annual rainfall of less than 50–80 mm. If the annual rainfall is no more than 150 mm, the planting of indigenous or drought-resistant species using microcatchments or along contour strips is suitable. Systems designed for livestock watering also can be used but will require storage tanks protected from evaporation losses as well as efficient catchment surfaces. Farming systems are possible in areas with annual rainfall greater than 250 mm if there are adequate water storage facilities. Drought-resistant crops should be used on sites with 250–300 mm of annual rainfall, unless the rainfall period coincides with the growing season. Conventional agricultural crops can be grown where the annual rainfall is 300 m or above.

The ultimate size of the catchment area should be determined by computing a weekly or monthly water budget of collected water (Eq. 16.1) and then comparing these values with the water requirement to help insure that there are no critical periods when there will be insufficient water. Smaller systems frequently can be used when the periods of maximum rainfall coincide with periods of maximum use. Larger systems with adequate storage capacity are necessary when the periods of greatest precipitation occur after the periods of greatest water needs. Here, it can be necessary to store water for 6–9 mo.

Materials, Labor, and Machinery

There is no best material for catchment and storage. The cost of alternative water sources and the importance of the water supply determine the costs that can be justified in a system (Fig. 16.2). Systems that supply drinking water are constructed from materials that, in general, are more costly than can be justified economically for runoff-farming applications. One must balance the cost of materials with the cost of labor.

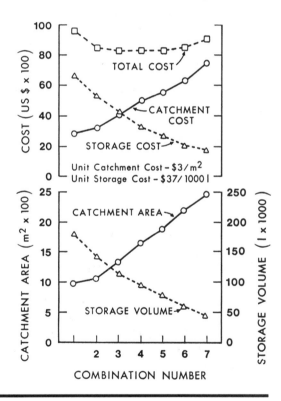

16.2. Cost estimates for different catchment sizes and storage volumes for water-harvesting systems (from Karpiscak et al. 1984).

Some materials and installation techniques are labor intensive but have a relatively low capital cost. Other materials can be higher in initial cost but require minimum labor for proper construction.

Maintenance

Failure to provide for maintenance will result in early failure of any system, and failure to repair minor damage can result in complete destruction of the system. Therefore, a maintenance program must be followed, even when the water collected is not being used. Some types of catchment treatments and storages require more frequent and intense maintenance than others. However, most water-harvesting systems can be maintained adequately with only annual inspection and repair visits.

All elements of the system should be inspected, including checks for leaks in any valves, pipes, or water storages, as well as the condition of the catchment for possible weed, animal, and insect control. Inspections and repair usually require only a few hours, but are as essential to the system as the initial installation.

■ SUMMARY

Water harvesting offers a method of effectively developing the scarce water resources of arid and semiarid regions. In contrast to the development of groundwater, which is usually a finite water resource, the method allows use of rainfall that occurs, even though in limited amounts, year in and year out. It is also a relatively inexpensive, small-scale method of water supply that can be adapted to the resources and needs of rural communities and small landholders who are several stages removed from the benefits of large-scale development projects. Despite this, water harvesting is not a panacea. There is some risk, dependent upon the uncertainties of climate; new skills, though simple, are required, maintenance is a constant necessity, and good design is imperative.

There is no universally "best" system of water harvesting; however, there will be some type of system that can be designed to best fit within the constraints of a given location. Each site has unique characteristics that influence the design of the most optimum system. All factors—technical, social, physical, and economic—must be considered.

During the past two decades, there have been many water-harvesting systems constructed and evaluated at different places in the world. Some of the systems have been outstanding successes, while others were complete failures. Some systems failed because of poor design or the materials used; others failed despite good design and proper materials because social factors were not integrated into the systems. These latter systems failed because of poor communication and lack of commitment by the local people both in planning and financing the projects. A successful system must be technically sound, properly designed, and maintained; economically feasible for the resources of the user; and capable of being integrated into the social traditions and abilities of the users.

After reading this chapter, you should be able to:

1. Determine the catchment area necessary to meet a specified annual water requirement, knowing the annual precipitation amount.

2. Present some examples of different catchment surfaces, and describe the desirable characteristics of catchment surfaces in general.

3. Describe some alternative methods of reducing an evaporative surface area.

4. Explain the constraints and strategies to be considered in developing a water-harvesting system.

CHAPTER 17

Hydrologic Methods

■ INTRODUCTION

Hydrologic information is needed for watershed management planning, performing economic and other types of analyses needed for project design, and making land use impact assessments. Sometimes, there may not be adequate hydrologic, meteorologic, and biophysical data available at locations of interest, and even when data are available, it can be difficult to decide which is the most appropriate method to use. Hydrologists must apply the appropriate tool or method for a given situation. When hydrologic information cannot be obtained from existing analytical methods, some type of field research or monitoring may be needed. This chapter presents an overview of analytical and field methods commonly used to obtain hydrologic information for watershed management and discusses guidelines for their application.

■ ANALYTICAL METHODS
Criteria for Selecting Methods

Numerous methods exist for estimating streamflow characteristics, such as peakflow, stormflow volume, annual water yield, and low-flow sequences. These methods range in complexity from simple equations to comprehensive computer simulation methods. Selecting the appropriate hydrologic method requires the careful consideration of:

1. The type and accuracy of information required.
2. All available data.
3. The physical and biological characteristics of the watershed.
4. The technical capabilities of the individual performing the study.
5. The time and economic constraints.

Study objectives usually dictate the type of information required (Table 17.1) and, in some cases, indicate which method should be used. For example, sizing culverts for rural roads requires peak discharge estimates associated with some predeter-

Table 17.1. Project objectives and the corresponding hydrologic information needed

Objectives	Hydrologic Information
Culvert design for storm drainage	Peakflow rates for small contributing area corresponding to a particular return interval
Floodplain delineation	Peakflow rates and associated stages (elevations) of large stormflow events
Spillway design for a dam	Hydrographs for extreme meteorological and hydrological events
Conservation storage requirements for a reservoir	Streamflow rates or volumes during critical drought periods
Water quality assessment	Volumes and discharge rates for selected events
Feasibility for mini-hydro project	Low streamflow sequences during dry-season flow and critical drought periods
Determine land use impacts on water yield	Runoff volumes over time for respective land uses

mined risk. Runoff is usually from small, simple drainages, and errors in the estimate of peakflow do not result in great economic loss. Therefore, simple, quick methods are applicable. Conversely, peak discharge estimates for floodplain mapping may require a more complex but reliable method. More time and effort can be justified in floodplain mapping, particularly if errors could result in large economic losses or losses of life.

After determining which hydrologic characteristics are of interest, the available data should be examined. Sometimes the data are insufficient for all but the simplest of hydrologic methods.

Watershed characteristics, including size, shape, vegetative cover, topography, soils, and geology, as well as some climatic and hydrologic data in proximity to the study area, are used to select an appropriate hydrologic method. Some methods are applicable only for small, homogeneous drainages, while others can be applied to large complex watersheds.

The capacity or capability of the individual or organization performing the study is another important consideration. One should be knowledgeable about the methods used and their limitations. A common constraint with current technology is the availability and type of computer facilities and software; when they are available, computer programs are invaluable for most large-scale hydrologic investigations.

Modeling Concepts

Hydrologic models are simplified representations of actual hydrologic systems that allow us to study the function and response of watersheds to various inputs and, thereby, gain a better understanding of hydrologic events. Furthermore, they may allow us to predict the hydrologic response of watersheds. For the most part, hydrologic models are based on the systems approach (Fig. 17.1) and differ in terms of how and to what extent each component of the hydrologic process is considered.

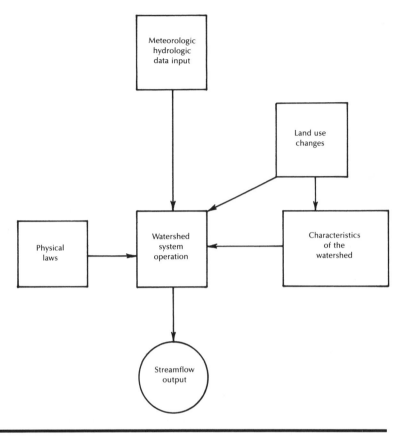

17.1. Systems approach for modeling the hydrologic response of watersheds (adapted from Dooge 1973).

TYPES OF MODELS

Models in general may be classified as *material* or *mathematical* (Woolhiser and Brakensiek 1982). Material models can either be *physical,* scaled-down versions of a real system, or *analog* models, which use substances other than (but analogous to) those in a real system. An example of a physical model would be a miniature, scaled version of a particular watershed and channel system; simulated rainfall can be applied in different patterns or quantities to evaluate differences in streamflow response. Physical models are used sometimes for channel and engineering structure (usually hydraulic) analysis, but they are expensive and cannot be used for general application. They also are not practical for most watershed hydrologic analyses because the physical and biological system cannot be reproduced. An example of an analog model is an electric analog in which the flow of electricity represents the flow of water. Analog models have been used with success in modeling groundwater flow. Because material models have limitations for most watershed applications, except for engineering purposes, we will confine our discussion to mathematical models.

Mathematical models can be either *empirical* or *theoretical* and can be further classified as *deterministic* or *stochastic*. Theoretical or physically based models rely on physical laws and theoretical principles. It is assumed that the hydrologic functions or relationships in a system are well understood and can be mathematically approximated directly from system characteristics. In contrast, empirical models are based on observed input-output relationships and do not necessarily simulate the actual processes involved. Empirical models rely on data and observations and simply relate output response to a given input.

Deterministic models mathematically characterize a system and give the same response or results for the same input data. For example, a given rainstorm with a particular intensity and duration will yield the same hydrograph response, once the model parameters and initial conditions are fixed. Conversely, stochastic models use the statistical characteristics of hydrologic phenomena to predict possible outcomes and have a random element that results in a different outcome for each execution of the model. Therefore, one can examine an array of possible outcomes that may never have been observed in the past, yet have some likelihood of occurring in the future. Stochastic models can be applied to specific problems, such as the estimation of drought sequences for the design of reservoir storage for irrigation (see Chapter 15). Several hundred years of simulated streamflow can be generated for the purpose of examining "potential" low-flow periods.

Deterministic models can be grouped according to how and to what extent hydrologic processes of a watershed are represented. The simplest are regression models that statistically relate one or more measurable watershed or climatological characteristics to some hydrologic response of interest, such as annual water yield. Regression models are empirical and useful for the watershed or perhaps the region from which they were developed, but they should not be applied elsewhere. In many instances, regression models have led to the development of simple formulas or equations that have more widespread application.

Although deterministic models can be either empirical or theoretical, most hydrologic models are a composite of mathematical relationships, some empirical, some based on theory. As one attempts to explain or predict events from complex systems, there is a need for more detail and complexity in the model formulation; however, the reality is that our understanding of hydrology is not sufficient to mathematically represent every process. This leads to the development of models, or parts of models, that need to be calibrated; relationships and parameters then must be fitted for a given watershed. Such a process involves adjusting parameters until the computed response approximates the observed response. Once calibrated, models then can be used to estimate the hydrologic response of the watershed to new, independent input data.

DEVELOPMENT OF MODELS

Models can be developed from source data in a number of ways. One common approach is through linear regression analysis (see Chapter 18). With this approach, the best equation for a scatter diagram of source data is calculated, with the dependent variable regressed against the independent variable. Theoretically, the line of best fit will predict the dependent variable from measurements of the independent variable. The line is positioned statistically such that the deviations of actual dependent values at observed independent value points, when squared and summed, are minimized.

Often, when source data are plotted in a scatter diagram, the equation for a straight line is not the appropriate relationship or "model" to use. In these instances, curvilinear (nonlinear) functions are selected to represent the data. Again, the regression constants are calculated to minimize the sum of squares of the deviations of observed and predicted values.

In the curve-fitting process, it generally is best to use a regression model that expresses a natural relation between the variables. Knowledge of the behavior of variables that are employed in a relationship allows the selection of one specific regression model over another. This process often leads to the development of more detailed field studies that can help to define cause-and-effect relationships. When cause-and-effect relationships cannot be identified, empirical relationships are derived.

Selection of the regression model to represent a particular set of data is somewhat of an art. The choice should be made with an awareness of the statistical properties of various regression models, among which the linear, polynomial, logarithmic, and semilogarithmic are encountered most frequently in watershed management. One or some combination of these forms usually will fit the source data being considered.

The assemblage of one or more appropriate "predictive functions," such as those defined by regression analyses, may allow for the simulation of a particular watershed system. Simulation of that system can help examine its response to different *inputs* and levels of inputs. The sensitivity of model outputs or response to changes in the value of regression constants (parameters) in the model can be determined, and the effects of modifying the structure of the system on response can be examined. Furthermore, assessments of subsequent development of a system and requirements for additional support data also can be determined.

Increasingly detailed computer-simulation techniques have come with the increasing sophistication of electronic computers. Mathematical models that previously were interpreted manually can now be analyzed, almost instantaneously, on a computer. The increased speed of computation allows the use of modeling procedures that have been seldom used previously because of excessive time requirements.

In a computer simulation, mathematical equations of a watershed system are assembled in a flow diagram. These models then are translated into a set of instructions in a higher-order computer language, such as FORTRAN (FORmula TRANslation). Next, the models expressed in a computer language are entered into a computer, along with the appropriate descriptive, or input, data. Finally, by executing the models, outputs that predict the response of the system to given inputs are obtained.

For ease of operation, many simulation models require input data that are introduced through answers to questions posed to the user by the computer program. These are termed *interactive* models, in contrast to assemblages of data records on magnetic disks or tape that are input to *batch* (or noninteractive) models.

As might be expected, computer-simulation modeling is used widely in many fields of science and management. Primary reasons for this are the savings of time and costs and the flexibility of modeling as an analytical tool. The users of models should not forget, however, that models are abstractions of real systems and that the output from models is only an estimate of hydrologic response. Moreover, confidence limits of the predicted output values are difficult to ascertain.

Simplified Methods and Models

The need for hydrologic information from ungauged watersheds has led to the development of a wide array of analytical methods, empirical formulas, and models. Simplified models relate some hydrograph characteristic to measurable watershed characteristics. Most are empirical models developed from observation or experimentation, without necessarily identifying or simulating the processes involved. Sometimes, these are called "black box" models that relate hydrologic output directly to input variables using one or more simple (regression) equations.

DIRECT TRANSFER OF HYDROLOGIC INFORMATION

Occasionally, hydrologic information can be transferred from a gauged to an ungauged watershed if the two watersheds are hydrologically similar. The hydrologic similarity depends on the following:

1. Watersheds should be within the same meteorological regime.
2. Physical and biological characteristics, such as soils, geology, topographic relief, watershed shape, drainage density, type and extent of vegetative cover, and land use should be similar.
3. Drainage areas should be about the same size, preferably within an order of magnitude.

The *direct transfer method* is quick, easy to use, and normally used only for rough approximations; however, it is applicable only if the assumption of hydrologic similarity is met. If a significant amount of adjustment is needed to transfer hydrologic information from a gauged to an ungauged watershed, there can be little confidence in the result.

Once it is determined that the involved watersheds are indeed hydrologically similar, direct transfer can be applied in two ways. First, the entire historical record from a gauged watershed can be transferred, with minor adjustments for differences in the size of drainage areas. For example, the observed streamflow record could be multiplied by the ratio of ungauged to gauged watershed areas. The second approach is to transfer hydrologic characteristics (such as the 100-yr return period annual flood peak), again, adjusting for drainage area differences. The entire flood-frequency curve for an ungauged location can be estimated by adjusting curves that have been developed from a similar but gauged watershed.

RATIONAL METHOD

The *rational method* is perhaps the most commonly used simplified formula that can be used to estimate peak discharge from rainfall. The basis of the rational method is that the maximum rate of runoff occurs when the entire watershed area contributes to flow at the outlet. Therefore, peak discharge estimates are valid only for storms in which the rainfall period is at least as long as the watershed *time of concentration*. Time of concentration (T_c) is the time required for the entire watershed to contribute runoff at the outlet, or, specifically, the time it takes for water to travel from the most distant point on the watershed to the watershed outlet.

Peak discharge from small (less than 1000 ha), relatively homogeneous watersheds is estimated from:

$$Q_p = \frac{CP_g A}{K_m} \qquad (17.1)$$

where Q_p = peak discharge in m³/sec; C = runoff constant (Table 17.2); P_g = rainfall intensity (mm/hr) of a storm with a duration at least equal to the time of concentration of the watershed; A = area of the watershed (ha); and K_m = constant, 360 for metric units (1 for English units).

Table 17.2. Values of runoff constants (C) for the rational method

Soil Type	Cultivated	Pasture	Woodlands
With above-average infiltration rates; usually sandy or gravelly	0.20	0.15	0.10
With average infiltration rates; no clay pans; loams and similar soils	0.40	0.35	0.30
With below-average infiltration rates; heavy clay soils with a clay pan near the surface; shallow soils above impervious rock	0.50	0.45	0.40

Source: Adapted from American Society of Civil Engineers (1969) and Dunne and Leopold (1978).

The assumption that rainfall intensity is uniform over the entire watershed for a period equal to the time of concentration is seldom met under natural conditions. To apply this method, rainfall intensity–duration values associated with an acceptable risk are used.

Models much like the rational method have been developed throughout the world and many express regionalized relationships (see Gray 1973, for examples). Such models are applicable for studies where peak discharge estimates are needed quickly or where few data are available. A typical application would be sizing a road culvert using regionalized rainfall data of some specified design criteria or recurrence interval (Ex. 17.1).

HYDROLOGIC RESPONSE FACTOR

The stormflow response of a watershed can be characterized by calculating the average ratio of *stormflow volume* or quickflow volume to precipitation volume for several periods of stormflow. Precipitation can be rainfall, snowmelt, or both. Stormflow volume, that portion of the hydrograph that responds quickly to a rainfall or snowmelt event, is determined by separating *baseflow* from total streamflow during the storm event (Ex. 17.2). By comparing response factors for watersheds with different vegetative cover and land uses within the same climatic region, the flood-producing potential for different areas can be estimated. In addition, the response factor can be used to develop quick estimates of peak discharge where a consistent relationship exists between stormflow volume and peak. A constraint with this method is that precipitation and streamflow data must be measured to determine the response

EXAMPLE 17.1

Using the rational method to size a culvert

A culvert system is to be designed with a risk of 10% for a design life of 5 yr for a 145-acre forested watershed, based on following information:

1. Soils are medium-heavy clays with good structure.
2. Maximum distance (measured from map) along the stream to the most distant ridgetop = 2430 ft.
3. Maximum elevation difference along the maximum stream pathway = 75 ft.

First the time of concentration must be calculated to determine the appropriate rainfall intensity to use. Using the Kirpich formula as reported by Gray (1973):

$$T_c = \frac{0.0078 L^{0.77}}{\left(\dfrac{H}{L}\right)^{0.385}}$$

where T_c = time of concentration (min); L = distance from main stream outlet to the most distant ridgetop (ft); and H = difference in elevation between main stream outlet and the most distant ridge (ft).

In this case:

$$T_c = 0.0078(2430)^{0.77} (0.031)^{-0.385} = 12 \text{ min}$$

The probability that a peak will be equalled or exceeded in the next 5 yr is $P_n = 1 - (q)^5$ where q is the probability of nonoccurrence (Eq. 2.8). Since we want the probability to equal the risk (0.10), the culvert must be designed to convey a peak with $(1 - q)$ probability or a $1/(1 - q)$ return period:

$$0.10 = 1 - (q)^5$$
$$5 \log q = \log 0.90$$
$$q = 0.98$$
$$\frac{1}{(1 - q)} = 50 \text{ yr}$$

From a rainfall intensity–duration frequency curve, the 50-yr rainfall event for 12 min is 2.90 in./hr; therefore:

$$Q = CP_g A = (0.30)(2.90)(145) = 126.2 \text{ cfs}$$

EXAMPLE 17.2

Baseflow separation

Baseflow or delayed flow must be separated from total streamflow for several single-event methods of stormflow analysis. The stormflow volume is that portion of the hydrograph above baseflow and sometimes is called direct runoff, or quickflow. There is no universal standard of separating baseflow because flow pathways through a watershed cannot be directly related to the hydrograph, which represents the integrated response of all flow pathways. This does not present a problem for most flood analyses, however, because the baseflow contribution is typically a small fraction of stormflow (10% or less). Therefore, efforts to devise elaborate baseflow separation routines are usually not warranted. The following is recommended:

1. Graphically separate baseflow from stormflow for several storm hydrographs, such as methods I and II (in figure below). Once one method has been adopted, it should be used for all analyses.

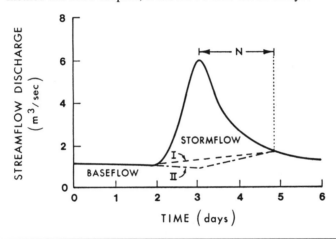

Methods of separating baseflow from stormflow; I and II are different approaches.

2. After examining several such storms, determine if there is a consistent relationship that can be expressed as follows:
   a. Draw a straight line from the beginning point of the hydrograph rise to a point on the recession limb defined by N days after the peak, where $N = A^c$ (see figure); A = watershed area (mi²); c = coefficient, typically a value of 0.2 is used (Linsley et al. 1982).
   b. Determine if the separation line I yields a consistent rate. Hewlett and Hibbert (1967) found that 0.05 cfs/mi²/hr was satisfactory for watersheds in the southeastern United States.

factor. Also, the factor is dependent on the antecedent moisture condition of the watershed. However, this does not preclude a regional analysis if regression models can be used to predict response factors based upon measurable watershed characteristics such as size, slope, vegetative cover, and land use.

Stormflow analyses of small watersheds in Georgia by Hewlett and Moore (1976) yielded prediction equations of the form:

$$Q_s = 0.22 \, R(SD)P^2 \tag{17.2}$$

where Q_s = predicted stormflow in the area (in.); $R = \sum_1^n (Q_s/P)/n$, for n observations and $P \geq 1$ in.; SD = "sine-day" factor = SIN [360 (Day No. / 365)] + 2, where Day 0 = November 21; and P = total storm precipitation in the area (in.).

The sine-day factor approximates antecedent moisture conditions as a seasonal coefficient for the region.

Comparisons of stormflow volumes and peaks (Q_p) yielded:

$$Q_p = 25 \, R(SD)^{0.5}P^{2.5} \tag{17.3}$$

where Q_p = predicted peak discharge above baseflow (cfs/mi^2).

Applications of the response-factor method are given in examples 17.3 and 17.4. Simple relationships (like the response factors above) are useful, but should not be applied to watersheds outside the region in which they were developed.

EXAMPLE 17.3

Using the stormflow response-factor method to estimate culvert size

Using the response factors developed by Hewlett and Moore (1976), the peak discharge for a 300-acre forested watershed with $R = 0.14$ for a rainfall of 3.5 in. is to be determined to select the appropriate size of culvert needed. The wettest month, February, will be used to obtain the maximum response ($SD = 2.99$).

$$Q_p = 25(0.14)(2.99)^{0.5} (3.5)^{2.5} = 138.70 \text{ cfs/mi}^2$$

For the 300-acre watershed:

$$\left(\frac{138.70 \text{ cfs}}{\text{mi}^2} \right) \left(\frac{300 \text{ acres}}{640 \text{ acres/mi}^2} \right) = 65.02 \text{ cfs}$$

If the average baseflow for the stream is 4 cfs, then the culvert(s) must be capable of conveying a discharge of 69 cfs.

EXAMPLE 17.4

Applying the response-factor method to estimate storage requirements

Determine the amount of storage required to hold the total discharge from a 24-hr, 50-yr return-period rainstorm (7.5 in.) on a 3000-acre watershed. The watershed has a 70% cover of old forest ($R = 0.10$) with 30% of the area in pasture and cultivated land ($R = 0.18$). Assume $SD = 2.99$ (February storm).

Forested

$$Q_s = 0.22(0.10)(2.99)(7.5)^2 = 3.70 \text{ area in.}$$
$$\text{Volume} = (3.7 \text{ area in.})(2100 \text{ acres})(1 \text{ ft}/12 \text{ in.})$$
$$= 647.5 \text{ acre ft}$$

Pasture and cultivated

$$Q = 0.22(0.18)(2.99)(7.5)^2 = 6.66 \text{ area in.}$$
$$\text{Volume} = (6.66)(900 \text{ acres})(1 \text{ ft}/12 \text{ in.}) = 499.50 \text{ acre ft}$$

Total storage required

1147 acre ft

Generalized Models

Generalized models are those mathematical methods that have been developed and tested on more than one watershed or stream system and that can be applied directly to similar systems elsewhere. Implicit with generalized models is that they require some level of data to describe a given hydrologic system so that one system can be distinguished from another. Generalized models include simplified formulas (for example, the rational method) that predict some hydrograph characteristic, techniques of hydrograph analysis, dynamic hydraulic routing, and continuous streamflow simulation. No matter how complex, each model is an abstraction of the physical system and uses generalized mathematical functions to estimate hydrologic relationships.

Projects and studies involved with flooding, structural design, and reservoir management require detailed and complex stormflow hydrographs that cannot be obtained with the simplified methods previously discussed. In addition, when the hydrologic response of more than one watershed within a larger basin is desired, hydrographs must be routed and combined to obtain an integrated response. The following paragraphs describe methods of developing stormflow hydrographs, estimating low-flow sequences, and predicting streamflow sequences over time.

UNIT HYDROGRAPH

One of the most widely used methods of stormflow analysis is the *unit hydrograph* (UHG), which is the hydrograph of stormflow (direct runoff, or quickflow) resulting from 1 unit (1 mm) of effective precipitation occurring at a uniform rate over some time period and some specific areal distribution over the watershed. It uniquely represents stormflow response (hydrograph shape) for a given watershed. The *effective precipitation* is the amount of rainfall or snowmelt that is in excess of watershed storage requirements, groundwater contributions, or evaporative losses. It is the portion of total precipitation that ends up as stormflow; therefore, the volume of effective rainfall equals the volume of stormflow.

The UHG method is simply a "black box" model that empirically relates stormflow output to a given duration of precipitation input. No attempt is made to simulate the various hydrologic processes involved in the flow of water through the watershed. The UHG concept provides the basis for several hydrologic models of greater complexity and wider application than simplified formulas such as the rational method.

Development of a Unit Hydrograph. The UHG concept can be best understood by examining the method for developing a UHG from an isolated storm (Fig. 17.2). Records of the watershed are examined first for single-peaked, isolated streamflow hydrographs, which result from short-duration, uniform rainfall or snowmelt hyetographs of relative uniform maximum intensity.

Once a hyeto-hydrograph pair is selected, the scale of the hydrograph is converted to centimeters or inches of depth by dividing streamflow by the watershed area. The total stormflow depth is determined from the hydrograph by separating the more uniform baseflow from the rapidly changing stormflow component (Fig. 17.2A). Each ordinate of the stormflow hydrograph then is divided by the total stormflow depth resulting in a normalized hydrograph of unit value under the curve (Fig. 17.2B).

The area-weighted hourly precipitation distribution that caused the stormflow hydrograph is the next factor to be determined (Fig. 17.2C). Effective rainfall is defined as being equal to stormflow; therefore, the total interception, storage, and deep seepage loss is determined as the difference between total rainfall or snowmelt and total stormflow (Fig. 17.2D). The magnitude of these losses is largely a function of antecedent moisture conditions. In Figure 17.2D a uniform-loss rate was assumed, but a diminishing-loss curve can be used if available. The effective rainfall in Figure 17.2D was uniform during the 2-hr period bracketed by the loss curve. This duration of effective rainfall characterizes the UHG, not the duration of the UHG itself. For example, a UHG developed from an effective rainfall of ¾-hr duration is a ¾-hr UHG, that of 1-hr duration is a 1-hr UHG, and of 6-hr duration is a 6-hr UHG. Unit hydrographs also can be developed from multipeaked stormflow hydrographs by means of successive approximations. Such complex storms are best analyzed with computer assistance.

The normalized shape of the UHG is characteristic for the watershed for a given intensity of effective rainfall and is actually an index of stormflow runoff for a particular watershed; it represents the integrated response of that area to a given rainfall input. The UHG method assumes that the effective rainfall and loss rates are relatively uniform over the entire watershed area. Also, the watershed characteristics that affect runoff response must remain constant from the time that the UHG is developed until the time it is applied.

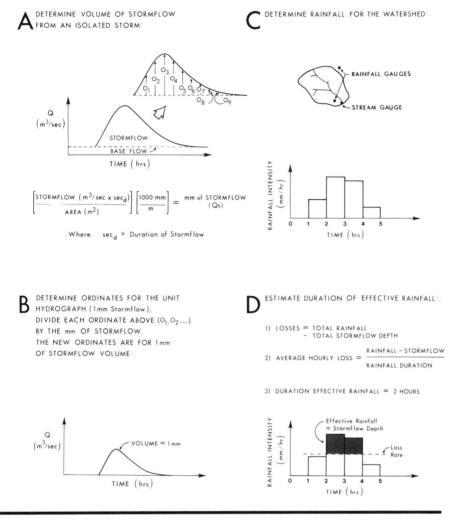

17.2. Development of an hourly unit hydrograph from an isolated storm. A: determination of stormflow volume; B: determination of ordinates; C: determination of rainfall; D: estimation of duration of effective rainfall.

Application of a Unit Hydrograph. To apply a UHG, the rainfall quantity and distribution over time from a design storm must first be obtained from the watershed (see Chapter 3). Estimated loss rates then are subtracted from total rainfall to obtain the quantity, distribution, and duration of effective rainfall. The rainfall duration is divided by the selected UHG duration to obtain the number of time periods to be added up for the total design storm. The ordinates of the selected UHG then are multiplied by the quantity of effective rainfall for each time period. For example, 20 mm of effective rainfall yields a stormflow hydrograph with ordinates 20 times that of the corresponding UHG for the first time period, and 30 mm of effective rainfall is 30 times the UHG, but delayed, for the second time period (Table 17.3). The calculated

Table 17.3. Application of a 1-hr unit hydrograph to a storm of 2 hr of effective rainfall

Time (hr)	1-hr UHG Ordinates (m³/sec)	Effective Rainfall (mm)	Stormflow			Base-flow (m³/sec)	Total Discharge (m³/sec)
			Time 1 (m³/sec)	Time 2 (m³/sec)	Subtotal (m³/sec)		
0	0.00	0	0.00	0.00	0.00	1.2	1.2
1	0.05	20	1.00	0.00	1.00	1.2	2.2
2	0.50	30	10.00	1.50	11.50	1.2	12.7
3	1.00	0	20.00	15.00	35.00	1.2	36.2
4	0.75	0	15.00	30.00	45.00	1.2	46.2
5	0.50	0	10.00	22.50	32.50	1.2	33.7
6	0.25	0	5.00	15.00	20.00	1.2	21.2
7	0.00	0	0.00	7.50	7.50	1.2	8.7
8	0.00	0	0.00	0.00	0.00	1.2	1.2

stormflows, plus any baseflow, then are added up for each time period to obtain the total runoff hydrograph.

The assumption of linearity is not always valid. As effective rainfall increases, the magnitude of the peak actually can increase more than the proportional increase in the rainfall amount. The consequences of ignoring such a nonlinear response can be to underestimate the magnitude of peak discharge for large storm events. If a nonlinear response is suspected, two or more UHGs should be developed from observed hydrographs resulting from substantially different rainfall amounts. The appropriate UHG then would be applied only to precipitation amounts similar to those used to develop the UHG in the first place.

It must be emphasized that the UHG developed from a specific duration of effective rainfall can be applied only to effective rainfall that fell over the same duration. For example, a 6-hr UHG cannot be applied directly to analyze a storm with an effective rainfall that occurred over 2 hr. The duration of a UHG must be changed in such cases. The most common method of converting a UHG from one duration to another is the S-*curve method* (Fig. 17.3). Once a UHG of a specified duration (say, 4 hr) is developed, an S-curve can be constructed by adding the UHGs together, each one lagged by its duration. The summation of the lagged UHGs is a curve that is S-shaped and represents the runoff response expected for a rainstorm of infinite duration, but at the same intensity of precipitation as the component UHGs (for a 4-hr UHG, the intensity would be 0.25 mm/hr). Once the S-curve is constructed, a UHG of any duration can be obtained by lagging the S-curve by the desired UHG duration, subtracting the ordinates, and correcting for precipitation-intensity differences as illustrated in Figure 17.3.

Before any empirical model such as a UHG is used for design or study purposes, the model should be tested on observed data. If historical streamflow responses can be reconstructed with a UHG model, then the model can be assumed to be valid.

One of the most difficult problems with the testing (verification) and application of UHGs is determining the appropriate loss rates. Such losses are dependent upon watershed characteristics and antecedent moisture conditions.

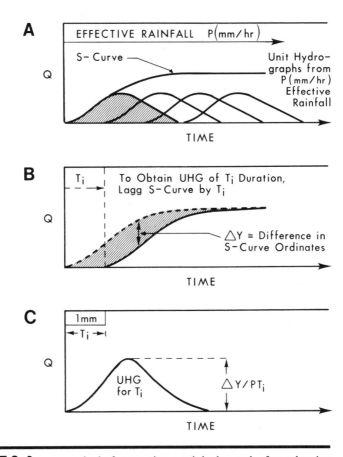

17.3. S-curve method of converting a unit hydrograph of one duration of P (mm/hr) effective rainfall to another duration (T_i). A: S-curve is the sum of UHG that result from P(mm/hr) of effective rainfall; B: S-curve is logged by T_i and the difference of ordinates $= \Delta Y$; C: the resulting UHG of T_i duration.

Loss Rate Analysis. Loss rates, as used in the UHG concept, represent the rainfall or snowmelt that occurs but that does not contribute to stormflow. Early engineering hydrology textbooks used the terms loss rates and infiltration rates interchangeably, which led to the idea that stormflow occurs only when infiltration capacities are exceeded and, therefore, result entirely from surface runoff. This is not the case, particularly for forested watersheds where subsurface flow predominates. As applied in the UHG, it is not necessary, and in fact not desirable, to equate loss rates with infiltration rates. Perhaps a more appropriate definition of losses would include precipitation that is stored on vegetative surfaces (interception), in the soils (where soil moisture deficits occur), as detention storage, or as water that percolates to groundwater or is otherwise delayed.

Therefore, a loss-rate function need not approximate infiltration curves and can be approximated in most instances with either a constant loss rate (ϕ index) or with a constantly diminishing loss rate. Loss rates have to be determined empirically for the entire watershed.

Synthetic Unit Hydrographs. The UHG method described above may be of limited value for many watershed studies because both rainfall and streamflow data must be available. Because streamflow data seldom are available at locations of interest, synthetic UHG models have been developed. These models consist of mathematical expressions that relate measurable watershed characteristics to UHG characteristics. Runoff hydrographs for ungauged watersheds can be estimated with synthetic UHG models if loss rates can be approximated.

The Soil Conservation Service (SCS) method (U.S. Soil Conservation Service 1972) incorporates generalized loss-rate and runoff relationships developed from watershed studies in the United States. The following equation, developed using English units, is used to estimate the stormflow volume from a given storm:

$$Q = \frac{(P - 0.2S_t)^2}{P + 0.8S_t} \tag{17.4}$$

where Q = stormflow (in.); P = rainfall (in.); S_t = watershed storage factor (in.); and $0.2S_t$ = an initial loss that was a consensus value determined in the original development of the method.

A watershed index or curve number (CN) is related to S_t as follows:

$$CN = \frac{1000}{10 + S_t} \tag{17.5}$$

Soil-vegetation–land use characteristics are related to curve numbers that indicate the runoff potential for a given rainfall (Table 17.4). Soils are classified hydrologically into four groups:

A = high infiltration rates; usually deep, well-drained sands and gravels with little silt or clay
B = moderate infiltration rates; fine to moderate-textured, well-structured soils, light sandy loams, silty loams
C = below-average infiltration rates; moderate- to fine-textured, shallow soils, e.g., clay loams
D = very slow infiltration rates; usually clay soils or shallow soils with a hardpan near the surface

Three antecedent moisture conditions (AMC) are considered, depending on the amount of rainfall received 5 days prior to the storm of interest:

AMC I = dry, < 0.6 in.
AMC II = near field capacity, 0.6–1.57 in.
AMC III = near saturation, > 1.57 in.

After the CN is determined, rainfall is converted to stormflow graphically (Fig. 17.4).

Table 17.4. Runoff curve numbers for hydrologic soil-cover complexes for antecedent moisture condition II

Land Use	Treatment or Practice	Hydrologic Condition	A	B	C	D
	Cover			Hydrologic Soil Group		
Fallow	Straight row		77	86	91	94
Row crops	Straight row	Poor	72	81	88	91
		Good	67	78	85	89
	Contoured	Poor	70	79	84	88
		Good	65	75	82	86
	Contoured and terraced	Poor	66	74	80	82
		Good	62	71	78	81
Close-seeded legumes[a] or rotation meadow	Straight row	Poor	66	77	85	89
		Good	58	72	81	85
	Contoured	Poor	64	75	83	85
		Good	55	69	78	83
	Contoured and terraced	Poor	63	73	80	83
		Good	51	67	76	80
Pasture or range		Poor	68	79	86	89
		Fair	49	69	79	84
		Good	39	61	74	80
	Contoured	Poor	47	67	81	88
		Fair	25	59	75	83
		Good	6	35	70	79
Meadow		Good	30	58	71	78
Woods		Poor	45	66	77	83
		Fair	36	60	73	79
		Good	25	55	70	77
Farmsteads			59	74	82	86
Roads (dirt)[b]			72	82	87	89
(hard surface)[b]			74	84	90	92

Source: U.S. Soil Conservation Service (1972).
[a]Close-drilled or broadcast.
[b]Including right-of-way.

For the SCS model to be valid, *CN* relationships should be determined for each hydrographically different region. The relationships developed in the United States generally are applicable to small watersheds (less than 13 km[2]) with average slopes less than 30%.

Once effective rainfall is determined, a hydrograph can be produced. Peak discharge (Q_p) can be approximated with the triangular hydrograph method (Ex. 17.5):

$$Q_p = \frac{K_o A Q}{T_p}$$

(17.6)

where K_o = constant, a value of 484 means that ⅜ of the UHG volume is under the rising limb, for mountainous watersheds a value near 600 may be appropriate, wetlands may be closer to 300, this is not a universal constant; A = area in square miles;

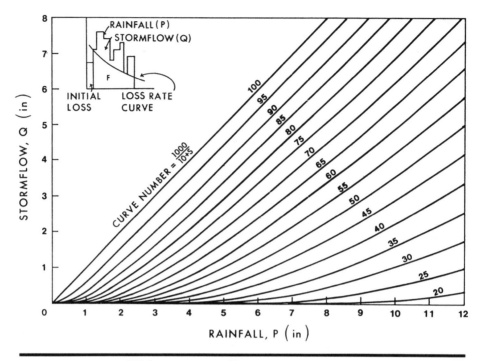

17.4. Rainfall-runoff relationships for curve numbers (from U.S. Soil Conservation Service 1972).

EXAMPLE 17.5

Application of the SCS method

A 4-in. rain fell over a 4.6-mi² watershed in good pasture condition, with soils in group D, and an AMC II. The duration of rainfall was 6 hr, and the time of concentration was estimated to be 2.3 hr. The stormflow and the corresponding peak discharge are estimated as follows:

1. From Table 17.4, $CN = 80$.
2. Enter Figure 17.4 with 4 in. of rain and a curve number of $= 80$. The stormflow is approximately 2.0 in.
3. Peak discharge for the watershed with a time of concentration (T_c) of 2.3 hr is determined as follows:

$$T_p = \frac{\Delta D}{2} + 0.6 T_c$$

$$= \frac{0.31}{2} + (0.6)(2.3) = 1.53 \text{ hr}$$

$$Q_p = \frac{(484)(4.6)(2)}{1.53} = 2910 \text{ cfs}$$

Q = stormflow volume (in.); T_p = time to peak in hours, where $T_p = \Delta D / 2 + 0.6T_c$; ΔD = duration of unit excess rainfall in hours = $0.133\,T_c$; and T_c = estimated time of concentration in hours.

Changes in stormflow associated with changes in the soil-vegetation complex are determined largely by the CN relationships. For example, changing from a good pasture condition, within hydrologic soil group C, with AMC = II, to a poor pasture condition, changes the CN from 74 to 86. In turn, this would result in an increase in stormflow volume from 3.2 in. to 4.6 in. for a 6-in. rain. In some instances, the time of concentration also could be altered, which would affect the peak and general shape of the stormflow hydrograph.

ANALYSIS OF RECESSION FLOWS

At the beginning of a dry season or in periods between isolated storms, the flow of water from a watershed usually diminishes with time. Without further replenishment, much of the water that reaches downstream users during such periods is recession flow. Typically, these flows originate from the upland watersheds, which are characterized by different vegetative cover types and land use patterns. Therefore, an analysis of recession flows can provide a basis for comparing different land management activities and their effects on streamflow between storm events.

Factors Affecting Recession Flows. While considerable information exists as to the influence of vegetative cover types and land use patterns on water yield (see Chapter 6), knowledge of recession-flow response to land management activities is less complete. It commonly is assumed that recession flows are dependent largely upon the storage characteristics of a watershed. The variability in recession flows is apparently due to the loss of water by evapotranspiration. The magnitude and duration of recession flows are both related to the rate of water movement through the soil, which is affected by vegetation and land use characteristics. Vegetative cover types, land use patterns, and the season determine the variability in soil moisture conditions and, hence, affect the rate of recession flow.

Hydrograph Analysis. To evaluate recession-flow characteristics, a number of regression models are available (Table 17.5). By consolidating variables such as evapotranspiration, soil moisture, and land use patterns into one constant term for a given recession-flow event, recession flows from different watersheds can be characterized and compared.

Of the regression models available, the equation reported by Barnes (1939) is used widely throughout the United States. This equation is:

$$Q_t = Q_o k^t \tag{17.7}$$

where Q_t = streamflow discharge after a time period t (cfs); Q_o = the initial discharge (cfs); k = the recession constant per unit of time; and t = the time interval between Q_o and Q_t in hours or days.

Table 17.5. Recession-flow equations

Type of Function	Reported or Reproduced by
$Q_t = Q_0 k^t$	Barnes 1939
$Q_t = Q_0 e^{-bt^n}$	Horton 1933
$Q_t = Q_0^{-at}$	Hall 1968
$Q_t = Q_0/(1 + at)^2$	Hall 1968
$Q_t = 1/(at + Q_0)$	Indri 1960
$Q_t = a/t^n + b$	Toebes and Strang 1964
$Q_t = a + (Q_0 - a)k^t$	Wicht 1943
$Q_t = Q_1^{-at} + Q_2^{-at}$	Hall 1968

Q_t = streamflow discharge after time t (cfs).
Q_0 = initial streamflow discharge (cfs).
k = recession constant.
b, n, a = constants defined by respective authors.
e = natural logarithm.

A linear form of the equation can be obtained by a transformation onto semilogarithmic paper, with discharge on the logarithmic scale and time on the arithmetic scale:

$$\log k = \frac{\log Q_t - \log Q_o}{t} \tag{17.8}$$

The slope k evaluated in this equation is considered to be indicative of differences in recession flows, attributed collectively to the effects of vegetative cover, land use patterns, season of the year, and soil moisture.

Streamflow data frequently are reported as daily averages; however, analysis of these averages can prevent the identification of individual hydrographs resulting from small storms not shown by the average streamflow for a day. Furthermore, the peaks identified by data points may not be representative of the actual peaks of the storms that caused the recessions.

For prediction purposes, it is a common practice to arrange the recession flows chosen for analysis in a manner such that a "composite" recession flow is formed to represent the complete recession for a particular watershed. However, such a procedure can be subject to judgmental errors and errors attributed to factors that contribute to the differences between short-event recessions (for example, evapotranspiration losses), which vary greatly from time to time. Therefore, evaluation of the constant k for a recession based on a "composite" curve may not be justified in a particular study. Instead, the average recession flow may be evaluated, with the variability measured as differences between slope constants of individual recession limbs.

From an analysis of recession flows of all major streams in Iowa, Howe (1966) found that there were no major differences in the values of the recession constants for watersheds that were less than 100 mi². It was concluded that the variability in recession flows due to area differences is small and, therefore, may not be important in most evaluations. However, Brown (1965) described the recession-flow characteristics of watersheds in the forests and woodlands of Arizona, and concluded that the average slope of the recession flows differed according to vegetative cover.

Generalized Continuous Simulation Models

The previous section dealt with single-event methods and models that allow estimates of certain hydrograph characteristics, such as peaks, stormflow volumes, or recession flows with limited data. For many hydrologic investigations, an estimate of streamflow response over an extended period of time is needed. Such information is useful for determining reservoir-conservation storage requirements (see Chapter 15), for investigating water quality, and for estimating differences in annual streamflow or streamflow patterns before and after watershed modifications. More complex models that require more extensive data usually are needed for such applications.

Continuous simulation models compute streamflow discharge over time periods that include more than one storm event and intermittent low-flow sequences. Such models use a water budget approach and simulate hydrologic processes such as interception, evaporation, transpiration, detention storage, and infiltration to varying degrees. Processes must be linked mathematically so that the conservation of mass principle is not violated. To be manageable, many such models are called *lumped* models, which means the spatial variability of processes and characteristics over the watershed unit are ignored; therefore, land units that are being modeled should be relatively homogenous in terms of hydrologic characteristics. However, for most watersheds of any size, the area usually must be subdivided into many relatively homogenous units that are modeled separately, and then streamflow values are combined and routed to obtain the overall system response. *Distributed* models attempt to characterize the spatial variability of a hydrologic property such as infiltration capacity.

Continuous simulation models should be conceptually sound, flexible in design, and physically relevant. Input data requirements should not be too detailed or complex, and the output should be presented in a way that it can be used conveniently. The utility of such models depends on input-output capabilities and on the applicability of its constants or parameters to ungauged or altered watersheds.

The utility of continuous simulation models is that they can be used for a variety of hydrologic investigations. For example, models like the Stanford, or a latter version called Hydrocomp Simulation Program (HSP), have been used as transport models for water-quality components. However, the temporal and spatial variability of most water-quality constituents limit their application to studies requiring only approximate answers.

Generalized continuous simulation watershed models evolved primarily as a result of engineering and flood-forecasting needs; most have the general form illustrated in Figure 17.5. The Stanford Watershed Model, the Streamflow Synthesis and Reservoir Regulation Model (SSARR), the "Sacramento" Model, and the U.S. Department of Agriculture Hydrograph Laboratory (USDAHL)-74 Watershed Model are examples. Hydrologic processes, represented mathematically, are calculated as flows and storages. Model parameters (or variables) of an *empirical* model usually cannot be measured exactly thus require fitting, which is accomplished by comparing observed and simulated streamflow. Parameter optimization routines are available sometimes, but even so they represent a trial-and-error procedure, which matches computed results with those observed. The greater the number of fitted parameters in a model, the more difficult the application to ungauged or altered areas. A regional analysis using regression techniques (described later) can be useful to estimate parameters for ungauged areas.

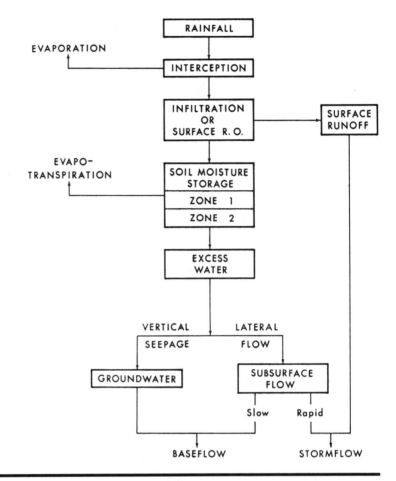

17.5. Hydrologic processes and runoff relationships commonly found in generalized continuous simulation models.

Soil and vegetation parameters in some of the above-mentioned models are not of sufficient detail to directly simulate the hydrologic effects of land use activities such as forest clearcutting or converting from rural agriculture to urban areas. As a result, detailed, more *theoretical* or *physically based* models have been developed to estimate the hydrologic effects of land management activities.

MODELING HYDROLOGIC EFFECTS OF WATERSHED MODIFICATIONS

The need to evaluate the hydrologic consequences of a specific activity, such as clearcutting forest cover or the implications of a comprehensive management plan that involves several different land use changes, led to the development of models oriented to land management. The hydrologic response of altered watersheds can be modeled in essentially two ways. The first and perhaps most appealing approach is the application of a physically based model in which all hydrologic processes changed by the modification must be represented and determined from measured characteristics (Larson 1973). The empirical approach, which offers a practical alternative to physically based models, links regional relationships, usually determined from experimental watershed studies, with readily available data and empirically predicts an outcome. The latter approach relies on extensive data from experimental studies.

Few physically based watershed models have been used in practice, although many have been developed and tested as part of research projects. Some physically based hydraulic models have been developed and used to estimate the effects of channel modification on streamflow. Extensive data are needed for even the more simple hydraulic models, but data requirements and the degree of complexity increase exponentially when water flow and storage processes are modeled for the entire soil-plant-atmosphere system. Examples of some continuous simulation models that have a more physical basis are listed in Table 17.6.

Models capable of predicting hydrologic effects due to changes in vegetative cover or land use practices have not been developed for global application. Rather, models have been developed that can simulate streamflow response to specific land use practices for a particular region and/or ecosystem, such as the subalpine Water Balance Model (WBMODEL) (Table 17.6), which is designed to simulate streamflow response due to timber management activities in the subalpine zone of the Rocky Mountains. The development of such regional models is continuing, and with the use of long-term watershed research data for testing and verification, useful models should be forthcoming for more areas in the world.

Statistical Methods

REGRESSION MODELS

Regression models are mathematical functions that describe relationships between a dependent variable (hydrologic response) and one or more independent variables, such as watershed and climatological characteristics. These models are approximations based on sampling and thus subject to sampling variation.

Linear regression models have been used extensively in streamflow studies and may be of the form:

$$Y = a + bX \qquad (17.9)$$

or

$$Y = a\,X^b \qquad (17.10)$$

transformed to

$$\log Y = \log a + b(\log X) \qquad (17.11)$$

where Y = dependent variable; a, b = regression constants; X = independent variable.

The dependent variable may be annual runoff in millimeters and the independent variable annual precipitation in millimeters for a given watershed. Many times, a nonlinear response such as Equation 17.10, is found but is transformed into the linear form

Table 17.6. Examples of continuous simulation models that have been used to examine the hydrologic effects of land use changes

Model	Processes Simulated				Flow		Application	Reference
	Rainfall	Snowfall	Infiltration	ET	Surface	Subsurface		
HSP	x	x	x	x	x	x	Simulates streamflow records for forested, rangeland, agricultural, and urban watersheds; engineering applications (PL/1 language, 250-K storage)	Hydrocomp (1976)
PROSPER			x	x	x	x	Simulates water flow through soil-plant-atmosphere system, computes water yield for different soil-plant systems (FORTRAN IV language)	Goldstein et al. (1974)
USDAHL-74	x	x	x	x	x	x	Simulates streamflow records for agricultural watersheds; considers zones of infiltration and exfiltration; similar to variable source area approach (FORTRAN IV language, 99-K storage)	Holton et al. (1975)
WBMODEL	x	x	x	x	x		Simulates hydrologic changes resulting from watershed management in Colorado subalpine zone; produces year-round water budget (FORTRAN IV language, 100-K storage)	Leaf and Brink (1973)

(Eq. 17.11) to simplify the analysis. For example, streamflow (Y) versus stage or water-surface elevation (X), or suspended-sediment concentrations in parts per million (Y) versus discharge in cubic meters per second (X), typically are represented by such a log-transformed relationship.

Multiple regression models are developed where the addition of other measured variables statistically improves the prediction of some hydrologic response. Such relationships are of the form:

$$Y = a + b_1 X_1 + b_2 X_2 + \ldots + b_n X_n \qquad (17.12)$$

where a = constant; and b_1, $b_2 \ldots b_n$ = slope of the relationships between respective independent variables X_1, X_2, $\ldots X_n$ with the dependent variable Y.

Multiple regression models have been useful for predicting streamflow characteristics for watersheds over a large area or region. Examples include regional relationships between peak discharge or low-flow discharge of a specified return period and other characteristics, such as watershed area, annual rainfall, percentage of area in lakes or wetlands, and watershed or channel slope. Models can be developed for an array of floods or low-flow duration events with different recurrence intervals. Regional analyses of this type are useful for estimating streamflow characteristics for ungauged watersheds.

Multiple regression also can be used to estimate hydrologic processes from readily obtained data. For example, potential evapotranspiration can be estimated by an equation using air temperature, wind velocity, and relative humidity. Such estimates then can be used as input to a water budget or other simulation model.

STREAMFLOW FREQUENCY ANALYSIS

Frequency analysis is performed for many purposes such as the design of water-control works, determining conservation storage requirements, and delineating a floodplain according to the flood risk. Frequency curves, the product of such analyses, are simply an expression of hydrologic data on a probability basis. The frequency with which some magnitude of a selected variable is equaled or exceeded can be determined from a frequency curve. Frequency curves can be developed for hydrologic variables, such as annual flood peaks, rainfall amounts (see Chapter 2), flood volumes, low-flow streamflow volumes or rates, river stages, and reservoir stages. This discussion focuses on streamflow frequency analysis.

In performing frequency analysis, the objective of the study first must be well defined: is the study to determine storage needs for low-flow augmentation or to estimate the chance of experiencing a critical low-flow value for a particular time duration? The objective will determine the type of data that are required. Important considerations include:

1. The appropriate streamflow characteristic needs to be identified. For example, are instantaneous peak discharges of interest (floodplain delineation) or are daily flood-flow volumes of interest (storage analysis)?

2. The data used in the analysis must represent a measure of the same aspect of each event. For example, mean daily peak discharges cannot be analyzed together with instantaneous peak discharges.

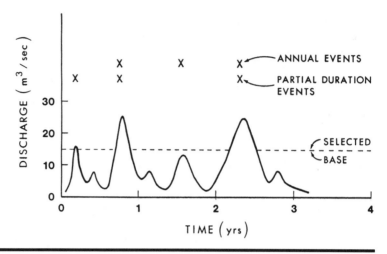

17.6. Annual and partial duration series approaches for flood peak analysis.

3. Streamflow data being analyzed should be controlled by a uniform set of hydrologic and operational factors. Natural streamflows of record cannot be analyzed with flows that have been modified by reservoir operations. Likewise, peak discharges from snowmelt cannot be mixed with peak discharges from rainfall.

4. If only a few years of streamflow records are available, a *partial duration series* analysis rather than *annual series* can be used to get a better definition of the frequency curve (Fig. 17.6). However, this does not necessarily make the curve more reliable.

The annual series approach uses only the extreme annual event (for peak discharge analysis, the largest peak flow) from each year's streamflow record, whereas the partial duration series uses all independent events above a specified base level in the analysis. For peak discharge analysis, the annual series analysis ignores the second highest peak discharge in a year (16 m^3/sec in year 1), which may be higher than the highest peak discharge in another year (14 m^3/sec in year 2). Including all major events in a partial duration series can better define a frequency curve when only a few years of data are available. As the number of years of record increases, a frequency curve developed from either method will yield essentially the same frequency relationship in the region of the curve that defines the more rare events (low probability).

The frequency curves based on the two methods are interpreted differently: for annual series, the exceedance frequency (frequency by which a value is equalled or exceeded) for a given magnitude is the number of *years* that magnitude will be exceeded per 100 yr; for a partial duration series, the interpretation is the number of events that will be exceeded per 100 yr.

Once the data sets are obtained, frequency curves can be developed by either graphical or analytical methods.

Graphical Frequency Analysis. The graphical method involves calculating the cumulative probabilities (plotting positions) for ranked events and then drawing the frequency curve through the data points. Several methods can be used to calculate cumulative probabilities. The median formula (Beard 1962) commonly is used for peak-discharge frequency curves:

$$P = \frac{m - 0.3}{N + 0.4} \tag{17.13}$$

where P = the cumulative probability (plotting position) for the event ranked m in N number of years of record.

The cumulative probability for the least severe events (probability $< 50\%$) can be calculated as follows:

$$P = \frac{2m - 1}{2N} \tag{17.14}$$

The graphical method does not assume any statistical distribution and is quick and easy to apply. Because the frequency curve is drawn by hand, one portion of a curve can be weighed more than another. It usually is recommended that the cumulative probabilities or plotting positions determined by the graphical method be plotted, even if the analytical method described below is used to define the curve.

Analytical Frequency Analysis. The analytical method requires that sample data follow some theoretical frequency distribution. For peak discharge frequency curves, the U.S. Water Resources Council (1976) recommends the log Pearson Type III distribution, which requires the following steps (Ex. 17.6):

1. The data are transformed by taking the logarithms of peak discharges.
2. The mean peak discharge (first moment) is calculated; this corresponds to the 50% probability of exceedance.
3. The standard deviation (second moment) is calculated; this represents the slope of the frequency curve plotted on log-probability graph paper.
4. The skew coefficient (third moment), an index of nonnormality, then is calculated; this represents the curvature in the frequency curve.
5. Adjustments then are made for small numbers of events. The skew coefficient usually is unreliable for short records; a regionally derived skew coefficient is recommended for less than 25 yr of record. If 25–100 yr are available, a weighted skew should be used. The skew derived from one station should be used only if more than 100 yr of record are available.
6. The frequency curve for the observed annual peaks (Q) then is determined for selected exceedance probabilities P, by the equation:

$$\log Q = \bar{x} + k_s s \tag{17.15}$$

where $\bar{x}$ = mean of log Q (m³/sec); k_s = factor that is a function of the skew coefficient and a selected exceedance probability; s = standard deviation of log Q (m³/sec).

7. Confidence limits can be calculated and plotted for the frequency curve as a final step.

EXAMPLE 17.6

Graphical and analytical frequency curves for a 19-yr record of annual peak discharges of the Little North Santiam River near Mehama, Oregon

Water Year	Instant. Peak Discharge (cfs)	Ranking Position of Peak Discharge	Cumulative Probability (Graphical Plotting Position)[a] (%)
1932	13,900	7	34.5
1933	10,600	10	50.0
1934	18,900	3	13.9
1935	10,400	11	55.2
1936	12,200	8	39.7
1937	8,200	18	91.2
1938	16,500	4	19.1
1939	8,570	15	75.8
1940	8,200	17	86.1
1941	8,330	16	80.9
1942	9,300	12	60.3
1943	19,400	2	8.8
1944	7,990	19	96.4
1945	11,700	9	44.8
1946	19,900	1	3.6
1947	15,300	5	24.2
1948	14,800	6	29.4
1949	9,120	13	65.5
1950	8,860	14	70.6

[a]Determined from equation 17.13.

Analytical Frequency Analysis Calculations

Mean log of peak discharge $\bar{x}$ = 4.0650
Standard deviation s = 0.1399
Calculated skew g = -0.6001

(Initial Plotting)	1.0	10	50	90	99
k_s*	2.33	1.28	0	-1.28	-2.33
$k_s s$	0.326	0.179	0	-0.179	-0.326
Log $Q = k_s s + \bar{x}$	4.391	4.244	4.065	3.886	3.739
Q**	24,600	17,540	11,610	7,690	5,480
P_N***	1.79	11.4	50.0	88.6	98.2

  *g = 0 from Table A (below).
  **Cubic feet per second.
  ***From Table B below, $(N - 1)$ = 18; the flow values are then plotted at these adjusted exceedance frequency values.

EXAMPLE 17.6

Table A. Pearson Type III coordinates

g (Skew Coefficient)	k_s = Magnitude in Standard Deviations from Mean for Exceedance Percentages of:								
	1.0	5	10	30	50	70	90	95	99
1.0	3.03	1.87	1.34	0.38	−0.16	−0.61	−1.12	−1.31	−1.59
0.8	2.90	1.83	1.34	0.42	−0.13	−0.60	−1.16	−1.38	−1.74
0.6	2.77	1.79	1.33	0.45	−0.09	−0.58	−1.19	−1.45	−1.88
0.4	2.62	1.74	1.32	0.48	−0.06	−0.57	−1.22	−1.51	−2.03
0.2	2.48	1.69	1.30	0.51	−0.03	−0.55	−1.25	−1.58	−2.18
0.0	2.33	1.64	1.28	0.52	0.00	−0.52	−1.28	−1.64	−2.33
−0.2	2.18	1.58	1.25	0.55	0.03	−0.51	−1.30	−1.69	−2.48
−0.4	2.03	1.51	1.22	0.57	0.06	−0.48	−1.32	−1.74	−2.62
−0.6	1.88	1.45	1.19	0.58	0.09	−0.45	−1.33	−1.79	−2.77
−0.8	1.74	1.38	1.16	0.60	0.13	−0.42	−1.34	−1.83	−2.90
−1.0	1.59	1.31	1.12	0.61	0.16	−0.38	−1.34	−1.87	−3.03

Source: From Beard (1962).

Table B. Expected probability (P_N) versus initial plotting position from normal populations

N-1	P_∞						
	50.0	30.0	10.0	5.0	1.0	0.1	0.01
1	50.0	37.2	24.3	20.4	15.4	12.1	10.2
2	50.0	34.7	19.3	14.6	9.0	5.7	4.3
3	50.0	33.6	16.9	11.9	6.4	3.5	2.3
4	50.0	33.0	15.4	10.4	5.0	2.4	1.37
5	50.0	32.5	14.6	9.4	4.2	1.79	.92
6	50.0	32.2	13.8	8.8	3.6	1.38	.66
7	50.0	31.9	13.5	8.3	3.2	1.13	.50
8	50.0	31.7	13.1	7.9	2.9	.94	.39
9	50.0	31.6	12.7	7.6	2.7	.82	.31
10	50.0	31.5	12.5	7.3	2.5	.72	.25
11	50.0	31.4	12.3	7.1	2.3	.64	.21
12	50.0	31.3	12.1	6.9	2.2	.58	.18
13	50.0	31.2	11.9	6.8	2.1	.52	.16
14	50.0	31.1	11.8	6.7	2.0	.48	.14
15	50.0	31.1	11.7	6.6	1.96	.45	.13
16	50.0	31.0	11.6	6.5	1.90	.42	.12
17	50.0	31.0	11.5	6.4	1.84	.40	.11
18	50.0	30.9	11.4	6.3	1.79	.38	.10
19	50.0	30.9	11.3	6.2	1.74	.36	.091
20	50.0	30.8	11.3	6.2	1.70	.34	.084
30	50.0	30.6	10.8	5.8	1.45	.24	.046
40	50.0	30.4	10.6	5.6	1.33	.20	.034
60	50.0	30.3	10.4	5.4	1.22	.16	.025
120	50.0	30.2	10.2	5.2	1.11	.13	.017
∞	50.0	30.0	10.0	5.0	1.00	.10	.010

Source: From Beard (1962).

Note: P_n values are usable approximately with pearson Type III distributions having small skew coefficients.

EXAMPLE 17.6

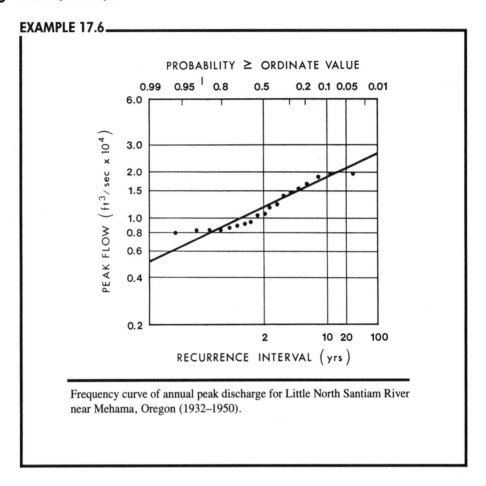

Frequency curve of annual peak discharge for Little North Santiam River near Mehama, Oregon (1932–1950).

The analytical method has the following advantages over the graphical method: the same curve is always calculated from the same data, which makes it more objective and consistent; the reliability of the curve can be calculated with confidence intervals; and the calculation of statistics by regional analysis (described later in this chapter) allows for the development of frequency curves at ungauged sites.

Frequency Analysis for Ungauged Areas. Because of limited stream-gauging sites in most watersheds, methods are needed to estimate streamflow frequency characteristics at ungauged sites. One method is to use hydrologic models. Frequency curves can be estimated for ungauged areas by modeling the streamflow response using the more readily available and longer record precipitation data. Care must be exercised with this approach to insure that a valid model has been developed, one that has been verified with gauged data of the region. A properly tested and verified continuous simulation model can be useful for such studies. The following steps are needed:

1. Calibrate the model using gauged data to establish the constants of the math-

ematical relationships. Hydrologic judgement and a reconstruction of historic stream-flow events are essential to this process. Model parameters can be mapped, and a regional analysis approach (described later) may be used to extend the mathematical relationships to ungauged sites.

2. Adapt the model to the ungauged watersheds using measurable data and esti-mated parameters.

3. Enter the historical precipitation data in sequence, which is estimated for the ungauged watersheds. A standard frequency analysis then can be conducted on the resulting streamflow output from the model.

4. The last step should be a critical analysis of the resulting frequency curve. Any "wide discrepancies" (perhaps on the basis of frequency estimates from gauged streamflow at a nearby station) must be resolved.

Comments on Frequency Analysis for Small Wildland Watersheds.
In rural watersheds, there are often few gauged stations available, and where gauges are present, the record periods are short. Therefore, the uncertainty associated with frequency curves developed in such regions is substantial. Uncertainty still exists with long-term records because even those records are still only a sample of the possible events that have occurred in the past or can occur in the future. The tendency is to "guess high" to provide conservative answers. However, the consequences of having substantial errors in a calculated frequency curve should be the guide for determining the acceptable risk.

Watersheds also are constantly undergoing changes that affect to some degree the hydrologic response. Fires, timber-harvesting operations, livestock grazing, road con-struction, and urbanization all affect the runoff response of watersheds. Such changes sometimes are abrupt, whereby the corresponding change in the hydrologic regime is readily identified. The more subtle, long-term changes are perhaps the most common and also the most troublesome for estimating streamflow frequency curves over a pe-riod of time.

Any time watershed modifications are such that a change in streamflow response is expected, special care must be exercised in the frequency analysis. One possible solution is to use a watershed model with sufficient sensitivity to simulate both land use change and the associated runoff response. Frequency analysis then can be made with the simulated data as previously discussed. Again, results are dependent upon the validity of the model and the adequacy of the input data.

REGIONAL ANALYSIS

A regional analysis is a statistical approach in which generalized equations, graphical relationships, or maps are developed for the purpose of estimating hydro-logic information at ungauged sites (U.S. Army Corps of Engineers 1975). Runoff factors, unit hydrograph coefficients, and streamflow frequency characteristics can be estimated for ungauged watersheds that are within the same climatic region as the gauged watersheds employed. Any pertinent information within the region should be used to relate watershed characteristics to hydrologic characteristics. For example, a regional analysis can be used to estimate runoff coefficients or peak discharge in cubic meters per second per square kilometer associated with a specified recurrence interval, or to estimate the constants needed to execute a complex hydrologic model.

Regional streamflow frequency analysis is most commonly applied. Equations and maps are developed that allow the derivation of exceedance frequency curves for ungauged areas in the following manner:

1. Select components of interest, such as the mean annual peakflow, 100-yr recurrence interval peakflow, etc.

2. Select explanatory variables (characteristics) of gauged watersheds, such as drainage area, watershed slope, and percentage of area covered by lakes or wetlands.

3. Derive prediction equations with single or multiple linear regression analyses, as previously discussed.

4. Map and explain the residual errors that are the differences between calculated and observed values at gauged sites.

5. Determine frequency characteristics for ungauged locations by applying the regression equation with adjustments as indicated by the mapped residual errors.

The residual errors constitute unexplained variance in the statistical analysis. Since it is impossible to include all variables that influence a particular hydrologic response, the mapping of unexplained variances sometimes can indicate other important factors. For example, sometimes mapped residuals will indicate a relationship between the magnitude of the residual error and watershed characteristics such as vegetative type, soils, or land use.

Regional analysis has been applied widely in the United States, where streamflow or other hydrologic data are available but are scattered throughout different climatic regions. The method must be used with care, however, since only one or perhaps a few components of the hydrologic system are included in the analysis. In any case, the results should be considered a rough estimate of the true hydrologic characteristics.

■ FIELD METHODS

Even though an array of analytical methods and models are available to address practically any type of hydrologic problem, there continues to be a need for hydrologic monitoring and field investigation. Monitoring is needed to better understand serial and spatial variability of hydrologic characteristics such as precipitation, streamflow, and water quality. Field research is needed to quantify the site-specific impacts of land use activities and watershed practices on the hydrologic response. Without monitoring and field studies, planning and implementing watershed practices will be hampered with uncertainty, and there will be little basis for developing better models. Field studies should be designed not only to improve our knowledge of hydrology but to lead to improved and more comprehensive predictive models.

Collecting data with little regard to objectives and needs does not necessarily improve our knowledge or ability to make decisions. There are many examples of field studies and monitoring that have resulted in copious data that cannot be used to answer any particular question. Financial resources are too scarce in most watershed management situations to allow for much data collection (particularly unusable data). Therefore, the purpose of this discussion is not to delve into the details of instrumentation and techniques of measurement, but rather to consider when and what type of monitoring and research studies are needed.

Plot Studies

Plot studies, where hydrologic investigations are carried out in small-scale trials, often have been conducted as a first step in testing a hypothesis relating to watershed management. They are justified at the initial stages of gathering knowledge about watershed management where the fundamental mechanics of a basic process need to be better understood. Early watershed management research consisted largely of small-plot studies aimed at measuring some particular hydrologic characteristic or process of a given soil-plant system. Much of what we know today about hydrologic processes is the result of such work. Yet, in hindsight, more information could have resulted had most of these studies been designed for practical solutions and directed toward the development of a predictive model.

EXAMPLE 17.7

Estimating evapotranspiration using plots with different vegetative cover conditions (from Johnston 1970)

A plot study was initiated in northern Utah to estimate evapotranspiration differences among three cover conditions: bare soil, herbaceous vegetation, and an aspen-herbaceous cover. Soil moisture depletion was measured to a depth of 9 ft in each $\frac{1}{10}$-acre plot. Four-year average evapotranspiration losses were 21.0 in., 15.3 in., and 11.3 in. for the aspen-herbaceous, herbaceous, and bare plots, respectively. Further, during the active growing season, soil moisture in the aspen-herbaceous plot was depleted to at least 9 ft in contrast to the bare plot that exhibited little soil moisture depletion below 2.5 ft. Soil moisture in the herbaceous plot was depleted mostly above a depth of 4 ft during the same period. The results of these plot studies helped to quantify the differences in evapotranspiration among cover types and indicated the potential for increasing water yield by manipulating vegetative cover in northern Utah.

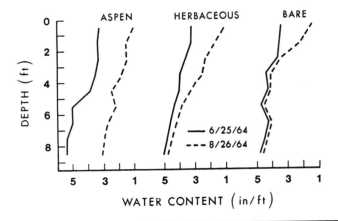

Soil moisture depletion for three plots in northern Utah (from Johnston 1970).

Plot studies are attractive to researchers because of the ability to study small, homogenous systems and to exert some level of control over inputs, or the ability to better measure certain characteristics and outputs from a plot. Plot studies have been used to estimate interception losses of forest communities, to estimate soil water depletion under different plant species or communities (Ex. 17.7), and to quantify infiltration, surface runoff, soil erosion, and other hydrologic properties of soils and land use conditions. Plot studies are easier to establish and less expensive to conduct than studies involving entire watersheds. For example, artificial barriers can be constructed to constrict flow or prevent leakage, which enables the water budget components to be measured more accurately. Comparisons of several land treatments or of different vegetation types can be made with a series of plots. To examine the same number of treatments or systems using watershed-scale investigations would be costly.

One of the major drawbacks of plot studies is the inability to extrapolate results of small plots to larger, more complex watersheds. For example, the differences in soil moisture depletion determined from plot studies in Example 17.7 cannot tell us how much water yield would change as a result of vegetation changes over an entire watershed. One should not think, however, that plot and watershed studies provide the same type of information. Plot studies should be designed to improve our knowledge of certain hydrologic processes that allow us to better interpret and understand the integrated response of larger watershed systems; therefore, plot studies should be closely linked to larger experimental watershed studies. The results of plot studies also should provide empirical data for the development and testing of mathematical relationships needed to simulate particular hydrologic processes. If such objectives are kept in mind at the start of a plot study, more useful information should result.

Lysimeters

Lysimeters are large tanks within which a soil-plant system is contained (see Chapter 3) and are constructed in such a way as to approximate field conditions. Water inputs and outputs are measured either by weighing or by keeping account of waterflow into and out of the lysimeter. Accurate water budgets can be obtained with lysimeters, but they have serious limitations: they generally cannot be used to investigate hydrologic processes for large trees and shrubs, or plant communities that contain such plants. Even for grasses or crop plants, disturbances of the soil system and the artificial boundary conditions that are created limit the interpretation and extrapolation of results. In summary, lysimeters are costly and have limited application for most watershed management studies.

Experimental Watershed Studies

An experimental watershed is one that has been chosen and instrumented for the study of hydrologic phenomena. Ideally, experimental watersheds are selected on the basis of their representativeness so that the results obtained from them might be transferred (at least qualitatively) to unmeasured watersheds with similar characteristics. The experimental watershed approach, particularly when used in the paired or multiple approach, has emerged as a principal means of evaluating the hydrologic effects of land use change on the quantity and timing of water yield from natural catchments. Experimental watersheds also are utilized for ecological studies, as field laboratories to investigate hydrologic processes, and as a source of data for calibrating or validating computer models.

BASIC APPROACHES

There are two general methods of calibrating experimental watersheds for hydrologic study: one is to use a single watershed and calibrate prior to treatment; the second is to use a control watershed as a basis for comparison with one or more treated watersheds. The single experimental watershed approach has been used extensively in the past. In using this method, a watershed is calibrated for a number of years until its behavior can be predicted from past performance, then a treatment is imposed and its effects measured in terms of deviations from the expected behavior. Success depends upon the ability to predict watershed behavior from climatic variables.

The paired watershed (described in Chapter 3) or multiple experimental watershed method involves the use of a control catchment and one or more catchments to be treated. These catchments are selected for their similarity in size, shape, topography, vegetative cover, past land use, climate, and general location. Typically, they are first calibrated against each other for a period of years to establish the response of each to a variety of precipitation events. The period of calibration is long enough to have confidence in the prediction of the behavior of one from that of the other.

Following the calibration period, a treatment is applied to one or more catchments while the control is left undisturbed, and the effects of the treatment are measured as departures from its predicted behavior. Usually, the predictions of expected behavior of the treated catchment are based solely on the control catchment. However, these predictions may be supported by predictions based on the period of calibration, or they may be further refined by climatic analyses. If the characteristics of the control catchment have remained unaltered, then changes in the water yield are attributed to the treatment. The paired or multiple experimental watershed approach is the principal method whereby the water yield improvement practices involving vegetation management have been evaluated.

APPLICABILITY OF EXPERIMENTAL WATERSHED RESEARCH

The experimental watershed technique generally has been criticized by many, as summarized by Hewlett et al. (1969):

1. Experimental watersheds often are unrepresentative.
2. It is difficult to transfer results obtained from experimental watersheds to other areas.
3. Experimental watersheds are costly to establish.
4. Experimental watersheds frequently leak.
5. Changes in water yield response following treatment often are too small for detection.
6. Integrated results obtained from experimental watersheds conceal hydrologic processes.

These criticisms, if valid, question the practical extension of experimental watershed research. However, before a final decision, they warrant discussion.

The most serious criticisms of small watershed experiments is that they are not representative and that it is difficult to transfer results to larger areas. This criticism stems from the frustration of water resource planners who attempt to apply the results of experimental watershed research to large river basins under the assumption that a small watershed is a microcosm of the larger river basin. However, an upland watershed is a subsystem within an overall river basin system, and homogeneity often is a reason for selecting the location of upland watersheds for experimental research. Thus, experimental watersheds should not be expected to epitomize the larger heterogeneous river basin with many different subsystems. It is unlikely that a small watershed represents more than one or two geologic features of larger basins. Similarly, the proportion of uplands and lowlands, soil groups, and vegetation cover types will not necessarily be represented on one small watershed.

Nevertheless, satisfactory results have been achieved when smaller experimental watersheds are representative of the larger river basin. Within major physiographic units, similarities in streamflows from small and large watersheds often are noted, as mean values for the entire physiographic unit. These similarities usually would be expected in terms of water yield, such as centimeters per year. However, peak discharge (cubic meters per second per square kilometer) and stormflow volumes (cubic meter) are greatly affected by the size of the watershed.

A basic problem of representativeness is in defining what the experimental watershed is to represent. Certainly, if removing the vegetation overstory on a 10-acre watershed increases runoff, it should do the same on a 10-mi^2 watershed with similar vegetation. However, the magnitude of the increase after the water moves off the small watershed and through the channels of a river basin is beyond the scope of experimental watershed research.

Bosch and Hewlett (1982) concluded that, although the results of many experimental watershed studies varied, there can be no real doubt about the main conclusion: evapotranspiration and streamflow are influenced by the type, size, and quantity of vegetative cover.

Experimental watershed research is costly. In the past, many experimental research projects were conceived hastily and poorly planned, and because of the emphasis on continuity, their termination was delayed far beyond the point of diminishing returns. Nevertheless, such projects provided an experience that no longer allows excuses for inadequately planned research efforts. Unfortunately, little rigorous benefits-cost analyses associated with experimental watershed research have been made to date, nor have realistic alternatives been advanced in lieu of experimental watersheds that would provide quantitative information on the influence of vegetation manipulation on the quantity, timing, and quality of streamflow.

Time is a major cost in experimental watershed research, and the need for quick results sometimes eliminates pretreatment calibration altogether. Calibration periods often have been 5 yr or longer, although some studies have indicated that, when the treatment period is longer, calibration periods as short as 3 yr may provide useful information. The number of years required to obtain adequate calibration between a control watershed and one or more treatment watersheds is not fixed; it depends on the objectives of the study and the variability of the data sets. If one is interested in annual water yield changes due to some treatment, each year represents only one data point in the regression equation. However, if stormflow changes are of interest, several storms can be analyzed in any given year; only a few years then may provide adequate calibration data. Furthermore, once a watershed has been instrumented, short-term interim studies can be superimposed at considerably less cost. Such studies should provide more information than if conducted independently, for their results are additive to the information being collected on the behavior of the watershed as a whole.

Nearly all watersheds leak, and there is no certain method for determining the amount of inflow or outflow across subterranean divides. However, with the paired or multiple experimental watershed approach, where differences rather than absolute values are of primary concern, leaks may present less of a problem when watersheds are properly calibrated against each other.

The principal advantage of the paired or multiple experimental watershed technique is the high degree of correlation that commonly is obtained between or among adjacent catchments. Although some problems in refining statistical analyses remain, treatment differences in streamflow of less than 10% have been detected with high confidence levels.

From a simplistic viewpoint, where only the difference in streamflow characteristics between catchments is considered, the criticism that integrated results conceal hydrologic processes may be valid. There is a need to explain experimental watershed effects so that results might be made more broadly applicable (as, for example, in the development of generalized synthesis models). This has led to increased emphasis on studies concerned with the difficult question of why a watershed reacts as it does, rather than simply what takes place following a vegetation manipulation.

Experimental watershed studies are indispensable to the complete understanding of watershed management effects, as demonstrated by catchment experiments. But, even with a more complete understanding, the circuitous argument of the uniqueness of individual experimental watersheds still must be faced. Thus, the empiricism of experimental watershed research must be relied upon as acknowledged by the most severe critics of this methodology. Small experimental watershed research still is needed, but such research efforts should be well planned.

The expense of experimental watersheds can be justified only if they are designed to provide information needed to manage watersheds for greater benefit or to avoid environmental degradation and economic cost. In many instances, the individual studies alone may not appear to be worth the cost, but one must recognize that the combined results of many experimental watershed studies represent some of the best data available to test and validate physically based simulation models. The models then become the vehicle for extending research results to other areas and represent a tool capable of estimating watershed responses to land management activities.

▌ SUMMARY

To be able to go beyond the purely descriptive treatment of watershed management, it is imperative to understand and be able to apply the methods that quantify the hydrologic response of watersheds. This chapter summarizes methods of quantifying streamflow characteristics that are more commonly used in streamflow forecasting for engineering design and other related applications, but that have direct application to forest and wildland watersheds. After completing this chapter, and relating the respective methods to other parts of the book, you should be able to:

1. Indicate the criteria used to select a hydrologic method for a particular purpose.

2. Define a hydrologic model and explain the different types of models, their applications, and their limitations.

3. Discuss the use of regression methods and other simple empirical methods for hydrology; under what conditions is it appropriate to apply them?

4. Define a unit hydrograph and explain the conditions under which it can be applied.

5. Explain how field methods can be used to acquire hydrologic information and develop methods that allow the prediction of a hydrologic response.

6. Select an appropriate hydrologic method to accomplish specific objectives, such as:

- determine the size of a culvert for a road
- determine the probability that a peak discharge of a certain magnitude will be equalled or exceeded in a specific number of years
- determine the peak discharge and stormflow volume for a watershed that has streamflow records
- determine how streamflow over the seasons will be affected when vegetation is altered
- examine the effects of different land use types on stormflow peak and volume

CHAPTER 18

Statistical Methods

■ INTRODUCTION

People often become frustrated when attempting to apply statistical methods to interpret the results of various actions, and to many, the use of statistical methods appears to limit progress. Much of this difficulty may be due to not fully understanding the basic objectives of statistics. Essentially, two primary objectives exist: to estimate population parameters, and to test hypothesis about these parameters. An example of the first objective is the application of statistical methods to estimate the mean (average) of a population. The statistician's task is to derive proper methods of collecting the required source data, and then to calculate the desired statistic (for example, the estimated population mean). An example of the second objective is to test the hypothesis (theory) that the estimated population mean equals or, perhaps, exceeds a predetermined value. It is the statistician's job to develop appropriate tests of hypothesis to satisfy this objective.

In this chapter, emphasis is placed on the first objective, specifically, to derive estimates of population parameters from a series of random values that are obtained from a population sample. Details of statistical methods used to test hypotheses about the estimates of population parameters are found in appropriate references.

■ BASIC DEFINITIONS

To apply statistical methods in watershed management, it is necessary to develop a working knowledge of the terms that are commonly employed in statistics. The term *statistics,* for instance, has two accepted meanings: statistics (plural) refers to the collection or organization of source data (such as the monthly streamflow from a watershed); however, statistics (singular) is the science of analyzing the collected measurements and, guided by the results of the analysis, inferring general truths.

A complete aggregate of individuals or items in one category is a *population.* An infinite population is composed of an unlimited number of individuals or items, while a finite population consists of a limited number of individuals or items. In many instances, the differentiation between infinite and finite populations is arbitrary.

Collectively, measurements or observations of small portions of a population are a *sample*. It is not information about the sample that is being sought, but rather about the population from which the sample was taken. The assumption is made that information obtained from a valid sample also holds for the population.

A *population parameter* (the mean, the variance, etc.) is a quantitative characteristic that describes and helps to quantify a population. A quantitative characteristic that describes a sample obtained from a population is a *statistic*. In essence, statistics based on samples are used to estimate population parameters.

A measurable characteristic that varies in amount or magnitude (precipitation, streamflow, or tree volume) is a *variable*. Variables capable of exhibiting every possible value within a specified range are *continuous variables*. Conversely, variables that are manifested in limited graduations or isolated values are *discrete variables*. For the analysis of many watershed measurements, it frequently is assumed that the source data are represented by continuous variables.

A variable of an associated pair whose value is considered to depend upon the value of that associated pair is a *dependent variable,* while a variable of an associated pair whose value is considered to determine (or predict) the value of the other variable in the pair is an *independent variable*. Relationships between dependent and independent variables are defined by regression analyses, as described below.

Definitions of other important terms that are relevant to statistical methods can be found in references on statistics, some of which are listed in the General References for this chapter.

■ DISTRIBUTION FUNCTIONS

Fundamental to the application of statistical methods in watershed management is an understanding of distribution functions, each of which exhibits unique properties. A definite pattern of frequency of occurrence of units in each of a series of equal classes is a *frequency distribution function*. For a population, a frequency distribution function shows the relative frequency with which different values of a variable, X, occurs. By knowing the frequency distribution function, it is possible to determine what proportions of the individuals in the population are within specified size limits.

Each population has its own distinct frequency distribution function. However, there are certain general types of functions that often occur, including the *normal*, the *binomial*, and the *Poisson*. Of these, the normal frequency distribution is perhaps the most frequently encountered.

The normal frequency distribution, which is the familiar bell-shaped distribution, is used widely in statistical analyses of watershed measurements (Fig. 18.1). Theoretically, the normal frequency distribution exhibits the following properties: the mean, median, and mode are identical in value; small variations from the mean occur more frequently than large variations from the mean; and positive and negative variations about the mean occur with equal frequency.

The binomial frequency distribution is associated with source data where a fixed number of individuals are observed on each unit; furthermore, the unit is characterized by the number of individuals having some particular attribute. The asymmetric Poisson frequency distribution can arise where individual units are characterized by a count having no fixed upper limit, particularly if zero or low counts tend to dominate.

There are a number of other frequency distribution functions that can be used to

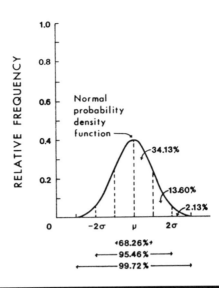

18.1. The bell-shaped curve of the normal frequency distribution function.

describe populations in nature. One of the more important tasks of a statistician is to identify the most appropriate function for the case in-hand and then apply the "proper" statistical methods to estimate population parameters and, if necessary, to test hypotheses about these parameters.

In addition to knowing the relative frequency that values of variable X occur in a population, it also may be required to know what proportion of a population lies between specified limits of X. For example, a hydrologist might wish to know what proportion of all precipitation events that occur on a river basin lie within a particular interval of X, where the interval of X defines a range of precipitation amounts. To obtain this kind of information, it becomes necessary to construct a *cumulative frequency distribution function*. Normally, to develop such a function, values of X are accumulated, starting with the smallest value and proceeding to the largest value in the source data (Fig. 18.2). Cumulative frequency distribution functions that are developed by starting with the largest, not the smallest, value of X and proceeding to the smallest value are referred to as *exceedance curves*.

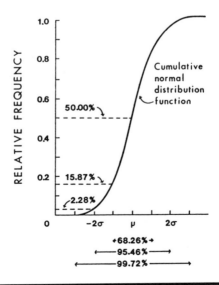

18.2. The cumulative frequency distribution function.

■ BASIC TERMS AND CALCULATIONS

To develop an understanding of statistical methods, it is important to obtain a working knowledge of basic terms and calculations. For source data that are obtained by simple random sampling, measures of central tendency and dispersion and the calculation of confidence limits are described below.

Measures of Central Tendency

Many situations require the determination of a central value of a series of random values obtained from a population sample. Some kind of "average" often is desired.

MEAN

The mean is the most familiar and commonly used measure of central tendency. Given the source data that are obtained from a simple random sample, the mean is calculated as:

$$\bar{x} = \frac{\Sigma X}{n} \tag{18.1}$$

where $\bar{x}$ = the estimated population mean; X = the individual random value in the sample series; and n = the sample size.

MEDIAN

Another measure of central tendency is the median. The median of a series of random values obtained from a population sample, arranged (ranked) in order of size, is the value halfway through the series. If the number of random values is odd (3, 5, 7, etc.), little problem exists in selecting the median. But, if the number of random values is even (4, 6, 8, etc.), the "true" median is the value halfway between the two central values.

MODE

Still another measure of central tendency is the mode. When a series of random values are arranged by classes and frequencies (a frequency distribution), one class (or a few classes) generally will show the highest frequency of occurrence; the class (or classes) with the highest frequency of occurrence indicates the mode (or modes).

As previously mentioned, in applying statistical methods to watershed measurements, it often is assumed that the basic measurements exhibit a normal frequency distribution. With a normal frequency distribution, the mean, median, and mode are identical; if the basic measurements are not normally distributed, these measures of central tendency are not identical. In the latter instance, care must be exercised to select the measure of central tendency that is most appropriate to the problem.

Measures of Dispersion

Measures of central tendency are fundamental descriptors of a series of random values that are obtained from a sample of a population. However, other measures also may be necessary for a "finer" definition of a series of random values. Measures of dispersion serve this purpose, since they define the extent to which the individuals in a series vary from the central tendency.

RANGE

The range is a measure of the total interval between the smallest and the largest values in a series of random values. Often, the range gives preliminary information on the variability of random values in a series.

VARIANCE

Perhaps, the most important measure of dispersion is the variance, which characterizes the variability of individual random values about the estimated population mean. From the variance, one obtains an idea of whether most of the individuals in a series are close to the mean, or spread out. Given the source data that are obtained from a simple random sample, the variance is calculated as follows:

$$s^2 = \frac{\Sigma(X - \bar{x})^2}{n - 1} \tag{18.2}$$

where s^2 = the estimated population variance and the other terms are defined as above.

Another mathematical expression of the variance, and a formula that is solved more easily, is:

$$s^2 = \frac{\Sigma X^2 - \frac{(\Sigma X)^2}{n}}{n - 1} \tag{18.3}$$

where all terms are defined as above.

The square root of the variance(s) is called the *standard deviation,* which is used in calculating the coefficient of variation, among other statistics.

COEFFICIENT OF VARIATION

In general, a series of random values that are obtained from a sample of a population that exhibits a large mean shows more variability than a series of random values from a population with a small mean. The coefficient of variation facilitates the comparison of variability about different-sized means. It is a measure of relative variability. With source data obtained from a simple random sample, the coefficient of variation is calculated as:

$$CV = \frac{s}{\bar{x}} \tag{18.4}$$

where CV = the estimated coefficient of variation; s = the standard deviation; and $\bar{x}$ = the estimated population mean.

STANDARD ERROR OF THE MEAN

There usually is variation among individuals in a series of random values, which can be measured by calculating the variance. It is conceivable, therefore, that variation also may exist among a series of estimated population means ($\bar{x}$) that are calculated from a set of different simple random samples obtained from a population. The *standard error of the mean* is a measure of dispersion among a set of sample means, just as the variance is a measure of dispersion among the individuals in a series of random values.

Fortunately, it is not necessary to obtain a set of simple random samples to calculate the standard error of the mean. Instead, a satisfactory estimate can be obtained directly from the source data of one simple random sample.

The calculation of the standard error of the mean depends upon how the simple random sample was selected. If the sample was drawn from an "infinite" population, the standard error of the mean is calculated as follows:

$$s_{\bar{x}} = \sqrt{\frac{s^2}{n}} = \frac{s}{\sqrt{n}} \tag{18.5}$$

where $s_{\bar{x}}$ = the estimated standard error of the mean and the other terms are defined as above.

Confidence Limits

The reliability of an estimated population parameter is indicated by confidence limits. Although confidence limits can be structured around many statistics, most commonly, they are established about an estimated population mean. Given basic source data obtained from a simple random sample, confidence limits about an estimated population mean are calculated as:

$$CI = \bar{x} \pm ts_{\bar{x}} \tag{18.6}$$

where CI = the estimated confidence limits about an estimated population mean; and t = the "t" statistic, a tabular value to define a statement of the level of probability for statistical inferences.

A portion of the distribution of the t statistic is given in Table 18.1. To use these tabular values with a simple random sample, the first column (degrees of freedom) equals the sample size less one ($n - 1$). The columns labeled "probability" refer to the odds specified by the user. For example, in the development of confidence limits at the 90% probability level, the t values in the 0.10 column are employed. If confidence limits at the 95% probability level are specified, the 0.05 column is used, etc.

■ SAMPLING TECHNIQUES

It may be desirable to have a complete enumeration of a population. A complete enumeration rarely is possible, however, and a sample usually is taken. To plan for the sampling of a population, the sample size, the size and shape of individual sampling units, and the sampling design must be considered.

Table 18.1. The distribution of the "t" statistic

Degrees of Freedom	Probability		
	0.10	0.05	0.01
1	6.314	12.706	63.657
2	2.920	4.303	9.925
3	2.353	3.182	5.841
4	2.132	2.776	4.604
5	2.015	2.571	4.032
6	1.943	2.447	3.707
7	1.895	2.365	3.499
8	1.860	2.306	3.355
9	1.833	2.262	3.250
10	1.812	2.228	3.168
11	1.796	2.201	3.106
12	1.782	2.179	3.055
13	1.771	2.160	3.012
14	1.761	2.145	2.977
15	1.753	2.131	2.947
16	1.746	2.120	2.921
17	1.740	2.110	2.898
18	1.734	2.101	2.878
19	1.729	2.093	2.861
20	1.725	2.086	2.845
25	1.708	2.060	2.787
30	1.697	2.042	2.750
∞	1.645	1.960	2.576

Source: This table is abridged from Table 18.1 of Fisher and Yates, *Statistical Tables for Biological, Agricultural, and Medical Research,* 6th edition, 1974, published by Longman Group, Ltd., London (previously published by Oliver and Boyd, Edinburgh), and by permission of the authors and publishers.

Sample Size

A primary objective of sampling is to take enough measurements to obtain a desired level of precision—no more, no less. The number of samples to be taken depends, in large part, upon two factors: the inherent variability within the population being sampled, and the desired level of precision (that is, the allowable error).

The basic equation used to calculate a sample size is derived by transforming the relationship for the confidence limits for an estimated population mean. In general, it is desired to have the product of t and $s_{\bar{x}}$ equal to or less than the specified level of precision. In other words:

$$E = ts_{\bar{x}} \tag{18.7}$$

where E = the specified level of precision, which is the sampling error and the other terms are defined as above.

The above relationship also can be expressed as:

$$E = t\sqrt{\frac{s^2}{n}} \tag{18.8}$$

The basic equation used to calculate a sample size is obtained by squaring all the terms in the above expression and then solving for n. Therefore, assuming that a simple random sample will be taken, the sample size is calculated as:

$$n = \frac{t^2 s^2}{E^2} \tag{18.9}$$

where n = the sample size and the other terms are defined as above.

To calculate the sample size, it is necessary to have an estimate of the variance of the population (s^2), which can be obtained from a preliminary sample of the population. Additionally, a t value at the specified level of probability is required and the level of precision must be specified.

Size and Shape of Individual Sampling Units

The size and shape of the individual sampling units will affect the precision and costs of sampling. In general, small plots exhibit more variability than large plots and circular plots are usually easier to establish than rectangular plots. However, many combinations of plot size and shape are available for use by watershed managers. It is necessary, therefore, to select the size and shape of individual sampling units that are compatible with the sampling objectives and the inherent variability of the population being sampled.

Sampling Designs

After calculating the sample size and selecting the appropriate size and shape of the individual sampling units, it becomes necessary to allocate the sampling units to obtain the source data necessary to estimate the required population parameters. The problem is to decide upon the most efficient design in terms of the sampling objectives and the characteristics of the population.

There are many sampling designs and variations of those designs. Three basic sampling designs often employed in watershed measurements are *simple random sampling, stratified random sampling,* and *systematic sampling.*

SIMPLE RANDOM SAMPLING

The fundamental idea behind simple random sampling is that when allocating a sample of n individual sampling units, every possible combination of the n units has an equal chance of being selected. Furthermore, the selection of any given individual sampling unit is completely independent of the selection of all other units.

Once again, all of the statistical formulas presented in this chapter have their roots in simple random sampling.

STRATIFIED RANDOM SAMPLING

Often, previous knowledge of the distribution of a population can be used to increase the precision of a sample. Stratified random sampling takes advantage of certain types of information about a population by grouping homogeneous units of a population together on the basis of some inherent characteristic (slope-aspect combination, vegetative cover, soil parent material, etc.). Then, each homogeneous unit (or stratum) is sampled by employing a simple random sampling design, and the group estimates are combined to estimate population parameters.

SYSTEMATIC SAMPLING

As the name implies, individual sampling units in a systematic sample are allocated, not randomly, but mechanically, according to a predetermined pattern. Systematic sampling has been used widely by watershed managers for two reasons: the location of the individual sampling units in the field often is easier and cheaper than is the case with other sampling designs, and there is a feeling that a sample that is deliberately spread over a population may be more "representative" than a simple random sample. Statisticians generally will not argue against the first reason, but they are less willing to accept the second. Estimation of sampling errors that are associated with a systematic sample requires more knowledge about the population being sampled than is usually available.

■ REGRESSION ANALYSIS

An important statistical tool that often is used in analyzing watershed measurements is regression analysis. The basic purpose of regression analysis techniques is to quantify relationships between two or more variables.

Simple Regressions

A simple regression defines a relationship between a dependent variable, Y, and one independent variable, X. A simple linear regression is used with a straight-line relationship between the two variables. Other simple regression analyses can involve nonlinear (parabolic, exponential, logarithmic, etc.) relationships.

The general model for a simple regression is:

$$Y = a + bX \tag{18.10}$$

where Y = the dependent variable; X = the independent variable; and a, b = regression coefficients estimated by statistical formulas, as given below:

$$b = \frac{\Sigma XY - \dfrac{(\Sigma X)(\Sigma Y)}{n}}{\Sigma X^2 - \dfrac{(\Sigma X)^2}{n}} \tag{18.11}$$

$$a = \overline{Y} - b\overline{X} \tag{18.12}$$

There are several methods of determining how well a simple regression line fits the sample data. Often, the coefficient of determination, r^2, is calculated, as follows:

$$r^2 = \frac{\left[\Sigma XY - \dfrac{(\Sigma X)(\Sigma Y)}{n}\right]^2}{\left(\Sigma X^2 - \dfrac{(\Sigma X)^2}{n}\right)\left(\Sigma Y^2 - \dfrac{(\Sigma Y)^2}{n}\right)} \tag{18.13}$$

A common means of interpreting the coefficient of determination is that if the coefficient of determination value of 0.65, then "65% of the variation in Y is associated with X." For example, 65% of the variation in annual precipitation is "explained" by elevation.

Multiple Regressions

Frequently, the dependent variable is related to more than one independent variable. If this relationship can be estimated by using multiple regression analysis, it can allow more precise estimations of the dependent variable than is possible by a simple regression.

The general model for a multiple regression is:

$$Y = a + bX_1 + b_2X_2 + \ldots + b_nX_n \tag{18.14}$$

◼ SUMMARY

Little has been offered in terms of "guidance" for the user of statistics in the foregoing discussion. If more specialized training in the applications of statistical methods is needed, until this is obtained, there are several points that users should keep in mind to improve their statistical performance (Thomas 1976). These are:

1. First and probably most importantly, *understand the statistical method* that you intend to use. It should be evident that statistics is an extensive and complex subject. In fact, statisticians often are unsure of their own conclusions and, as a result, commonly discuss them with their colleagues for verification. Be sure that you know the method thoroughly, then you will be much less likely to misuse it.

2. *Keep it simple.* Where there is a choice, use the simpler statistical method. There is no need to apply the latest analytical tool if an older, simpler one tells us what we want to know. Also, there may be less chance of going wrong when the simpler method is applied.

3. *Plan ahead.* To obtain an adequate performance, sampling design and analysis must be planned from the outset. Be sure to allow enough time for all aspects of an investigation. Unfortunately, a common practice is to leave analysis and interpretation to a time when there is no possible way to do an adequate job.

4. *Adopt a critical attitude* when examining the results of a statistical analysis. Try to let the source data, rather than your preconceptions, lead your thoughts.

5. Statistical analysis cannot be completely reduced to a routine process. Do not be led astray by computer analysis packages. While many computer programs are good tools, it should be kept in mind that *computers do not analyze*—and they never will. Become familiar with computer programs that are useful, but do not surrender your analyses to them. Statistics is only a helpful tool for summarizing data.

6. *Respect your professional judgment.* Your training and experience give you an ability to see the elements and relationships in watershed resources management better than a layman.

APPENDIX

■ **Common Standard Conversion Factors from English to Metric Units**

Quantity	English Unit	Metric Unit	Convert English to Metric Multiply by
Length	inches (in)	centimeters (cm)	2.54
	inches (in)	millimeters (mm)	25.4
	feet (ft)	meters (m)	0.3048006
	yards (yd)	meters (m)	.9144
Area	square inches (in^2)	square millimeters (mm^2)	645.16
	square feet (ft^2)	square meters (m^2)	0.0929034
	square yards (yd^2)	square meters (m^2)	0.8361274
	acres	square meters (m^2)	4046.873
	acres	hectares (ha)	0.4046873
	square miles (mi^2)	square kilometers (km^2)	2.589998
Volume	cubic inches (in^3)	cubic centimeters (cm^3)	16.38706
	cubic feet (ft^3)	liters (l)	28.31685
	cubic feet (ft^3)	cubic meters (m^3)	0.02831685
	cubic yards (yd^3)	cubic meters (m^3)	0.7645549
	acre-feet	cubic meters (m^3)	1233.489
	pints	liters (l)	0.4731765
	quarts	liters (l)	0.9463529
	gallon	liters (l)	3.785412
	bushels	cubic meters (m^3)	0.03523907
Velocity	miles/hour (mi/h)	kilometers/hour (km/h)	1.609344
	feet/second (ft/s)	meters/second (m/s)	0.3048
Acceleration	feet/second^2 (ft/s^2)	meters/second^2 (m/s^2)	0.3048
Flow	cubic feet/second (ft^3/s)	cubic meters/second (m^3/s)	0.02831685
	gallons/minute (gpm)	liters/second (l/s)	0.06309020
Rates & Yields	pounds/acre (lb/acre)	kilograms/hectare (kg/ha)	1.1208465
	short tons/acre	metric tons/hectare (t/ha)	2.241693
	inches/hour (in/h)	millimeters/hour (mm/h)	25.4
	inches/day (in/day)	centimeters/day (cm/day)	2.54
Mass	ounces [avdp] (oz)	grams (g)	28.34952
	pounds [avdp] (lb)	kilograms (kg)	0.453592
	short tons (t)	metric tons (t)	0.90718474

■ **Common Standard Conversion Factors from English to Metric Units**

Quantity	English Unit	Metric Unit	Convert English to Metric Multiply by
Density	pounds/cubic foot (lb/ft³)	grams/cubic centimeter (g/cm³)	0.01601846
	pounds/cubic foot (lb/ft³)	kilograms/cubic meter (kg/m³)	16.01846
Force	pounds force (lbf)	Newtons (N)	4.448222
Pressure or Stress	Atmosphere (Std)	kilopascals (kPa)	101.325
	inches of mercury @ 60°F	kilopascals (kPa)	3.37685
	millibars	kilopascals (kPa)	0.100
	feet of water @ 30.2°F	kilopascals (kPa)	2.989
	inches of water @ 60°F	kilopascals (kPa)	0.24884
	pounds/square inch (lb/in²)	kilopascals (kPa)	6.894757
	pounds/square inch (lb/in²)	kilopascals (kPa)	0.04788026
Temperature	Degrees Farenheit (°F)	Degrees Celsius (°C)	$t_{°C} = (t_{°F} - 32) / 1.8$
	Degrees Farenheit (°F)	Degrees Kelvin (°K)	$t_{°K} = (t_{°F} + 459.67) / 1.8$
Energy	British thermal unit (mean) (BTU)	joule (J)	1055.87
	Calorie	joules (J)	4.186
	Watt-hours	joules (J)	3600.
Power	foot-pound/second (lbf/s)	watts	1.355818

Source: Adapted from: American Society for Testing and Materials (ASTM). 1976. *Standard for Metric Practice*. Philadelphia: ASTM.

CITED REFERENCES

American Society of Civil Engineers (ASCE). 1969. *Design and construction of sanitary and storm sewers*. Man. and Rep. Eng. Pract. No. 37.

Anderson, E. A. 1978. Streamflow simulation models for use on snow covered watersheds. In *Modeling of snow cover runoff*, ed. S. C. Colbeck and M. Ray, pp. 336–350. U.S. Army Cold Regions Research and Engineering Laboratory. Hanover, N.H.

Anderson, H. W., M. D. Hoover, and K. G. Reinhart. 1976. *Forests and water: Effects of forest management on floods, sedimentation, and water supply*. USDA For. Serv. Gen. Tech. Rep. PSW-18.

Baker, M. B., Jr. 1986. Effects of ponderosa pine treatments on water yield in Arizona. *Water Resour. Res.* 22:67–73.

Baldwin, H. I., and C. L. McGuinness. 1963. *A primer on groundwater*. U.S. Geol. Surv.

Bange, G. G. J. 1953. On the quantitative explanation of stomatal transpiration. *Acta Bot. Neerl.* 2:255–297.

Barnes, B. S. 1939. The structure of discharge recession curves. *Trans. Am. Geophys. Union* 20:721–725.

Bartsch, A. F., and W. M. Ingram. 1959. Stream life and the pollution environment. *Public Works* 90:104–110.

Baumol, W. 1968. On the social rate of discount. *Am. Econ. Rev.* 58:788–802.

Beard, L. R. 1962. *Statistical methods in hydrology*. U.S. Army Corps of Engineers, Sacramento District. Sacramento, Calif.

Berglund, E. R., A. Ahyoud, and M. Tayaa. 1981. Comparison of soil and infiltration properties of range and afforested sites in north Morocco. *For. Ecol. Manage.* 3:295–306.

Berris, S. N., and R. D. Harr. 1987. Comparative snow accumulation and melt during rainfall in forested and clearcut plots in the western cascades of Oregon. *Water Resour. Res.* 23:135–142.

Blake, G. J. 1975. The interception process. In *Prediction in Catchment Hydrology, National Symposium on Hydrology*, ed. T. G. Chapman and F. X. Dunin, pp. 59–81. Melbourne: Aust. Acad. Sci.

Bonell, M., D. S. Cassells, and D. A. Gilmour. 1982. Vertical and lateral soil water movement in a tropical rainforest catchment. In *First National Symposium on Forest Hydrology*, ed. E. M. O'Loughlin and L. J. Bren, pp. 30–38. National Committee on Hydrology and Water Resources of the Institution of Engineers. Melbourne, Aust.

Bosch, J. M., and J. D. Hewlett. 1982. A review of catchment experiments to determine the effect of vegetation changes on water yield and evapotranspiration. *J. Hydrol.* 55:3–23.

Bowie, J. E., and W. Kam. 1968. *Use of water by riparian vegetation, Cottonwood Wash, Arizona*. U.S. Geol. Surv. Water Supply Pap. 1858.

Brooks, K. N., H. M. Gregersen, E. R. Berglund, and M. Tayaa. 1981. Economic evaluation of watershed projects—an overview methodology and application. *Water Resour. Bull.* 18:245–250.

Brown, G. W. 1980. *Forestry and Water Quality*. Corvallis: Oregon State Univ. Bookstores.

Brown, H. E. 1965. Characteristics of recession flows from small watersheds in a semiarid region of Arizona. *Water Resour. Res.* 1:517–522.

———. 1969. A combined control-metering section for gaging large streams. *Water Resour. Res.* 5:888–894.

Brown, H. E., M. B. Baker, Jr., J. J. Rogers, W. P. Clary, J. L. Kovner, F. R. Larson, C. C. Avery, and R. E. Campbell. 1974. *Opportunities for increasing water yields and other multiple use values on ponderosa pine forest lands*. USDA For. Serv. Res. Pap. RM-129.

Brown, T. C., and M. M. Fogel. 1987. Use of streamflow increases from vegetation management in the Verde River Basin. *Water Resour. Bull.* 23:1149–1160.

Burdass, W. J. 1975. Water harvesting for livestock in western Australia. In *Proceedings of the water harvesting symposium,* ed. G. W. Frasier, pp. 8–26. USDA Agric. Res. Serv. ARS-W-22.

Calder, I. R. 1982. Forest evaporation. In *Hydrological Processes of Forested Areas,* pp. 173–193. Proc. Can. Hydrol. Symp. 1982, National Research Council, Canada. Fredericton, N. B.

Cheng, J. D., T. A. Black, J. DeVries, R. P. Willington, and B. C. Goodell. 1975. The evaluation of initial changes in peak streamflow following logging of a watershed on the West Coast of Canada. *Int. Assoc. Hydrol. Sci. Publ.* 117:475–486.

Chiarella, J. V., and W. H. Beck. 1975. Water harvesting catchments of Indian lands in the southwest. In *Proceedings of the water harvesting symposium,* ed. G. W. Frasier, pp. 104–114. USDA Agric. Res. Serv. ARS-W-22.

Churchill, M. A., R. A. Buckingham, and H. L. Elmore. 1962. *The prediction of stream reaeration rates.* Tennessee Valley Authority, Chattanooga.

Clyde, C. F., C. E. Israelsen, and P. E. Packer. 1976. Erosion during highway construction. In *Manual of erosion control principles and practices.* Utah Water Research Laboratory, Utah State Univ., Logan.

Davis, S. N., and R. J. M. DeWiest. 1966. *Hydrogeology.* New York: John Wiley and Sons.

DeBano, L. F. 1981. *Water repellent soils: A state-of-the-art.* USDA For. Serv. Gen. Tech. Rep. PSW-46.

Dissmeyer, G. E., and G. R. Foster. 1980. *A guide for predicting sheet and rill erosion on forest land.* USDA Tech. Publ. SA-TP11.

―――. 1985. Modifying the Universal Soil Loss Equation for forest lands. In *Soil Erosion and Conservation,* ed., S. A. El Swaify, W. L. Moldenhauer, and A. Lo, pp. 480–495. Ankeny, Iowa: Soil Conserv. Soc. Am.

Dixon, J., and M. Hufschmidt (eds.). 1986. *Economic Valuation Techniques for the Environment: A Case Study Workbook.* Baltimore: John Hopkins Univ. Press.

Dixon, R. M., and A. E. Peterson. 1971. Water infiltration control: A channel system concept. *Soil Sci. Soc. Am. Proc.* 35:968–973.

Dooge, J. C. I. 1973. *Linear theory of hydrologic systems.* USDA Agric. Res. Serv. Tech. Bull. 1468.

Douglas, J. E. 1983. The potential for water yield augmentation from forest management in the eastern United States. *Water Resour. Bull.* 19:351–358.

Dyrsdale, P. J. 1981. Status of general and forest hydrology research in Fiji. In *Country papers on status of watershed forest influence research in southeast Asia and the pacific.* Working Pap. East-West Center. Honolulu, Hawaii.

Duffy, P. D., J. D. Schreiber, and S. J. Ursic. 1986. Nutrient transport by sediment from pine forests. In *Proceedings of Fourth Federal Interagency Sedimentation Conference.* pp. 57–65. Las Vegas, Nev.

Dunin, F. X., and S. M. Mackay. 1982. Evaporation of eucalypt and coniferous forest communities. In *First National Symposium on Forest Hydrology,* ed. E. M. O'Loughlin and L. J. Bren, pp. 18–25, National Committee on Hydrology and Water Resources of the Institution of Engineers. Melbourne, Aust.

Dunne, T., and L. B. Leopold. 1978. *Water in Environmental Planning.* San Francisco: W. H. Freeman and Co.

Edwards, K. A., and J. R. Blackie. 1981. Results of the East African catchment experiments, 1958–1974. In *Tropical Agricultural Hydrology,* ed. R. Lal and E. W. Russell, pp. 163–188. New York: John Wiley and Sons.

Environmental Protection Agency (EPA). 1976. *Quality criteria for water.* EPA Rep. 440/9–76–023.

―――. 1980. *Acid rain.* Off. of Res. and Dev., EPA-600/9–79–036.

Fetter, C. W., Jr. 1980. *Applied Hydrogeology.* Columbus: Charles E. Merrill.

Ffolliott, P. F., and D. B. Thorud. 1974. A technique to evaluate snowpack profiles in and adjacent to forest openings. *Hydrol. Water Resour. of Arizona and the Southwest* 4:10–17.

Foster, G. R., and W. H. Wischmeier. 1973. *Evaluating irregular slopes for soil loss prediction.* Am. Soc. Agri. Eng. Pap. 73–227.

Frasier, G. W. 1975. Water harvesting: A source of livestock water. *J. Range Manage.* 28:429–433.

Frasier, G. W., and L. Myers. 1983. *Handbook of water harvesting.* USDA Agric. Res. Serv. Handb. 600.

Fritschen, L. J., J. Hsia, and P. Doraiswamy. 1977. Evapotranspiration of a Douglas-fir determined with a weighing lysimeter. *Water Resour. Res.* 13:145–148.

Frye, P. M., and G. S. Runner. 1970. *A proposed streamflow data program for West Virginia.* U.S. Department of Interior, Geological Survey, Charleston, W.V.

Gary, H. C. 1975. Airflow patterns and snow accumulation in a forest clearing. In *Proceedings of the 43rd Western Snow Conference,* pp. 106–113. Coronado, Calif.

Gilmour, D. A., D. S. Cassells, and M. Bonell. 1982. Hydrological research in the tropical rainforests of North Queensland: Some implications for land use management. In *First National Symposium on Forest Hydrology,* ed. E. M. O'Loughlin and L. J. Bren, pp. 145–152. National Committee on Hydrology and Water Resources of the Institution of Engineers. Melbourne, Aust.

Gittinger, J. P. 1982. *Economic Analysis of Agricultural Projects.* 2d ed. Baltimore: John Hopkins Univ. Press.

Goldstein, R. A., J. B. Mankin, and R. J. Luxmore. 1974. *Documentation of PROSPER: A model of atmosphere-soil-plant-water flow.* Oak Ridge Natl. Lab. EDFB-IBP-73-9. Oak Ridge, Tenn.

Gosz, J. R., C. S. White, and P. F. Ffolliott. 1980. Nutrient and heavy metal transport capacities of sediment in the southwestern United States. *Water Resour. Bull.* 16:927–933.

Gray, D. M. (ed.). 1970/1973. *Handbook on the Principles of Hydrology.* Reprint. National Research Council, Canada. Port Washington: Water Information Center, Inc.

Gregersen, H. M., and A. H. Contreras. 1979. *Economic analysis of forestry projects.* FAO For. Pap. 17. Rome.

Gregersen, H. M., and A. Lundgren. 1986. An evaluation framework. In *Alternative approaches to forestry research evaluation and assessment,* pp. 2–6. USDA, For. Serv. Gen. Tech. Rep. NC-110.

Gregersen, H. M., K. N. Brooks, J. A. Dixon, and L. S. Hamilton. 1987. *Guidelines for economic appraisal of watershed management projects.* FAO Conserv. Guide 16, Rome.

Guertin, D. P., P. K. Barten, and K. N. Brooks. 1987. The peatland hydrolic impact model: Development and testing. *Nordic Hydrol.* 18:79–100.

Guy, H. P. 1964. *An analysis of some storm-related variables affecting stream sediment transport.* U.S. Geol. Surv. Prof. Pap. 462-E.

Haan, C. T. 1977. *Statistical Methods in Hydrology.* Ames: Iowa State Univ. Press.

Hall, F. R. 1968. Base-flow recessions—a review. *Water Resour. Res.* 4:973–984.

Hamon, W. R. 1961. Estimating potential evapotranspiration. *J. Hydrol. Div., Proc. Am. Soc. Civil Eng.* 87(HY3):107–120.

Hanks, R. J., and G. L. Ashcroft. 1980. *Applied Soil Physics.* New York: Springer-Verlag.

Hanks, R. J., H. R. Gardner, and R. L. Florian. 1968. Evapotranspiration-climate relations for several crops in the central Great Plains. *Agron. J.* 60:538–542.

Harr, R. D. 1983. Potential for augmenting water yield through forest practices in western Washington and western Oregon. *Water Resour. Bull.* 19:383–393.

Harr, R. D., and F. M. McCorison. 1979. Initial effects of clearcut logging on size and timing of peak flows in a small watershed in western Oregon. *Water Resour. Res.* 15:90–94.

Harvey, M. D., C. C. Watson, and S. A. Schumm. 1985. *Gully erosion.* USDI Bur. Land Manage. Tech. Note 366.

Hawkinson, C. F., and E. S. Verry. 1975. *Specific conductance identifies perched and groundwater lakes.* USDA For. Serv. Res. Pap. NC-120.

Heede, B. H. 1967. The fusion of discontinuous gullies: A case study. *Bull. Int. Assoc. Hydrol. Sci.* XII(No. 4):42–50.

———. 1976. *Gully development and control: The status of our knowledge.* USDA For. Serv. Res. Pap. RM-169.

Heede, B. H., and J. G. Mufich. 1973. Functional relationships and a computer program for structural gully control. *J. Environ. Manage.* 1:321–344.

Helvey, J. D., and J. H. Patric. 1965. Canopy and litter interception by hardwoods of eastern United States. *Water Resour. Res.* 1:193–206.

Helvey, J. D., A. R. Tiedemann, and T. D. Anderson. 1985. Plant nutrient loss by soil erosion and mass movement after wildfire. *J. Soil Water Conserv.* 40:168–173.

Hem, J. D. 1970. *Study and interpretation of the chemical characteristics of natural water.* 2d ed. U.S. Geol. Surv. Water Supply Pap. 1473.

Hewlett, J. D. 1982a. Forests and floods in the light of recent investigations. In *Proceedings of the Canadian Hydrology Symposium 82 on Hydrological Processes of Forested Areas,* pp. 543–559. National Research Council, Canada.

———. 1982b. *Principles of Forest Hydrology.* Athens: Univ. of Georgia Press.

Hewlett, J. D., and J. D. Helvey. 1970. Effects of forest clear-felling on the storm hydrograph. *Water Resour. Res.* 6:768–782.

Hewlett, J. D., and A. R. Hibbert. 1967. Factors affecting response of small watersheds to precipitation in humid areas. In *Forest Hydrology,* pp. 275–290. New York: Pergamon Press.

Hewlett, J. D., and J. B. Moore. 1976. *Predicting stormflow and peak discharge in the Redland District using the R-index method.* Georgia For. Res. Pap. 84, Athens.

Hewlett, J. D., and C. A. Troendle. 1975. Nonpoint and diffused water sources: A variable source area problem. In *Proceedings of a Symposium on Watershed Management,* pp. 21–46. Am. Soc. Civ. Eng. New York.

Hewlett, J. D., H. W. Lull, and K. G. Reinhart. 1969. In defense of experimental watersheds. *Water Resour. Res.* 5:306–316.

Hewlett, J. D., H. E. Post, and R. Doss. 1984. Effect of clearcut silviculture on dissolved ion export and water yield in the Piedmont. *Water Resour. Res.* 20:1030–1038.

Hibbert, A. R. 1983. Water yield improvement potential by vegetation management on western rangelands. *Water Resour. Bull.* 19:375–381.

Hillel, D. 1967. *Runoff inducement in arid lands.* USDA Final Tech. Report, Proj. A 10-SWC-36.

Hitzhusen, F. J. 1982. *The "economics" of biomass for energy: Towards clarification for non-economists.* Mimeogr. Ohio State Univ., Columbus.

Holtan, H. N. 1971. A formulation for quantifying the influence of soil porosity and vegetation on infiltration. In *Biological Effects in the Hydrological Cycle,* pp. 228–239. Proc. Third Int. Sem. Hydrol. Professors. Purdue Univ. West Lafayette, Ind.

Holtan, H. N., G. J. Stiltner, W. H. Henson, and N. C. Lopez. 1975. *USDAHL-74 model of watershed hydrology.* USDA Agric. Res. Serv. Tech. Bull. 1518.

Hornbeck, J. W. 1973. Storm flow from hardwood-forested and cleared watersheds in New Hampshire. *Water Resour. Res.* 9:346–354.

Hornbeck, J. W., R. S. Pierce, and C. A. Federer. 1970. Streamflow changes after forest clearing in New England. *Water Resour. Res.* 6:1124–1132.

Horton, J. S., and C. J. Campbell. 1974. *Management of phreatophyte and riparian vegetation for maximum multiple use values.* USDA For. Serv. Res. Pap. RM-117.

Horton, R. E. 1919. Rainfall interception. *Mon. Weather Rev.* 47:603–623.

———. 1933. The role of infiltration in the Hydrologic Cycle. *Trans. Am. Geophys. Union* 14:446–460.

———. 1940. An approach to the physical interpretation of infiltration capacity. *Proc. Soil Sci. Am.* 5:399–417.

Howe, J. W. 1966. *Recession characteristics of Iowa streams.* Iowa State Water Resource Research Institute, Iowa City.

Hudson, N. W. 1981. *Soil Conservation.* 2d ed. New York: Cornell Univ. Press.

Hufschmidt, M. M., D. E. James, A. D. Meister, B. T. Bower, and J. A. Dixon. 1983. *Environment, Natural Systems, and Development—An Economic Valuations Guide.* Baltimore: Johns Hopkins Univ. Press.

Hydrocomp. 1976. *Hydrocomp simulation programming operations manual.* Hydrocomp Inc. Palo Alto, Calif.

Indri, E. 1960. Low water flow curves for some streams in Venetian Alps. *Int. Assoc. Hydrol. Sci. Publ.* 51:124–129

Johnson, A. W. 1961. Highway erosion control. *Am. Soc. Agric. Eng. Trans.* 4:144–152.

Johnson, M. G., and R. L. Beschta. 1980. Logging, infiltration capacity, and surface erodibility in Western Oregon. *J. For.* 78:334–337.

Johnston, R. S. 1970. Evapotranspiration from bare, herbaceous, and aspen plots: A check on a former study. *Water Resour. Res.* 6:324–327.

Karpiscak, M. M., K. E. Foster, R. L. Rawles, N. G. Wright, and P. Hataway. 1984. *Water harvesting agrisystem: An alternative to groundwater use in Avra Valley area, Arizona.* Office of Arid Land Studies. Univ. Arizona, Tucson.

Kattelmann, R. C., N. H. Berg, and J. Rector. 1983. The potential for increasing streamflow from Sierra Nevada watersheds. *Water Resour. Bull.* 19:395–402.

Kleinberg, K. 1984. Hydrology of north central Florida Cypress Downs. In *Cypress Swamps,* ed. K. C. Ewel and H. T. Odum, pp. 72–82. Gainesville: Univ. of Florida Press.

Lane, E. W. 1955. The importance of fluvial morphology in hydraulic engineering. *Proc. Am. Soc. Civ. Eng.,* Vol. 81, Pap. 745, pp. 1–17.

Lane, L. J. 1983. Transmission losses. In *National Engineering Handbook.* Section 4, Hydrology, Chap. 19. USDA Soil Conservation Service. Washington, D.C.

Larson, C. L., and W. Albertin. 1984. Controlling erosion and sedimentation in the Panama Canal watershed. *Water Int.* 9:161–164.

Larson, C. T. 1973. Hydrologic effects of modifying small watersheds—is prediction by hydrologic modeling possible? *Trans. Am. Soc. Agric. Eng.* 16:560–564, 568.

Leaf, C. F., and G. E. Brink. 1973. *Hydrologic simulation model of Colorado subalpine forest.* USDA For. Serv. Res. Pap. RM-107.

———. Brink. 1975. *Land use simulation model of the subalpine coniferous forest zone.* USDA For. Serv. Res. Pap. RM-135.

Lee, R. 1964. Potential isolation as a topoclimatic characteristic of drainage basins. *Bull. Int. Assoc. Hydrol. Sci.* 9:27–41.

———. 1978. *Forest Climatology.* New York: Columbia Univ. Press.

———. 1980. *Forest Hydrology.* New York: Columbia Univ. Press.

Linsley, R. K., Jr., M. A. Kohler, and J. L. H. Paulhus. 1982. *Hydrology for Engineers.* 3d ed. New York: McGraw-Hill.

McConnon, R. J., D. I. Navon, and E. L. Amidon. 1965. Efficient development and use of forest lands: An outline of a prototype computer-oriented system for operational planning. In *Proceedings of a Conference on Mathematical Models in Forest Management,* pp. 18–32. Edinburgh, Scotl.

McMahon, T. A., and R. G. Mein. 1978. *Reservoir Capacity and Yield.* Developments in Water Science, Vol. 9. New York: Elsevier Scientific.

Mace, A. C., Jr., and J. R. Thompson. 1969. *Modifications and evaluation of the evapotranspiration tent.* USDA For. Serv. Res. Pap. RM-50.

Marques, J., J. M. Santos, N. A. Villa Nova, and E. Salati. 1977. Precipitable water and water flux between Belem and Manaus. *Acta Amazonica* 7:355–362.

Martin, C. W., R. S. Pierce, G. E. Likens, and F. H. Bormann. 1986. *Clearcutting affects stream chemistry in the White Mountains of New Hampshire.* USDA For. Serv. Res. Pap. NE-579.

Megahan, W. F. 1977. Reducing erosional impacts of roads. In *Guidelines for watershed management,* ed. S. H. Kunkle and J. L. Thames, pp. 237–261. FAO Conserv. Guide 1. Rome.

Mehdizadeh, P. Howsar, A. Vaziri, and L. Boersma. 1978. Water harvesting for afforestation, efficiency and life span of asphalt cover 11, survival and growth of trees. *Soil Sci. Soc. Am. J.* 42: 644–657.

Meriam, R. A. 1960. A note on the interception loss equation. *J. Geophys. Res.* 65:3850–3851.

Milliman, J. D., and R. H. Meade. 1983. World-wide delivery of river sediments to the oceans. *J. Geol.* 91:1–21.

Monteith, J. L. 1965. Evaporation and the environment. *Symp. Soc. Exp. Biol.* 19:205–234.

Morisawa, M. 1968. *Streams—Their Dynamics and Morphology.* Earth and Planet, Sci. Ser. New York: McGraw-Hill.

O'Connel, P. F., and H. E. Brown. 1972. Use of production functions to evaluate multiple use treatments on forested watersheds. *Water Resour. Res.* 8:1188–1198.

Omernik, J. M. 1976. *The influence of land on stream nutrient levels.* EPA Publ. 600/3–76–014.

Organization for Economic Cooperation and Development (OECD). 1986. *The Public Management of Forestry Projects.* Paris.

Patric, J. A., J. O. Evans, and J. D. Helvey. 1984. Summary of sediment yield data from forested land in the United States. *J. For.* 82:101–104.

Penman, H. L. 1948. Natural evaporation from open water, bare soil and grass. *Proc. R. Soc. London, Ser.* A 193:120–145.

Penman, H. L., D. E. Angus, and C. H. M. van Bavel. 1967. Microclimate factors affecting evaporation and transpiration. In *Irrigation of Agricultural Lands.* Vol. 2, *Agromony,* ed. R. M. Hagen, H. R. Haise, and T. W. Edminster, pp. 483–505. Madison, Wis.: Am. Soc. Agron.

Philip, J. R. 1957. The theory of infiltration: The infiltration equation and its solution. *Soil Sci.* 83:345–357.

Pilgrim, D. H., D. G. Boran, I. A. Rowbottom, S. M. Mackay, and J. Tjendana. 1982. Water balance and runoff characteristics of mature and cleared pine and eucalypt catchments at Lidsdale, New South Wales. In *First National Symposium on Forest Hydrology,* ed. E. M. O'Loughlin and L. J. Bren, pp. 103–110. National Committee on Hydrology and Water Resources of the Institution of Engineers. Melbourne, Aust.

Ponce, S. L. 1974. The biochemical oxygen demand of finely divided logging debris in stream water. *Water Resour. Res.* 10:983–988.

———. 1980. *Water quality monitoring programs.* Watershed Systems Dev. Group, Tech. Pap. 00002. USDA For. Serv. Ft. Collins, Colo.

Postel, S. 1984. *Air pollution, acid rain, and the future of forests.* Worldwatch Pap. 58. World-watch Inst. Washington, D.C.

Rango, A., and J. Martinec. 1979. Application of a snowmelt-runoff model using LANDSAT data. *Nordic Hydrol.* 10:225–238.

Reifsnyder, W. E., and H. W. Lull. 1965. *Radiant energy in relation to forests.* USDA For. Serv. Tech. Bull. 1344.

Roehl, J. W. 1962. Sediment source area delivery ratios and influencing morphological factors. *Int. Assoc. Hydrol. Sci. Publ.* 59:202–213.

Rose, C. W. 1966. *Agricultural Physics.* New York: Pergamon Press.

Rosgen, D. L. 1980. Total potential sediment. In *An approach to water resources evaluation, nonpoint sources silviculture.* pp. VI.1-VI.43, Environ. Res. Lab. EPA-600 18–80–012. Environmental Protection Agency. Athens, Ga.

Roth, F. A., II, and M. Chang. 1981. Throughfall in planted stands of fourth southern pines species in east Texas. *Water Resour. Bull.* 17:880–885.

Salati, E., and P. B. Vose. 1984. Amazon basin: A system in equilibrium. *Science* 225:129–138.

Schuster, E. 1980. Economic impact analysis of forestry projects: A guide to evaluation of distributional consequences. In *Economic analysis of forestry projects.* FAO For. Pap. 17, Suppl. 2, pp. 63–132. Rome.

Shen, H. W., and R. M. Li. 1976. Water sediment yield. In *Stochastic Approaches to Water Response,* ed. H. W. Shen, pp. 21–68. Colorado State Univ., Fort Collins: H. W. Shen.

Sidle, R. C. 1985. Factors influencing the stability of slopes. In *Proceedings of the workshop on slope stability: Problems and solutions in forest management,* ed. D. Swanston, pp. 17–25. USDA For. Serv. Gen Tech. Rep. PNW-180.

Sidle, R. C., and D. M. Drlica. 1981. Soil compaction from logging with a low-ground pressure skidder in the Oregon coast ranges. *Soil Sci. Am. J.* 45:1219–1224.

Sinha, B. 1984. Role of watershed management in water resources development planning—need for integrated approach to development of catchment and command of irrigation projects. *Water Int.* 9:158–160.

Slatyer, R. O. 1967. *Plant-Water Relationships.* New York: Academic Press.

Stromquist, L., B. Lunden, and Q. Chakela. 1985. Sediment sources, sediment transfer in a small Lesotho catchment—a pilot study of the spatial distribution of erosion features and their variation with time and climate. *S. African Geol. J.* 67:3–13.

Swank, W. T., and J. B. Waide. 1979. Interpretation of nutrient cycling research in a management context: Evaluating potential effects of alternative management strategies on site productivity. In *Forest Ecosystems: Fresh Perspectives from Ecosystem Analysis,* ed. R. H. Waring and J. Franklin. pp. 137–158. Corvallis: Oregon State Univ. Press.

Swanson, R. H., and R. Lee. 1966. Measurement of water movement from and through shrubs and trees. *J. For.* 64:187–190.

Swanston, D. N. 1974. *The forest ecosystem of southeast Alaska*. USDA For. Serv. Gen. Tech. Rep. PNW-7.

Swanston, D. N., and F. J. Swanson. 1980. Soil mass movement. In *An approach to water resources evaluation, nonpoint silvicultural sources*. pp. V.1-V.49. Environ. Res. Lab. EPA-600/8–80–012. Environmental Protection Agency. Athens, Ga.

Tan, C. S., and T. A. Black. 1976. Factors affecting the canopy resistance of a Douglas-fir forest. *Boundary-Layer Meteorol*. 10:475–488.

Tennyson, L. C., P. F. Ffolliott, and D. B. Thorud. 1974. Use of time-lapse photography to assess potential interception in Arizona ponderosa pine. *Water Resour. Bull*. 10: 1246–1254.

Thomas, R. 1976. *Numerical nonsense: A discussion of commonly unrecognized problems in collecting, analyzing, and drawing conclusions from data*. USDA Forest Service Region Five. San Francisco, Calif.

Thornthwaite, C. W., and J. R. Mather. 1955. *The water balance*. Laboratory of Climatology, Publ. 8. Centerton, N.J.

Thut, R. N., and E. P. Haydu. 1971. Effects of forest chemicals on aquatic life. In *Forest Land Uses and Stream Environment Symposium*, pp. 159–171. Corvallis: Oregon St. Univ. Press.

Todd, D. K. 1970. *The Water Encyclopedia*. Port Washington, N.Y.: Water Information Center, Inc.

Toebes, C., and D. D. Strang. 1964. On recession curves. 1—recession Equations. *J. Hydrol.* (N.Z.) 3:2–15.

Troendle, C. A., and R. M. King. 1985. The effect of timber harvest on the Fool Creek watershed 30 years later. *Water Resour. Res*. 21:1915–1922.

Trustrum, N. A., V. J. Thomas, and M. G. Lambert. 1984. Soil slip erosion as a constraint to hill country pasture production. *Proc. N.Z. Grassl. Assoc*. 45:66–76.

U.S. Army Corps of Engineers. 1956. *Snow hydrology*. North Pacific Division. Portland, Oreg. (Available from U.S. Dept. Commerce, Clearinghouse for Federal Scientific and Technical Information as PB 151660).

———. 1960. *Runoff from snowmelt*. Eng. Man. 1110–2–1406.

———. 1972. *Program description and users manual for SSARR model, Streamflow Synthesis and Reservoir Regulation* (revised 1975). North Pacific Division. Portland, Oreg.

———. 1975. *Hydrologic Frequency Analysis*. Hydrologic Engineering Methods for Water Resources Development, Vol. 3. Davis, Calif.: Hydrology Engineering Center.

———. 1977. *Reservoir System Analysis for Conservation*. In Hydrologic Engineering Methods for Water Resources Development, Vol. 9. Davis, California: Hydrology Engineering Center.

U.S. Forest Service. 1980. *An approach to water resources evaluation of nonpoint silvicultural sources*. Environ. Res. Lab., EPA-600/8–80–012. Environmental Protection Agency. Athens, Ga.

U.S. Soil Conservation Service. 1969. *Engineering Field Manual for Conservation Practices*, p. 995.

———. 1972. *National Engineering Handbook*. Sec. 4, Hydrology.

———. 1977. *Procedure for computing sheet and rill erosion on project areas*. Tech. Release No. 41.

U.S. Water Resources Council. 1976. *Guidelines for determining flood flow frequency*. Hydrol. Comm. Bull. 17.

Van Hylckama, T. E. A. 1970. Water use by Salt Cedar. *Water Resour. Res*. 6:728–735.

Varnes, D. J. 1958. Landslide types and processes. In *Landslides and engineering practice*, ed. E. B. Eckel, pp. 20–47. Highway Res. Board Spec. Rep. 29, National Academy Science. Washington, D.C.

Vashistha, R. N., M. L. Pandita, and R. R. Batra. 1980. Water harvesting studies under rainfed condition in relation to growth and yield of okra. *Haryana J. Hort. Sci*. 9(314):188–191.

Vergara, N. T. 1982. *New directions in agroforestry: The potential of tropical legume trees*. East-West Center. Honolulu, Hawaii.

———. 1985. Agroforestry systems: A primer. *UNASYLVA* 37(147):22–28.

Verry, E. S. 1976. *Estimating water yield differences between hardwood and pine forests: An application of net precipitation data*. USDA For. Serv. Res. Pap. NC-128.

————. 1986. Forest harvesting and water: The Lake States experience. *Water Res. Bull.* 22:1039–1047.

Verry, E. S., J. R. Lewis, and K. N. Brooks. 1983. Aspen clearcutting increases snowmelt and storm flow peaks in north central Minnesota. *Water Resour. Bull.* 19:59–67.

Vigon, B. W. 1985. The status of nonpoint source pollution: Its nature, extent and control. *Water Res. Bull.* 21:179–184.

Weitzman, S., and R. R. Bay. 1963. *Forest soil freezing and the influence of management practices, northern Minnesota.* USDA For. Serv. Res. Pap. LS-2.

Wicht, C. L. 1943. Determination of the effects of watershed management on mountain streams. *Trans. Am. Geophys. Union,* Pt. II: 594–605.

Williams, J. R. 1975. Sediment yield predicted with universal equation using runoff energy factor. In *Present and prospective technology for predicting sediment yields and resources,* pp. 244–252. USDA-ARS-S-40.

Wischmeier, W. H. 1975. Estimating the soil loss equation's cover and management factor for undisturbed areas. In *Present and prospective technology for predicting sediment yields and sources,* pp. 118–124. USDA-ARS-S-40.

Wischmeier, W. H., and D. D. Smith. 1965. *Predicting rainfall-erosion losses from cropland east of the Rocky Mountains.* USDA Agric Handb. No. 282.

————. 1978. *Predicting rainfall-erosion losses—a guide to conservation planning.* USDA Agric Handb. No. 537.

Wischmeier, W. H., C. B. Johnson, and B. V. Cross. 1971. A soil erodibility nomograph for farmland and construction sites. *J. Soil and Water Conserv.* 26:189–193.

Woodruff, J. F., and J. D. Hewlett. 1970. Predicting and mapping the average hydrologic response for the eastern United States. *Water Resour. Res.* 6:1312–1326.

Woolhiser, D. A., and D. L. Brakensiek. 1982. Hydrologic system synthesis. In *Hydrologic modeling of small watersheds,* pp. 3–16. Am. Soc. Agric. Eng., Monogr. No. 5.

Zadroga, F. 1981. The hydrological importance of a montane cloud forest area of Costa Rica. In *Tropical Agricultural Hydrology,* ed. R. Lal and F. W. Russell, pp. 59–73. New York: John Wiley and Sons.

Zon, R. 1927. *Forests and water in the light of scientific investigation.* USDA For. Serv. Rep. unclassified.

GENERAL REFERENCES

CHAPTER 1

Food and Agriculture Organization (FAO). 1985. *Tropical forestry action plan*. Rome.

————. 1986. *Strategies, approaches and systems in integrated watershed management*. FAO Conserv. Guide 14. Rome.

Gregersen, H. M., K. N. Brooks, J. Dixon, and L. Hamilton. 1987. *Guidelines for the economic appraisal of watershed management projects*. FAO Conserv. Guide 16. Rome.

Kessel, M. L. 1985. Timber harvest, landslides, streams, and fish habitat on the Oregon Coast. *J. For.* 83(10):606–607.

Kunkle, S. H., and J. L. Thames (eds.). 1977. *Guidelines for watershed management*. FAO Conserv. Guide 1. Rome.

CHAPTER 2

Baumgartner, A., and E. Reichel. 1975. *The World Water Balance*. München: R. Oldenbourg.

Brakensiek, D. C., H. B. Osborn, and W. J. Rawls (coord.). 1979. *Field manual for research in agricultural hydrology*. USDA, Agric. Handb. 224.

Clary, W. P., and P. F. Ffolliott. 1969. Water holding capacity of ponderosa pine forest floor layers. *J. Soil Water Conserv.* 24:22–23.

Helvey, J. D. 1971. A summary of rainfall interception by certain conifers of North America. In *Biological Effects in the Hydrologic Cycle*, pp. 103–113. Proc. Third Int. Sem. Hydrol. Professors. Purdue Univ. West Lafayette, Indiana.

Lee, R. 1980. *Forest Hydrology*. New York: Columbia Univ. Press.

Leonard, R. E. 1967. Mathematical theory of interception. In *International Symposium on Forest Hydrology*, ed. W. E. Sopper and H. W. Lull, pp. 131–136. New York: Pergamon Press.

Swank, W. T., and N. H. Miner. 1968. Conversion of hardwood covered watersheds to white pine reduces water yield. *Water Resour. Res.* 4:947–954.

Todd, D. K. (ed.). 1970. *The Water Encyclopedia*. Port Washington, N.Y.: Water Information Center, Inc.

CHAPTER 3

Federer, C. A. 1970. *Measuring forest evapotranspiration—theory and problems*. USDA For. Serv. Res. Pap. NE-165.

Hillel, D. 1982. *Introduction to Soil Physics*. New York: Academic Press.

Houghton, D. D. 1985. *Handbook of Applied Meteorology*. New York: John Wiley and Sons.

Lee, R. 1978. *Forest Climatology*. New York: Columbia Univ. Press.

Sellers, W. D. 1965. *Physical Climatology*. Chicago: Univ. of Chicago Press.

Swanson, R. H. 1972. Water transpiration by trees is indicated by heat pulse velocity. *Agric. Meteorol.* 10:227–281.

Thom, A. S. 1975. Momentum, mass and heat exchange of plant communities. In *Vegetation and the Atmosphere*. Vol. 1, ed. J. L. Monteith, pp. 57–109. London: Academic Press.

U.S. Forest Service. 1961. *Handbook on soils*. No. 2212.5.

CHAPTER 4

Brakensiek, D. C., H. B. Osborn, and W. J. Rawls (coord.). 1979. *Field manual for research in agricultural hydrology*. USDA, Agric. Handb. 224.

Branson, F. A., G. F. Gifford, K. G. Renard, and R. F. Hadley. 1981. *Rangeland Hydrology.* 2d ed. Dubuque, Iowa: Kendall/Hunt.

Hewlett, J. D., and A. R. Hibbert. 1963. Moisture and energy conditions within a sloping soil mass during drainage. *J. Geophys. Res.* 68:1081–1087.

Taylor, S. A., and G. L. Ashcroft. 1972. *Physical Edaphology, the Physics of Irrigated and Nonirrigated Soils.* San Francisco: W. H. Freeman and Co.

CHAPTER 5

Carter, V. 1986. An overview of the hydrologic concerns related to wetlands in the United States. *Can. J. Bot.* 64:364–374.

Dunne, T., and L. B. Leopold. 1978. *Water in Environmental Planning.* San Francisco: W. H. Freeman and Co.

Leopold, L. B. 1974. *Water—a Primer.* San Francisco: W. H. Freeman and Co.

Mitsch, W. J., and J. G. Gosselink. 1986. *Wetlands.* New York: Van Nostrand Reinhold Co.

Todd, D. K. 1980. *Ground Water Hydrology.* 2d ed. New York: John Wiley and Sons.

CHAPTER 6

Anderson, H. W., M. D. Hoover, and K. G. Reinhart. 1976. *Forests and water: Effects of forest management on floods, sedimentation, and water supply.* USDA For. Serv. Gen. Tech. Rep. PSW-18.

Harr, R. D. 1982. Fog drip in the Bull Run municipal watershed, Oregon. *Water Resour. Bull.* 18:785–789.

Harr, R. D., W. C. Harper, and J. T. Krygier. 1975. Changes in storm hydrographs after road building and clear cutting in the Oregon coast range. *Water Resour. Res.* 11:436–444.

Harr, R. D., A. Levno, and R. Mersereau. 1982. Streamflow changes after logging 130-year-old Douglas fir in two small watersheds. *Water Resour. Res.* 18:637–644.

Lull, H. W., and K. G. Reinhart. 1972. *Forests and floods in the eastern United States.* USDA For. Serv. Res. Pap. NE-226.

Pereira, H. C. 1973. *Land Use and Water Resources.* Cambridge: Cambridge Univ. Press.

Swank, W. T., and D. A. Crossley, Jr. (ed). 1988. *Forest Hydrology and Ecology at Coweeta.* New York: Springer-Verlag.

U.S. Forest Service. 1980. *An approach to water resource evaluation of nonpoint silvicultural sources.* Environ. Res. Lab., EPA-600/8–80–012, Environmental Protection Agency. Athens, Ga.

CHAPTER 7

Branson, F. A., G. F. Gifford, K. G. Renard, and R. F. Hadley. 1981. *Rangeland Hydrology.* 2d ed. Dubuque, Iowa: Kendall/Hunt.

Dissmeyer, G. E. 1982. Report on application of the USLE to desert brush and rangeland conditions. In *Proceedings of the Workshop on Estimating Erosion and Sediment Yields on Rangelands,* pp. 214–225. USDA, Argic. Res. Serv., ARM-W-26.

Dissmeyer, G. E., and G. R. Foster. 1981. Estimating the cover management factor (C) in the universal soil loss equation for forest conditions. *J. Soil and Water Conserv.* 36:235–240.

El-Swaify, S. A., E. W. Dangler, and C. C. Armstrong. 1982. *Soil erosion by water in the tropics.* Res. Ext. Ser. 024. College of Tropical Agriculture and Human Resources, Univ. Hawaii, Honolulu.

Food and Agriculture Organization (FAO). 1985. *Sand dune stabilization, shelterbelts and afforestation in dry zones.* FAO Conserv. Guide 10. Rome.

Kunkle, S. H., and J. L. Thames (eds.). 1977. *Guidelines for watershed management.* FAO Conserv. Guide 1. Rome.

Meyer, L. D. 1984. Evolution of the Universal Soil Loss Equation. *J. Soil Water Conserv.* 39:99–104.

Morgan, R. P. C. 1986. *Soil Erosion and Conservation.* New York: John Wiley and Sons.

Renard, K. G. 1980. Estimating erosion and sediment yields from rangelands. In *Proceedings of a Symposium on Watershed Management, 1980,* pp. 164–175. Am. Soc. Civ. Eng. New York.

Smith, S. J., J. R. Williams, R. G. Menzel, and G. A. Coleman. 1984. Prediction of sediment yield from Southern Plains grasslands with the Modified Universal Soil Loss Equation. *J. Range Manage.* 37:295–297.

Trott, K. G., and M. J. Singer. 1983. Relative erodibility of 20 California range and forest soils. *Soil Sci. Soc. Am. J.* 47:753–759.

Williams, J. R. 1982. Testing the modified universal soil loss equation. In *Proceedings of a workshop on estimating erosion and sediment yield on rangelands,* pp. 157–165. USDA-ARS, ARM-W-26.

Zingg, A. W. 1940. Degree and length of land slope as it affects soil loss in runoff. *Agric. Eng.* 21:59–64.

CHAPTER 8

Brown, G. W. 1980. *Forestry and Water Quality.* Corvallis: Oregon State Univ. Bookstores.

Dunne, T., and L. B. Leopold. 1978. *Water in Environmental Planning.* San Francisco: W. H. Freeman and Co.

Food and Agriculture Organization (FAO). 1977. *Guidelines for watershed managmeent.* FAO Conserv. Guide 1, Rome.

———. 1985. *Sand dune stabilization, shelterbelts, and afforestation in dry zones.* FAO Conserv. Guide 10, Rome.

Gil, N. 1979. *Watershed development with special reference to soil and water conservation.* FAO Soils Bull. 44, Rome.

Gray, D. M. (ed.). 1970/1973. *Handbook on the Principles of Hydrology.* Reprint. National Research Council, Canada. Port Washington, N.Y.: Water Information Center, Inc.

Heede, B. H. 1977. *Gully control structures and systems.* pp. 181–222, FAO Conserv. Guide 1, Rome.

O'Loughlin, C. L., and A. J. Pearce (eds.). 1984. *Symposium on the effects of forest land use on erosion and slope stability.* East-West Center. International Union of Forestry Research Organizations (IUFRO). Honolulu, Hawaii.

Toy, T. J., and R. F. Hadley. 1987. *Geomorphology and Reclamation of Disturbed Lands.* Orlando, Fla.: Academic Press.

CHAPTER 9

Dunne, T. and L. B. Leopold. 1978. *Water in Environmental Planning.* San Francisco: W. H. Freeman and Co.

Food and Agriculture Organization (FAO). 1981. *Arid zone hydrology.* Irrig. and Drain. Paper 37. Rome.

Swanson, F. J., R. J. Janda, T. Dunne, and D. N. Swanston. 1982. *Sediment budgets and routing in forested drainage basins.* USDA For. Serv. Gen. Tech. Rep. PNW-141.

Toy, T. J. (ed.). 1977. *Erosion: Research Techniques, Erodibility, and Sediment Delivery.* Norwich, Conn.: Geo Abstracts Ltd.

CHAPTER 10

Lamb, J. C. 1985. *Water Quality and Its Control.* New York: Wiley and Sons.

Lee, R. 1980. *Forest Hydrology.* New York: Columbia Univ. Press.

Likens, G. E., F. H. Bormann, R. S. Pierce, J. S. Eaton, and N. M. Johnson. 1977. *Biogeochemistry of a Forested Ecosystem.* New York: Springer-Verlag.

McKee, J. E., and H. W. Wolf. 1963. *Water quality criteria.* 2d ed. Calif. State Water Qual. Cont. B., Publ. No. 3-A, Sacramento.

Novotny, V., and G. Chesters. 1981. *Handbook of Nonpoint Pollution, Sources and Management.* New York: Van Nostrand Reinhold Co.

CHAPTER 11

Barraclough, S. L., and E. M. Gould, Jr. 1955. *Economic analysis of farm forest operating units*. Harvard For. Bull. No. 26.

Biesterfeldt, R. C., and S. G. Boyce. 1978. Systematic approach to multiple use management. *J. For.* 76:342–345.

Gregory, G. R. 1955. An economic approach to multiple use. *For. Sci.* 1:6–13.

Hewlett, J. D., and J. D. Douglass. 1968. *Blending forest uses*. USDA For. Serv. Res. Pap. SE-37.

Kneese, A. V., and S. C. Smith. 1966. *Water Research*. Washington, D.C.: Resources for the Future.

Lloyd, R. D. 1969. Economics of multiple use. In *Proceedings of the Conference on Multiple Use of Southern Forests*, pp. 45–54. Georgia Forest Research Council and Georgia Forestry Association. Pine Mountain, Ga.

Miller, R. L. 1969. Progress in developing multiple use forest watershed production models. *Ann. Reg. Sci.* 3:135–142.

Muhlenberg, N. 1964. A method for approximating forest multiple-useoptima. *For. Sci.* 10:209–212.

Ridd, M. K. 1965. *Area-oriented multiple use analysis*. USDA For. Serv. Res. Pap. INT-21.

Satterlund, D. R. 1972. *Wildland Watershed Management*. New York: Ronald Press Co.

Seckler, D. W. 1966. On the uses and abuses of economic science in evaluating public outdoor recreation. *Land Econ.* 42:485–494.

U.S. Forest Service. 1980. *IUFRO/MAB conference: Research on multiple use of forest resources*. USDA For. Serv. Gen. Tech. Rep. WO-25.

Worley, D. P. 1965. *The Beaver Creek watershed for evaluating multiple use effects of watershed treatments*. USDA For. Serv. Res. Pap. RM-13.

———. 1966. Economic evaluations of watershed management alternatives—the Beaver Creek watersheds. *N.Mex. Water Conf.* 11:58–65.

Worley, D. P., G. L. Mundell, and R. M. Williamson. 1965. *Gross job time studies—an efficient method for analyzing forestry costs*. USDA For. Serv. Res. Note RM-54.

CHAPTER 12

Gregersen, H. M., and A. Contreras. 1979. *Economic analysis of forestry projects*. FAO For. Pap. 17, Rome.

Tillman, G. 1981. *Environmentally Sound Small-scale Water Projects: Guidelines for Planning*. Arlington, Va.: Volunteers in Technical Assistance (VITA) Publ.

CHAPTER 13

Brown, T. C. 1976. *Alternative analysis for multiple use management: A case study*. USDA For. Serv. Res. Pap. RM-176.

Gregory, G. R. 1987. *Resource Economics for Foresters*. New York: John Wiley and Sons.

O'Connell, P. F. 1972. Valuation of timber, forage, and water from national forest lands. *Ann. Reg. Sci.* 6:1–4.

O'Connell, P. F., and H. F. Brown. 1972. Use of production functions to evaluate multiple use treatments on forested watersheds. *Water Resour. Res.* 8:1188–1198.

Organization for Economic Cooperation and Development (OECD). 1986. *The Public Management of Forestry Projects*. Paris.

Worley, D. P., and J. H. Patric. 1971. Economic evaluation of some watershed management alternatives on forest land in West Virginia. *Water Resour. Res.* 7:812–818.

CHAPTER 14

Gray, D. M., and D. H. Male (eds.). 1981. *Handbook of Snow*. New York: Pergamon Press.

Harr, R. D. 1976. *Forest practices and streamflow in western Oregon*. USDA For. Serv. Gen. Tech. Rep. PNW-49.

Harr, R. D., W. C. Harper, J. T. Krygier, and F. S. Hsieh. 1975. Changes in storm hydrographs after road building and clear-cutting in the Oregon Coast Range. *Water Resour. Res.* 11:436–444.

Harris, D. D. 1977. *Hydrologic changes after logging in two small Oregon coastal watersheds.* U.S. Geol. Surv. Water Supply Pap. 2037.

Rango, A. 1987. New technology for hydrological data acquisition and applications. In Water for the future: Hydrology in perspective. *Int. Assoc. Hydrol. Sci. Publ.* 164:511–517.

Swanson, R. H., and G. R. Hillman. 1977. *Predicted increased water yield after clear-cutting verified in west-central Alberta.* Northern For. Res. Cent., Can. For. Serv. Info. Rep. NOR-X-198.

Troendle, C. A., and J. R. Meiman. 1984. Options for harvesting timber to control snowpack accumulations. In *Proceedings of the 52nd Western Snow Conference.* pp. 86–97. Colorado State Univ., Fort Collins.

U.S. Army Corps of Engineers. 1981. *HEC-1 flood hydrograph package* (revised 1985). Hydrology Engineering Center. Davis, Calif.

U.S. Soil Conservation Service. 1972. *Snow survey and water supply forecasting.* S.C.S. Natl. Eng. Handb., Sect. 22.

CHAPTER 15

Bruk, S. 1980. Reservoir sedimentation. In *Pollution and water resources,* Columbia Univ. Sem. Ser., Vol. 13 (P. 2):31–47.

Chow, V. T. (ed.). 1964. *Handbook of Applied Hydrology.* New York: McGraw-Hill.

Drysdale, P.J. 1981. Status of general and forest hydrology research in Fiji. In *Country papers on status of watershed forest influence research in southeast Asia and the pacific.* Environ. and Policy Inst. Work. Pap. East-West Center. Honolulu, Hawaii.

Fritz, J. J. 1984. *Small and Mini Hydropower Systems.* New York: McGraw-Hill.

Goodman, L. J., J. N. Hawkins, and R. N. Love (eds.). 1981. *Small Hydroelectric Projects for Rural Development, Planning and Management.* New York: Pergamon Press.

Jackson, W. L. (ed.). 1986. Engineering considerations in small stream management. *Water Resour. Bull.* 22:351–415.

Linsley, R. K., and J. B. Franzini. 1969. *Water Resources Engineering.* New York: McGraw-Hill.

Linsley, R. K., M. A. Kohler, and J. L. H. Paulhus. 1982. *Hydrology for Engineers.* 3d ed. New York: McGraw-Hill.

Tillman, G. 1981. *Environmentally Sound Small-scale Water Projects: Guidelines for Planning.* Arlington, Va.: Volunteers in Technical Assistance (VITA) Publ.

U.S. Army Corps of Engineers. 1967. *Reservoir Storage-Yield Procedures, Methods Systemization Manual.* Davis, Calif. Hydrology Engineering Center.

CHAPTER 16

Cooley, K. R., G. W. Frasier, and K. R. Drew. 1978. Water harvesting: An aid to range management. In *Proceedings of the First International Rangeland Congress,* ed. D. N. Hyder, pp. 292–294. Society Range Management. Denver, Colo.

Duckstein, L., and M. M. Fogel. 1972. A stochastic model of runoff-producing rainfall for summer type storms. *Water Resour.* 8:410–421.

Myers, L. E. 1975. Water harvesting—2000 B.C. to 1974 A.D. In *Proceedings of a water harvesting symposium,* ed. G. W. Frasier, pp. 1–7. USDA Agric. Res. Serv. ARS-W-22.

Thames, J. L., and J. N. Fischer. 1981. Management of water resources in arid lands. In *Arid Land Ecosystems: Structure Functioning and Management.* Vol. 2, ed. D. W. Goodall, R. A. Perry, and K. M. W. Howes, pp. 519–547. New York: Cambridge Univ. Press.

CHAPTER 17

Bedient, P. B., and W. C. Huber. 1988. *Hydrology and Flood Plain Analysis.* New York: Addison-Wesley.

Chow, V. T. 1964. *Handbook of Applied Hydrology.* New York: McGraw-Hill.

Haan, C. T., H. P. Johnson, and D. L. Brakensiek (eds.). 1982. *Hydrologic modeling of small watersheds.* Am. Soc. Agric. Eng. Mono. No. 5.

U.S. Army Corps of Engineers. 1972. *Hydrologic data management.* Hydrologic Engineering Methods for Water Resources Development, Vol. 2. Davis, Calif. Hydrology Engineering Center.

CHAPTER 18

Cochram, W. G. 1963. *Sampling Techniques.* New York: John Wiley and Sons.

Dixon, W. J., and F. J. Massey, Jr. 1957. *Introduction to Statistical Analysis.* New York: McGraw-Hill.

Ezekial, M., and K. A. Fox. 1959. *Methods of Correlations and Regression Analysis: Linear and Curvilinear.* New York: John Wiley and Sons.

Freese, F. 1964. *Linear regression methods for forest research.* USDA For. Serv. Res. Pap. FPL-17.

Green, R. H. 1979. *Sampling Design and Statistical Methods for Environmental Biologists.* New York: John Wiley and Sons.

Haan, C. T. 1977. *Statistical Methods in Hydrology.* Ames: Iowa State Univ. Press.

Natrella, M. G. 1963. *Experimental statistics.* U.S. Natl. Bur. Stand., Hadb. 91.

Steel, R. G. D., and J. H. Torrie. 1960. *Principles and Procedures of Statistics.* New York: McGraw-Hill.

Williams, E. J. 1959. *Regression Analysis.* New York: John Wiley and Sons.

Yates, F. 1960. *Sampling Methods for Census and Surveys.* New York: Hafner Co.

INDEX

383